NATIVE NEW YORKERS

NATIVE NEW YORKERS

The Legacy

of the

Algonquin People

of New York

E V A N T. P R I T C H A R D

Council Oak Books
San Francisco / Tulsa

Grateful acknowledgment is made for permission to reprint excerpts from Susan Tarrow's translation of Verrazzano's letter to Francis I from *The Voyages of Giovanni da Verrazzano 1524–1528*, by Lawrence Wroth, copyright © 1970 by Lawrence Wroth, published by Yale University Press. Used with permission.

Council Oak Books, LLC

1290 Chestnut Street, Ste. 2, San Francisco, CA 94109

1615 S. Baltimore Avenue, Ste. 3, Tulsa, OK 74119

NATIVE NEW YORKERS: *The Legacy of the Algonquin People of New York*

Copyright © 2002 by Evan T. Pritchard. All rights reserved.

Library of Congress Cataloging-in-Publication Data

Pritchard, Evan T., 1955–
     Native New Yorkers : the legacy of the Algonquin people of
New York / Evan T. Pritchard.
     p. cm.
    Includes bibliographical references and index.
     ISBN 1-57178-107-2
     1. Algonquin Indians—New York (State) I. Title.
E99.A35 .P75 2001   974.7'004973—dc21
2001032389

First edition / First printing.
Printed in Canada.
02 03 04 05 06 07 5 4 3 2 1

Contents

Maps may be found on pages 36, 214, and 304

INTRODUCTION

N*ative New Yorkers* is a book for readers who love New York. It is also for those who are possessed by a deep and abiding interest in Native American tradition, whether by birthright or passion. These two subjects seem to lie at the extreme opposite poles of the universe, yet they have coexisted for centuries. They still coexist today, not just in the wilds of upstate New York and Long Island, but right in New York City, the economic hub of the world.

There is an over-arching glory and fame to New York City, one that shines on everyone who lives there. Go to Thailand or Italy, and tell someone you live in New York, and you too are an instant celebrity. As you walk down Fifth Avenue, New York's singularity and opulence make you imagine you are walking along the colonnades of the pharaohs of Egypt.

New Yorkers proudly boast of the toughness it takes to survive in their city and speak openly to strangers about its blemishes and pit-falls. It's not perfect, but it is magnificent. Some say it's not even a good place to live, but it is a great place to be.

But ask them who or what was there before the Dutch, before New York was called New Amsterdam, and people become timid, unsure, and quiet. They don't know or perhaps are afraid to learn about the real Native New Yorkers, those ghosts that, from time to time, haunt their dreams at night. Many suspect that the "original owners" of New York were somehow swindled, because no deed has ever been found for Peter Minuit's $24 Manhattan deal, even though the Dutch West India Company kept careful records of all business transactions. So many people—educators and Native Americans alike—have asked me, "What *really* happened to whoever the Indians were here in New York?" that I was compelled to write this book. Although I had already taught Native American history at the college level, and had been on a committee as an advisor to New York State on teaching Native American history in the public schools, what I learned while preparing to write *Native New Yorkers* was utterly astounding.

At one time the land and the people of New York were one. The timeless harmony with nature and neighbor known to the northernmost Algonquin today was also known to the original people of New York City. I was touched by the brutal loss of that fragile world to "progress," and felt driven to reconstruct their world—the language, philosophy, customs, and ecology, but especially the landscape of the state as the Algonquin people knew it—on paper. As I researched and taught myself the names and stories of the villages, mountains, lakes, trails, and forests, the entire region took on a new character for me. I began to see the land beneath the buildings as a living entity, one still worthy of respect and even reverence. What started as a scholarly endeavor soon became a spiritual quest, and I struggled page by page to find a way to acknowledge both pursuits in my choice of words.

DISCOVERING NATIVE NEW YORK

In 1524, according to Giovanni da Verrazzano, the first chartered explorer[1] to reach what is now the Atlantic Coast of the United States, the original Native New Yorkers had a high population density with almost no negative impact on the environment. He found them highly intelligent and sociable.[2] Close your eyes and imagine what their world was like: Fed by a small lake where City Hall now stands, Canal Street was once a stream that led to the Hudson River. The environment was pristine. The air smelled unusually sweet and dry, and schools of playful dolphins escorted ships into harbor. The air was so filled with birds that sometimes you could hardly hear conversation.[3] Algonquin people were able to hunt bottlehead whales in the ocean, using harpoons and flotation devices made from the inflated bladders of large game animals such as deer and moose.[4] They wore whale fins and tails as ornaments.

New York City dwellers are amused when I tell them Manetta Creek was named after a primeval monster of Lenape legend,[5] one that was banished to the sea to make way for Native American civilization, and that Greenwich Village was an actual Indian village that stood on the banks of Manetta Creek (spelled Minetta by the Dutch, thus today's Minetta Lane). The apartment building at #2 Fifth Avenue even has a fountain in the lobby whose waters are still drawn from Manetta Creek below.

Bowling Green was the site of a sacred council fire and council elm in the realm of the Kapsee, a group of Canarsie people. It lay at the end of one of the longest trails along one of the longest rivers—now called the Hudson—in the New World. There can be no doubt to its pre-Columbian importance—it was geographically a place of power. According to a 1920 archaeological map,[6] and in accordance with traditional Algonquin custom, this spot was the site of a Kapsee chief's house—ironic because George Washington's plan was to build his new "White House" on that spot, where the Heye Center of the National Museum of the American Indian now stands. The first presidential "White House" was actually in Manhattan, not far from Bowling Green, at 1 Cherry Street, named after a Lenape cherry orchard located there. Cooper Union—where Lincoln gave one of his greatest speeches—was a gathering place for orations by Lenape "sagamores," or wise chieftans, for hundreds of years. Manhattan has always been an ideal location for commerce and political power.

Of course, the Canarsie Shipping Lines were named after Native Americans (via the Brooklyn neighborhood by the same name), but did you know that there were Canarsie shipping lines in 1300 to 1500, run by New York City's Native tribe, which traded all over North

America? Or that archaeological finds make it likely one would have seen a fur market five hundred years ago near the site of today's "fur market" at Sixth and Twenty-seventh? Whatever location Native people used to trade certain items, the Dutch would go there too. Later the English took over but allowed the Dutch to continue their practices uninterrupted by politics.

In many respects, the Algonquin created the template by which New York City was designed. They followed the lay of the land and utilized its features to maximum advantage, and the colonists followed their lead, setting a chain of events in motion that is still roaring forward. For example, canoe commuters used to come from Hoboken and land near the spot the PATH train now stops (because it was the narrowest spot on the Hudson) to do business in Manhattan for the day and then go home. Why did they commute? Because Manhattan was a tough place to live, due to the rocky soil, but a good place to visit—and make a deal. Broadway was the main road long ago because it followed the high ridge of the island, but it was called the Mohican Trail then. It led to Montreal, another Algonquin site on a river that was colonized rather early, giving the Dutch settlers a head start in international commerce.

Flatbush Avenue and King's Highway in Brooklyn were important Canarsie trails that followed the lay of the land; King's Highway circles the perimeter of the area, following the shoreline a mile or so inland, while the trail that became Flatbush Avenue began at the best boat crossing from Manhattan and led across Brooklyn to the best boat crossing to the Rockaway Islands on the Atlantic side. The Dutch couldn't improve on that plan.

It was the combination of New York's ready availability of wampum and the marketing ingenuity of the Dutch that set the stage for New York to become the economic capital of the New World. The Lenape had a plentiful supply of wampum shells, which they valued for making ritual objects and ornaments, and the Dutch had the muxes, a steel tool from Europe that happened to make drilling the hard shells easier. The Dutch needed land and beaver pelts, of which the Lenape had plenty. The Dutch needed a form of currency in order to acquire those things, and when it was clear that wampum did the trick, it was soon the first legal tender in the New World. Other objects held value, but wampum was portable and easy to evaluate in a trade, at least until inflation set in due to oversupply by the Dutch.[7]

THE ALGONQUIN CIVILIZATION

Most people I meet are shocked to learn that there was a great civilization in New York State alongside the famous Iroquois Confederacy—one with a larger population and with an incredibly ancient history, dating back at least nine thousand years. Over thirteen million New York State citizens in twenty-eight counties now live on what was Algonquin territory when the Dutch first arrived. There may have been over eighty thousand Algonquin-speaking people in those twenty-eight counties of what is now New York State between 1300 and 1600 C.E.,[8] which means several million Americans living today may be descendants of those eighty thousand Algonquin. According to Edwin G. Burrows and Mike Wallace in their book *Gotham*, there may have been as many as fifteen thousand Algonquins in the five boroughs of New York City—Brooklyn, the Bronx, Manhattan, Queens, and Staten Island (Kings, Bronx, New York, Queens, and Richmond counties, respectively), an area many think of as being uninhabited before the Dutch. They further state that there may have been between thirty and fifty thousand more Algonquin living in the surrounding metropolitan area—a large region taking up parts of present-day New Jersey, Long Island, and the lower Hudson Valley, all with little if any negative impact on the environment.[9]

Algonquin occupation in New York State divides easily into three great territories: Long Island, the Hudson Valley, and in between the two, the complex of islands now known as the City of New York.

While Long Island and the Hudson Valley are obviously much larger, the importance of New York City as America's cultural center during the last one hundred years gives it a defining presence. It was one of the first European towns to be developed in North America, and one of the first to forget its Native American roots. Therefore I feel compelled to give it primary importance.

◦

People say, "Why wasn't I taught this in school?" The best answer is, "there were no books about it, so teachers couldn't teach it." I hope that *Native New Yorkers* will change that state of affairs. To accomplish this, I have compiled and woven together thousands of pieces of information from dozens of out-of-print or rare books and manuscripts, and have filled in the holes with my own knowledge of Algonquin culture as a person of Micmac ancestry. I have spoken at length with Munsee Chief Mark Peters of the Munseetown band, and Chief Walter Van Dunk of the Ramapough Mountain band, plus many Munsee elders, and representatives from many of New York State's other Algonquin nations. It has been an extraordinary journey.

The ancient ancestors of the Algonquin, those who have been called "The First Peoples" of North America and who covered perhaps a third of the continent at one time, were great lovers of nature, and this affection is reflected in the way they named and took care of the land. For those who sincerely seek it out, much fascinating information is available elsewhere on the Iroquois history within the state,[10] but the Algonquin part of the puzzle is much more difficult to reassemble. What you hold in your hands constitutes a first volume in this study, one that emphasizes the sacred geography of the Native land before New York changed its name and became famous.

LAYERS OF LENAPE CULTURE

Archaeologists do dig in New York, and they do occasionally find skeletons, but the public doesn't often hear about it. The skeletons are merely sequestered in storage by museums, such as the Peabody Museum in Boston, which has eighteen thousand Native American skeletons hidden there.[11] If full-sized gravesites were made for each of those Native Americans, it would take a graveyard half the size of Central Park to lay them all to rest. Yet this is less than half the number of Lenape who lived in the New York metropolitan area at the time of first contact in 1524. The island of Manhattan was once hilly and green for the most part, but then it was either leveled or land-filled to make it unnaturally flat and more convenient for urban living. Most artifacts that have been found have been broken and buried deep within the earth. Early subway and skyscraper construction pulverized some sacred burial sites beyond recognition.

Many tribes have passed through New York City, and most of them were somehow related to the Lenape at various phases of their development. The Lenape, usually translated *len*, or "human," and *ape*, or "person,"[12] are an ancient riverine people of Algonquin stock. Their unique nature-revering but sophisticated culture took shape at least as early as 1000 B.C.E. in and around Manhattan, and eventually spread at least two hundred miles in every direction before any known contact with white explorers.

There are actually seven layers of Lenape culture underneath New York City, usually referred to as the Orient Point Phase, the Sebonac Phase, the Fox Creek Phase, the Minisink Phase, the Bowman's Brook Phase, the Clason Point Phase, and the Colonial Phase, not to mention the many phases of greater antiquity. Together they make up what we recognize today as "Lenape."

The Mohican developed out of the Orient Point phase, the Munsee from the Minisink Phase, the Unami from the ensuing Bowman's Brook Phase, and the Unalatchtigo thereafter. The last three became members of the Lenape Confederacy, which was in alliance with the Mohican. At time of contact, the Lenape Confederacy was a loosely organized but wide-ranging entity: the Munsee occupied lower New York and upper New Jersey, the Unami occupied central New Jersey and parts of Pennsylvania, and the Unalatchtigo occupied lower New Jersey. Their symbols—the wolf, the turtle, and the turkey, respectively—are emblazoned on the *wanaque*, a "coat of arms" of the Lenape. These three groups were not clans, per se, but totem states or territories, with clans within each territory.

However, the predominant nation of Lenape to occupy New York City during the last millennium were the Munsee, a people virtually written out of the history books not because of their insignificance, but precisely because of their painful significance in United States and Canadian history. Out of the Munsee culture sprang not only the other two Lenape nations of the confederacy, the Unami and Unalatchtigo, but over time, dozens of other nations as well. Although the ancient Algonquin civilization gave birth to the Lenape in the cradle of Long Island, the infant soon outgrew its parent, forming the great southern tier of Algonquin culture that covers much of the United States as far south as Cape Hatteras and as far west as Iowa. For the most part, these Lenape were the Indians the early settlers married and made families with. Let us therefore call the Lenape the "mother" of America and the Munsee of New York her "father." The section of this book on the Hudson Valley reveals much about the Munsee history.

The Lenape were not the only Algonquin to inhabit New York State. Equally renowned are the Mohican[13] of the upper Hudson region. No book on the New York Algonquin would be complete without discussing their presence upon the land from Rhinebeck to Lake George, and the Mohican influence eastward and westward from there. The Mohican are not generally called Lenape, however they are also "People of the River," and the two were once one great people, thousands of years ago. Sometime, around a thousand years ago, the Munsee opened their council circles to new ideas from the south, while the Mohican retained their ancient northern traditions and language. Chapter 15 is devoted to the Mohican of the upper Hudson Valley.

Chapters 16 and 17 will focus on Long Island, home to both the most ancient and most recent of Lenape traditions in the state. The Matouac, the "young warriors" of Long Island, became "the thirteen tribes" of Long Island. However their roots run very deep to the very beginning of Lenape history.

The other Algonquin of the state also arose out of the seven layers of Lenape culture mentioned earlier: the Corchaug from the Orient Point Phase, the Shinnecock and other Long Island Indians from the Sebonac Phase, and the Wappingers, Matinecock, Canarsie from the Clason Point Phase. All these tribes existed at the time of first contact with whites, and most still exist today in some form. Together the speakers of the Munsee, Unami, and Renneiu languages (in cooperation with the Mohican sachems, or chiefs, from the north) combined to establish the great population center that became New York City. The contemporary descendants of these people represent an Algonquin culture that is profoundly different from modern American culture, and yet one that has been making important contributions to American life for thousands of years. The accomplishments of New York's Algonquin population have gone almost completely unnoticed in the history books. *Native New Yorkers* attempts to correct this deficit by documenting the geography, population, philosophy, fashion, customs, ecology, spirituality, diplomatic ability, and the several beautiful and poetic languages of the Algonquin in the New York State region. It will also briefly answer the question, "Where did they go?"

CULTURAL GENOCIDE AND DISPERSION

What followed the political defeat of the Munsee was cultural genocide, not so vicious as total genocide such as attempted with the Jews perhaps, but devastating nonetheless. It was a slow and complex process, carried on in relative secrecy within almost every avenue of New York's huge bureaucracy. Some of this cultural devastation has been slow to be reversed, but much of Algonquin culture still exists and can be reexamined in the light of new discoveries and under-standings in the fields of body-mind medicine, environmental science, and sociology, to name a few, and applied by anyone who wishes to do so.

How the Munsee were defeated or made to disappear is a story with two sides to be told. Their history was suppressed, their lan-guage driven out of them, and their New York settlements, in the words of New York State historian James Folts, were "cartographically submerged."[14]

The exodus saga of these real Native New Yorkers was one of the greatest tragedies in U.S. history. Descendants of New York City Lenape were removed by treaty at least twenty times and sent to Oklahoma, Ontario, and Wisconsin, where they were subjected to poverty, disease, and death.[15] They became so destitute that in 1849, a U.S. group of Munsee, among the most proud and stoic of Native Americans, wrote a letter begging President Zachary Taylor for "a crust of bread." Taylor was not known for kindness even to his friends, and though his response is unknown, most of the Munsee who signed the paper had to leave the United States shortly thereafter. Some joined the thousands moving west, further and further from home.

On their way west, the Lenape who founded New York City also founded, with help from a variety of Algonquin relatives, several dozen other great American cities, including Corning, and Binghamton, New York; Wilkes-Barre, Harrisburg, Pittsburgh, and Punxsutawney, Pennsylvania; Muncie and Fort Wayne, Indiana; Kansas City and Leavenworth, Kansas; as well as Muncie, Ontario, Canada, to name only a few. They even lent one of their words to name the state of Wyoming. All of this will be explained in more detail in Chapter 18, "Lenape Exodus," and in the Epilogue.

I sometimes use the term "Delaware," which developed during the Colonial Phase, to include Munsee, Unami, and Unalatchtigo peoples. It is somewhat synonymous with "Lenape," however it is commonly used to refer to people who are a mixture of the three, plus all of their relatives who intermarried for survival's sake as they were driven west. These "Delaware" are, at least to some extent, descendants of the Munsee of New York and upper New Jersey. The heroic story of the Delaware in their westward exodus is the story of the Munsee of New York City as well.

Those Delaware descendants of New York City's founders befriended a child named Stephen F. Austin, the future founder of the political entity known as Texas, and taught him Native ways that later saved his life. Still later they helped him to manage conflict with the Comanche, making possible the establishment of Texas.[16] Very few Americans know that eleven of the twenty-five or so Native American state-names refer to the Algonquin people of which the Lenape are considered "Grandfathers," or that the Lenape played an important role in the history of at least half the states in the United States.[17]

Few know that some of the Munsee and Unami whose grandparents lived in or around New York City, such as the great Delaware scout Black Beaver, moved to Kansas, Texas, and Arkansas, became expert horsemen and lived part of what is now called the saga of the Wild West, as stereotypically depicted in movies and radio and television shows such as *The Lone Ranger*.[18]

These Delaware played pivotal roles in helping the United States win its various wars. In many cases, they were promised land if victorious, helped win the war, and were left homeless with empty pockets afterward. Ironically, the only leader to make good on such a promise was America's enemy, King George III. He gave the Munsee land in Canada as many of them helped in the war effort, but then placed them on Chippewa land, which was later sold out from under them. The wampum treaty belt commemorating the promise now stands on display at New York City's American Museum of Natural History, on land which the Munsee once possessed but lost. Although there were as many as fifty thousand Munsee in New York, New Jersey, and Connecticut during the 1500s, no Munsee group has ever been awarded a reservation of their own in the United States, except as additional baggage on Unami, Mohican, Seneca, Delaware, Shawnee, or other reservations. Although the Munsee have contributed greatly as scouts in every American war effort up to World War II, no tribe or nation that was solely "Munsee" has ever been federally recognized in the United States.

Most of this Delaware saga is unknown to New Yorkers today—especially the part of it which occurred under their own feet. In the heart of the information center of the world, there is a vacuum of information about that center itself, and its early history. Manhattanites have difficulty imagining what their city was like before the streets were installed and the massive buildings erected.

The Munsee have words that help us see the natural world a little bit closer up. Their way of life helps us see each other's hearts as "real human beings" more closely, too. By sharing some of the spirituality and ceremonies of the greater Lenape culture, I hope to help bring a more intimate view of the spirit world as well.

Understanding Munsee history can help us see New York State, not to mention the United States and Canada, which they helped to build, in a new light. Aside from being a land war, the struggle of the Native New Yorkers was an ideological war, one that challenged the understanding of the term "Western civilization." It was a conflict of ideas between two great civilizations, two ways of seeing the world, two types of languages and ways of speaking to one another, two ways of fighting, loving, raising children, doing business, and sharing land. Both sides wanted to come out heroes and be proven "right." A surprising number of families on both sides were eager to adopt the other's children and raise them with love—"the right way" as they saw it. Largely due to the ideological element of the conflict, neither was willing to compromise and the Algonquin were gradually outnumbered, outspent, and outmaneuvered, at least as a political force. According to Burton J. Hendrick, author of *Statesmen for a Lost Cause*, even among evenly matched war machines, it takes at least a three to one ratio to successfully invade and conquer a settled population.[19] It is little comfort to the Lenape survivors that it took a much greater ratio to drive the Lenape political presence out from New York and New Jersey, and that it took roughly from 1624 to 1789, a period of 165 years, to accomplish it. As an ideological force, however, the Lenape have never been completely defeated.

Interestingly, reports of the paranormal in North America frequently refer to appearances and communications from Native American guides. Perhaps these are Native spirits fulfilling their vow to be sacred Land Keepers. I believe that these spirits have been trying to convey the sacredness of the land to all New Yorkers who will listen since the day Peter Minuit cleared the land to build his thirty homes in lower Manhattan, and that their messages are meant to help us individually and as a society. I also believe that by understanding their culture, we will find it much easier to see the world through Lenape eyes and perhaps help make New York an even better place to live.

To the four directions I dedicate this writing, and to the grandmothers and grandfathers of the four directions as well. Only six fluent Munsee speakers remain today, but thanks to John O'Meara's dictionary and the language programs on the Munsee reserves, there is a chance the language will survive. If enough of the culture is recorded and passed along, it will allow us to gain a foothold in the Munsee conceptual world, or at least open a small window. Once we can see through this boarded-up window, perhaps we will catch a glimpse not only of the minds of the Lenape, but of the other side of history as well.

Many people mistakenly call the Lenape a tribe. In fact they are simply a "hoop" or "circle" of similar people within the Algonquin Civilization which is made up of circles within circles. Or they could be described as branches of a tree. There are so many levels to the structure of Lenape Society that there are no equivalent English terms to sort them out. This chart focuses on the Munsee branch of the tree and how its subtribes relate to the others mentioned in the book.

ALGONQUIN

Northern Algonquin (Mohican, etc.)

Southern Algonquin
Lenape, Shawnee, Illinois, Miami, Powhatan, etc.

LENAPE

The Three Confederated* Lenape Nations————}

Munsee	**Unami**	**Unalatchtigo**	**Renneiu**
(Northern Lenape)	(Middle Lenape)	(Southern Lenape)	(Eastern Lenape)
			Long Island/Conn.

The Three Munsee Bands: All prominent in Manhattan————}

Hudson Valley Munsee	**Upper Delaware Munsee**	**Southern Munsee**
(The Esopus)	(Minsi or Minisink)	(Ramapough, etc. of N. J. *Rechgawank, etc. of Manh.*)

The Five Esopus Tribes————————————————}

Waoraneck	**Warranawongkong**	**Wawarsing**	**Esopus**	**Catskill**

*There are several non-Confederated Lenape, including the Nanticokes, the Brandywine, the Long Island groups, the Wappingers, and so forth.

1

THE NAMING
OF THINGS

N*ative New Yorkers* is very much a book about the naming of things. By naming something, we take possession of it; by losing that name, we lose possession of it. New York State has been a battleground of words for centuries, as different peoples struggled to take control, to own, to erase, and to rename. I will be focusing on the original people, what they named things, and why, in order to give readers a glimpse of New York as it was when the land and the people were one.

Just about everyone knows what a "native New Yorker" is: someone who is born, raised, and lives in the unique and sometimes chaotic environment that is New York City. It's the accent, the clothes, the style, the survivor attitude. There's an intangible quality about a "native New Yorker," and you can spot it anywhere in the world he or she might happen to be. But these are not the people that this book is about. While the memory of most modern New Yorkers goes back at least to the blizzard of '78, the collective memory of the real "native New Yorkers" stretches back to the Ice Age. They are the Lenape, the "Real People" of New York City.

Who are the Lenape? *Len* means "common" or "real," and *ape* (a-pey*)* means "people." The word is used to mean "human," including both men and women.[1] Therefore, the *Lenape* are the "Real People," although some interpret the word as "We the people." This could be to distinguish them from the "stone people," the "tree people," the "four-legged people," and other nonhuman "people" in the Native American tradition. The prefix *Lenni-* has often been placed in front, for "man," but this is passing out of favor. In this book, I will use the term "Lenape" to refer to all the direct descendants of the original people of New York and New Jersey. The Lenape are river people, and it should be at least mentioned that Len-nape can also mean "the people of that river there," although this is not the usual interpretation.

Regardless of what they called themselves, it remains clear, judging by several first-contact observations, that the Lenape had learned to cultivate the art of being human to its finest form. They knew how to live on the earth, and in brotherhood and sisterhood with each other.

THE ART OF BEING HUMAN

When challenged by adversity or placed under extreme restrictions, either by political pressure or social expectations, the great Lenape Chief Teedyuskung would loudly exclaim, "I am a MAN! Nee Lenni! I am a MAN!" [2] I believe Chief Teedyuskung was standing up for his "humanity," and all that implies, fighting to get a moral foothold in his soul. Throughout their history, the Lenape have been trying to hold on to the sense of what it once was to be human. They have risen to the occasion with amazing moral courage. They have decided to be forgiving even when being eviscerated as a people.

Algonquin storyteller Ken Little Hawk of the Micmac shares a story that intimates how hard it is to be a "real human being" in this world, and how important it is to try. A young half-breed boy kept asking his full-blooded grandfather, "Teach me to be an Indian! Teach me to be an Indian!" After some weeks, Grandfather finally promised to teach him. He brought the boy to the edge of a beautiful lake. He gave the boy a big stick and said, "See this stick? I want you to take it over to the edge of that lake and stir up the water."

The boy did so. Then Grandfather instructed the lad to stir up the stones, sand, and even the plants that grew under the water with that stick. The boy, being a boy, was happy to do so, and soon the water was a cloudy mess of leaves and mud and sand whirling around. The boy stepped back to admire his work.

After the cloudy water began to clear, Grandfather said to the boy, "Now I want you to put everything back exactly as it was before." The boy sat down and cried, "I cannot do that! It can never be the same! I thought you were going to teach me to be an Indian!"

"Yes," Grandfather answered, "but before you learn what it is to be an Indian, first you must learn what it is to be a human being!"

The boy was on his way to learning an important lesson: The power to change things that comes with being human must be used responsibly—you cannot simply put things back as they were.

Is New York's Past the Key to Its Future?

For a thousand years, the "Real People," the Lenape, lived in a beautiful gardenlike paradise surrounding what is now called New York Harbor. Like the Algonquin elder in Little Hawk's story, they were well aware of their destructive potential as human beings, and strove to interact gracefully with their environment and fellow humans without causing permanent damage whenever possible. In doing so, they developed the art of being "real people" to its highest form.

All the major races of the world have contributed greatly to the international culture that exists in New York State today. They each possess different parts of the truth, different types of wisdom. Why does it matter that a few of these groups happen to be native to this continent and native to this state?

Wherever you live, you owe it to yourself to know the history of the land you live in and who lived there before. How did it come into your possession? The spirit of the people before you is still there in some sense, so it is appropriate and necessary to do a spiritual and moral "title search" wherever you live. "Title" denotes the right of ownership in law,[3] and "right" implies moral responsibility. When we acquire ownership from someone, don't we also inherit their duties? *Native New Yorkers* is part of my own "title search" to help me understand the New York land I have lived on for over half my life, and the responsibility I have to take care of the land, as expressed by the Lenape land keepers four hundred years ago as they "transferred" title to the Dutch colonists, either knowingly or not.

There is a difference between being born in America and being Native American. The term *Native American* denotes a culture, not a state of circumstances. A Lenape or Cherokee born in Europe would still be Native American. Some people born on American soil are of this culture, but most are not, so the distinction must be made. Native American refers to a people whose civilization was born and raised in America, regardless of where they as individuals were born.

The true story of the contribution Native Americans have made to the culture of New York has yet to be told. These Native people, like those of the Hopi mesas, Rosebud, or Wind River, have a folk wisdom that now belongs to all the people. This wisdom includes how to live in harmony on and with the earth, and with each other. This is an important message that has yet to be transmitted successfully. In spite of five hundred years of confusion, it is still not too late for understanding and change.

The message of the New York "Indians," as Henry Hudson incorrectly called them, is not a surprise: "Honor the earth. We belong to our mother, and without her we are lost." This is a timely call to action because there is evidence that the biosphere may be disintegrating rapidly; ice caps are melting, water tables are down, temperatures are vacillating, storms are increasing, and species are becoming extinct. With the exception of Los Angeles, New York City generates more carbon monoxide than any other city in America. New Yorkers use a lot of clean water and generate more garbage and sewage than some entire countries. It is a place that is ecologically out of balance, where each person is totally dependent on distance sources for food and water.

Another important message of the New York Indians is this: "We are all medicine for each other. We need to treat each other with respect. We are all related." In *No Word for Time: The Way of the Algonquin People,* I listed seven principles of respect that I had observed among the Algonquin peoples, which include the Lenape. They are (1) respect for feelings and for suffering, (2) respect for individual space, (3) respect for limitations as well as strengths, (4) respect for boundaries and individual differences, (5) respect for truth, (6) respect for the earth and all paths, peoples, cultures, and customs growing here, and (7) respect for yourself. The Algonquin from New York City embraced this way of life, honoring the earth and each other.

One thing is clear: we need a better understanding of how people should live on the earth, and a belief system that gives us the strength to do it. This is one of the gifts of the Native American culture: they held this wisdom long ago, and have held onto it for millennia with amazing tenacity. To uphold this truth is something worth living or even dying for.

CITY OF AMNESIA

Perhaps more than anywhere else in the world, New York is a city of immigrants. It is a city of displaced people in a displaced world. Once, though, it was a circle or hoop, *Woch-ah-ga-po-ay* in Munsee (the root language of the Lenape), of many great nations. New York doesn't know its own past. Without a true a sense of the past, it steams blindly toward the future without a rudder. It is a city with amnesia. Like a person so afflicted, it doesn't know that anything is missing. I love New York City dearly; it just feels hollow to me sometimes. I feel a huge emptiness, like there's no one really there. While I often get a strange sense of peace standing on a street corner at lunchtime in midtown, feeling totally alone with my thoughts, sometimes I also feel the city's pain—its lack of direction or roots. Then it seems that nothing really matters, since everyone else is lost in self-distraction or caught up in the fast pace and vast energy of city life.

Nowhere else is the displacement of a great people by another great people so complete or more devastatingly significant for the course of world history. Nowhere else is the contrast more dramatic between what was lost and what replaced it. The great nature-loving metropolis of the Lenape of New York City has, over the last five hundred years since Columbus sailed from Spain, been completely eradicated and replaced with another totally different culture, a culture in denial of the natural world. The long history, geography, wisdom teachings, ecology, and language of the previous culture were almost completely cast aside in a frenzied rush toward the future, their humble pathways *(aneyk mettelen)* buried deep beneath the dust of progress; their ochred bones crushed and crusted over with miles of concrete and asphalt.

But in a thousand subtle ways, the influence of the Lenape remains. Through five hundred years of extermination, of building, bulldozing, and dishonoring Mother Earth in every way imaginable, the spirit of the Lenape still abides in the land. It is very strong, and getting stronger. It touches the life of everyone who visits the land, and yet they are unaware of it. Once you see New York City through Algonquin eyes, though, you will never be the same. The legacy of the great Lenape city is everywhere—the triumph of their persistence, the tragedy of their loss.

What's in a Name?

The Munsee and Unami called it Lenape Hoking, "Dwelling-Place of the Lenape," or E-hen-da-wi-kih-tit,[4] "Where the Ordinary People Dwell." The Mohawk called it Knonoge, or "Place of Reeds." The explorer Giovanni da Verrazzano called it Angouleme in honor of King Francis, Count of Angouleme. Later the Dutch called it New Netherlands, and parts of it New Amsterdam. Finally, in 1664, the British called it the colony of New York, and the rest is history. Or is it?

We can learn a lot by understanding the origins of place-names throughout the colony that has become New York State. Each place-name in the world has an ethnic flavor due to its language. We don't taste that flavor if the language is our own. We don't notice the ethnic bias that builds up over the years, but the indigenous people do.

It's a global phenomenon. From school to school, the globes in New York City's classrooms all consistently present the same country, city, county, province, river, and mountain names, and the students believe these are not only the correct names, but are the only names that ever existed. As they grow up and travel around the world—or around New York—they talk to people of different ethnic groups and find out the truth. A large percentage of the world's place-names—as we in America are taught to say them—are not only imposed by conquerors, but are often distasteful to the conquered.

Nowhere more than in geography do the winners write history. We use awful names that glorify bloody conquests and blatant human rights violations, and we remain blissfully unaware. It is important to acknowledge this, even if we don't change the maps.

What we call New York is a land that people have visited on business for some twelve thousand years, and have called home uninterruptedly for about seven thousand. It is not new, nor does it resemble York, England, in any way. This name implies that the land was "discovered" by the people of England, which we know wasn't true. And to name it "new" repeats the sin of "Columbus Day"; it subtly implies that no one was here, so it was "all right" to move in and take over and build a reproduction of England on this vacant lot. This is sheer Albionic fantasy, and names like New York, New Jersey, New Hampshire, New Brunswick, and New England, not to mention

New Bedford, New Salem, Newark (after Newark, England) all vali-
date this fantasy.

What Is Old York?

York is a very old town in England that dates back to prehistoric
times. The name was changed from Eburacum to York even before
the Romans packed up their gear and went home. York is short for
eoforwyc-ceastre, the place of the wild boar. Eburacum, which is what
the Romans called it, means the same thing in Latin. In ancient
European mythology, the wild boar is the creature that wounds[5] or
slays the son of the cosmos, the savior, the sun god.

According to Joseph Campbell, Tammuz, Adonis, and Attis were
all gods or demigods slain by the wild boar; Odysseus, Wotan (Wodin),
and others were crippled. A stone sculpture of a wild boar made in
Roman times and unearthed near London also attests to the importance of the boar in Roman mythology. York, England, was and shall
always be thought of as the place of the wild boar. The boar is the hero's
downfall. The pig, whose skin is most similar to that of humans, has
had associations with fertility and sexuality throughout the history of
the Western world, and the sharp-tusked boar is a symbol of the
Goddess's power to avenge the mistreatment of women, as well as of
the animal kingdom and Mother Earth herself. The woman-boar, as in
the Arthurian story of Ragnell, who sat at the crossroads, was a symbol
of love and death in ancient times, the destructive/seductive power of
life and procreation. That's New York in a nutshell, the place at the
crossroads where the strongest and most heroic are tempted and
destroyed by the seductive attractions of earthly life. Some Lenape
sachems—sages and leaders—were among those fallen heroes,
seduced by rum, money, and trinkets. New York is therefore the "new
place of the wild boar," a place of mythic importance for our times.

But why name it after York, England, when it had such a history
of its own?

The Dutch towns of New Amsterdam and Fort Orange were renamed "New York" and "Albany" respectively by the English in honor of a certain Duke of York, who was also Duke of Albany. He later became King James II.

Other colonists in Lenape Hoking created New Sweden, New Amsterdam, New Holland, New Haven, and New Utrecht, but the English have branded us all "New Yorkers" even though England had control of the area for only 119 of its twelve thousand years of human habitation.

This choice to retain the name New York in 1781 eliminated seven thousand years of Algonquin/Iroquois history. The names of the counties of Essex, Sussex, Kings, Orange, Queens, Richmond, and Westchester all come from England, but all of this land is still part of Turtle Island, where the spirits of the Native American Land Keepers still keep silent watch over the terrain.

Some geographers try to downplay the importance of place-names, because it's a lot of work to change a map or learn a word in a different language. They call the study of the etymology of place-names "toponymics," but fail to see the potentially enlightening lesson in social studies. Whether you call it toponymics, or cultural genocide, erasing the original name of a nation sweeps generations of human occupation, oppression, and removal under the rug of semantics. It removes the fingerprints from the body of everyday history. It is a way of insuring that children don't ask the wrong questions, the ones that are hard to answer. Where there are no bones, there is no murder. There are only "missing persons."

THE RIVER THAT FLOWS BOTH WAYS

For at least seven thousand years, Algonquin people lived along the Hudson River, which has a long lineage of names. Some of the oldest known inhabitants were the Mohican, who named themselves after the river, which they called Mohicanituk, "The River That Flows Both

Ways." The Iroquois, or Hodenosuannee as they call themselves, named the upper part of the river Skanehtade Gahunda, "The River That Lies Beyond the Opening" (the opening to the Mohawk River). The lower Hudson was named Cohatatea.

The Mohican word for Albany is Pem-po-tow-wut-hut—Muh-he-can-neuw, which means "It Is the Place of Fire of the Mohicans." Schodack Island, in the Hudson River, was the site of their great council fire for centuries. There was nothing new about Albany either. The Mohawk called it Sha-neh-ta-de, or "Beyond the Opening." The mapmakers inadvertently gave that name to Schenectady, which should have been called by its Mohawk name, Onoalagoneh, "In the Head."

The Portuguese explorer Esteban Gomez reputedly called it "The Deer River," an appropriate name. Then Henry Hudson sailed it as far as Albany, referring to it as "The River of Steep Hills." The French came and called it La Riviere de la Montagnes, or "River of the Mountains," all very appropriate by Algonquin standards. In 1611, it was renamed the Mauritius River, after the Dutch *stadtholder* (land-holder) Prince Maurice of Nassau. In 1624, they nicknamed it the "Noort River," or North River, to distinguish it from the South River, now known as the Delaware, and the East River. It retained the name "North" for four decades during the seventeenth century. When the English took over in 1664 they named it after Henry Hudson, who had first come there looking for a more direct route to India. Sooner or later, it became Hudson's River, the least appropriate of names, as viewed from the losers' side of history, and yet later, the Hudson.

Over eighty years earlier, French-backed Verrazzano glimpsed the mouth of the Hudson River but was driven back by a chance storm and never realized what he'd found. Verrazzano named the upper bay at the entry to the river the "Bay of St. Marguerite" after the king's sister. That chance storm may have saved the lives of thousands of people, as we now know that some of Verrazzano's men carried smallpox. According to one Native account, the storm was a strange one, carrying a bitter smell with it, brimming with bad omens.

The Dutch followed closely on the heels of Henry Hudson, their heads bursting with names, and within fifteen years had left a permanent imprint on Manhattan. Even though we don't call it "New Netherlands" any longer, we still call the island of the bear clan of the Canarsie "Coney (or 'rabbit') Island," and we still call Mannahatting "Brooklyn," both of which mean "Broken Land." We still call the Muscoota village "Harlem," and the Muscooten River the "Harlem River."

The Dutch also named Breedewegh (which we now call Broadway), Gansevoort Street, Kill Van Kull, Vly (Creek) Street, Varick Street, Staten Island, New Dorp, Tottenville, Arthur Kill, the Bronx, Cortlandt, Van Duzer, Todt Hill, and Governor's Islands. They also gave us Stuyvesant Place, Van Wyck Expressway, and Roosevelt Island as well.

The so-called "Dutch" have a complex ethnic history of their own and have been subjected to much misnaming. "Holland" was only one of about ten provinces that make up the modern-day Netherlands. Holland, the lowest province, lies below sea level, although Netherlands also means "lowest or furthest land." But to call the people who settled Manhattan "Dutch" is problematic for many reasons. The word "Dutch" refers to the language and it is spoken not only in Holland, but in Belgium where it is spoken by the Flemish, and on the Frisian Islands, some of which are German. Secondly, most of the settlers of New Amsterdam were Walloons from Belgium who spoke Old French.[6] The word *walloon* means "foreigners,"[7] as they were named by their conquerors, the "French." No one was any less foreign than the Walloons, descendants of the Gauls and fathers of the French tongue itself.

Some of the early "Dutch" settlers were really "Flemish," a people who live on the corner of France, Belgium, and the Netherlands, at a place called "Flanders," or "The Flat Lands," which is also what they named the section in Brooklyn where they built the First Dutch Reformed Church of the Flatlands. They also built Flanders, New Jersey. The Flemish and the Walloons were named Belgique or Belgae by their conquerors, the Gauls; it means "the angry ones." The Gauls and all Gallic people are now called "French," and their money "francs," after their Frankish German conquerors in the ninth century, but the French now call the Welsh "Galls," which is where the term Gaelic comes from. This is at least better than "Welsh," which also means "foreigner." The same pattern of misnaming the vanquished is found all over the world. The Germans, Albanians, and Greeks were named by the Romans, the Hungarians by the Huns, the Japanese by the Chinese.[8] Thus Native Americans are not the only toponymically oppressed people. America has no monopoly on land grabbing, yet dispossessed people around the world know what happened in America, chapter and verse, and are quick to identify with the Indians. Those "homeless, tempest-tossed" refugees who now live in New York City—including people from Taiwan, Bosnia, Armenia, China, Somalia, Columbia, or Pakistan—have more in common with the original Native New Yorkers, whose children were born in exile, than New Yorkers of the more common variety.

Mapping Out a New (Subtitled) World

Each geographical place-name in the world, be it a city, country, province, state, river, or mountain, is loaded with ethnic significance and ethnic bias. There is no way to avoid it. One people name a mountain or river in praise of its beauty, and often its own specific way of beauty, humbly submitting to its preeminence over the area, whereas another people will name it after their past leaders, who strut for a time upon the political stage and are gone. Mount Washington, the Jefferson Peaks, Mount Rushmore, Cadillac Mountain, the Columbia River, for example, once had Native American names that have been all but forgotten.

Given history, it is not surprising that the Dutch and English—both conquered by the Romans—gave most places around the New York area new names they could pronounce. What's surprising is that so many were left in the Native tongue. This attests to the importance the Algonquin and Iroquois still held well into the 1800s. The colonists needed their help, respected them, and in many cases, tried to imitate them.

I have sometimes seen world maps with subtitles for almost every country in the world. If we can see movies with subtitles, why not maps? If geography is supposed to be part of social studies, what better way to learn about social studies than by studying not what Rand McNally calls people, but what the people call themselves? Perhaps eventually we can create a map of New York with subtitles in the Munsee and other Algonquin languages.

MALAPROPIAN-AMERICANS

Many Native American tribes and nations are horribly misnamed. The Delaware nation is a good example. Although I use the term to define a latter phase of Lenape culture, for cases in which all its survivors were blended together, the word *delaware* is not a proper term. The Lenape Seepu, "River of the Lenape," is approximately three hundred miles long, and lies west of New Jersey, which was formerly the heart of Lenape Hoking. (Lenape Hoking, which means "The Dwelling Place of the Lenape," included not only much of New York but also New Jersey and parts of Delaware, Maryland, and Pennsylvania.) The majestic bay at the mouth of the river was named after Thomas West, Baron de la Warr, in 1610. The baron, the first governor of Virginia and the first in a long line of Virginia politicians, was supposed to visit the bay, but he never actually saw it. Soon the whole river was named De La Warr, and became known as the Delaware River shortly thereafter.

Eventually the Lenape people along its shores were nicknamed "De

La Warr" Indians, or "Delaware." The people spread along that long river were mostly of one confederacy, called the Lenni-Lenape Confederacy, consisting of Unami, Munsee, Unalimi, and Unalatchtigo people, all closely related. The Nanticoke were also an adjunct to the Delaware confederacy, and some of their villages were within sight of the bay. The newly named "Delaware" were one of the largest groups east of the Mississippi, and outnumbered the colonists until 1700. The Lenape eventually gave up resisting and adopted the name Delaware.

The term Mohican, or "Mohicanner" as the Dutch said it, is similar to the actual word Muhheakunnuk ("People of the River That Flows Both Ways"), but Wappingers (an "R speaking" branch of the Munsee who formed an alliance with the Mohicans around 1675) are precariously close to being misnamed. Wappingers derives from Moo-wha-pink-us, which means "possum," or "he has no fur on his tail." The *us* means "little." The other Lenape at the time apparently called them Wappinks or Wappinkus, short for possum.[9]

Many Wappinkus Indians moved via Stockbridge, New York, along with the Munsee, to Canada around the time of the Revolutionary War. Munsee oral tradition holds that they escaped through a secret passageway behind Niagara Falls that has since been eroded away.[10] The name "Canada" is a malapropism. An interesting video clip is shown to visitors of the Canadian Museum of Civilization in Hull, Quebec, just as they arrive: In the reenactment a pompous missionary comes up to a small Huron (Iroquoian-speaking) village for the first time, translator in tow, and gesturing grandly, says, "And what do you call this . . . this . . . country . . . of yours?"

The Huron man points to his humble village and says, "Canada." ("This is my village.") The missionary responds, "Then we shall call this entire land, Canada." The translator tries to explain the blunder to no avail. The missionary had decided! The entire northern half of the continent is now named "This is my village" in Huron. It could be worse.

The name Iroquois is an unfortunate choice of terms. The French adopted this nickname from the term *irinakoiw* of the Algonquin tribe of Canada. It means, "they are real adders," or "they are mean." So "Irinakoiw" ("Iroquoian") may have been taken out of context and mistaken for a proper name by the French.

Indeed, geographic toponymics have a penchant for worst-case scenarios, and so the insulting term "Iroquois" was applied to an entire language group. This language group today includes the Seneca, Cayuga, Onondaga (all dialects of a single language), and the languages of the Huron, Mohawk, Tuscarora, Oneida, and Cherokee. It also once included the Erie, Wenro, Tobacco, Neutral, and Susquehanna. The commonly accepted word for these people is Hodenosuannee which means "People of the Longhouse," although elders say Ongwe-Oweh is more correct. Nonetheless, I use the term Iroquoian to refer to this complete language group, since there isn't a more appropriate recognizable word.

The same thing that happened with the Iroquois also happened to the Sioux. They call themselves Dakota, but when those same French, or their offspring, came to the Dakotas, they asked the Ojibway who these people were. The Ojibway, relatives of the Lenape, the Narragansett, and the Algonquin, said the same thing about their "Sioux" rivals as the Algonquin had, Na-do-we-ees-eew, "They are like adders." It was yet another worst-case scenario; the term "Sioux" was then used to refer to the entire language group, which now includes Lakota, Nakota, Dakota, Mandan, Crow, Omaha, Hidatsa, Osage, Iowa, Tutelo, and Saponi.

The most prominent of the Iroquois nations are the Lenape's northern neighbors, the Mohawk. The term "Mohawk," from the Narragansett *mohowauuck,* means "cannibals" or "man-eaters." There is a beautiful story of how Iatwenta, "He Combs Their Hair," better known as Hiawatha, was so angry and stricken by grief that he had been lowered to a state of cannibalism. One day he was preparing a stew made of human meat from people he had killed when the Great Peacemaker of the Iroquois arrived. The Peacemaker climbed upon Iatwenta's roof and looked down the smoke hole. When the cannibal saw the reflection of this great saint's face in the water of the soup pot, staring down at him compassionately, he was immediately over-come, thinking it his own countenance, and gave up the practice of cannibalism forever. He threw away the soup, and became a man of peace, who "combed the hair" of the despotic Atotarho, and planted the Great Tree of Peace at Onondaga Lake.[11] This is a great story about a change of heart; it seems sad that we only know the term "Mohawk" today. The name these people call themselves is Kanienkahageh, "People of the Flint," which is a name of honor with a deep history.

The Seneca people wandered all over the greater Lenape region creating trails and roads, all the way down to Virginia. Although they were great road builders like the Romans, they were never Roman statesmen as their English name implies, and are not descended from the balding Roman, as far as we know. It is a mispronunciation of Sennacaas, from the Mohican translation *a'sin-nee-ka*, from "People of the Standing Rock," which is Oneniute in Oneida. Their homeland is the Genesee River area in New York.

Susquehanna means "water crossing the big plain" in the Iroquois language.[12] Near the mouth of the Susquehanna, at Parryville, Maryland, there is a place where the high tide rolling in off the Chesapeake Bay covers a grassy field in a way that fits the descrip-tion perfectly.[13] The Susquehanna Trail can still be seen today on the other side of that watery plain at Havre de Grace. The term "Wyoming," which was later applied to a slice of the Susquehanna River Valley, is a Lenape translation of Susquehanna, also meaning "water crossing a big plain." Unfortunately that slice now called Wyoming—Pennsylvania—is not a plain at all but a mountainous valley. It was more appropriately applied to the new state of

Wyoming by a former Pennsylvanian,[14] who wished to honor all Native Americans. Much of the state of Wyoming is big open plains. Wyoming is also the name of two counties where the Delaware lived, one in New York and one in Pennsylvania.

How ironic that the three states named after the Lenape—Delaware, Wyoming, and to some degree Indiana—are all incorrectly named in some regard,[15] while the land they occupied so utterly and cared for so lovingly for a thousand and more years is now named New Jersey.

The Algonquin themselves, having played a role in the misnaming of other people (and the "Delaware" have been guilty of this as well), have also been misnamed. The word was first used, by mistake, by Samuel de Champlain in 1603. He was referring to a specific group of Indians he had met at Tadoussac, which the Maliseet had told him were *Elaegomogwik,* which means either, "these people are our allies," or "the people on the other shore." Champlain, for some reason, had trouble with this word and called them "Algoumekin." This term was gradually altered to "Algonquin." Even though it has no real meaning, I use this term frequently in this book to refer to the cultural linguistic group that the Lenape belong to. The Algonquin, Ottawa, Menominee, Potawatomi, and Ojibway nations call themselves collectively "Anishinabi," which Micmac elder Grandfather William Commanda has said could be translated as "good people."

My own Micmac people have similar names they call themselves, such as *meegamooatch* or *meegamaw,* meaning "we are all related by blood" or "my relatives" or "allies." But the demeaning term Micmac seems to have been derived from the French slang term *micmac,* or "this and that, all mixed together." Maliseet derives from an Algonquin word for "they talk funny," which is far from complimentary. Many Maliseet would rather return to the name Etchimen, "People of the Sandy Berries," referring to blackberries and raspberries, a name that honors the abundance of Maine's beautiful shoreline.[16] The Montagnais and Naskapi of northern Quebec are currently engaged in a struggle to be recognized as a single nation known as the Innu, which means "we the people."

Pequot, or Pequotanoag, means "People at the Shallow Water," but the English translated it as "Destroyers of Men," which they somehow derived from the word pequanock, which means "a cleared field."[17] After defeating them at Mystic, the English forebade them by law to use the term "Pequot." This made it difficult for them to regroup, yet they succeeded in only ten years, under two other names. That terrifying definition "destroyers" persists today in most textbooks, along with exaggerations of their warlike nature, yet it was probably only a nickname before his Majesty's Royal experts linked the two unrelated words pequanock and Pequot. Quahogs and conches are both found only in shallow salt water, and the Pequotanoag were dependent on them for their famed wampum–shell bead production, hence the poetic, "People at the Shallow Water."

The term *illinois* relates to the Delaware Indians. The French recognized these prairie people as closely related to the Lenni Lenape, and called them "Ils Lenni-uois," similar to how we say "Le Quebequois." Hence the name Illinois. Their Illinois language is so similar to Lenape that they call themselves Lenni, or "real men," as the Lenape do.

The Fox should really be called Mesquakee, "People of the Red Clay." It was their French adversaries who called them sly "foxes" because of their reddish complexion. Arapaho is a word for "People with Many Skins" in the nomenclature of their enemies, the Crow. They would rather be called Kananavich, "Bison Path People." Likewise, the term Cheyenne is a Lakota word for "they speak jibberish!" They would *much* rather be called Tsitsista or "The People." They too are currently engaged in a struggle to be recognized by the preferred name. The name of the Algonquin-speaking Piegan means "small or humble robes," in other words, "po' folk." It was said that in the early 1800s, their buffalo robes were tattered and inadequate due to hard conditions. They call themselves Kainah, or "Many Chiefs," which sounds more impressive.

One Delaware Indian told me that when she and her siblings were growing up their grandma told them they were descended from "nanny goats." Naturally they were embarrassed to tell their friends about this strange family tree. It was only years later, after grandma had passed away, taking her knowledge with her, that they discovered that indeed they were descendants of "nanny goats": Nanticoke Indians, an ancient branch of the Lenape of eastern shore Maryland.

There is even a story that America was not named after Columbus because of a rivalry between two secret Masonic societies in Europe. Columbus had been part of the first group, but defected to the second, a competing pious religious community. Although he did win the boat race to the new world, the first "jilted" group had more media clout, and was able to publish an atlas which had Amerigo Vespucci, their new poster boy, on the cover, with his first name written across the contours of the "New World," making all of us living in the Western Hemisphere "Malapropian-Americans."

Now that we have stripped away the modern veneer of names that stands as a block to a more profound understanding of ancient geography, we can explore the terrain as the Lenape knew it, as a landscape dominated by the will of nature, not of man. For the purposes of orienting the reader who may be new to Algonquin geography, we will keep our travels within the boundaries of New York State, conceptual lines that didn't exist before the 1600s, and also recognize the modern boundaries of New York City. Given these concessions to practicality, the Algonquin territories within the boundaries of the state fall into three distinct hoops: Long Island to the east, the Hudson River Valley to the north and west, and in the center, the islands and land masses that make up New York City.

Although tiny in comparison to the other two regions, there is something about New York City that has captivated the curiosity of people all over the world. More people are familiar with the street and neighborhood names of New York than any other city on earth. Therefore we will start our journey by exploring the Natives of New York City first, followed by those of the Hudson Valley, and then the Natives of Long Island. In this way we will leave no stone unturned in our exploration of New York State's ancient Algonquin civilization and geography.

2

HOW GREEN
WAS MANHATTAN

Manhattan has been known by many names. The Unami Delaware called it Menatay, or "island." The Munsee nicknamed it Mahatuouh, "the place for gathering bow wood" (usually hickory or cherry). Most people called it Manhattan or Manahatta, "rocky island" in Munsee. However it was also known as Mahahachtanienk, "A Place of General Inebriation." Manhattan received this nickname because on more than one occasion, Native people were found drunk there, apparently after being convinced by the colonists that receiving rum instead of trade goods for their furs was a good idea. Alcohol, with the possible exception of hard cider, was new to the Native Americans, who didn't realize its powers and hazards. Even squirrels can become tipsy from eating fermented apples on the ground, according to Native botanist James Flowers, and the Lenape would have noticed this. However, there is no record of any ritual or social use of alcoholic beverages in any Algonquin society. Anthropological maps such as those of Molly Braun in *Atlas of the Native American Indian* shows alcohol use to be a Southwestern phenomenon. There, its use is strictly controlled by taboos and penalties for misuse. It's ironic that Manhattan was called "place of general inebriation" after only a few years of exposure to alcohol because today it is known for being a big party town,

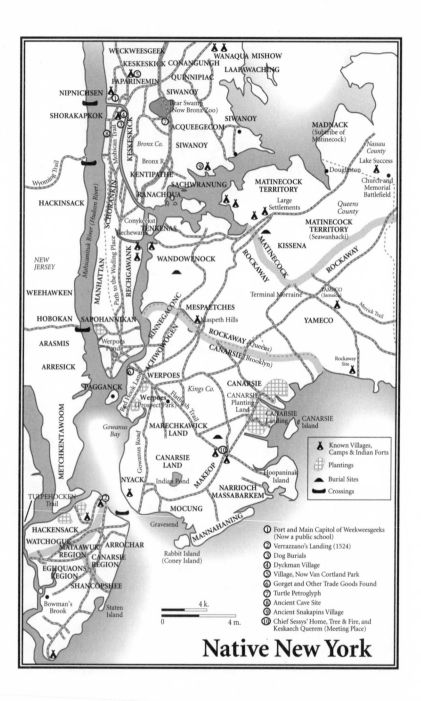

Native New York

with well over one thousand drinking establishments on Manhattan Island alone.

Manhattan was called "The City of the Manhattoes" by Herman Melville in *Moby-Dick*, and his characters include the Algonquin whale-hunter, Tashtego. Today we call it by the Munsee term Manhattan.

Not all of Manhattan's nicknames were so prosaic. According to author Will Grant, the Delaware called the island Hay-la-py-ee-chen-quay-hee-lass or "The Place Where the Sun Is Born." The Unami, looking eastward from what is now New Jersey through the doors in their wigwams as they rose to greet the dawn, would see that rocky island stretching across the horizon, and beyond it, the shining face of grandfather sun. Mohawk people called Manhattan Knonoge, "A Place of Reeds."[1]

If the number of names a place possesses is a measure of its mythological and practical importance, the island of Manhattan is certainly a place of power. But the way the Europeans used that power differed dramatically from the ways of the gentler Lenape.[2]

PARADISE-ON-HUDSON: YOU ARE STANDING ON SACRED LAND

The following summation of life in New York City before European contact is from a plaque placed at the tip of Manhattan by the Heye Museum: "Farming communities thrived around Menatay (Manhattan) where the soil was well drained and the water was good. Following the round of the seasons, the first people planted, hunted, and fished in the spring. In the warmest season when the smell of wild flowers perfumed the air, they traveled for trade and adventure, meeting here to exchange goods, share knowledge, give thanks, and show respect to the spirits. When the leaves changed color, the villagers gathered to harvest, hunt, and collect food for the winter. During the cold moons of long nights they made objects for trade, repaired tools, told lesson stories, and celebrated festivals."

The Lenape were devoted to the land and to the natural world, for it was the root of their spiritual life. According to eyewitness accounts, the land was fragrant and bountiful under their care, in spite of a dense population on both sides of the Mohicanituk (Hudson River).

The earliest Dutch descriptions of Manhattan are so beautiful they are difficult to believe today. They describe "vast meadows of grass as high as a man's middle, forests of walnut, cedar, chestnut, maple, oak." These were large healthy specimens, not the blighted type you find today. There were also healthy elm trees and hemlock in the area, both now struggling to survive.[3] Dutchmen wrote of "birds too loud to hear yourself talking." Elsewhere, Dutch huntsmen wrote of being able to "kill 170 blackbirds with one shot of buckshot, and eleven 16-pound geese with another single shot." According to other accounts, at the sound of the blunderbuss, an early, wide-bore rifle with poor accuracy—the word was actually *donderbus,* or "thunderbox,"[4]—the sky would fill up with wild swans flying to safety.[5] All of this is hard to imagine standing on Manhattan Island today.

Swedish botanist Peter Kalm wrote of "a kind of wild duck with immense numbers upon the water." English cleric Andrew Burnaby spoke of "delightful prospects of rivers, islands, fields, hills, woods, the Narrows, New York City, vessels sailing to and fro, and innumerable porpoises playing upon the surface of the water."[6] Johannes de Laet, one of the first Dutch historians to describe the region, wrote, "The land is excellent and agreeable, full of noble forests, trees, and grapevines. [Working it will] render it one of the finest and most fruitful lands in that part of the world."[7]

In 1653, Adriaen van der Donck, a Dutch chronicler, wrote, "The sweet ruler that influences the wisdom, power, and appearance of man, of animals, and plants, is the air. Many name it the temprament [*sic*] or the climate. The air in New Netherlands is so dry, sweet, and healthy, that we need not wish that it were otherwise. In purity, agreeableness, and fineness it would be folly to seek for an equal of it in any other country."[8] Four hundred years later, you can take an hour's walk on a summer day in Manhattan and you will find your skin covered with a thin gray film that you can rub off and examine on your hands. The Lenape would have been horrified to think of breathing such air. Some still are.

GROWTH INDUSTRIES

Dutch sailors described "boats escorted by whole schools of playful whales, seals, and porpoises."[9] They also told of twelve-inch oysters and monster lobsters. When the first Europeans arrived, the fish were so plentiful that according to accounts, they could be caught by hand. Archaeologists have found huge shell middens on both sides of the Hudson at least as far north as Beacon, and also at Tottenville, Staten Island, and Tuckerton, New Jersey, which produced oyster and clam shells twice the size of those found today. Some oysters would have been over forty years old, indicating careful harvesting and management of shellfish. The Lenape bred lobsters for size as well. (Since lobsters regenerate their organs, they can live well past one hundred years, growing to lengths reputedly of six feet in cold seawater, as described by the first Dutch sailors.)[10]

Whippoorwills were abundant then, and were still abundant even a hundred years ago; now they are nearly extinct due to DDT and other pesticides.[11] The cedar waxwing was equally abundant in upper New York State, even twenty years ago, but it too is rarely seen, or seen in small flocks. Once there were clouds of them winging by.[12]

"Orchards bore apples of incomparable sweetness, and 'pears larger than a fist.' Every spring the hills and fields were dyed red with ripening strawberries."[13] Certain types of apples, including Lucullian and Esopus,[14] were apparently already being grown by the Lenape, as were cherries and watermelons.

The Lenape's farming practices rotated around the "three sisters": corn, beans, and squash. Planted together, they work as a team, or family. First the Lenape would plant the corn on a small mound so that it took root better. They would place dead fish and plant material in the mound so that it would rot and keep the roots warm in the cold nights of early spring. Then when the corn was a foot high, they would plant red beans, which use the corn stalk as a bean-pole. When it became warmer, they would plant squash between the mounds. The squash leaves repel bugs, kill weeds, and shade the roots of the corn and beans, keeping the ground cool.[15] Then in the late summer, they harvested them and made succotash out of the beans and corn, throwing in tasty tidbits such as fish brains for flavor.

Native Americans as a whole enjoyed over three hundred kinds of corn and all the types of beans we have today except horse and soy, which is from China. They also enjoyed seventy-nine varieties of so-called "Irish" potatoes, developed by Indians and sent to the Irish to help them survive the famines of the 1700s and early 1800s, caused in part by the English taking their grain as taxes. Native Americans had been enjoying the "Irish" potato for five hundred years before the first Irishmen came to the New World. When a blight wiped out the potatoes in Ireland in the 1840s—the Potato Famine—a large percentage of the population emigrated to the New World, birthplace of the potato. It should also be noted that the Choctaw of Oklahoma, neighbors to the absentee Delaware, sent money to the Irish during the 1840s, even though they had so little themselves.

Other Natives to the south had developed and bred tomatoes and peppers out of the nightshade family, thought by Europeans to be too poisonous to be useful.[16] The Lenape also grew Jerusalem artichokes and sunflowers for food, and goosefoot for the tiny, edible seeds that are harvested later in the year.

The Lenape had, according to Dutch accounts, many peach trees, well laden with fruit, as well as apple orchards and also cherry trees. They had well over two dozen planting fields and eighty campsites in Manhattan and the surrounding territories. The women took care of most of the agricultural duties, although accounts suggest that the men grew and cured tobacco. A Dutchman wrote that "their tobacco is not as good as ours ... [yet] they still prefer their practices to ours. Our methods require too much labor and care to please them."

What the writer didn't realize is that the Dutch plowing methods were damaging to the soil, while Lenape methods were much more ecologically sound, preserving the nitrogen in the soil many times more efficiently, and disrupting the land hardly at all, except for the controlled burning of crop fields in the early spring, which seems to have had a positive effect in the long run. The Dutch were in the habit of stealing the "burnt" Lenape cornfields because the soil was so good, then bragging about their crops. Their success was short-lived due to subsequent soil damage.

"The Last Fish"

Today one can walk for many blocks in Manhattan without passing a single tree or blade of grass. The fish in the rivers and bay are unfit to eat, and few if any porpoises, unless they are sick and disoriented, come up the Hudson anymore. Despite forty years of environmental activism, there are still sturgeon-killing PCBs in the river. There are few birds other than pigeons feeding on garbage, and the air often smells of diesel.

There is no more food for the taking as in ancient times. One cannot just lie down anywhere on the grass to take a nap in the sun. Streets are everywhere you look, yet now there is no place to park. To an Algonquin observer it would seem that it is a place where the needs of the car have eclipsed the needs of person, yet most people who live in Manhattan do not even own a car.

The Algonquin had strict rules concerning the use of the land. The bottom line, later adopted by the Boy Scouts, was "Pack it in, pack it out," "Leave the land as you found it," "Leave no traces." This means that every hole in the ground should be filled up after you're done, that everything should return to the earth. That is why Owasco[17] stone-lined or box graves were never adopted by the Lenape; boxes take too long to decay. The Lenape used bark to line the grave pit instead. Algonquin sweat lodges were torn down after four days of ritual, the stones returned to the earth, and the pits and holes filled up and covered with carefully preserved clumps of grass so that only the most trained eye could tell someone had been there. The Lenape built no monuments, libraries, or museums, so that the earth would not be marred by blocks of stone.

There is a famous Cree saying, not attributed to any one chief or sachem, which expresses the way many Munsee and Native Americans in general feel about what has become of their island, Manhattan: "Only after the last tree has been cut down, only after the last river has been poisoned, only after the last fish has been caught, only then will you find that money cannot be eaten."

Where else on Turtle Island (North America) can one so clearly see that prophecy coming true? Surely encountering the environment of Manhattan and most of the surrounding boroughs today would make a woodland Indian feel that something had gone terribly wrong with the world.

POPULATING THE ANCIENT CITY

Some may say, "Of course the land was beautiful; there was almost nobody there. New York City today is relatively spotless when you think of how many people live there." However, there is every indication that the native population in 1524 was quite high, and that the vigorous abundance of every aspect of nature found by the first white visitors was the result of their remarkable stewardship of the land, most notably their soil conservation techniques, but also the careful husbandry of ocean life. This stewardship, not luck, had brought them the fruits of paradise.

To get an idea of the environmental planning skills of the first

New Yorkers, we need to have an idea of their populations and the extent to which they built up permanent settlements. Few subjects have eluded historians more completely, but every few years, new research brings the pre-contact population estimates up.

The Charter of the English Governor Dongan, a document written in 1686 when the English city of "New" York was only twenty-two years old, declared New York to be "an ancient citie." By the time the Americans declared their independence nearly a century later, declaring New York their political as well as financial capital, all knowledge of that ancient past had already been lost. Few seemed to realize how large a population had been displaced to make room for their thriving metropolis.

Most New Yorkers today don't realize that a great nation existed here a thousand years before Columbus. At the time of European contact, Edwin G. Burrows and Mike Wallace, the authors of the Pulitzer Prize–winning *Gotham,* state, "What is now New York City had as many as fifteen thousand inhabitants—estimates vary widely—with perhaps another thirty to fifty thousand in the adjacent parts of New Jersey, Connecticut, Westchester County, and Long Island."

Dr. Dean Snow at the University of Pennsylvania disputes these figures based on the assertion that the land can only sustain so many people per square mile. He asserts that the highest density along the southern New England and New York coast around 1600 c.e. was no more than four people per square kilometer. As the area of the five boroughs is about 950 square kilometers, his formula suggests that the Native population of the five boroughs was only around 3,800 people, about a quarter of what Burrows and Wallace permit. These are pre-epidemic figures. Snow calculates there were "probably about 40,000 Delawares" (including the Munsee) total before decimation.

Although these "probable" figures are higher than the conservative estimates of only fifteen years ago, they are by no means the highest *possible* figures. Dr. Snow himself, in his book *The*

Archaeology of New England, states possibility ranges for Algonquin populations in New York State, which, on the high end, are astounding in their ecological implications. For Munsee people of the Lower Hudson Valley, he estimates a range of 18,300 to 32,300. For the Munsee of the Upper Delaware in New Jersey, he estimates between 9,000 and 19,000. This means there were between 24,500 and 51,300 Munsees total, between the Lower Hudson and the Upper Delaware Valleys combined. Snow also estimates a population range of 24,300 to 51,300 Mohican before contact.

Unfortunately most of Manhattan and the other four boroughs have been so severely altered that little archaeological record survives. But what is known—the diggings, the early trail maps, the numbers of distinct tribal units and their available food sources—does not disprove the higher figures.

If, as some believe, the Lenape population in the New York area was 65,000 at its height in 1524, the date of Verrazzano's arrival, it would have ranked with the top cities of Europe. By comparison, in that same year of 1524, the population of Rome was 90,000. Rome was sacked three years later, and its population fell to 40,000. In 1300 c.e. there were only sixteen cities in Europe with populations equal to or greater than 50,000, mostly within three European urban centers. In 1500 there were a few additional cities rising above the 50,000 mark in population, plus sixteen additional cities with populations over 20,000. In 1524 there were less than thirty-two European cities that matched the 15,000 figure cited in *Gotham* by Burrows and Wallace for the Lenape of New York City.[18]

No Longer at This Address

In *The Archaeology of New England,* Snow estimates that of the 24,300 to 51,300 Mohicans living before contact, only 4,500 remained after the epidemics that swept through the Native population, fourteen epidemics between 1640 and 1690 alone.[19] The Iroquois fared better as they were further from the coast; their population had an original range of 9,000 to 11,300, and was reduced to between 4,100 and 5,100 after the epidemic. Much better warriors, this ratio gave Iroquois dominance over the Mohican for the first time.[20]

Snow estimates the probable population of the Lower Connecticut and Long Island Quiripi and Unquachaug was between 24,700 and 29,000 before the epidemics. Smallpox hit them especially hard, and their numbers were reduced to 1,200, a mortality rate of 95 percent. He estimates the Pequot of Eastern Connecticut and Eastern Long Island (Montauk) at 13,300, with 3,000 surviving the holocaust of germs. The Canarsie alone may have had 4,000 members, including at least eighteen subtribes. They also had vast cornfields, and a large trading network that stretched for hundreds of miles—by land, sea, and waterway. According to SUNY New Paltz's Professor Laurence Hauptman, the effect of smallpox, diphtheria, and fever were truly decimating for the people of ancient New York, with as many as 90 percent dying of disease in some areas. This means that a population of 65,000 would have been reduced to 6,500 by the decimation. From 1664 to 1670, the number of Lenape villages in Manhattan shrank from six to a desperate two. In *Denton's Description of New York,* published in 1670, Denton wrote, "The Indians disappear by disease by the hand of God." The English considered it divine intervention.

The aftermath numbers are well known, as the people were subject to European census counts by then, but what is so important, and so elusive, is the size of the original population. That would give us a clearer picture of the very nature of Algonquin civilization in the region.

The Unknowing Multitudes

The land that was sacred to the Lenape for millennia is now home to millions of people. New York City is only a small part of Lenape Hoking, "Dwelling-Place of the Lenape." The land of a single Lenape-speaking nation, the Canarsie, is now home to over two million people who hail from all over the world. These squatters are called "Brooklynites." Another two million live on the land of the Rockaway and Matinecock Indians, the neighbors of the Canarsie to the north, in what is now Queens, and eastward.

Including the Unami, Munsee, Renneiu, Unalatchtigo, Piscataway, Nanticoke, Powhatan, and Hatteras dialects as part of the Lenape Delaware Confederacy of languages and its extended peoples (all linguistic descendants of the Munsee people of New York), and including the closely related and intertwined Mohican group of languages, all peoples who frequented Manhattan, it could be said that their traditional territory is now occupied by approximately thirty-four million people, covering all or parts of ten states and the District of Columbia. Thirteen million of those are in New York State alone. Albany and New York, New York; Philadelphia, Pennsylvania; Washington, D.C.; Baltimore, Maryland; Roanoke, Virginia; plus all of New Jersey and Delaware were once the gardens and villages of the Lenape. Their trails are now paved highways, their footprints buried underneath the cement.

If we also include the territories of the peoples who spoke closely related languages, such as the Prairie Algonquin (a.k.a. Wakashan), the Shawnee, Illinois, and even the New England nations, the figure would be two to three times higher. This expanded Lenape region would include much of Ohio, Indiana, Illinois, and northern Kentucky, plus, for a brief period, the eastern edge of Iowa.

English was not widely spoken in New York and New Jersey until 1664, when the Dutch surrendered to English forces after a long series of skirmishes. From 1598 to 1664, Dutch, Lenape, and Mohican were the important tongues, and before that, only Lenape and Mohican, which are closely related languages. Perhaps to a much lesser degree, Mohawk was spoken. It's hard to imagine now, but not that long ago, the entire eastern seaboard from Hartford down to Cape Hatteras was highly populated with Native Americans living tribal lives, and all speaking a similar language, the many dialects of Lenape. Native American researcher Lee Sultzman has written that there is no doubt that the Lenape, Shawnee, Miami, Illinois, Mohicans, and their cousins throughout New England were once one people speaking one dialect, in fairly recent time.

The Lenape and their close kin are all Algonquin-speaking people, an even larger group of Native Americans who are also all related. The territories of the five hundred or more bands and nations of the Algonquin are now occupied by at least 111 million people throughout the United States and Canada. There are sixty-five yet more distantly related Algonquin groups in the Pacific Northwest, and among all those people, the Lenape are referred to respectfully as "The Grandfathers."

Manhattan Still Beautiful into Her 1700s

In spite of the devastation of the Native people, the natural beauty of the land did not disappear overnight. In the early 1700s, New York City north of Roosevelt Street was still lovely, still a bit untamed. The "Collect," as the Dutch called the seventy-acre pond near where City Hall now stands, drained both east and west in rivulets, depending on the season. Nearby Beekman's Swamp stretched from the East River near Gold Street, almost to the City Hall area, part of a quagmire of springs and streams that crossed the entire island along the axis of today's Canal Street, prohibiting northward expansion until it was filled in around 1730. It was said that Dutch families skated from river to river in wintertime on the frozen waters. The swamps were death traps to wandering cows and a nuisance for travelers, so most citizens were relieved when much of it went underground or was filled in. The names of Spring and Canal Streets still bear testimony to the struggle to remove all above-ground running water from the island.[21]

Before the pond that was home to the Werpoes was destroyed, the ground between Roosevelt and Catherine Streets was so soft, only the desperately poor would live there, their yards becoming "little islands" in the springtime. In 1728, when the municipal authorities lost their taste for the ripe and pungent smell caused by curing leather, tanners and shoemakers were forced to live there, adding to the misery of the tenants of Manhattan's Beekman's Swamp. Breweries, distilleries, and slaughterhouses followed. What had been a key wetlands area, home to ducks, water animals, and eventually, Dutch cows, became a toxic wasteland of "problem industries."

Even in 1763, the part of town that is now at the foot of the Manhattan Bridge was green hills covered with sheep and cows in the midst of grazing, with hill-roaming split-rail fences and rustic dirt roads. It was said that oats did not thrive there, but that "Indian corn stalks rise to seven or eight feet, the blades are a deep green, and make at this season a very luxuriant appearance."[22] At that time the city was home to eighteen thousand people, had only expanded north to a point halfway between today's Brooklyn and Manhattan Bridges, and only as far west as Broadway. Even Broadway only extended to Worth Street before reverting back to a trail. In 1773, the city paid Abraham Mesier for "carting ye stumps from Broadway."[23] After the colonial rebellion, it expanded like a wave of brick and stone, swallowing everything that was green before it.

THE GREAT VILLAGE ON THE WATER

Many Algonquin today feel pity for New Yorkers, some feel angry at what has been done to their Mother Earth, while others feel disoriented or even hopeless. However, despite the harm to the environment, New York does retain something of the quality of a village, where everyone walks along the same pathways every day, greeting and conversing with the same people. There's a feeling of neighborhood pride and identity, and people stick together just because they are from the same block. In some ways, each of the thousand "little New Yorks" has something that most of North

America has lost, a face-to-face way of living and sharing space and a sense of belonging that is very specific to a certain place called home. The Munsee of Canada still call New York City and the surrounding area "home," even though most of them have never seen it. Today they refer to it as "back east," or Wundjiyarlkun.

WALKING GENTLY ON THE EARTH

Among the descendants of the Native Americans of New York are those who insist there have been as many as thirty thousand Algonquin living in certain counties upstate. Archaeologists generally scoff at these figures, but they agree that the postholes from Algonquin movable wigwams were so tiny, four centimeters in some cases, and so temporary that they don't register in the archaeological record. They truly left no impact on the land, as was their desire. Whereas the Iroquois left large shell midden heaps off the sides of hills, the midland Algonquins were more likely to compost.[24] In Micmac today there is no word for garbage, but there is a word for potato peelings, which implies "nearly useless." Archaeologists have found ancient composting sites in Algonquin settlements deep under the ground. It is hard for people today to believe that such a large population could have "walked so gently on the earth."

3

A Paradise for the Living

The New York City area before the Dutch was not only a paradise on earth ecologically. For those who knew the passwords to the secret lodges, it was a paradise for the spirit as well. New York was home to "enlightened masters" or *neolinuk,* wisdom teachers, not to mention seers, visionaries, and saints. *Gitschach summen* means "one who is enlightened."

The Lenape respected and had their own terms for each of these types of people. Any sign of disrespect to others or to the earth would have been challenged. Among the Algonquin, it is generally said that if you don't have visions and communication with animals and spirit guides, you're doing something wrong. You should follow no man or woman, but follow spirit itself, wherever it leads. Nevertheless, from time to time truly gifted men or women would rise to prominence, and crowds would gather at council oaks and elms throughout the city to listen to them speak, or to be more exact, to listen to see if spirit was speaking through them. The ashes from those council fires are still buried beneath New York's streets, the bones of those saints still rest encased by cement. All of them spoke of loving the earth as if she were their own mother.

A Kind and Loving People

Mores and modes of behavior have changed drastically over the last five hundred years in Manhattan since "wild savages," as the Dutch called them, roamed. As a matter of fact, they've gotten much worse.

In speaking of the character of the American red man, the early French Catholic missionary, Father La Jeune said that "in point of intellect" he ranked highly. "The Indian I can well compare to some of our own French villagers who are left without instruction. I have scarcely seen any person who has come from France to this country who does not acknowledge that the savages have more intellect or capacity than most of our peasantry."

The French traveler Charlevoix was even more emphatic: "The beauty of their imagination," he says, "equals its vivacity, which appears in all their discourses. They are very quick at repartee, and their harangues are full of shining passages that would have been applauded at Rome or Athens. Their eloquence has a strength, nature, and pathos which no art can give and which Greeks admired in the Barbarians."

In 1634, Captain Thomas Young described the Delaware as "very well proportioned, well featured, gentle, tractable, and docile." He went on to say, "I do not believe that there are any people on earth who are more attached to their relatives and offspring than these Indians are." John Heckewelder, who published *An Account of the History, Manners, and Customs of the Indian Nations* in 1819, commented, "The Delawares always treated their women with respect and reverence and even in council their voices were heard, and rarely were they forced to do anything against their wills."[1]

In "an account of the conduct of the Society of Friends toward the Indian tribes," published in London in 1844, the head of the Society of Friends of England wrote: "Amidst all the devastating incursions of the Indians in North America it is a remarkable fact that no friend who stood faithful to his principles in the disuse of all weapons of war, the cause of which was generally understood by the Indians, ever suffered molestation from them."

Wherever the Dutch and English settled, it was found that the Algonquin would not attack those believed to be peaceful. For example, the Bull house in Hamptonburg, New York, in Orange County, was surrounded by Native American settlements, but even during the bloody French and Indian War, it was not harmed by the Native people because the Bull family were nonaggressive.

William Penn, who interacted mostly with Lenape, and with the Iroquois to a lesser extent, said of Native people, "In liberality they excel, nothing is too good for their friend. Wealth circulateth like the blood, though none want what another hath, yet they are exact observers of property."[2]

Penn opposed the British point of view that any Indian "living on land discovered by Englishmen who made any effort to oppose the exploitation of their country, were to be treated as enemies of England." Penn suggested just the opposite: "Don't abuse them, but let them have justice, and you win them."[3] A Dutch observer in 1655 made a similar observation: "They are all free by nature, and will not bear any domineering or lording over them."[4]

Penn observed, "I have never seen more natural Sagacity, and he will deserve the name of Wise, that outwits them in any treaty about a thing they understand." Weslager adds, "Time and again, the Delawares proved to be excellent diplomats and negotiators."[5] The Lenape, as part of the Algonquin world, were inheritors of what Eunice Bauman Nelson, an elder of the Penobscot tribe has called "The Way of the Heron." In Lenape the translation would be *Aaney Talika.* It is the way of the peacemaker, and it is a great tradition throughout the Algonquin world. Penn's observations on Lenape statesmanship were astute and accurate, for the Lenape were the Grandfathers, the elder statesmen of the realm.

Penn summed up much of what is best about the Algonquin

"government by communication not force," when he said, "'Tis admirable to consider how powerful the Chiefs are and yet how they move by the breath of the people."[6]

In *North American Indians*, George Catlin, the foremost portrait painter of Native Americans in history, wrote, "By nature they are discreet and modest, unassuming and inoffensive, and all history proves them to have been found friendly and hospitable on all parts of the American Continent. And from what I have seen I am willing and proud to add, for the ages who are only to read of these people, my testimony to that which was given by the immortal Columbus . . . 'I swear to Your Majesties that there is not a better people in the world than these, more affectionate, affable, or mild. They love their neighbors as themselves, and they always speak smilingly.'"[7]

It is hard to describe in words the deep inner fire of the surviving Lenape when they speak of the spirit world or the natural one; the silence between the words is as eloquent as the words themselves. It defies proper translation, though some have tried. The New Netherlands office in the middle 1600s wrote that the Lenape "used few words, which they previously well consider." Also, according to that office, "they are quick witted and quite modest."[8] The Dutch historian Van der Donck wrote in the 1650s that the Lenape "said no more than is necessary. They despise lying, yet are still not very precise in performance of their other engagements. Swearing and scolding are not common."[9]

Van der Donck also observed that the Lenape refused to let an enemy win control over their spirit by making them cry out. Free will was the basis for living a spirit-guided life; allowing someone else to make one yell or cry would be giving up free will. The Lenape men would sing when being tortured, and would continue singing until death rather than show reaction to pain.

One Dutch account reported that the Lenape were "mild except when aroused, and greedy for vengeance,"[10] when their rules for self-government were violated, perhaps not as pretty a picture, but realistic nonetheless.

THE OTHER '60S

According to James Folts, New York's state historian, the Munsee experienced a powerful upsurge of renewed interest in their spiritual and mystical traditions after only a hundred years of "missionary zeal." Not unlike the 1960s in twentieth-century New York, the 1760s brought all kinds of sages, philosophers, prophets, and holy men to the forefront of the Munsee nation, and their "gurus" ranged from cult leaders to truly powerful visionaries.

Around 1760, the now industrialized cities of the Ohio Valley were all Algonquin villages, and several "prophets" walked the trails among them. The Delaware knew and listened to the teachings of Neolin, the "Enlightened One," who was called "The Delaware Prophet," by some, and "The Imposter" by the English. (Apparently the Enlightened One had critical things to say about them.) Another great teacher who rose to influence after Neolin, Oneeum, was called "the Munsee prophet." Tunskwatawa, "the Shawnee prophet," was an important player in Delaware history, as was his brother Tecumseh, who was truly enlightened, *gitschach summen* (in Unami), and whom some compare with the Buddha.

According to 1960s environmental advocate and Algonquin author Manitonquat, or "Medicine Story," the famous peace symbol with two fingers spread in a "V" did not originate with Winston Churchill, whose "V" was for victory, but with the Native American peace activist camp in the '60s. He believes it may actually represent the Iroquois "Tree of Peace" in Native American sign language, many details of which have been carried over into American Sign Language. During the revolutionary times of Pontiac and Tecumseh, the Iroquois and Algonquin were working more closely together than ever before, in spite of their language differences, and were using

Native American sign language to communicate. Certainly the Algonquin could have learned it from the Iroquois at that time, and passed it on two hundred years later.

Of the eighteenth-century surge in spirituality Folts writes, "Some of them [the Munsee] tried to revive old customs to reduce their dependence on European culture. Others were converted to Christianity by missionaries of the Moravian Bretheren based in Bethlehem, PA. Both movements—the 'pagan' revival and Christian conversion—had a common origin" in the repeated visits of the missionaries to Minisink settlements along the Susquehanna in the 1740s. Folts continues:

> Some Munsees decided to preach a different message. Possibly in response to Christian proselytizing, Munsee traditionalists active in the Wyoming Valley in the 1750's, at Assinisink in the 1760's and on the upper Allegheny in the 1770's, taught that the Creator had made three races of humankind [the brown, the red, and the white], with a separate salvation for each. They denounced liquor and other European corruptions; they revived ancient ceremonies; and they preached a message of reconciliation to native communities that were often torn by factions. The Munsee cultural revival was not only a reaction to cultural deprivation, but also a positive, creative attempt to re-establish a system of social and spiritual values. The message of these traditionalist reformers had a persistent appeal among the non-Christian Munsees. Wangomend, who lived at Assinisink and relocated to Goshgoshunk and later to the Ohio, was an influential traditionalist and became a leader of the Ohio Delawares during the Revolutionary War. Oneim [spelled Oneeum by some], active as a "sorceror" [*sic*] among the Susquehanna Munsees in the 1770s, preached the same traditionalist message at Muncy Town in Ontario over thirty years later.

Neolin began preaching around the year 1762 among the Delaware of the Muskingum Valley in Ohio. He spoke against intertribal war, drunkenness, polygamy, and the use of magic, and he promised his hearers that if they would but heed his words, the Native Americans would be strong again and able to resist the whites. He prepared symbolic charts of his message on deerskin and left them in various villages to help his converts teach others. The religious fervor spread rapidly and is said to have been an inspiration to Pontiac.

The Munsee prophet Oneeum also played an important role after Neolin's downfall. He was described but not named by historian John Heckewelder as living and preaching his prophecy in the upper Susquehanna Valley, and was found again at Cattaragus by missionary David Zeisberger, teaching the same way, and was then identified as the Munsee prophet "Oneeum." As they did with other spiritual leaders of the traditional ways, the missionaries took an immediate dislike to Oneeum and had little good to say of his teachings, implying that any such talk was "dangerous," which it probably was, just as Moses' talk among the Hebrews was dangerous during their captivity. Oneeum died at Munsey Town in 1819 without a successor. A missionary claimed a deathbed conversion to Christianity, but there were apparently no witnesses other than the missionary himself. Folts continues:

> The cultural and religious ferment at the Minisink town on the Susquehanna during the 1750's also resulted in the formation of a separate, reformist Munsee community that eventually became Christian. *Papunhank* was its leader. He had been a resident of the Minisink town on the Susquehanna, and he undoubtedly heard the missionaries who visited the area. After the death of his father, he experienced a spiritual crisis, climaxed by a vision in the woods—a transforming experience that many Delaware have experienced. Papunhank now established his own community at Wyalusing—the town is still in existence; a Lenape research library is located there. It was there in Wyalusing that he and other Munsees tried to live in a spirit of brotherly love as the

Creator had intended. (Papunhank had visited Philadelphia, the "City of Brotherly Love," and was much influenced by the Quakers as well as by the missionaries who visited the Wyoming Valley.) In the spring of 1763, the Moravian missionary David Zeisberger accepted the Wyalusing Munsee's oft-repeated invitation to visit them. Convinced by Zeisberger of his sinfulness, Papunhank was converted to Christianity, along with many of his people.[11]

This surge of traditionalist enthusiasm for seeking guidance and protection from spirit in utter faith was not invented by these rebels. It was a delayed echo of the song their New York and New Jersey ancestors had sung for a thousand years. The teaching tales of Oneeum, Wangomend, Neolin, and Papunhank were the offshoots of stories they had heard from their grandfathers, stories that were told in, and in many cases originated in, the territory of New York City.

Teaching Tales from Ancient New York City

Like all Algonquin teaching tales, Lenape stories are not just for entertainment. They often contain messages from the spirit world. Only a few of the fantastic, dreamlike stories and folk tales from the Munsee of New York City have survived. Four are known to anthropologists, which I will retell here in my own words. Many other Munsee tales probably have their origins in the wigwams and longhouses that once graced New York City's landscape, but the exact locations are unknown and cannot be verified. The people were always looking for new stories to tell, and a good one spread quickly, even across cultural and linguistic boundaries.[12]

The Hackensack Munsee of Bayonne and Staten Island told this now well-known story of the creation of the world:

> At first there was only water; then a small dark green area appeared in the center. It was the topmost peak of a gigantic tortoise's shell. As the tortoise raised its back, water ran off in every direction until the full size of the turtle was revealed, and it was the

size of Turtle Island, all of North America, today. There was a lot of
mud on that turtle, which eventually dried and became the surface
of the earth. Over the years a great tree grew up in the middle of
the earth, and the first man sprouted from the tree's root. The tree
eventually became bent over and the tip of one of its long branches
touched the earth. In that spot the first woman sprang up from the
tip of the tree, naked as a baby. The first man was very pleased with
her. They separated themselves from the tree and from the earth in
order to be together but never forgot their origins—rooted in the
earth. They raised a family, and their children had children and so
forth, and the story continues today. Staten Island today looks a bit
like that turtle, with his big head pointing to the southwest.

There is another story that has survived the move from New York
City, however it is only a fragment. Passed down by a man named
Charles Wolley in *Two Years' Journal in New York*, it dates from about
1678. This is my own telling of the story:

> Five hundred years ago, a man called Wach-que-ow came
> down from above, riding upon a barrel's head let down by a rope.
> He lived among the Lenape near what is now New York City. He
> stayed sixty years, and taught the people many things. Then he told
> them that the place he came from was a happy place, where every-
> one worked together in harmony and peaceful cooperation, and
> where people spoke truthfully to one another. He said that in that
> other world were many of their Native American nations, and so
> he left them to return to that world. The Lenape took his stories to
> heart and have tried their best to live by them ever since.[13]

Charles Wolley also recorded two other tales in a similar spiritual
vein. Again, I will tell them in my own voice:

> Meco Nish, a good Lenape man, was everyone's friend. One
> day he disappeared into the woods and failed to come back at the

usual time. They searched for him for sixteen days, worrying about him and praying for him, and on the sixteenth day found him lying there in the forest as if dead. They revived him, and asked him what it was like to have been dead for sixteen days. He answered that during the interval he had been in a fine place where he saw all the people that had been dead, and he spoke to them at length. It was a great experience for him, and he said he wouldn't mind returning if they'd have him back. When the time came for his actual departure from this world, he went happily. There was no mourning for him, for he had told everyone where he was going with great joy.

Wolley also tells the story of the origin of corn:

The Lenape have a tradition that their corn was brought to them from the west by Grandfather Crow. He was flying so long that he accidentally dropped a kernel of corn from his beak. It was found by children and brought to their parents, who planted it to see what would happen. From then on, the Lenape people had corn, and no matter how annoying the crows became, trying to eat from their cornfields as they worked, the people were not allowed to kill the old Grandfather Crow who had brought them such an important gift. However, they were allowed to build a sturdy platform high above the cornfield, climb up on the platform and throw rocks at him with their best aim, just to keep him humble.[14]

Keepers of the Sacred Land

It is well established that, among the living, the Lenape consider themselves keepers of the sacred land, just as the Ramapough Munsee are "Keepers of the Ramapough Pass," and the Nissequogue are "Keepers of the Nissequogue River" on Long Island. In addition, Lenape-speaking wisdom-keepers, like other Algonquin, long believed that part of their spiritual duty was to look after the land even after death. Many people living today who are gifted with "second sight" or visions report seeing Native American ghosts and departed spirits working as guardians over the land and the people living there. These spirit guides are often described as great in stature and nobility. Part of the explanation for these unexpected sightings in North America is that these souls, during their lives, made a vow that they would continue to protect and watch over the land of their forefathers, and to be of spiritual benefit to those who were born on that land and who care about that land. Psychics from all over North America are continually visited by and receive messages from Native American guides, whether they look for them or not. These Native spirits are fulfilling their vow to be Sacred Land Keepers. With pollution, traffic, and overpopulation, their job is getting harder every day. We can help them by being open to their prayers and their wisdom.

THE NATIVE NEW YORKER AS METAPHOR

According to author and Jungian analyst Dr. Stephen Larsen, the concept of a beautiful village being replaced by rows of cold gray buildings is a common one in his clients' dreams. It is an archetypal dream of our time, the loss of our own innocence, the dark side of "growing up" in industrial society. Such a dream is a warning that we are in danger of becoming hardened, and no longer nurturing. Dr. Larsen's mentor, the late Joseph Campbell, in his writings on the hero myth, described the robotized "dark father" figure who could not feel emotions anymore as a mythic archetype of increasing importance. This image was later given form in George Lucas's movie *Star Wars* as Darth Vader, which means "dark father."

Joseph Campbell would take the position that we don't want to know about Manhattan's former self because it awakens in us the recognition of the same possibility of a similar downward transformation in ourself, the possibility of "selling out" to the point where there is nothing left to save. In *The Mythic Imagination*, Stephen

Larsen recounts a patient's description of a vivid dream: "I am going along through an area I've been to before—old desiccated villages— now replaced by one long row of buildings. Not much room in front, so I have to go underneath. . . ."

It is underneath where one finds the "underground," the sur- vivors who remember the dreamtime, in this case, the Native New Yorkers who live secret lives as invisible tools of the Creator.

Following in the wake of this image is that of the indigenous shaman, wandering the streets of the dark city—a healer in disguise, playing whatever role is acceptable to both the shaman and the industrial society, meanwhile making sure no one around him gets too rigid and unfeeling. Often the only option is the role of "crazy woman," "floor scrubber," "beggar," or "trickster."

Larsen recounts how two men, one a friend, one a client—two people who didn't know each other—had the same dream at the same general time: "An old scrubwoman, often in tatters, or in sordid circumstances; yet with a goddess-like quality of concealed power." A few months later, the analyst himself had the same dream about "an old crazy scrubwoman who lives in the basement of the Empire State Building. She runs the elevators, and we ride from level to level, just barely in control. She seems full of power and secret mystery. There are winds, and sometimes it feels like we are inside the *Sushumna* of the world."[15]

To me the Empire State Building is, by its own self-named recognition, a symbol of "the power structure" and the state of "empire building." The janitor or charwoman is the healer and transformer who touches everyone's lives without any empire build- ing at all. Many of the mixed-blood Native Americans living in New York City today find themselves in that dream, only for them it is very real. They are gifted with the knowledge of radical healing and transforming, handed down from their ancestors, and the only role they are allowed to play is janitor, floor scrubber, or crazy man.

Another powerful archetype of New York City is the massive subway system, the great American symbol of the underworld. Larsen describes a dream by a middle-aged client who was "lost in a dark woods in the middle of his life": "I am crossing a city park with a friend when a group of tough-looking youths approaches. My friend flees; but it seems all they want to do is bring me to their 'master,' who is underground, in a basement or subway. But the Master presents an aura of great knowledge and power, and shows me all kinds of allegories about life. Then we go to a movie kiosk where all kinds of perverted, horrible and unnatural things are depicted. He says, 'I am this, too.' In the last part we are walking together in the mountains and talking. We seem to be looking out upon the whole world." Larsen comments that the subway-master is to the dreamer as Virgil is to Dante, and he keeps the dreamer moving and flexible. He describes it as "soul-education."[16]

What Larsen sees as "soul-education," I see also as shamanic initiation. The Hudson Valley's storehouse of legends is filled with stories of "Indians," usually the "last of their tribe" guiding adventurous white citizens through wondrous caves. It is acknowledged that the Native American way of life is well grounded in the natural world and not afraid to look at the underside of things. There was nothing airy-fairy about real Native American "shamanic" ritual as it was actually practiced. Today such things are prohibited, and we feel the resultant fragility, the loss of power in the spiritual arena. We need to be reminded that the roots of the oak tree lie deep underground where it is dark and brooding with worms.[17]

REACHING IN FOR HELP

I lecture in New York City on a regular basis. Recently I have felt more and more compelled to encourage people to open up their hearts and minds to the most benevolent of those "grandfathers" who still guard this city and its land to ask for help. It is with their help we can make

New York a better place to live; it is with their guidance we can rekindle the fire in our own heart, and help rekindle it in others. If we learn how to protect our spirits from injury the way the old Lenape did, we can grow strong-hearted and courageous like those philosopher-sachems of long ago. With their help we can even bring back a taste of the earthly paradise that was once Manhattan.

Some readers already feel a strong need to form a bond with the people who took such good care of the lands east of the Appalachians for so many centuries. They may want to speak to the Creator in the Native language, make prayers to the land and to the Creator in the Native tongue of their region, or simply learn the meanings of some of the names of the lakes and rivers of their homeland. They may want to make contact with what might be referred to as guardian spirits of the Algonquin, whom so many have dreamed about or seen in unexpected visions. These guardians are often nameless and work in a humble manner to help those in need. Once in a while, the seer will be given the name of the guardian, either in English or a Native tongue. This is as it has always been. The truly spiritual Algonquin see no racial differences, they only see what is in a person's heart, and they observe and see how good one is to the Mother, the earth we walk upon. From time to time they will help those who live in a good way, or will show the way, or help connect them with animals, or other people of good heart and mind who can guide them.

If you look around at the cement and pollution, and say, "I wish I could help heal this land," you are not alone. The spirit of the departed Lenape are there with you. When they were alive, they prayed to Mun-ih-toh (in Munsee; Manitou in other dialects), "Great Spirit," to help protect the land. These prayers need to continue, both in the Lenape language and in your own.

These guardians are men and women, young and old. There is a belief among the Algonquin that some of the truly great souls who come to this world pass away just before puberty for mysterious reasons. It is said that they have completed one quarter of the wheel and go into the spirit world as pure souls, and help to watch over the people and the land. I was visited by one of these spirits in a wooded area in Putnam County, which until the Revolutionary War was a Wappingers Indian reservation and a Nochpeem village before that. The young woman who appeared to me was finely dressed and her quillwork moccasins were a picture of perfection. She stood there during a private ceremony, not saying a word and not moving. I got the impression she was of the Ottawa Nation, but she was clearly one of those who had passed away just before reaching adulthood. I saw five such spirits together in eastern Pennsylvania a few years later, in the heartland of the Unami Delaware. They stood around me in ceremony when I was grieving and needed healing. Again, they were silent.

As the Algonquin elders say, everything is interconnected. You can't change one thing without changing another. Your spiritual life affects every aspect of your physical life; the reverse is also true. The way you live your life affects your spirit deeply. The oldest teaching of all, and the most respected one among the Algonquin, is the teaching that the earth is sacred, and that a good, loving relationship with the earth is a foundation for a good spiritual life, as well as good health and happiness.[18]

I think that if the Munsee and the other nations of New York are all honored once again and given their proper place in U.S. history, it will be a good sign that, in the words of the old Munsee blessing, "The sun will shine on our wigwams, and our moccasins will not get wet." We will then begin the great healing of all our people that must take place—the red, white, yellow, and black nations coming together as four parts of the hoop of life. Only then can the earth be healed. As the Cree say, "Animals don't have problems, we do!" It's our healing that will ensure a more bountiful earth and a better place for children to grow up. And that's something we can all do for each other.

4

A WALK AROUND
OLD MANHATTAN

THE CIRCLE AND THE SQUARE

Look at any map of Manhattan and you will see an endless grid of
square blocks and rectangles. New York City arguably has more
squares than any other city on earth. Everything in midtown is measured in city blocks. From Houston Street to Harlem on the east side,
and from Fourteenth Street to 154th Street on the west side, the lay-
out is as boxy as a bookshelf. It harkens back to the Egyptian roots of
civilization, or more specifically the Roman model of city planning,
not the circular or curvilinear model of the Algonquin. The Egyptians
based their squares and much of their geometry on the circle. The
Romans somehow lost the "circle in the square" concept and began
building boxes. New York, like its namesake Eboracum, is a very
Roman city, filled with boxes.

Squares are plentiful in New York: Herald Square, Times Square,
Sheridan Square,[1] Sutton Square, Minetta Square, Hancock Square,
Foley Square, Chatham Square, Chelsea Square, Cooper Square,
Abingdon Square, and Madison Square Park. Gramercy Park is a
square, one kept under lock and key. Only those whose apartment
buildings face the park have keys to the front gate.[2]

The only circles around Manhattan are near Central Park, which is
a rectangle: Columbus Circle, Cathedral Circle, and Frederick Douglas

Circle, to the north of the park. Bowling Green is actually an oval. Manhattan clearly illustrates the ideological war between European and Algonquin belief-systems, and who won. The square dominates— the circle is almost extinct.

The first thing the elders teach is the importance of the "hoop," or circle. Nature is full of circles—the sun, the full moon, the iris and pupil of the eye, a pond, a bird's nest. When sitting in council, the Algonquin people sit in a circle, which is a symbol of equality as every person has an equal chance to be heard. The fire in the center burns a circle in the grass and leaves a circle of ashes behind. The gourd bowl they pass clockwise around the circle is round. When the elders throw back their heads and sing the old songs, their mouths form a circle. The head of the water drum is a circle, as is the end piece of the buffalo-horn rattle. The painted turtle rattle is an oval. The beater on the drumstick is round. The hole in the pipe is a circle as well. The Hopi of Arizona use a circle in their petroglyphs to represent the good way of spiritual life. It represents wholeness.

Before the Dutch built the square Fort Amsterdam at the base of the island, circles were everywhere. The berries were round, as were the apples, pears, cherries, and the kernels of the maize that grew in abundance. Stones were round. Wigwams made circles on the ground; pottery was often round, as were soapstone bowls and clay vessels. Oyster shells were mostly circular, as were wampum beads whose strands formed circles around the necks of the people. When Lenape people made faces on pottery and dolls, they tended to make eyes and mouths circular. It was part of their way of seeing things. In the ancient city one rarely found a square or rectangle anywhere. The Lenape may not always have placed their wigwams in circles or had circular paths around their great council oaks, but they did follow the form of nature, which is curvilinear, not boxy, in everything they created. A straight line is likely to conflict with the lay of the land, which is rich with spirals, undulating curves, and circles.

The ancient city was a place of natural beauty to which people from miles around came for trade and exploration. It was a very busy place, highly populated, with miles of trails, and many traditional marketplaces. In the following pages we'll attempt to revisit the city as it was in the days of the Lenape.

BATTERY PARK AND THE KAPSEE

There is a ten-foot-tall, square-shaped monument that stands at Battery Park (Battery Place) near the location of the original Dutch fort. Carved inscriptions are found on all four sides and a flagpole rises out of the top. Carved on one side are the words: "On the 22nd of April, 1625, the Amsterdam Chamber of the West India Company decreed the establishment of Fort Amsterdam, and the creation of ten adjoining farms. The purchase of the island of Manhattan was accomplished in 1626. Thus was laid the foundation of the city of New York. In testimony of ancient and unbroken friendship, this flagpole is presented to the city of New York by the Dutch People, 1926."

It sounds like they forgot or glossed over some of the details, doesn't it? As for the twenty-four dollars (60 guilders) in trinkets that Governor Peter Minuit is said to have traded for Manhattan in 1626, there are many versions of the story. However, although the Dutch West Indies Trading Company kept meticulous business records, no deed has ever been produced. The only document that refers to it is a personal letter back home to Holland from a Pieter Jansen Schagenauer,[3] a citizen of no particular authority or involvement, who reported the trade to his friends back in the Netherlands. He wrote (in Dutch), "Minuit bought the island of Manhattan from the wildmen for the value of sixty guilders." The story seems to have grown out of this casual account, later picked up and codified by Washington Irving in *Knickerbocker Tales* in 1809.

The trade reportedly took place at the great council elm at the foot of the Mohican Trail. Council elms were where people met, and this one was near the tip of Manhattan where the Lenapes went to trade. That place is now Bowling Green, and the trail, called Breedewegh by the Dutch, is now Broadway, which started at that spot. It is said that the Kapsee people of the Canarsie were the sellers, which is possible, since they had long claimed usage of Manhattan island from the southern tip northward as far as Fourteenth Street. If the story is true, they would have thought it an agreement to share their region with the small group of Dutch traders for two years, which was the Lenape custom. The concept of permanent land ownership was relatively unfamiliar to them, as the Lenape tended to burn agricultural land after two years and let it lie fallow for a season or two while moving on. Villages were moved seasonally, although some were permanent. The idea that the Dutch would try to grow the same crop on the same land each year would have embarrassed the Kapsee, and possibly offended their sense of justice toward Mother Earth because of the depletion of the soil that would inevitably follow.

The Lenape at this stage in colonial history were exceedingly polite to the Europeans. It was customary to "share the pot"[4] with travelers and those in need. What supposedly happened after the "sale" is a good example. The Dutch went northward to the Werpoes' village at the edge of the small lake just north of where City Hall now stands, showed them a document, and told them to leave. According to this story, the gentle Werpoes, also Canarsie, simply said something to the effect of, "Oh, we're sorry. We didn't know,"[5] and moved to Brooklyn.

In that first year of "New Amsterdam," the Dutch collected an impressive total of 7,246 beaver pelts, in addition to 65 otter, 48 mink, and 36 wildcat pelts.[6] Before long the forest wildlife was being drastically depleted. Demand was outstripping supply. The Lenape had been coming to the lower end of Manhattan to trade for two thousand or more years. The Dutch settled there because they knew the Lenape would know where to find them and trade with them. It is ironic then that the Dutch immediately built a 2,340-foot wall around their city, which Kryn Frederych, a civil engineer and New York's first urban architect, had already designed for the spot the year before. The same wall with the same design was built at Fort Orange, now Albany, with similar street names such as Beaver and Broad. It was designed with the British in mind, but also the Lenape. As the Dutch had no standing army, the wall was their main defense against possible attack. Although most employees of the Dutch West India Company owned weapons, few were trained for military expeditions. Nonetheless, the wall must have seemed like an unfriendly gesture from the Lenape point of view. Ironically it wasn't too many years before the Lenape were building forts of their own, not only to keep out the Dutch, but as a result of the economic chaos brought by the Dutch traders. The growing dependence on certain trade objects— muxes (shell drills), copper kettles, metal knives, and hatchets— caused fights to break out in times of scarcity. People are people.

MANHATTAN GEOGRAPHY: A JOURNEY ACROSS THE ISLAND

We begin our tour of the city beneath the City standing on State Street, at the upper edge of Battery Park, looking south to the statue of Giovanni da Verrazzano. On April 17, 1524, Verrazzano became the first known European to visit New York. Today New York Harbor is far in the distance; in 1524 we would have been standing right at the edge of the bay. This place was called Kapsee, "The Point of Rocks," and its people were the Kapsee people, leaders among the Canarsie group of the Lenape.

Directly to the south of Manhattan we can see Governor's Island. The Kapsee call it Pagganck,[7] which means "Nut Island," specifically hickory. There was once a village of Canarsie-speaking Pagganck Indians living there. Almost all the people living on the small islands in the region were Canarsie.

On March 28, 1624, the first colony of Dutch traders settled where we now stand. Two days later a group of thirty families, mostly Walloons, would leave Holland to settle on Pagganck, later Governor's Island and the site of the governor's mansion where many of New York's notable governors would live throughout the early years of New York history, including the sworn enemy of the Munsee, Governor Robert Morris.[8]

Heading north, to our right we would once have seen a Lenape pathway running along the East River. Piles of discarded oyster shells as high as a man's head, or "shell middens," lined the riverbanks. The native Lenape were not that interested in pearls. When a Dutchman found a pearl in a discarded oyster right along here, it caused a frenzy of searching through the heaps of Lenape castoffs, and ultimately lent the street its name: "Perel" in Dutch,[9] later Pearl. When I see the street sign for Pearl Street, it makes me think of how the pearls of wisdom buried in the Lenape language were discarded by the Dutch, who were more interested in exploiting the land and water than in Lenape teachings. More than three city blocks of landfill have pushed Pearl Street to the *middle* of lower Manhattan today.

Somewhere along here on the right a path once led down to a canoe landing. Right across the East River was another landing, from which point the path continued. This is Fulton Street in Manhattan, and the path on the other side is Fulton Street, Brooklyn. If you follow it many miles then turn right at Stuyvesant Avenue, you will come to the location of the Canarsie landing in Jamaica Bay, where Native canoes departed for destinations all along the Atlantic.

HISTORIC BOAT LANDINGS

In Dutch times, a "Brooklyn Ferry" left from Maiden Lane, a few feet south of the spot where we began. A second ferry left from Peck's Slip, also landing at what is now Fulton Street, Brooklyn, approximately the same path taken by Canarsie canoes centuries earlier.

The Dutch built one of the first inns along the path that is now Pearl Street, at the place where a stream cuts in from the East River. Fraunce's Tavern was built on the site in 1719,[10] and then rebuilt in 1763. It still stands at 56 Pearl, at the corner of Pearl and Broad Street. In the 1600s, Broad Street didn't really exist except as a stream with pathways on either side and a boat landing on the East River, so the tavern was conveniently located, to say the least.

The boat dock at Broad Street and Pearl was the first one in New Netherlands, and one of the earliest European docks in America. The Fulton Street dock, a few feet to the north, came soon after. Bridge Street is one of the oldest in the city. It was once called Brugh Street and led to a bridge that spanned a canal running where Broad Street is now. Broad Street ran on both sides of the canal, which was equipped with facilities for off-loading cargo adjacent to warehouses. In the mid-1600s, the canal was filled in and the two side roads were joined to become one broad thoroughfare. Nearby Beaver Street was named in recognition of the animal whose pelts formed the basis of early trade between the Indians and the Dutch in New Netherlands.[11]

The first actual wharf was added to the East River shoreline in 1649, a few blocks to the south at Whitehall Street, near the Staten Island Ferry terminal. Called "The Great Dock," it still left much to be desired, and was eventually bypassed by smaller docks, particularly those at Hanover Square and John Street.

BOWLING GREEN: AN ANCIENT PLACE OF POWER

Strolling along the Pearl Street path as far as an inlet, and then turning south, we come to Bowling Green, New York's oldest park. The Dutch called it "The Plain." The Dutch used to play duckpins there, which is why it is now called Bowling Green. No one actually bowls there anymore.

The old Mohican trail—Broadway—started here. This would have been a likely site of a Kapsee chief's hut: at the confluence of the two rivers, which were like highways to the Canarsie, at the access to the bay, at the tip of the island, and at one end of the ancient Mohican Trail, which runs along the entire length of the Hudson River and up to Oka, now Montreal. In addition, the spot was within sight of Long Island and New Jersey.

Beneath a large elm where the Mohican Trail actually starts would have been a sacred spot where council fires were held, and great orators came to speak from time to time. People would also have met here to trade and make conversation. Early drinking taverns would be built along the foot of Broadway to refresh the Dutch bowlers, viewed with suspicion by the traditional Lenape. Later, in 1775, one of the architectural descendants of those taverns, Burns Tavern, was called a "seminary of sedition" by King Charles and viewed with equal suspicion by the Whigs and Loyalists.

Broad Way, as the English came to call this twisting and turning road, heads north along the ridge of the island. We follow it past the stream that is now Broad Street, past the place where, in 1653, the Dutch built a palisaded wall to keep the Lenape out, site of today's Wall Street. That wall came down in 1699, when the English felt securely rid of their predecessors. Near here the Dutch, in the early 1600s, exchanged stocks of food, wood, and furs with the Natives. The New York Stock Exchange may be traced back to this shady spot along the road where a large buttonwood tree once stood.[12]

THE CHERRY ORCHARD

Not far from the East River, a path no longer reflected in any modern road stretched from what is now Park Row to the Lenape's vast cherry orchard at the corner of Cherry Street and Franklin Square. The orchard was later taken over by the Dutch, who created the street and named it after the orchard.

New York was the capital of the nation under the Articles of Confederation from 1785 to 1789, and then of the United States under the Constitution from 1789 to 1790. During that one year in which New York served as the U.S. capital, George Washington himself lived at Franklin Square, #1 Cherry Street, in a classic cube-shaped white building, literally the first presidential White House. This was meant to be a temporary accommodation until a real White House mansion could be completed just south of Bowling Green. To do this it was necessary to dismantle the first Dutch fort (which in turn occupied the likely site of a Kapsee chief's residence) where today's Heye Museum stands.[13] Before that White House could be completed, the U.S. capital would move to Philadelphia, and ultimately Washington, D.C., but the Executive Mansion in Washington, D.C., would look just like the house on Cherry Street,[14] with an added portico.

An important landing site for the Canarsie lay several blocks to the north. The corresponding landing site across the river is the foot of the main trail we now know as Flatbush Avenue, which leads directly to the Keskaech Querem, the "Great Gathering Place," the Canarsie Nation's capital, and beyond that, to the best ocean launching spots.

Early Natives would have set off from here in dugout canoes. Making a dugout was a labor-intensive job. The craft was carved from a single piece of wood. The log had to be burned out and then chopped out over and over to get it right. It took a skilled workman ten to twelve full days to do a good job. Long ago such a canoe sank to the bottom of the East River in an area that was later landfilled, now beneath Oliver Street. In the early twentieth century, during construction of the Oak Street Station subway stop, this canoe was excavated at the corner of Cherry and Oliver Streets. Crowds came to watch, but the workmen became impatient and destroyed the rear half of it in the space of an hour, accidentally chopping up all but seven feet of it.

David de Vries, a friend to the Lenape and the first to farm Staten Island, mentioned an incident in New York Bay when "twenty of us went sitting in a canoe or hollow tree which is their boat, and the

edge was not more than a hand's breadth above the water."[15] That is
how low in the water these heavy boats could sail.

The wealthy William Walton cleared out some of the cherry trees
to build one of New York's finest houses here in 1752, but left a beautiful garden across the way that was later destroyed to make Franklin
Square. The Brooklyn Bridge construction destroyed all remaining
traces of the cherry orchard, #1 Cherry Street, and the Walton estate
later in the 1800s. All are now entombed deep beneath the massive
stones of the Brooklyn Bridge's foundation.

Returning to the Mohican Trail and walking further north, our
trail passes through the Bowery (Dutch *Bowerji* for farm), which
actually *was* a bowery, a place of farming. Here, and many other
places, the Lenape planted the three sisters—corn, bean, and squash.
The Dutch would take over their fields as soon as the Lenape left
them fallow. The size of the plants in their first crops amazed them,
but their farming methods quickly depleted the soil and ruined the
land. Nearby was the site of Peter Stuyvesant's large farm at around
Eighth Street and Second Avenue, his retirement project during the
last four years of his life. Yet another stream ran along his property
and into the East River.

The Werpoes Village by the Pond

Five hundred years ago, just to the north of City Hall, beneath Centre
Street (formerly Collect Street) lay a great pond surrounded by lush
thickets, and close by, a Werpoes village. In Canarsie, Werpoes means
"beautiful field by the thicket."[16] Fresh waters ran freely above the
ground in this area of the island. One spring flowed north from the
future site of Spring Street into the stream where Canal Street would
be, which fed the beautiful pond at the Werpoes' village. Another
spring fed it from the east. Later, the Dutch called the pond Kalch-
hook, then abbreviated it to "Kalch" or "collect" in Dutch. The banks
of these bubbling streams were soon walled up by the Dutch, and

then covered over completely in later times. The sixty-foot deep, spring-fed pond is now landfill. The first Dutch were amazed by a huge shell heap on the western shore, and later named that neighborhood Shell Point Hill. Near where Chatham Square now stands was a place called Indian Lookout, on a hill that no longer exists.

In Dutch times a spring still ran along the path of Spring Street, leading to the stream where Canal Street now stands. It is said that as late as the 1960s there was a passageway underground, accessible through one of the old subway stations, by which one could reach the original stream. It still runs underneath New York, much like the spirit of Native American culture in America.

Just to the east of this spot the Dutch built a brewery that became a very important meeting site in the 1630s, and in 1642 the City Tavern was constructed by the pond. It later became the Dutch City Hall for many years, called *Stadt Huys,* the architectural remains of which can still be seen under plexiglass in a hole in the ground at Pearl Street.[17]

A Rechtank village lay along the shore farther east; Rechtank means "a sandy place" in the Renneiu language of the coastal Munsee people of lower Manhattan. Rechtank was later called Corlear's Hook, after the Dutch Captain Corlear and a massacre he led in which thirty Native Americans lost their lives the same night as the Pavonia Massacre near today's Jersey City. This area south of the Williamsburg Bridge is still considered dangerous today. These same "sandy place" people called themselves by different names according to local dialect: Rechgawonk in upper Manhattan, Reckgawank in the Bronx, and Reckgawawank in Westchester. Many scholars consider these to be the real "Manhattan Indians."

THE SAPOHANNIKAN VILLAGE

A brook once followed the course of today's Canal Street, from one block east of Broadway where the great pond ended, running west almost to the Hudson River where it became swampy. In the spring it created a wide swamp on either side. By the early nineteenth century the pond had become seriously polluted, and in the wake of a yellow fever epidemic, the stream was widened into a canal to drain off the pond. A decade later, both were filled in.[18] Walking along beside that brook in the early sixteenth century, we would have passed through acres of lush strawberry fields and wooded patches of walnut, cedar, and chestnut trees filled with a wide variety of birds.

Arriving at the future course of Varick Street, we enter into the small territory of the Unami-speaking Sapohannikan people. Their territory stretched from the Bowery to the Hudson and from Grand Street up to Eighteenth Street, angling northwest to Chelsea Park. The Sapohannikan were originally from what is now New Jersey, on the mainland.[19] Some moved here to support their trading post at Fourteenth Street and Eighth Avenue, at the end of Gansevoort Street. Following Varick Street to the north, in 1524 we would soon have arrived at a Lenape village with a number of wigwams set beside a small stream, with Native people busy making crafts and garments of hide to trade.

The Lenape called this place the Sapohannikan or "Tobacco Field," or *Lapinikan,* which meant "Plowed Fields."[20] The Dutch called it "the Indian Village." In 1664, the English renamed it after Greenwich, England, though some sources say the name derives from a Dutch farm called Greenwjck, meaning green inlet or cove. (Wick in Old English can mean "camp.")[21] Most New Yorkers call this area "the Village" today, an unusual name for an urban area, but if you consider that it was once an actual Indian village, it makes perfect sense.

All of these names, including Greenwich Village, were at various times given to the entire area between the Bowery and the Hudson, or Noort River, as the Dutch called it. A stream ran just below West Third Street between McDougal and Sixth—Manetta Creek, called Minetta by the Dutch. *Manetta* means "evil spirit" or "snake water" in Lenape. Minetta Street and Minetta Lane are named after the creek. It's said that Minetta means "little one" in "double Dutch," a practice of making witty translations of Lenape terms.[22] In fact, the Dutch called it Bestavaar's Kill. Here you would once have seen traders with their wares: a man offering a stack of tobacco leaves for an old birchbark scroll, a woman trading a wampum necklace for a basket of herbs. Two blocks south of Minetta Street, the stream curved, and here you might have seen Sapohannikan village women doing their wash. In that same spot today you can still find "Village" women doing their laundry at The Village Cleaners.

THE EVIL UNDERGROUND

The meaning of Manetta is clear. It refers to the evil snake that hampered and tormented humanity at the dawn of time, until vanquished by that great Lenape hero, Nanabush. When Manetta was driven underground, all that was left was the winding, snakelike creek, and now that creek is underground as well.

The creek used to be near the Village Smoke Shop, where one can still find tobacco. The Lenape used tobacco as currency as it was portable, useful, and plentiful. A large leaf of tobacco could be used similar to a dollar bill today. If you examine the back of the U.S. one-dollar bill, you'll see tobacco on it.[23] Algonquin people today still exchange tobacco in a wide variety of situations.

There is an apartment building on the north border of Washington Square Park, #2 Fifth Avenue, the first one on the left at the base of the avenue, with a fountain in the lobby. The waters of that fountain are drawn from the waters of the original stream—and thus linked to Manetta, the evil serpent who was forced underground thousands of years ago by Nanabush. Nanabush is basically the same person as Natabozu in Mesquaki, Waynaboozhoo in Ojibway, Anishinabi or Weesuckerjack in Cree, Glooskap in Micmac, Glooskabee in Abenaki, and Mestapeo in Innu or Naskapi.[24] He made some mistakes in the past, but he learned from them and was able to accomplish many great deeds. Some Lenape thought the white men arriving on ships from the east were Nanabush coming back. Tradition has it that when the Native people need him most, he will return.

Manetta is not the devil but the original, genuine trickster spirit who has plagued humanity since the beginning of time. It is said that when Manetta was free to maraud among the Lenape, they could accomplish nothing; all effort was futile. This sounds as if refers to something inside of ourselves, something real, a cancer of the human spirit. Is it selfishness? Lust? Anger? The answer is not clear, but the old Algonquin word *loowaywoodee,* which is literally "bad things in my heart" in Lenape, has come to mean "fear, anger, and confusion." Some translate it as "evil." However as the missionary David Zeisberger stated in 1776, "They seem to have no idea of the devil until in modern times preachers arose among them who proclaimed that there was such a being, having secured their knowledge from the whites." Otherwise, Manetta comes closest.

The waters of Manetta ran from a swamp stretching from the Flatiron District at 21st and Fifth Avenue, down along Broadway to Eleventh Street. There it became Manetta Creek and ran diagonally across Madison and Fifth Avenues, diagonally across the foot of Bleeker and Houston Streets, and entered a swamp at Hudson Street, from which it fed into the river to the west.

Manetta returns to the Village every spring to haunt and torment the tenement owners near Minetta Street. They look down into the basement of their building, and there he is, his black shining waters, gurgling and rising up to greet them.[25]

Walking along the old Manetta Creek long ago would bring us to a gathering place where a trail crosses the stream. This is now Washington Square Park; the trail was the Sapohannikan Trail.[26] This path arched down from the Sapohannikan Fort at West Fourteenth

Street to the northwest, roughly following today's Greenwich Street (formerly Monument Lane), and then continues along West Fourth Street. The people at the fort used the trail to haul fresh water from the stream, because the Hudson is briny this far south. Then the trail headed east until it met the Bowery path to the Shepmoes' (a group of Canarsie people) village at East Fourteenth Street.[27] The clearing would not only have been a spot for water gathering, but also a marketplace, a gaming area, and a cultural space where the Lenape might gather with their drums at night. Here, Lenape youth would be seen playing Hubbub (a game of chance with discs in a bowl), Dice, Stick and Hoop, Archery, and other games of chance and skill, including several varieties of Indian arm wrestling.

This gathering place is now Washington Square Park, a popular space with a large water fountain, where young people still gather for drumming circles and group singing, and perhaps some buying and selling. In the late 1950s, signs reading "No Bongo Playing" were posted, which put a temporary halt to the drumming tradition. Those signs recently came down by popular demand, so the practice the Lenape started here long ago has been resumed.

Then as Now

Washington Square Park today is a major chess-playing conclave, with wagers occasionally placed on the outcome. I have also seen these outdoor chess tables used for Indian arm wrestling contests, with bystanders betting on the contest. In this way, the outdoor gaming contests of the Lenape continue, five hundred years later.

Today mental wrestlers of the chess tradition hold council all day and have sparring matches for warriors of all ages at the Village Chess Shop, only a short walk from the train stop at Bleeker and Seventh Avenue, which lies at the south end of the old Indian village.

Nearby Bleeker Street, running parallel to the Sapohannikan Trail, was named after the A. L. Bleeker farm, which lay right next to the

Trinity Church farm to the west, with a long strip reaching to the Bowery road to the east. An obelisk was erected in Dutch times near the former site of the Sapohannikan Fort, and Greenwich Street, which leads to Washington Square Park from there, was for a time called "Monument Lane," after the obelisk. This stone pillar was similar to the one called "Cleopatra's Needle," which stands in Central Park today.

A farm belonging to a Peter Warren started at the obelisk and reached southward on both sides of Monument Lane approximately to Houston at its lowest point, and the center of Washington Square Park at its easternmost point. Christopher Street, known for its markets and businesses, was a path to the Hudson River. Even in the 1820s, twenty-seven of the thirty-two businesses in the Village were on Christopher Street (named for Charles Christopher Amos, an heir to Warren's farm).[28]

The course of today's Bleeker Street runs parallel to and just over a hundred feet to the south of the Sapohannikan Trail. Walking here, it's fascinating to note the number of trades practiced in the area that likely had Lenape counterparts similarly located in ancient times. Imagine for a moment you've been transported back five centuries to that long-ago village. Peer back in time as you stand in front of the Village Apothecary at 346 Bleeker Street. Is that an herbalist's wigwam over there? The woman crushing herbs with a mortar and pestle must be a hundred years old. We would call her *Chaux-scheesis* in Unami, "Really Old Woman," a name of respect. On the future site of Native Leather Ltd., 203 Bleeker, an elderly man sews moccasins for trade, spreading them out on a blanket.

Here is a young Lenape woman with a gutted deer hanging from the frame of her portable outdoor shop. She is brain tanning the skins with water and stretching them on a frame, using a deer bone to rub the leather. Later she will cut the leather and sew clothes, pouches and shoulder bags from the skins. The Lenape might have called her something like *Chey-ee-noo-tay-sis,* or "Shoulder Bag

Woman," in Unami. At this very spot—173 Bleeker Street—a woman opened a shop in the 1970s called The Village Tannery which remains in business today. She created many shoulder bags and pouches from scratch, the last in an old Manhattan tradition.[29]

The Village Community School is near the site of places where Lenape children once ran and played under the watchful eyes of their community. There's Village Furs at 29th and Sixth, which is near the site of a pelt market from the old times. Over there is yet another marketplace. Some day it will be The Village Bazaar. The Village Art Gallery is in close proximity to the site of a former hut of an Indian hide painter. The underlying patterns have never changed, just the window dressing. One wonders if the spirits of those ancient craftsmen and women are watching over the land still, helping and inspiring their modern-day counterparts.

Following the Eastern Path

There were three major groups of Lenape on Manhattan in 1523: the Renneiu-speaking Canarsie to the east of the Bowery path, the Unami-speaking Sapohannikan people to the west of that same trail as far south as Canal Street, and the Munsee-speaking "Manhattan" people to the north.[30] The great intertribal gathering place where the boundaries of these three major Lenape groups met was called Kintecoying. Not only did three languages meet there, but three great roads as well. Today we call it Astor Place.

In old times we would have continued north along the Bowery trail to reach this Great Gathering Place where there is a great **Y**, or splitting of the trails. To the north is "The Path to the Wading Place"; to the West, the trail to the Sapohannikan fort; to the east, the short trail to the Shepmoes; to the south, the Bowery trail to Bowling Green. This was where the great orations of influential sachems would have taken place. Here we would have seen great intertribal meetings and councils, intertribal games, and the usual buying and selling of trade goods. It was a place of politics, trade, and diplomacy. It was also a place where leaders inspired by the Great Spirit would speak to the people about the Algonquin ideals of equality, freedom, dignity, and courage.

There would have been a council elm at this spot. According to widespread Native custom, there was always an elm or oak planted at a great crossroads, such as the oak at what is now Oak Park near Boston, Massachusetts, where the Nonantum people met to talk, listen to orators, and trade at the conjunction of several trails. The Lenape used to bury a great leader or orator with an acorn in his or her mouth. The resulting oak would sometimes have two trunks, because the sprouts would have to exit the skull in a roundabout manner, usually splitting into two parts. Although whole skulls are rarely found, occasionally pieces of skull are found at the root of such trees. Their minds and bodies became food for this new growth. These acorn burials often took place at crossroads, where such great leaders gave speeches. Next time you see a place called Twin Oaks, consider who might be buried there.

Astor Place may even have been the site of a scaled-down version of Bagettaway, "The Creator's Great Game," a sacred ritual now known by its French name, "La Crosse." The space at the Kintecoying would have been limited, used only for practice games. Important Bagettaway games needed to be played in large, open, level areas, which downtown Manhattan didn't have even then. A great bluff in the upper part of Manhattan, future site of the Polo Grounds, could have served for a playing field. Bagettaway involved endless daylong clashes where teams from two rival villages battled for victory as if pitted in real warfare, with half the players covered with blood or lying injured on the field at the end of the contest. The New York Giants played football there, a game that has much in common with Bagettaway. Jim Thorpe, an Algonquin Indian and probably a great Bagettaway player, was a star runner for the New York Giants who played at that location.

Given the confluence of Native people coming through Astor Place, it seems certain that the ubiquitous fur traders would have operated there as well. It is interesting that John Jacob Astor (1763–1848), perhaps the most successful fur trader in history, lived at and gave his name to that spot. Astor was America's first millionaire and a man who employed many Lenape fur trappers and guides at the bottom of the corporate pyramid of his American Fur Company from 1808 until his retirement in 1834. Only two blocks away at 404 La Fayette Street is the present-day American Indian Community House, where Native Americans and their friends from all over still gather to honor their culture and traditions.[31]

In the central spot where the three trails converged, there is now a traffic island with a large black cube set on its corner.[32] Next to it, painted on the cement pavement in yellow and blue, is a Native American medicine wheel, aligned to the four directions. It was crafted by Native Americans in 1992, and is inscribed "500 Years of Resistance, 1492–1992." Someone thoughtfully painted as an addendum the words "and dignity" under the word resistance. Someone else added numbers over the last digits year by year, so that in 1999 it read "507 Years of Resistance and Dignity: 1492–1999." I wonder if those souls who painted that powerful message in 1992 knew just how significant a spot they had chosen for their handiwork? Perhaps the ancestors were at work again, trying to keep the worlds connected throughout creation.

ECHOES OF ALGONQUIN ORATORY

There can be no doubt that Astor Place/Kintecoying, the crossroads where three nations came together, was of great political importance to Native New Yorkers. Standing there today one can almost feel the lingering spirits of those great orators and sachems. It is relevant to note that this powerful spot was the site of one of the most decisive moments in our nation's political history. It was in the spacious auditorium of Cooper Union College, overlooking Astor Place, that Abraham Lincoln, the great sachem of the American people, delivered one of his most important, if not most famous, speeches on February 27, 1860. Although he had the Lincoln-Douglas debates behind him,[33] Lincoln was still not taken seriously as a candidate. Indeed he had only lasted as an Illinois congressman for two years, and that was ten years earlier. Originally he was to give a talk at Henry Ward Beecher's church in Brooklyn, but the pro-Republican Cooper Union took over the arrangements and made the occasion more political.

The night of the speech, Lincoln's candidacy was still unannounced, but word got out that he would be speaking in defense of the new Republican party, responding to Southern states' threats to secede if a Republican won the presidency.

Slavery was the burning constitutional issue.[34] Lincoln had researched the notes and minutes of the Constitutional Convention and found that a majority of the signatories, twenty-one of thirty-nine, had made statements against slavery during the discussion over what the United States Constitution should say. The speech had taken him four months to prepare. When he ascended the podium, he looked out over a sell-out crowd of fifteen hundred New Yorkers, including some of the most influential men of the time. He was visibly nervous, his voice shaky at first, but his experience as a trial lawyer came to his aid. In a real sense, he "cross-examined" the South in soliloquy, and found their position on slavery to be criminal. They say some spirit came over him, as if he were a biblical prophet, the mouthpiece of the Creator. By the time he finished, the crowd was on its feet, and people were "yelling like wild Indians."[35] It was a brilliant speech that not only made him an overnight celebrity, but also won him the nomination he had not even sought. For those in the North, it was a blueprint for a new truly *United* States, free of slavery.

I can't help but feel that in Lincoln we hear echoes of the eloquence and courage of the long ago Lenape sachems. Lincoln was not even remotely Native American, but it is interesting that this historic location—or perhaps the invisible spirit guides of this location—inspired the events that made the humble Abe Lincoln commander in chief at a critical moment in Turtle Island's history.

CONTINUING THE JOURNEY NORTH

Following the Path to the Wading Place northward, we would come to the small village of the Shepmoes at what is now the corner of Fourteenth Street and Third Avenue. To the east was Shepmoes Creek, running through a strip of wetlands area that reached to the East River at the place where Avenue A now sits.

I once went to Fourteenth Street and Third Avenue at night, and found an out-of-the-way place to sit down and relax. I went into "dreamtime," and one of the Shepmoes came to me in spirit and told me that he thought their graves had been covered over by the sea. I asked why. He said that from the distance of the spirit world he heard the repeated sound of waves rolling over his body, and that it was beautiful. He must have been hearing the sound of car tires, hissing across the pavement that now covers his body, and that due to traffic lights and patterns, they were coming in waves, high tide at noon every day, low tide at midnight or 2:00 A.M. I told him what I thought it was, and showed him the cars. He had mixed feelings about what had been built up there and about the strange vehicles, and we walked together for a while along the old path that still exists in the spirit world. When I returned to my waking world, there were still cars, cement, and the city buses to shock me back to reality.

Just north of the Shepmoes spot is East Seventeenth Street, specifically the southwest corner, where Washington Irving (1783–1859), author of *The Legend of Sleepy Hollow*, was to live from 1853 to 1856, before moving to Sunnyside, now part of Irvington, New York. He wove into his works more than a few Indian tales and legends. East Seventeenth Street is now called Irving Place in his honor.

There is a present-day Native arts and crafts shop on West 27th Street and Sixth Avenue, not far from the old path. The Third Avenue path bends to the west and becomes Fifth Avenue, which runs along the east side of Central Park. This area was once lush with evergreens, but few Native people lived here as it was too rocky and without fresh water.

This was the land of the Rechgawonk, who lived mainly down by the shore on the East River, where, in this century, archaeologists discovered a grooved stone ax beneath 77th Street and East Side Drive, near the shore, just south of Gracie Mansion.

To the left is Central Park and the site of the city reservoir. This was also the site of a slave village in the 1800s, and a slave cemetery, which, when excavated, yielded many Native American remains as well. The old path bore to the left, and then to the right one would have observed a large seasonal camp of about sixty wigwams, but no longhouses. Lenape people made their hunting and gathering base at this location for hundreds of years. They called it Konaandekongh. It wouldn't have been unusual for two hundred Lenape people at a time to live at these campsites, complete with herbalists, curers, sweat-lodge pourers, and soothsayers. This camp was at approximately 98th Street and Park Avenue; nearby is today's Mount Sinai Medical Center.[36]

SWIMMING TO THE BRONX

To our east, at 105th Street on the East River, was Rechewanis, "The Great Sands," where two more villages were located. The pathway north led to the middle of Central Park's northern end, at Harlem Meet, and beyond. At 110th Street and Sixth Avenue, the paths split again, the Path to the Wading Place branching to the right. The other path led back to the Mohican Trail and the Hudson River to the left. There was a rather large stream—the largest in Manhattan—running along what is now East 108th Street. Traveling upstream by canoe, one would enter at the East River and come to Fifth Avenue and Central Park, heading due east. One would then turn and head north to 116th, then travel northwest to Morningside Park at 125th Street where the source of the stream lies. The Rechewanis Lenape would have lived along both sides of this stream, probably in considerable numbers.

Duck Blind

As we walk along the Path to the Wading Place, we see a Lenape village on our left, near the future Marcus Garvey Memorial site. We soon come to the Harlem River, named after the city of Haarlem in the Netherlands. But the Harlem River was Muscooten until the mid-1700s. This word means "blindwater," which means that the banks are full of rushes one would use as a duck blind. Red oyster shells have been excavated from 209th to 211th Streets on the west bank of the river in a line with Ninth Avenue, along with European glass throughout the deposit, interestingly enough.

Looking across the Muscooten River in Lenape times, we would have seen gently sloping agricultural land and many villages of the Ranachqua, who remained there in strength until 1639, when the Dutch farmer Jonas Bronk settled in the region. Later, in the 1800s, the river was dredged so that larger boats could pass, and most of the reeds and cattails were cleared away. By 1900, no barefoot humans with bundles would attempt to cross the river. Today the FDR Drive goes over one of the two crossing sites, but like the Harlem River today, it is dangerous to those on foot.

Taking the other branch of the trail, along the south shore of the Muscooten River, we would come back to the little crossroads, and then continuing north by northwest along the upper panhandle of Manhattan, we would find ourselves walking along today's St. Nicholas Avenue, which was paved right over the Indian trail. The lower extension was Columbus Avenue, a common naming irony. On our right was a village situated at 139th Street and Seventh Avenue, near the Harlem Hospital.

Continuing north, we would come to a broad ridge, with the Hudson to our left and the Harlem River to our right. Another small village stood on our right at 169th Street and Tenth Avenue; here we would join up again with the western branch of the trail. To our left is the present-day George Washington Bridge. Beneath the bridge is a boat landing that connects with one at the southern end of the Palisades,[37] just a few hundred feet south and across the Hudson. This landing opposite was the beginning of a great trail, later part of the Wyoming Trail, also called "The Pocono Road," which connected with Dreamer's Rock, at "The Delaware Gap," where Native people went to fast, pray, and seek visions. Lenape ancestors lived there as long ago as 5000 years B.C.E.

Now our path would have led directly along a straight road, or *schachack geeay* in Unami, to the ancient cave site at Inwood. The Cloisters area is sacred to many people now, but it was sacred to the Lenape too. There are three rock shelters near Cold Spring, from 194th to 198th Streets between Fort Washington and Bennett Avenue. People have taken shelter from the wind and snow here for at least five thousand years.

Between Academy and 204th Streets at Seaman Avenue lay a Weckweesgeek village. The tribal name means "People of the Birchbark," but the English called them "Wickercreek." There was a large planting field at the intersection of Seaman Avenue and Isham Street. This location appears to have been settled for a very long time because pottery shards of many different styles have been found there. One of the very few unbroken pots ever found in Manhattan was unearthed near here at 204th Street and Tenth Avenue.

A little further along was a small ridge where Native people settled from time to time. The burial site of a dog, *mo-ay-can-nay-oo*, or "it is like a wolf" in Unami, was found at 209th Street near the

Harlem River and Ninth Avenue. As with all other Lenape pet dog burials, the remains were covered with a layer of crushed oyster shells. Another such dog burial was found fifty yards away, again with oyster shells covering it. (The lime in the oyster shells helps slow down the decay of the organic material and kills bacteria.) An ancient human burial was found at the west end of the rise between 210th and 211th Streets at Tenth Avenue in the early twentieth century. Typically there were no crushed oyster shells, further evidence that this practice was reserved for animals only.

At Inwood, right on the banks of the Hudson at the foot of Dykman Street, is a cave or rock formation where some of the earliest Lenape ancestors camped. One of the reasons for the light occupation of Manhattan during early times was the fierce winter wind. Thus the cave was one of the first places to be settled. There was a sloping field south of this spot, at 194th and Broadway, a Lenape village site which later became Zerrenner's farm.[38] At the very northern tip of the island, beyond which the waters churn and bedevil unwary sailors, lay another early settlement. This area is now called Spuyten Duyvil, based on the old Dutch creek to the immediate north, actually part of the Harlem River watercourse, whose name means "Spite the Devil." Next to it is Cold Spring, where fresh water bubbles up from the rocks. Three heaps of refuse were excavated here, and evidence of fire. The fire would have been shielded from the wind, and the spring provided fresh water.

FOLLOWING THE WESTERN PATH

Starting out back at the Kintecoying (Astor Place), the path to the Sapohannikan Fort runs along Eighth Street, then crosses Seventh Street, then traces the north edge of Washington Square Park. It then heads northwest to Eighth Street again and follows Greenwich Avenue to Fourteenth Street. This was the site of the Sapohannikan Fort, where the Hoboken ferry terminal was built, and today the

PATH trains come in. It is here that the Hoboken and Sapohannikan of New Jersey crossed the Hudson or Mohicanituk River to commute to work and trade. The reason for this coincidence is obvious: it is the narrowest place on the river.

After landing their canoes on the western shore of Manhattan island, the Sapohannikans walked a beautiful trail every day that led from the banks of the Mohicanituk, where they fished and raised corn at what would some day be West End Avenue, to the fort. This path inland follows along what is now the sticky pavement of Gansevoort Street. The location of the great fort is now a great open star-shaped cobblestone plaza just south of Fourteenth Street.

Here the Sapohannikan "commuters" set about their business, trading their corn for other goods acquired by the Manhattan traders from the north, their own people at the village, and especially the Canarsie further to the south. Here is where the Sapohannikan Trail began, used at first to haul water to the fort but then developing into a main thoroughfare through the village. A Dutch inn later called the Old Homestead was built just north of the site of the Sapohannikan Fort, for the comfort of white fur traders. No one knows the original date the Old Homestead was constructed, but it looks to have been rebuilt in the early 1700s. There is still a restaurant in operation today in that old edifice.

Returning to the Kintecoying and walking along The Path to the Wading Place from there, we would once have come to a fork in the road at Broadway and Fifth Avenue where the Manetta Creek's head-waters start. Finding archaeological evidence of the Mohican Trail from the Flatiron District to what is now Columbus Circle has proved problematic, due to intensive use and development of the area. However common sense indicates that the east and west side paths connected here. We know that Saint Nicholas was a major trail as far south as Columbus Circle, and The Path to the Wading Place veered eastward at the Flatiron District, i.e., Madison Square Park. The earliest British colonial maps show Bloomingdale Drive (now known as Broadway) connecting these two points or crossroads. It was named after the Bloomingdale farm, located at what is now Times Square. There is every reason to believe Bloomingdale followed the route of an earlier trail, either the Mohican Trail itself or a subsidiary trade route.

The (Pre-)Historic Garment District

Walking north along this stretch of the Mohican Trail in Lenape times, we would eventually have come to an open air trading spot where one would have seen Lenape men tending blankets covered with small pelts of otter, rabbit, and fox. At the trading post we would be likely to find the skins of bear and deer. This long-ago shady, forested area was located at Broadway and 28th Street. Today the New York Fur Market, a multimillion-dollar piece of the Garment District, is housed in skyscrapers, one block to the west.

Although present-day Broadway reaches its busiest and most congested area at Times Square where it crosses Seventh Avenue, in ancient times, this was one of the most tranquil and peaceful (*gunt-a-woagan*) spots along the trail, suitable for contemplation and undisturbed rest for the wandering trader. Broadway passes Eighth Avenue on its way westward at one of those rare circles, this one named for Christopher Columbus. This one-time oasis of peace, like most of the metropolis beneath which Lenape Hoking lies dreaming, is now a traffic-jammed thoroughfare.

5

EXPLORING THE
ANCIENT CITY

The Bronx, Brooklyn, Queens,
and Staten Island

Manhattan was a busy island before the advent of white traders, but the remaining four boroughs, the Bronx, Queens, Brooklyn, and Staten Island, were even more populated, with a more complex web of trails weaving together their many villages of mixed descent and dialect. Unfortunately comparatively little is known about these Algonquin people. Their precontact history is sketchy; still I will attempt to pass along what I have been able to reconstruct to date in the clearest manner possible.

There were several trails from Manhattan to the Bronx, across the shallow Muscooten, now the Harlem River. The whole northern panhandle of Manhattan, called Shorakapkok, "Sitting-down Place"[1] by the Munsee, was lined with many branching trails and crossings. The mile-long stretch of the river that divides the two boroughs at 218th Street had three crossings. That stretch is also known as Spuyten Duyvil Creek, although today it is a deep channel connecting the Harlem River to the Hudson. The modern Manhattan street called Indian Road follows the path of an Indian trail leading from the site of an old village of the Rechgawawank to Spuyten Duyvil.[2]

The Harlem River then bends at a right angle and runs south four miles with few known trail crossings before reaching The Path to the Wading Place. Here the river widens into the Bronx Kill before reaching Randall's Island. There are two trails north from The Wading Place as well, plus one from Randall's Island. We'll visit those later.

The bluff where the Mohican Trail fords the river is now the foot of Tenth Avenue, which runs to the right of Baker's Field, an athletic field now operated by Columbia University. A spur branched off to the left, fording across to a small Reckgawawank settlement (the "sandy place people" of the Bronx). The main course enters into the extensive settlements of the Keskeskick, meaning "short, sharp sedge grass,"[3] a territory that stretches for many miles from Melrose north to Westchester.

The Mohican Trail was called the King's Highway from the British conquest in 1664 to 1758. After that time it was known as the Albany Post Road, or, as some preferred to call it, the North Road. Many Route 9 postal destinations in Poughkeepsie are still properly written as "North Road" today. It was this Post Road that united the new nation after 1776. Old stone mile markers, silent testaments to the location of the old pathway north, can still be found along dusty side roads up and down the Hudson Valley.

Entering the North Bronx

As we head north today, the main trail will bring us into the Bronx at the Paparinemin village, meaning "diverting, or turning aside,"[4] in reference to the sharp left turning of the river here, which is one of the more remarkable geographical features in these parts. This village was once an island in ancient times, and later a gathering place for Reckgawawank people (the "sandy place people" of Westchester).

Across the river stood the fortified village of Nipnichsen, "Two Waters Come Together,"[5] which indeed stands on the point where the two rivers meet, the Mohicanituk (Hudson) and the Muscooten

(Harlem). After crossing at the old fording place, we come to a landing that is now part of Kingsbridge. Here, in Lenape days, was a
bustling village, with many longhouses and trade blankets, populated
by a vibrant people.

Long ago, two important trails split off from a point at West
230th Street in present-day Kingsbridge Heights in the Bronx. One
was the Mosholu Trail, a subsection of the Mohican Trail, which led
to the Mosholu village to the north and then to Westchester and
beyond; the other was the Sacherah Trail to the Bronx River.

To the immediate west was a small Reckgawawank village. These
people moved here in the fifteenth century from a sandy place on the
west bank of the Hudson, south of Fort Lee. Passing through the
Paparinemin territory into the northern section of the vast Keskeskick
territory, we come to a bubbling stream now called Tibbett's Brook—
just about where Manhattan College is today—where we would once
have found the old Mosholu Village, not too far from where the
Parkway by the same name now runs. No one passed along to the
white colonists what the name means, but *mosholu* in the language of
the Lenape west of the Hudson, the Unami, indicates an area that has
been burned to make a clearing.[6] This was surprisingly common
among the Lenape, despite their renowned reverence for trees, though
it seems they had mastered the art of controlled burning.

This northern footpath was widened at the time of the British
conquest when it became the Albany Post Road, the name it still
bears. This path takes us past what is now Van Cortlandt Park, and
then we find ourselves in Westchester.

The other important trail that branched off back at Kingsbridge
Heights was the Sacherah Trail, now Old Gun Hill Road, which led
northeast to the Conangungh "river crossing" village of the
Quinnipiac on the Bronx River. Also called Wikison, the village was
located where Willis Avenue begins, and again, though nothing about
its meaning was passed on to the settlers, the word means "homes in

the wilderness" in Unami.[7] There the trail crossed the "Common Path" now called the Bronx River Parkway, and eventually connected with what is now Route 1. This Sacherah Trail became the Old Boston Post Road in 1672.

The corner where the Albany Post Road and the Boston Post Road met was a popular stopover spot among the Algonquin. They placed their tents and lodges there, both as long- and short-term settlement camps, sharing tales and songs, throwing dice, and smoking tobacco. In 1693, Frederick Philipse built The Philipse Inn at that fork in the road; as a result, he became a very successful man. The inn, also known as Cock's Tavern, stood for many years, and was mentioned in a novel by James Fenimore Cooper.[8] The Algonquin of the time must have been upset, since they were used to spending the night there for free. The Isaac Varian house was built there in 1770, and still stands today.

The Old Boston Post Road was made up by interconnecting several well-worn Algonquin trails that stretched from the Canarsie territory to the land of the Pawtuxet and Wampanoag in what is now Massachussetts. It followed the Old Gun Hill Road, or Sacherah Path to the Bronx River. Working its way northeast, it traveled through the Conangungh territory, connecting to what is now Route 1, and extending through the Siwanoy village at modern-day Larchmont, and the village of Mamaroneck, both now part of Westchester. This stretch is still called the Old Boston Post Road today. Then it ran up the east side of Westchester, becoming Barnes and Bussing Avenues, and entered Connecticut near the colonial town of Horseneck, now Greenwich, Connecticut.

ENTERING THE SOUTH BRONX

The Path to the Wading Place in Manhattan branched off the main trail at what is now 113th Street, and passed between the Muscoota village on the left and the Conykeekst,[9] or "narrow tract of land," village on the right, before descending to the beautiful river, now called the Harlem River, full of wild ducks and rushes.

Crossing over the shallow water here in 1524, we would land at the base of the pleasant rolling hills called the Ranachqua, "the end place,"[10] now Morrisania, and walk through a small village. These were the people who later, in 1639, deeded Jonas Bronk the land for his farm, thus the name "the Bronx." Their main village was at Stony Point, at what is now called Hell Gate. We come to a fork in the road, the Keskeskick ("short sedge grass") road to the left, and the Acqueegecom ("crossing place") path to the right.

The Keskeskick road heads northwest and becomes what is now the Grand Concourse passing Yankee Stadium and then Morrisania. It winds to the west around Morris Heights, before reconnecting with the Mohican Trail at Kingsbridge Heights.

The other trail heads northeast from the FDR Drive (named when Franklin Delano Roosevelt, a descendant of Lenape-raised Susanna Hutchinson, died near the end of World War II), to Melrose Avenue. Then it follows Westchester Avenue and merges with the current route of the Bruckner Expressway. Near that spot was Acqueegecom, where the path crosses over the Bronx River, the dividing line between the Munsee-speaking people and the Renneiu dialect Quinnipiac and Siwanoy to the east.

Taking the Common Path due south from Acqueegecom brings us to one of the largest villages of the Bronx, Snakapins, "The Land between River and Open Water,"[11] at what is now Clason Point. A large wampum manufacturing area, Snakapins village was known to have had sixty or more lodges at one time. This area was heavily populated from the 1300s, and this is the site where the newer Lenape type of pottery culture was first discovered. That important new development, linked to the origins of the Renneiu dialect, was called Clason Point culture.[12]

To the immediate west of the Clason Point group were the Hunt's

Point villages, known as the Sachwranung and the Quinnahung. Quinnahung means "Long High Place" in Narragansett,[13] one of the older languages, related to Mohican. Sachwranung has not been translated.

The people to the east of the Bronx River, where the Bronx River Parkway now runs, were of this Renneiu dialect, and were called Siwanoy, which means "People of the Wampum Trade."[14] These are the people who massacred Anne Hutchinson's family, and captured their daughter Susanna Hutchinson during Kieft's War. Hutchinson Parkway, or the "Hutch" as most New Yorkers call it, was named after Anne Hutchinson.

If we take the Common Path due north a few hundred yards from Acqueegecom, we enter into the Ketchee Machk Poodunk, the "Great Bear Swamp."

THE GREAT BEAR SWAMP

This almost impenetrable region was full of bears and other wild animals. When the filth and noise of European industry had almost completely driven off the nature-loving Algonquin, they took refuge here with the last remaining undomesticated animals and hid out for generations in the dark swamp. The Siwanoy people maintained a semisecret traditional village here until 1782, when they were finally expelled.

In one of the interesting ironies of New York history, the Great Bear Swamp is now the site of the Bronx Zoo. The last vestige of wilderness where animals were able to roam free is now the only place where animals can exist at all, but only as captive guests of the state.

A clear, well-articulated, well-preserved turtle petroglyph was recently found along the Bronx River on the grounds of the New York Botanical Gardens, adjacent to the Bronx Zoo and to the north. It was probably carved some time between 1000 and 1600 C.E. The turtle, with its head expressively turned to the left, may have been a symbol for Turtle Island, now known as North America; however it was also a clan symbol for the proud Unami people of the Delaware and may have been a boundary marker.[15]

A trail split off to the east, merging with modern-day Tremont Avenue and leading to three Siwanoy villages of Throgs Neck, one at what is now Sunterville Cove, another at Locust Point, and another near Ferry Point Park. Other pieces of trail have been identified here and there around the Bronx, but do not have modern counterparts.

PRINCIPAL ALGONQUIN VILLAGES IN THE AREA

The Algonquin villages of the Bronx are scattered throughout the landscape, the lesser of which have not been mentioned. Here are some additional villages alphabetically by current location. At Castle Hill, there was a stockaded village, which has not been named. At Eastchester, there was a village called Asumsowis, no translation of which has been passed on to us. The Wanaqua and Mishow, untranslated, were at Hunter's Island, a name that evokes images of Siwanoy archers bagging deer in the forest. At Pelham Bay Park, there was the Pelham Neck village and the village of Laaphawaching, a Munsee word meaning "a place of stringing beads." Like Clason Point, it was a center of the wampum industry.

THE BROKEN LAND

The Brooklyn Dodgers were founded in 1890. Their original name was the Brooklyn Bridegrooms, but everyone called them "the Trolley Dodgers," and the name "the Dodgers" stuck. That's about as far back in history as most Brooklynites can remember, but Brooklyn in 1523, with a vast network of trails and villages, was perhaps the greatest population center east of present-day New Jersey.

The original people of Brooklyn were the Canarsie, which translates as "Grassy Place,"[16] or more commonly "Fenced-In Place." They maintained a large trading network that stretched to the Gulf of

Mexico and probably Central America to the south, and Lake Superior to the west. Lenape travelers and traders explored the Carolinas and the Mississippi Valley in their wanderings, as well as the western Great Lakes. Their wampum and pottery are found here and there throughout the eastern half of Turtle Island, though mostly where copper can be acquired. A large, ancient gorget (a piece of armor to protect the throat), forged from Native copper, was found during the excavation of the foundation for the Brooklyn Bridge at Flatbush Avenue. This would have been a trade item of great value, having been carried over a thousand miles by foot or boat from where copper is mined in Lake Superior.[17] The Canarsie were importer-exporters par excellence. Theirs was the original Canarsie Shipping Lines, employing swift sea-going canoes capable of holding ten people or more. Canarsie canoes were easily forty feet long, and were constructed without nails. They carved their oars deeply scooped for better propulsion in the water. The navigators of the dugout canoes would place their coats on the end of a pole to catch the wind and pick up speed in warm weather, creating a rudimentary sail.[18]

Their main port was across from Canarsie Island. There is now a cement pier about fifty feet east of the Canarsie Landing site. Although part of New York City, Canarsie Island still retains much of its original untamed wildness.

The area of Bay Ridge belonged to the Nyack ("point of land") tribe of Canarsie Indians. Fort Hamilton Parkway was once a trail that led to the boat landing for Staten Island, which continued on the other side of the narrows. Early in colonial times the Nyack were forced to move in with the Tappan further up the Hudson due to Dutch expansion; a town in Rockland County now bears their name. Others of the Nyack moved across the narrows to Staten Island.

In 1635 the Dutch laid out a few villages in Canarsie territory, and named the area Bruckelen. It means "Broken Land," which is what the Canarsie called Coney Island Beach from Sea Gate to

Manhattan Beach, Mannahaning, although the Dutch didn't buy Coney Island itself until 1654.[19] The homesick Dutch had a town back home by the name of Breuckelen, so the name stuck. (There was no standard spelling system in those times, hence the missing letter.) The Dutch town was linked by rowboats to the fort of New Amsterdam across the East River. As mentioned elsewhere, they landed at Fulton Street, Brooklyn, and could travel on the trail now traced by Fulton Street as far as Bedford-Stuyvesant, and turn south on Stuyvesant Avenue to the landings, or continue east on Jamaica Boulevard. Another popular route from the Brooklyn Bridge crossing was what is now Flushing Avenue, a trail that led across north Brooklyn to Flushing Bay in Queens.

The Great Crossroads

The grand sachem of the Canarsie during the Dutch occupation was Sessys.[20] His longhouse dwelling stood just to the northeast of the great crossroads of two of the main Canarsie trails. This great meeting place was called Keskaech Querem. Those two roads are now Flatbush Avenue and King's Highway. Nearby was another of those great trees that often marked the site of an important meeting place. Many of these towering sentinels survived into colonial times. The settlers called them "council oaks" or "treaty elms," depending on the species.

The Dutch, offering considerable amounts of dry goods and promises of protection from enemies, managed to get Sessys to agree to give up his longhouse, which was located next to the Canarsie sacred burial ground. By this time, disease had already decimated the Canarsie, and many had moved further east on Long Island or further west to New Jersey.

The Dutch razed the chief's house and built a church, which was called the First Dutch Reformed Church of the Flatlands.[21] The Flatlands were named after Flanders ("flat land"), a place on the border of Holland and Belgium where the Flemish among them had been born. That church, rebuilt twice, is still there. What is most unusual is that they placed their own church cemetery right over the Canarsie one, and the remains still lie together today. This Dutch cemetery is still at that site, marking some thread of continuity between the great metropolis of the Lenape and the urban sprawl of the city of Brooklyn.

From the great crossroads, Flatbush Avenue ran northwest across the settlement of Flatbush, crossing Prospect Park, which is what much of Brooklyn once looked like, crossing Fulton Street, also an ancient trail, to the landing where Brooklyn Bridge now stands. From there the Canarsie paddled across to where the cherry orchards stood. In the opposite direction from the crossroads, the Flatbush Trail crossed the Flatlands, the Brooklyn Marine Park and Golf Course, and led to the Hoopaninak ("enclosed island") and Shanscomacocke ("a crossing place") villages at Bennett Field. There the Canarsie traveler arrived at the best crossing to the Far Rockaways, now the site of the Marine Parkway Bridge.

The other trail that made up the great crossroads was the King's Highway, an old pathway that circled the area of Brooklyn about a mile, on average, from shore—the prehistoric equivalent of the Belt Parkway. These two paths, plus the Fulton Street path and the Flushing Avenue path, all merged at the Werpoes new village south of the Brooklyn Bridge crossing, where the Brooklyn Academy of Music now stands. This site is just a block north of the Long Island Railroad Terminal today, but it was already one of the major transportation hubs of Lenape Hoking in 1523.

A trail approximated by Avenue D today, leading from the Flatbush Trail to the cornfields, created a triangle of pathways north of the great crossroads. At the same time, it created two more intersections. One, to the northeast of the Keskaech Querem, was called Mikyttey Houll by the Dutch, a meeting place; the other, was at the corner of Avenue D and Flatbush Avenue.

Flatlands Avenue, Fifth Avenue, and Pennsylvania Avenue in Brooklyn were all trails as well. Many of Brooklyn's trails, however, meandered a little too much to please the British, and were discontinued and built over with straighter routes, or became lost under the now familiar grid of streets in New York's most populated borough.[22] One important trail that passed through what is now Sunset Park on the way to the village of the Marechkawick chief Gowanus ("Young Pine") on Gowanus Bay, has been completely obliterated by development. *Marechkawick* means "gathering at the sandy place." The Marechkawick were unjustly attacked by the Dutch during the Kieft War period, an error the Dutch later admitted. Much weakened by the attack, they left the area in1685 and joined the Weckweesgeek to the north and the Canarsie to the south. Some went east to the Poospatuck. Others moved west and joined the Unami and Munsee. By that time, they were a forgotten people.

The Massabarkem[23] lived south of the Canarsie, not far from Coney Island, in the area north of Neptune Avenue. Their name has been translated as "Land by the Great Water." To the west, along Leif Ericson Drive and north to Indian Pond, were the Mocung, "Black Muddy Place."[24] The powerful Canarsie had treatied the outer areas of their land along the shore to other related tribes, creating a barrier between themselves and the shore.

CONEY ISLAND

The day the first Dutch sailor landed on what is now called Coney Island, learned the word Mannahaning, and translated it, marked the beginning of two classic New York place names: Manhattan, the modern spelling of a word for "hilly or broken-up island," and "Brooklyn," a modern spelling of a Dutch term for "broken land."

Coney Island *was* actually an island at one time. The section from Sea Gate eastward past 33rd Street was the old island the Canarsie called Narrioch, "a point of land."[25] The ten blocks eastward

from 33rd Street were actually under the ocean. During the "storm of
the century" on December 10, 1992, this man-made piece of landfill
was for a time submerged again. The Dutch name for this island was
Koynen Eyland, "rabbit island," hence the name Coney Island.[26] After
the island became attached to the mainland, this name was erroneously applied to the entire area, which is not an island. The
Narrioch people moved inland, keeping their name, although it too
was now made inappropriate by the change in geography.

SOUTH BROOKLYN

There was once a great cornfield in Brooklyn. The breadbasket of the
Canarsie, it stretched for several miles across the southeast corner of
Brooklyn, from Ralph Avenue in the west to the water in the east and
north. Within a decade, the Dutch had somehow managed to buy
most of the cornfields from the Canarsie. There is an expansive
Dutch plantation shown on early maps of the area. Its heart-shaped
boundary enclosed a large portion of the Canarsie cornfields.

There are still wild maizelike grass plants growing along the Belt
Parkway in southeastern Brooklyn, at the outer edge of where the
great cornfields once stood. Driving by, I have often wondered if
these grasses are the direct descendants of that vast acreage of maize
that fed the Canarsie long ago.

There was an Indian Pond in southwest Brooklyn, also the site
of an ancient settlement that probably existed for thousands of
years. At contact, the Makeop, "a great clearing or open field,"[27] were
living there. As their population dwindled to almost nothing at the
height of New Amsterdam's expansion, an elder signed away the
rights to this large planting area "for one gun, one blanket, and one
kettle." The large pond was filled in during the 1930s and the name
Indian Pond forgotten by all but a few. It is now part of New
Utrecht, the landfill area stretching from Avenue O to King's
Highway.

QUEENS

The modern borough of Queens was not heavily populated in ancient times, but it provided good hunting grounds and hosted many villages nonetheless. The main indigenous people of Queens were the Matinecock, which meant "the place to search," implying "good hunting ground."[28] The Matinecock language was the new Matouac-type, what I call the Renneiu language, rather than the older, more traditional Munsee as spoken in Manhattan.

The Rockaway also claimed an equally large section of Queens. The word derives from Rechquaakie (a variation on "people of the sandy places"), the name of their capital city on Long Island, now called East Rockaway. Not much is known about them, but their language was of the Matouac, the Long Island Confederacy of people who speak Renneiu languages.

The Old Rockaway Trail is now called Jamaica Avenue. The name Jamaica may derive from *Yau-may-ko*, the old Algonquin word for "Place of the Beaver."[29] The long trail starts as Fulton Avenue in Brooklyn, travels along Jamaica Avenue in Queens, and continues along Jericho Turnpike across Long Island. The northern border of the Rockaway territory (abutting that of the Matinecock) was the terminal moraine of the Wisconsin Glacier, the high point of which is now called Forest Park. The line of the terminal moraine divided not only types of terrain—exposed rock to the north and sandy outwash to the south—but also types of Algonquin peoples. The glacier was several thousand feet thick, and it peeled off the top layer of rock in the Bronx and upper Manhattan with its great weight. That terminal moraine line runs along the ridge of Long Island, then moves to the southwest across Brooklyn, then across the south side of Staten Island to the high point at 410-foot-high Todt Hill, the highest point on the coastal seaboard south of Cadillac Mountain at Bar Harbor, Maine. The line then passes through New Jersey and into Pennsylvania and west to Ohio.

The boundary line between the Matinecock to the east and Rockaway to the west was a north-south trail that started at Flushing Bay, and followed the Van Wyck Expressway near Flushing Meadow Park. The Rockaway territory bent in an **L** shape under the Matinecock's from there. The boundary line between the Matinecock to the north and the Rockaway to the south was the terminal moraine itself, and on that high ridge was a trail that is now Grand Central Parkway. At Bellerose, the boundary line shifted south then ran along a trail that is now Hempstead Turnpike. The Rockaway territory extended south to the ocean, embracing today's Long Beach, Atlantic Beach, and the Rockaways.

Although the villages are not well known, there are many trails in the region, indicating considerable habitation. The important north-south trail upon which the Van Wyck is built can be traced today as follows: Go south on the Van Wyck until it crosses Jamaica Boulevard, then follow Sutphin Boulevard and continue south along Rockaway Boulevard at least to Inwood near the John F. Kennedy Airport. At the beginning of what is now JFK, the journey along Rockaway Boulevard ended as terra firma gave way to marshy wetlands, then seawater.

The Old Rockaway Trail was an important Algonquin route that ran west to east. It can be traced today as follows: Starting at the eastern terminus of Fulton Street in Brooklyn, continue on Jamaica Avenue to its end in Bellerose. Then continue on Route 25, also known as Washington Avenue, until it reaches Westbury, then continue on the Jericho Turnpike out of Queens. In this way you can complete in a single hour a journey that would have taken a Matinecock a full day, although the scenery is not quite the same.

Another major boulevard that is actually built on top of an ancient trail is Flushing Avenue from the Brooklyn Bridge through Brooklyn and Queens. When it crosses Queens Boulevard, continue on Grand Avenue, then Cerone Avenue. From there the trail cut directly to Flushing Bay near Shea Stadium, however no road today follows the last leg of its route. Another major trail coincides with parts of Fresh Pond Avenue and Cypress Hills Avenue. Woodhaven Boulevard is also concealing an ancient trail that wound through Astoria, starting at a canoe landing across from Ward's Island and continuing east to Flushing Bay.[30]

MASPETH: THE BAD WATER PLACE

New York City's drinking water comes from reservoirs all associated in some way with the Delaware. Some of it comes through the Delaware Aqueduct, which lies underneath Central Park West. Some of it comes from the Ashokan Reservoir, named after an Esopus chief who never existed. (See "The Minisink Trail" in Chapter 14 for details.) But the Maspeth, "bad water place" tribe, a subdivision of the Rockaway Nation, didn't have very good water. They lived along the salt waters of Flushing Bay where La Guardia Airport now stands, and along Mespaetches Creek, meaning "bad water."[31] This is now Newtown Creek, dividing King's County from Queens. Many people lived on the La Guardia site, overlooking Flushing Bay. The airport was built without excavating the land, so we don't know how much archaic debris is underneath or how many people may have lived there at one time. The Maspeth produced great quantities of wampum belts for trade. In 1642, Willem Kieft, Dutch governor from 1638 to 1645, granted the Maspeth, Corona, and Elmhurst areas of Queens to Francis Doughty in a land grant. In 1645, after Kieft was fired, the Dutch established the town of Vlissingen in Queens. That village is now called Flushing. It is known to have been an important sachemdom, with at least thirty Native American families in residence, according to R. P. Bolton.[32] In 1662, a smallpox epidemic spread like wildfire through Queens and almost all Native Americans in the area perished.[33]

The Maspeth joined the Matouac Confederacy, which included the Matinecock and the Rockaway, around 1400 C.E. Both the Matinecock and Rockaway peoples spoke the Renneiu language, although different dialects. This large confederacy has also been called Paumanauke (also spelled Paumanoc or Pomonok by non-natives). There is a Pomonok Housing Project today in Queens near Kissena Boulevard. The owners of the project are probably unaware that the word means "place of tribute" in Lenape. Long Island was often called upon to pay wampum to the natives of the mainland.

An equally important term for old Long Island is Matouac, which is translated as "young men." Macouac is interpreted as "young man" in the Nahautl language. Around 1400 C.E., Montauk became the territory of the grand sachems of the Long Island Confederacy. The alliance was also known as the Montauk Confederacy or the Matouac Confederacy with all three terms used equally and interchangeably.

LITTLE PEOPLE

Queens was once forest and wetlands and a good area to hunt, but for the most part, not a good place to live, judging by its small human population. But the Lenape and all the related tribes, including those of the Matouac Confederacy, believed that the landscape was highly populated—with "little people."

The Lenape say there are "little people" everywhere in the woods. Most Algonquin elders have a name for these little people. The Unami call them *Mesingw wemahtekenis* and consider them to be the most powerful spirit forces in the forest. These three-foot-high dwarves, dressed in leather, help lost hunters find their way and are especially nice to lost children. One who encounters a *Mesingw wemahtekenis* is given great power, strength, and stamina.

The Irish call them Leprechauns, the Greeks have their Hammadryads, the English their wood nymphs and fairies. Some Ojibway call them *mimigess;* the Munsee, *womptchakaneesh-sha;* the Micmac, *madjaweenoodjeek.* The Micmac also believe that the first man, Glooskap, created the little people himself. Many Algonquin elders who remember these traditions describe them as having mouths like rabbits (with folds that come down on either side and teeth showing in the middle) and butterfly wings. The "little people" are mostly seen in the early morning or at dusk, and more in the spring and fall of the year when they have a lot of work to do.

THE FORGOTTEN PEOPLE OF STATEN ISLAND

Staten Island was known to the Lenape as Eghquaons, "high sandy banks" or at least that's what the Dutch were told. In actuality, while the southern half of the island was certainly known as such, and was within the domain of the Unami-speaking Raritan Indians, the northwest of the island, called Matawuck or Monocknong, "the place of bad woods," belonged to the Hackensack, and a tiny piece of the northeast belonged to the Canarsie. Meanwhile almost every other Lenape nation, including the Tappan, Nyack, and Rockaway, claimed part of the island at one time. It is highly likely that there was even a form of "time sharing," as some historians today have called it— treaties within treaties that allowed two or more tribes to share a plot of land on the island.

Staten Island, with its strange, twisting roads and high hills, was well populated with Lenape in the days before the Dutch. To the north was the Hackensacks, "land of broken-up ground." The rolling hills of their territory extended south to Meadow Brook and east to Sea View Hospital, the eastern boundary slanting through the College of Staten Island, Wagner College, and finally Stapleton. This area includes the most heavily populated areas of Staten Island today, St. George and New Brighton, as well as the least populated, in the northwest corner near the Goethal's Bridge. Large Lenape village sites have been found at Snug Harbor, at the corner of Forest Avenue and Victory Boulevard, and at the corner of Cebra Avenue and Van Duzer Street. The lengthy route known as Victory Boulevard, home to many of Staten Island's businesses today, was built on top of one of the main indigenous trade routes that stretched across the island hundreds of years ago. Richmond Terrace, from Jersey Street and the Arts and Industries Museum, past Sailor's Snug Harbor and around Fresh Kills inlet, was also an Indian trail in ancient times. A third trail connected modern-day Burgher Street with Clove Road.

The area where Giovanni da Verrazzano first landed in 1524, near Tompkinsville, was well within the area currently identified as Hackensack. His descriptions seem consistent with the fact that the Hackensack were one of the larger and more prosperous groups in the region. The people he met were an offshoot branch of a much larger group based on the mainland. This mainland territory of the Hackensack stretched for thirty miles, from the south tip of Staten Island at Perth Amboy all the way to Hackensack, New Jersey, and perhaps further. According to one early map, the Hackensack people of the Jersey coast (stretching from Bayonne, which is across the Kill Van Kull from St. George, up to where the Palisades begin at Englewood Cliffs) were called Metchkentawoom. "A Great, Beautiful Gathering of People."[34] Further inland were the "unfriendly" Sanhikan, "The People with the Firemaking Drills." Verrazzano's friendly welcoming committee must have been from the Metchkentawoom.

South of that region were the Raritan, whose huge sandy territory extended as far east as Great Kills Park. The SIRT—Staten Island Rapid Transit—was built along a lengthy trade route that stretched from Grymes Hill area (in Canarsie territory) to Tottenville. Richmond Road and Amboy Road cover up this trail today. Both are still somewhat scenic, but it must have been quite a beautiful twelve-mile hike in ancient times. The Nyack of the Canarsie had a settlement on the border between the territories at Great Kills Park, which in the contact period was called Shancopshee or Shawkopoke, "a midway haven."[35] There is an ancient Indian burial ground near the Old Conference House, which was built in 1668 on the south shore of Staten Island in Tottenville. The unusual town name, which means "village of the dead" in Dutch, derives its morbid tone from the discovery there of a large Native American burial ground. The full extent of the burial ground wasn't discovered until 1898. Some of the skeletal remains found show that bows and arrows were used, and that these bows, six feet or more in length, were so powerful they sent arrows right through bones and out the other side. These skeletons were placed in the American Museum of Natural History.[36] Historians including R. P. Bolton and Alanson Skinner believe there to have been a permanent settlement near that spot dating back several thousand years. The site would have been ideal for a fortress or defense point overlooking traffic on the Arthur Kill to the west and Raritan Bay and the Lower Bay to the east.

In the northeast corner of the island was a small area where the Canarsie people made their home in later days, a territory extending only as far west as Van Duzer Street and as far north as Stapleton. It was only one and a half miles from Brooklyn, the land of the Canarsie, so it is not surprising these boat-loving people would have settled there. Along the shoreline just south of Fort Wadsworth, within sight of the modern Verrazzano Bridge, was an ancient village some historians have referred to as the "Arrochar Village," named after an unknown Canarsie chief. The Rockaways also had an interest in this area, and a Rockaway sachem Orasguy sold his lot in 1670.

The Canarsie, Raritan, and Hackensack territories met at a high point where Sea View Hospital now stands.[37]

Within the memory of most older Staten Islanders is the old Brooklyn Ferry, which was discontinued when the enormously expensive Verrazzano Narrows Bridge was put into place. What most Staten Islanders don't know is that there was a free Brooklyn ferry at that same site five hundred years ago, as the Canarsie traveled each day from their Staten Island settlement back to the homeland of Bay Ridge. A Canarsie trail used to run from the main trail, near where Hylan Boulevard now meets with Interstate 278, directly toward where the bridge now stands. The Canarsie would sail across the water along the same ferry route, and then pick up the trail just south of present-day Bay Ridge Parkway.

The Amboy Trail

Perth Amboy, in New Jersey, was once a very sacred site. The earliest Unami soapstone carvings and pottery show up here about 1100 c.e. Directly across the way is Bowman's Brook, Staten Island, where the earliest Unami settlements have been found. They would have chosen that spot right on the ridge of the terminal moraine because it had the most diverse collection of stones, a sandy soil to the south, and a rocky soil to the north. They advanced quickly as an artistic culture, with the Arthur Kill as their eastern center.

Ascending the Amboy Trail from Bowman's Brook and heading north we eventually reach Amboy Road and the SIRT railroad. Passing Great Kills, at Emmet Avenue we enter into the Canarsie region at what is now Oakwood. At New Dorp, we climb to the summit of Gryme's Hill. In April 1524, a Lenape traveler standing on this blustery hilltop might have noticed a small speck on the southern horizon that would turn out to be Verrazzano's ship, the *Dauphine*—and the beginning of the end for the Lenape.

6

VERRAZZANO
AND HIS LEGACY

It must have seemed like paradise on earth to Giovanni da
Verrazzano and his men when they first set foot on New
York soil on April 17, 1524. The spot, near Bay Street on Staten
Island, is now a stone's throw from the post office, the ferry terminal,
and the new Yankee minor league stadium. His arrival was the first
known contact between the inhabitants of Lenape Hoking and those
of the troubled continent to the east. It triggered a series of events
that would turn that forest paradise into a fortress of concrete.

The first result of this contact was the first and most catastrophic
of the countless[1] epidemics to follow, and it was carried by Captain
Giovanni da Verrazzano's crew. The invisible biological army that followed on Verrazzano's flank brought about the downfall of the
Algonquin civilization like no ideology or weaponry could. When the
next boat from Europe arrived some eighty-odd years later, the
"dense populations" Verrazzano had described were gone, with only
a fraction remaining.

Verrazzano was a rather enlightened man. It is no discredit to
him that he brought about the deployment of this ultimate weapon;
he couldn't have foreseen it. Many of the explorers sent on these dangerous missions were people no one wanted to have return home, but

Verrazzano was not among them. Some, like Cortés and Columbus, exhibited strikingly antisocial tendencies. It seemed to be part of the explorer mentality of the time.

The famous explorer Martin Frobisher is a good example. Born eleven years after Verrazzano's trip to New York, he was orphaned early and in 1544 became a cabin boy at the age of nine. He became an officer in his early twenties, and in his thirties became "a notorious and well-known pirate,"[2] marauding French ships along the English Channel, and turning over the oceans' bounty to Her Majesty. He was tried several times for piracy but was never convicted thanks to a series of royal interventions. He had a reputation for strict discipline bordering on cruelty. He commanded a number of ships doing battle with the Spanish Armada and personally involved himself in the fighting, though most ship captains were unwilling to serve under him. He found a backer in Michael Lok, a known gambler and swindler, as well as a pioneer in public relations. Lok changed Frobisher's image from cunning pirate to romantic court gallant, using many amusing publicity stunts and commissioning songs to be written about the dashing Martin Frobisher.

The former pirate was given a commission in 1576 to find a passage to Cathay using a northwest route to cut down the distance. He found Canada's desolate Baffin Bay instead, just south of the Arctic Ocean between Baffin Island and Greenland, and landed on Baffin Island. He captured an Inuit and tossed him in the cargo bin, took the poor man back to London, and paraded him around in an Oriental costume, then disposed of him somehow. He also brought back black rocks with fool's gold in them and had a dishonest assayer assert that they contained gold from the Orient. Although he arrived in safety, none of the other ships in his fleet were ever seen again. Upon returning, he admitted that he hadn't taken many notes or made maps. In fact, he had never been to school. He died in 1594, his reputation suspect.

Christopher Columbus was obsessed with status, acquiring any titles, positions, coats of arms, and wealth that he could. More importantly, recent studies portray him as having become ruthless and gold-crazed by the time of his second and third voyages to the New World, ordering the slaughter of countless native people. The ill will he left in the once-peaceful islands became very costly. Subsequent European captains mistaken for Columbus were killed and even eaten. According to Verrazzano's own brother, or at least from accounts of his words, one of these unfortunate seafarers to suffer for Columbus's sins was Verrazzano himself. The most accepted theory about the explorer's death four years after discovering New York was that he was eaten by cannibal warriors in the Caribbean in the wake of Columbus's massacres, possibly a case of mistaken identity.

Samuel de Champlain gave guns to some Algonquins and had them open fire on a group of Mohawks who had declared war on them. The Mohawks turned against the French because of this, and in the long run nearly drove them from the New World by siding with the British. Henry Hudson was so disliked by his crew that on a later trip to the north, he and his son were set loose in a rowboat on the open sea near Greenland in cold weather and never seen again. Johan Printz, governor of the Swedish West India Company, was probably the model for the villainous "governor" of Virginia in the Disney version of *Pocahontas*. Hernán Cortés was a virtual killing machine, whose slaying statistics have yet to be accurately tabulated.

These were the types of white people that Native Americans had to contend with for two centuries, and it didn't leave a very savory impression of the race. In comparison to many of his contemporaries, Verrazzano was a saint. A quiet, cautious man, Verrazzano was a father-figure to his crewmen, concerned about their welfare. He was also one of the most brilliant mathematicians of his time and widely read in the classics and metaphysics.

VERRAZZANO'S ARRIVAL

In 1524, New York welcomed its first official visitor, Giovanni da Verrazzano. However, according to Steven Sora in *The Lost Treasure of the Knights Templar: Solving the Oak Island Mystery*, the Knights Templar had already initiated the Micmacs of Oak Island in Nova Scotia's Mahone Bay, south of Halifax, and there were scattered fisherman's shacks, built mostly by men from France, England, Breton, Portugal, and the Basque country along some rivers in Canada when Verrazzano arrived.

Fishermen were sailing the Grand Banks of Canada by the time Cabot arrived on St. John's Feast Day, June 24, 1497. Sora writes, "Though not potential colonists, their tiny shacks dotted the St. Lawrence Seaway," but they weren't in search of a passage to Cathay, so no one mentioned them.[3]

Verrazzano wrote several accounts of his encounters with the Algonquins. Usually a moody and withdrawn man, easily lost to polite company by mathematical calculations, it was reported that he seemed of unusually high spirits after meeting with the "Lenni" and other people of Turtle Island. His disposition was for once sunny and outgoing. Glimpsing a world with such freedom must have been quite a revelation to him.

In a letter to King Francis I (see Appendix III for full text), Verrazzano described his first landfall in the New World and the Algonquins of Virginia he encountered: "They have big black eyes and an attentive, open look." This was the first account by a European of a Lenape, and in fact an Algonquin Indian. The only other European to have met an Algonquin before this was John Cabot, in Canada's Maritimes in 1497, but Cabot failed to write about his journeys.

Verrazzano first caught sight of land near what is now Wilmington, North Carolina, where the sailors saw huge fires built on shore, possibly to help the visitors navigate. He wrote, "We left this place continually, skirting the coast, which we found turned to the east. Seeing everywhere great fires on account of the multitude of the inhabitants, anchoring there off the shore because it did not contain any port. On account of the need of water we sent the little boat to land with twenty-five men." This was Pamlico Sound.

His comment on "seeing everywhere great fires on account of the multitude" is fascinating. This mainland area today is Croatan National Forest, a swampland practically devoid of human population. In his day, it was home to the eastern flank of the Hatteras Confederacy of Algonquin, including the Neuusioock, after whom the Noose River was named,[4] Paumuvatock, Sekota, Aquasco, Setuoock, Iramaskekoock, and Mosquepanang.

He did not find a place to land until he reached Cape Lookout in the Hatteras area. Here he noted that the inhabitants wore the furs of martens. The pine marten, or sable, is an animal with dark brown shiny fur and an arching back, sacred to the most ancient Algonquin traditions. However few accounts exist of the Lenape hunting pine martens. He described the Natives wearing "tails of other animals," and tying their hair in ponytail fashion. They were very helpful, although cautious at first.

Verrazzano landed again a hundred miles further north on the Virginia coast. The people he met in Virginia must have been grandfathers of the Powhatan, and therefore relatives of the Lenape. He explored near what is now Richmond, Virginia. It is ironic that his two principal landing spots in North America are both now named Richmond—Staten Island is now Richmond County, New York, and Richmond, Virginia, is in Richmond County, Virginia. Undoubtedly the thing that impressed Europeans the most about the Algonquin was how rich their land and vegetation were. The fact that it was not by accident, but by design, has been lost to general knowledge.

One of the younger sailors who swam to shore to offer gifts to the Natives was caught in the tide and nearly drowned. He was rescued by Natives and revived and healed by a great fire as he lay resting near a hill. The Natives of the area included the Sekota, Aquascocok, Pequipotac, and the Pomeetuoc,[5] who later became the eastern flank of the Powhatan Confederacy.

"Where, the youth, seeing himself carried in such a way, stricken with terror, uttered very loud cries, which they did similarly in their language, showing him that he should not fear. After that, having placed him on the ground in the sun at the foot of a little hill, they performed great acts of admiration, regarding the whiteness of his flesh, examining him from head to foot. Taking off his shirt and hose, leaving him nude, they made a very large fire near him, placing him near the heat. Which having been seen, the sailors who had remained in the small boat, full of fear, as is their custom in every new case, thought that they wanted to roast him for food. His strength recovered, having remained with them awhile, he showed by signs that he desired to return to the ship; who, with the greatest kindness, holding him always close with various embraces, accompanied him as far as the sea, and in order to assure him more, extending themselves on a high hill, stood to watch him until he was in the boat."

With the young man safely aboard, they set sail. Soon they anchored again, possibly south of Chesapeake Bay. It was here Verrazzano felt it necessary to accomplish the perfunctory taking of a specimen to prove to those back home he had actually made the journey. Because of this incident, many have discredited Verrazzano, categorizing him with the other more oppressive explorers mentioned earlier.

He wrote to the king, "[With] twenty men going about two leagues inland, we found the people through fear had fled to the woods. Seeking everywhere, we met with a very old woman and a damsel of from eighteen to twenty years, who through fear had hidden themselves in the grass. The old one had two little girls whom she carried on the shoulders, and back on the neck a boy, all of eight years of age. The young woman had as many of the same but all girls.

Having approached toward them, they began to cry out [and] the old woman to make signs to us that the men had fled to the woods. We gave them to eat of our viands, which she accepted with great gusto; the young woman refused everything and with anger threw it to the ground. We took the boy from the old woman to carry to France, and wishing to take the young woman, who was of much beauty and of tall stature, it was not however possible, on account of the very great cries which she uttered, for us to conduct her to the sea. And having to pass through several woods, being far from the ship, we decided to release her, carrying only the boy."

Soon they passed a large bay with a river that they called Vandome, probably Chesapeake Bay, but this is disputed, and found a safe cove where they landed. Some scholars believe Vandoma was Verrazzano's name for Lenape Seepu, that which later became known as the Delaware River further north. (If so, then the Lenape could well have ended up as "Vandoma Indians" if history had twisted differently.) There, a young Native man, who was probably a pipe carrier, stood hesitantly in the shadows. As he was alone and naked, it is possible he was on a sort of fast or vision quest, seeking signs or visions either in the outer world or the inner one, that distinction being secondary during the vision quest. Upon seeing the ship and twenty large, strangely dressed men land on shore and walk toward him, he must have felt as if he was about to be taken through the twelve levels of the heavens. As they approached, he offered them a smoke of his pipe. It could have been an important moment in history, for educated European noblemen to experience the remarkable power of the Algonquin pipe ceremony. It would have opened for them a new portal into the spirit world, and would have made the young faster feel he had been well blessed by a visit from the Manitowak, the principal deities of the spirit world under Manitou, the Great Spirit, in answer to his prayers.

Perhaps if Verrazzano had humbly accepted the great gift that was being offered, he would have developed a better connection with not only the protector spirit of the eagle and the bear, but with Native people as a whole and their ways of communicating. He might also have saved himself from a fatal encounter in the jungle four years later.

Here is the incident in Verrazzano's words: "Land of Angouleme, Bay of Santa Margarita. [I believe this was the Delaware Bay, but it is impossible to be sure.] In Arcadia we found a man who came to the shore to see what people we were: who stood hesitating and ready for flight. Watching us, he did not permit himself to be approached. He was handsome, nude, with hair fastened back in a knot, of olive color. We were about twenty (in number) ashore and coaxing him he approached to within about two fathoms, showing a burning stick as if to offer us fire. And we made fire with powder and flint-and-steel and he trembled all over with terror and we fired a shot. He stopped as if astonished and prayed, worshipping like a monk, lifting his finger toward the sky, and pointing to the ship and the sea, he appeared to bless us."

The rowdy sailors, too long at sea, shot guns into the air to impress the pipe carrier with their "fire" power, and the moment of opportunity was lost. Birds scattered, and the young man fell to his knees and began to pray in his language, appearing to bless them and the ship. Satisfied they had educated the Native American in the ways of their world, they reboarded the ship, and lifted anchor.

Verrazzano passed the Navesink Highlands of New Jersey, south of Sandy Hook, which he named San Polo.[6] Soon he sighted the entrance to New York Bay. It was the afternoon of April 17, 1524. Two worlds were about to collide.

It would have been a great boon to history if Verrazzano had been able to walk the trails of the island and make an estimate of the population, as John Smith did along the Potomac. But Verrazzano was always eager to move on and see more. By the time the next boat from Europe arrived, over eighty years later, most of the once-teeming population had vanished. The Dutch estimated the Native population of Staten Island in the early 1600s at only 600. It had certainly been much more at the time of Verrazzano. Did smallpox and other illnesses kill 90 percent of them after Verrazzano left? Half? We don't know.

Verrazzano wrote, "After a hundred leagues, we found a very agreeable place between two small but prominent hills; between them, a very wide river, deep at its mouth, flowed out into the sea." Verrazzano had discovered the Narrows that now bear his name.

"And with the help of the tide, which rises eight feet, any laden ship could have passed from the sea into the river estuary. Since we were anchored off the coast and well sheltered, we did not want to run any risks without knowing anything about the river mouth. So we took the small boat up this river to land which we found densely populated." This landing spot is somewhere between St. George and Tompkinsville, [7] Staten Island.

"The people were almost the same as the others, dressed in birds' feathers of various colors, and they came toward us joyfully, uttering loud cries of wonderment and showing us the safest place to beach the boat. We went up this river for about half a league [about a mile and a half], where we saw that it formed a beautiful lake, about three leagues in circumference." This was New York Harbor before the Statue of Liberty, the Ellis Island Immigration Center, or Fort Jay at Governor's Island were constructed. To his right was Bay Ridge, Brooklyn, and above that Gowanus Bay.

"About thirty of their small boats ran to and fro across the lake with innumerable people aboard who were crossing from one side to the other to see us." Again Verrazzano talks about an incredibly dense population, living in harmony with the environment, with little or no negative impact on the ecosystem.

Verrazzano describes their canoes, their cleverly built round huts, and "worked mats" of straw, which protected them from wind and rain. He noted the care and respect they showed toward their women. He mentioned the fine workmanship of their arrows, which were tipped with hard marble, and wrote of cherries, plums, filberts, and many kinds of fruit that differed from European varieties. The plucky Renaissance man was also something of a botanist.

They then returned in their small craft to *The Dauphine*, and navigated the large vessel northward through the Narrows and entered into the Upper Bay itself. Directly ahead lay the entrance to the Hudson River. If Verrazzano had found it, he might have thought it was the entrance to the passage to Cathay, and gone at least as far as Albany, where the water becomes shallow. As it turned out, a storm blew in, with unfavorable winds. They were forced to return to sea, with regrets on account of the great beauty they had to abandon. While weathering the storm he wrote in his diary about New York Harbor and the area that he named "Angouleme."

"Suddenly, as often happens in sailing, a violent unfavorable wind blew in from the sea, and we were forced to return to the ship, leaving the land with much regret on account of its favorable conditions and beauty; we think it was not without some properties of value, since all the hills showed signs of minerals."

If the people were dressed in their feather cloaks, they must have realized it was a high social occasion, which means they spotted his ship fairly far off, as it sailed along what is now Raritan Bay. The two prominent hills were Grymes Hill—now the site of the College of Staten Island at Route 278 and the western foot of the Verrazzano Narrows Bridge—and Bay Ridge in Brooklyn, at the other end of the bridge to the east. If someone were to sail north through the Verrazzano Narrows today, they would see these two hills, though the one in Brooklyn has been flattened a bit by development.

Verrazzano first set foot in New York near the place where the Staten Island Ferry now lands. Thousands of New Yorkers who live on Staten Island but work in Manhattan—also jokingly referred to as "the boat people"—land at this same spot every day.

Verrazzano was the first European to explore the two thousand miles of coastline that constituted the eastern border of the Algonquin civilization, now one of the most populated areas in the Western Hemisphere. His descriptions of Algonquins are glowing, his encounters mostly friendly, though certainly not all. Verrazzano's statue now stands at the southern tip of Manhattan where the Statue of Liberty Ferry and the boat to Ellis Island depart. It is a fitting spot for New York City's first white European immigrant.

ARCADIA

Verrazzano is credited for giving the New World one of its earliest names, which he is said to have put on the maps as "Arcadia." For initiates, the theme of Arcadia and the transmission of an underground stream of knowledge passed through generations is of paramount importance.[8]

Steven Sora observes, "Giovanni Verrazzano too, might have been part of an elite group, as were several of the important world explorers. . . . Verrazzano's family crest included a six-pointed star, which some believe indicated he was not the Christian he was purported to be . . . [while] the religion of Columbus is still a nagging debate." In other words, Verrazzano may well have been Jewish.

Many say Columbus was a "Morano," or a Jew. As Jews were being burned at the stake all over Europe, it was understandable for Jewish intellectuals to claim to be Christian, while belonging to secret societies bent on preserving their knowledge and seeking a new holy land. Assuming Verrazzano to have been a Jew, his exploration of the New World was part of that same vast underground effort to build a New Jerusalem across the water, where all minorities would be safe from persecution, a new Holy or "Promised" Land.

Reports of the early explorers and mapmakers do not always agree as to where Verrazzano placed the name Arcadia on his final navigational charts. One mapmaker shows Arcadia as being north of the Hudson River, along the shoreline of Long Island. Others say it was the Outer Banks of North Carolina. Because Verrazzano correctly noted the latitude, thanks to his excellent skill as a mathematician, the historian Morison for one believes that Maine and the Canadian Maritimes are Arcadia.[9] But at first he obviously thought of the entire coast as Arcadia. Why is this term so important?

Sora writes: "Arcadia was the true Garden of Eden, lost to the modern medieval world. It was life in a pure state, where thought and deed were free . . . from the threat of official punishment by church and state. The [later] English philosopher Sir Francis Bacon [1561–1626], and others, believed this world could exist only outside Europe. They believed in the creation of a new country in which certain freedoms would be guaranteed and all religions would be tolerated. Bacon described this country in his classic work, *The New Atlantis*. Interestingly enough, the French name for Nova Scotia was 'L'Acadie,' a label they applied from the native Micmac word for 'the land' *akkah*, related to the Lenape *hakee*. Mapmakers may have made the two names into one, and Nova Scotia was for a while called (both) L'Acadie and Arcadia."[10]

Sora goes on to speculate, "If these selected families [that backed the first New World explorers] had a secret society that mysteriously placed great value on Saint John the Baptist, it is more than coincidence that John Cabot, Jacques Cartier, and Samuel de Champlain all [are said to have] reached the New World on his feast day. It is then by design that the capital of Newfoundland (Saint John's) the original name of Prince Edward Island (Ile-St-Jean, or Isle of Saint John) and the capital and harbor of New Brunswick (Saint John) all commemorated that saint."[11] Verrazzano arrived at Nova Scotia a month too early to be part of this trend, and John Cabot's visit to the Maritimes is surrounded with mystery and a lack of detail, so we don't know when he really landed. It is supposed that he sailed around Cape Breton Island, landed in Nova Scotia, planted a large crucifix in the ground, and then left. The Micmac have a story, as part of their oral tradition, that the Micmac chief found Cabot saying, "I hereby declare this land…." The chief confronted him and asked why he put the cross up on Micmac ground. He answered that it was "to help other ships navigate." The Micmac chief, who may have already met other white men bearing crosses, flags, and other symbols of propriety, replied in words to this effect: "Please remove it immediately. I'm sure your friends will find their way." The Micmac chief then chased him off. All that is known for certain historically about Cabot's visit is that he left in a great hurry.

John Cabot's principal backer was Sheriffe Richard Amerike. The same year that Columbus reached America, relatives of Columbus's jealous ex-employer sent Amerigo Vespucci to Seville to make maps and perform other services to downplay or distract from Columbus's success and protect their interests. In 1524, an Italian banker named Bonacorso Rucellai backed another expedition to the New World. Rucellai was based in Lyons, where the Carolingian dynasty was no longer able to protect the Jews against those who coveted their property. Many Jews had converted to Christianity to escape persecution, often more in name than in spirit. This was a good time for finding a promised land, quickly. Again, quoting Sora, "Rucellai hired a captain from another noble family to take charge of his exploratory journey. The Captain was Giovanni da Verrazzano."[12]

Sora continues, "Verrazzano took the Prieure' de Sions' (an esoteric religious group in Europe) passion for the Arcadia theme to the New World. Sailing by a coast with tall trees, Verrazzano said that it reminded him of Jacopo Sannazaro's idyllic Greek land, and called the place Arcadia. The harbor now called Newport, Rhode Island, is the place he dubbed Rhodes after the harbor in Greece. Newport's modern harbor city still debates the origin of the 'Viking Tower' that Verrazzano labeled as a 'Norman villa' on his map." However, historian and author Jack Dempsey[13] feels sure it was built by Prince

Henry Sinclair's men in 1398 on the same latitude as Rome, in hopes of starting up a new Jerusalem for the powerful Knights Templar, a religious group of Masons who were being persecuted at the time.

New Jerusalem

Francis Bacon wrote of the New World as a so-called "New Atlantis" very much like the Arcadia of the Catholic religious orders, the d'Angous and St. Clairs—a proposed "utopia where the true Renaissance man could be free to publish and study science without fears of a censoring government or a church inquisition."[14]

The name of Bacon's speculative utopia was Bensalem. Some equate Salem with shalom, or "peace," which is related to *salaam* in Arabic. Jerusalem means "foundation of Salem" and Bensalem means the "son of Salem," in the context of a second holy place. Bacon made a point of declaring that Jews would be "allowed to reside on the secret island and practice their arts and sciences."

If New York City is that "New Jerusalem," the "secret island,"[15] then from this perspective it has been highly successful. In the 1970s there were more Jewish people in and around New York City than anywhere else in the world.

There are 1.1 million Jews in New York City today. If you add Long Island and Westchester, the total is 1.5 million. Adding northern New Jersey and Connecticut, the total is 1.9 million. In other words, there are just under 2 million Jews in the New York metropolitan area. There are approximately twice that number of Jews in Israel today—4 million—however it was not always thus. In 1970 New York's Jewish population reached its highest mark, 2,742,000, higher than Israel's, which was approximately 2,200,000 at that point. By 1990, Israel's Jewish population had surged past 3 million, while half of New York's Jewish population migrated south to Florida, or other warm climes.

The number of Jews has increased in Israel over the years, with large numbers of immigrants from the Soviet Union and other areas.

The Jewish population of New York reached its peak in the 1970s, with 2.74 million or so. The population of Jews in the United States is 6 million. In another twenty years, Israel might exceed the United States in numbers of Jews.[16] Chicago, Los Angeles, and Houston also have large successful Jewish communities, but New York City has the largest of all.

George Washington wrote, "May the children of the stock of Abraham . . . enjoy the good will of the other inhabitants. For happily the government of the United States gives to bigotry no sanction, to persecution no assistance."[17] For the record, George Washington had over four hundred slaves.

During the New Amsterdam period, from 1621 to 1664, Manhattan welcomed immigrants from all over—Huguenots from France, Lutherans from Sweden, Presbyterians from Scotland, Moravians and Anabaptists from Germany, and Jews from the four corners of the earth. It was a Babel of confusion, as one visitor, a French priest, observed. New Amsterdam was a place of business and so all were welcome, or almost all. Governor Peter Stuyvesant tried to keep the Jews out of the city by any means necessary, saying it would create a still greater confusion if the "obstinate immovable Jews come to settle here." In September 1654, twenty-three Sephardic Jews came seeking refuge from the Spanish Inquisition in Brazil. Stuyvesant protested, writing home to Holland, "Let none of the Jewish nation be permitted to infect New Netherlands." But his efforts were unsuccessful—some of the financiers of the promising little venture called New Amsterdam were Jewish, and paying his salary.

Stuyvesant then said, "Okay, but no public worship." On September 12, 1654, a Rosh Hashanah service was held in Manhattan at a private residence, located at what is now the corner of Broad Street and Mill Lane. It was the beginning of Shearith Israel, the oldest Jewish congregation in the New World, which is still holding services just a few blocks over from where Stuyvesant's body lies in a vault at St. Mark's Place.[18]

The Jewish people were not the only ones longing for a new Jerusalem. Many Christian refugees were looking as well. The Salems of northern Westchester, New York, and other Salems, such as those in Massachusetts and Ohio, may be part of this underground "New Jerusalem" (considering Jerusalem means "foundation of Salem") cult from Europe. All of them were built on Algonquin village sites. All of them experienced bloody conflicts within a hundred years, either whites versus Indians or whites versus whites. Like Jerusalem itself, Manhattan has been coveted as a prize worth dying for by practically every band and conqueror that passed by, adding to its colorful history and complex toponymics, although most of its pre-Columbian history has yet to be reconstructed.

Francis Bacon, who died at the age of sixty-five in 1626, the year New Amsterdam was founded, saw the New World as a place of intellectual and artistic freedom, and a place where Jews would be free from persecution. If Verrazzano was looking for a New Jerusalem in New York Harbor, he didn't stay long enough to create it, departing within a day. By his own accounts, and those of the early Dutch, the area was indeed a "garden of Eden," but perhaps too populated for easy settlement.

The usually conscientious Verrazzano would probably have been horrified to know that either he or one of his men unwittingly transmitted the smallpox disease to that "dense population," killing thousands in a matter of a few years. Lenape medicine men eventually discovered that sassafrass, well known as a remedy for skin aliments and infections, was also a useful treatment for "the great pox,"[19] but the good news came too late to save the old and the weak.

There is a famous expression in Latin, in which Death says, *"Et in Arcadia, Ego!"* "Even in Paradise, I am!" an ironic quotation not only because so many Lenape died, but because Verrazzano himself, who named the land Arcadia, died a horrible death in the New World paradise in 1528.

Whether New York or America in general has lived up to Bacon's dream of a place "of liberty and justice for all" has been debated by patriots and natives for four hundred years. For some, it is indeed, but for others, it is far from perfect. George Washington wrote, "I hope ever to see America foremost among nations in example of justice and liberality."[20] Washington visited the Delaware in 1756, and attempted to keep good diplomatic relations at least until the Declaration of Independence. Once the Revolution was over, however, Washington had little time for talk with Indians.

Thomas Crawford's Statue of Freedom was altered before its placement and unveiling atop the Capitol Building in Washington, D.C., so that it wore an eagle headdress with feathers and talons as "a reference to Native American costume," at the suggestion of Jefferson Davis. Davis is a common Lenape and Wampanoag name. There is a chance that Davis was part Lenape as his Quaker family lived in the old Lenape stronghold of Philadelphia before moving to the south. In portraits made after he became president of the Confederacy, one can see in his features the eagle-like stare of a proud sachem. Unfortunately while he was in charge of the Bureau of Indian Affairs, he was able to do little to help the Native American cause.

In 1933, 409 years after Verrazzano first called it paradise, Albert Einstein came to the Lenape region seeking refuge from Hitler, settling in Princeton, New Jersey, after landing at Ellis Island in New York Harbor, not far from where Verrazzano landed. In many ways, Manhattan was indeed the fulfillment of Bacon's utopian dream

There are interesting parallels between Verrazzano and Einstein. According to Steven Sora, Verrazzano, like Einstein, was Jewish. Einstein, like Verrazzano, was a brilliant mathematician who could grasp the movements of stars in the cosmos, and who mastered the problems of traveling over great distances, charting the oceans of subatomic and galactic space. For Einstein, too, the words *Et in Arcadia, Ego* carried a fatal message. Einstein, like the earlier explorer, quite accidentally brought with him the means for destroying thousands of lives, the atomic bomb.

New York now hosts both the Verrazzano Narrows Bridge and the Albert Einstein College. The Morgan Library now houses both Verrazzano's travel diary letter to King Francis I, and several of Einstein's letters and his travel diary as well. The same collection also has an original draft of Einsten's article for *Nature Magazine* in 1919 outlining a theory of relativity, which led eventually to the Manhattan Project. It was at Columbia University in Manhattan that some of the first experiments on $E=mc^2$ were attempted, on paper. This is why the race for developing the atom bomb was called "The Manhattan Project."

That the gentle Munsee-speaking people coined the term that would be linked forever in the human memory with the development of nuclear war is one of the great ironies of history.

7

WE BELONG
TO THE EARTH

D utch, English, and French privateers and pirates had
explored the New York City area since at least the mid-
sixteenth century, if not before.[1] The early Lenape were reluctant to
trade with the Europeans; most had received such rigorous training in
the stoic philosophy of self-sufficiency and unselfishness that they
refused to see themselves as needy. *Tschee-tah-nee*, "strength," was
their byword. A strong man doesn't beg for material comforts.

Before New Amsterdam was built, the Dutch traders commented
with frustration that they couldn't seem to induce enough greed in
the Lenape to coerce them or involve them in high-volume trade.
Plus, as they commented ruefully, "They share everything," so one or
two pots, blankets, or trinkets would suffice for all. Later, when fur
trading became necessary for Lenape survival, traplines made for disputes among neighbors, and the newly acquired guns made the
disputes deadly.

First Landing in Manhattan:
The European Side of the Story

As with any meeting between leaders of two countries, there are two
sides to this story. The leaders who are lucky enough to be on the winning side usually get to pass on their story. This is especially true in

Algonquin history. Many Americans only know of the Algonquin who may once have lived in their vicinity, because that's the only fragment of the true story they ever hear. In fact, the Algonquin occupied a wide geographic area, from North Carolina to the Arctic Circle and as far west as the Rocky Mountains. They most certainly comprised the main population of Manhattan before 1609. The Algonquin Hotel, at 59 West 44th Street in Manhattan, famous for literary lunches in the Round Table Room and $400 suites, has not hosted many Native American elders since it opened its doors in 1902, but it has done one thing for the aboriginal people of the island: reminded the world of who lived in New York before first contact.

The following somewhat Eurocentric account of first contact in New York was recorded by Charles C. Trowbridge in the mid-1800s, and cited by John Heckewelder and later by Charles A. Weslager in *The Delaware Indians,* all three considered Lenape experts. Note the stereotypes, such as the "animal sacrifice" and the implied cowardice of the Lenape, as well as the patronizing language and false sense of self-importance throughout. In *Indian Tribes of Hudson's River,* E. M. Ruttenber argued that this account was actually a description of Henry Hudson's ship in 1609, flying under an English flag. Although the arrival the following year may have been under a different captain and a different flag, presumably that of the Dutch, Ruttenber notes that the Lenape believed it to be the same people.[2]

> Some coastal Algonquins who were fishing in their canoes saw something on the horizon that appeared to be an uncommonly large fish or a huge canoe. They paddled to shore and reported what they had seen. Runners were sent to carry the news to their scattered chiefs, who came with their warriors to view the approach of the strange object. Meanwhile, as the vessel came closer it appeared to be a large house in which *Keeshaylum-mookawng* [The Great Chief of the Spiritual World] lived, and they thought he was coming to pay them a visit. Preparations were

made to greet the Creator; the women prepared the best food, [animals] were brought for sacrifice, and arrangements were made for [an evening of] dance and entertainment.

As the vessel approached the shore, the Indians saw that it was full of strangely dressed men whose faces were of a white color, different from the Indians, and their leader wore a red coat with lace cuffs. They felt certain he was *Keeshaylummookawng*. Terror seized the Indians. Some wanted to run off and hide in the woods, but their chiefs prevailed on them to stay lest they give offense to their guests.

The vessel finally came to anchor, and a smaller boat was sent ashore with a landing party, including the leader with the red coat. The chiefs and councilors formed a large circle, and the Dutchmen strode into the center; the Indians were lost in admiration. The leader filled a glass of liquor, which he drank. Then he refilled the glass and gave it to the chief next to him to drink, but the chief smelled it and passed it to the next chief, who did the same until the glass had been handled by everyone without being tasted. Suddenly one of the Indians, a spirited man and a great warrior, jumped up and harangued the assembly on the impropriety of returning the glass with its contents untasted. He said this would displease the Creator and might be the cause of his destroying all of them. He said if the contents were poisonous it would be better for one man to die than for the whole nation to be destroyed. [This man's name, according to author Lee Francis, was "Bender of the Pine Bow."[3]]

He then took the glass and, bidding the assembly farewell, drank it. Every eye was fixed on him. Soon he began to stagger around, and then he fell to the ground in a sleep as though dead. The spectators were almost paralyzed with terror, but in a little while the warrior opened his eyes, jumped to his feet, and declared that he had never been so happy before as after he had drunk the liquor. He asked for some more, and the wish was granted, following which the whole assembly started to drink, and everyone became intoxicated.

The Dutchmen returned to their vessel while the Indians were carousing, and then came ashore again with a quantity of presents, including beads, axes, hoes, and stockings, which they distributed. This represented untold wealth to the Indians and further convinced them they had been honored by a visit from their deities.

After several encounters, the Indians began to realize that these visitors were not Gods, but men like themselves from a faraway country, and they called them *Swanakens*, "salty people." Familiarity increased daily between the Dutch and the Indians, and the former asked for a small piece of land in order to sow some seeds and raise herbs to season their broth. The Dutch said they needed only so much land as the skin of a bull would cover, and they spread the hide on the ground in front of the Indians to show its size. The request was granted, whereupon a Dutchman took a knife and beginning at one place on the hide, cut it into a rope no thicker than the finger of a little child. When he was done, there was a large coil. This hide rope was then drawn out to a great distance and brought around so that both ends would meet, and it encompassed a large piece of land. The Indians were surprised by the superior wit of the *Swanakens*, but they did not complain about allowing their guests to have this small plot of land since they had more than they needed.

This Euro-centric version of what happened is quoted verbatim from Weslager's *The Delaware Indian Westward Migration*.[4] The Munsee records substantiate the story, but in their words, it comes rather differently.

THE FIRST LANDING IN MANHATTAN: THE MUNSEE SIDE OF THE STORY

The following is an excerpt from a previously unpublished letter written by Munsee leaders to President Zachary Taylor on March 29, 1849, a copy of which was generously provided to me by Chief Mark Peters of the Munsee band of Thames River, Ontario, Canada. (The complete text is included in Appendix III.)

Previous to your arrival into our vast Continent, our Ancient Prophets and wise men had a Vision and Revelation in regard to your coming, though they did not understand fully the meaning of it, whether it was to be the almighty himself or our fellow men, this was a matter of deep consideration for a while with our forefathers until you did arrive.

Our ancient wise men without any delay made a Song concerning their expectation of your coming. Likewise a Drum was made for the purpose, out of the shell of a Sea Turtle. The drumming and their singing of the song were connected together and were performed jointly together, and also dancing, which was performed with great solemnity in honor of your coming.

This foreknowledge of our forefathers of your coming was one year previous to your arrival; our forefathers collected together frequently and performed these celebrations until you did arrive, and when the vessel came at last in open sight to the eyes of our forefathers at the shore, the appearance of the vessel at sea was truly a great mystery to our forefathers, and immediately many wise men and counselors of high respectability among our ancient forefathers were called and collected together by the rumors and influential men of our Nation in order to ascertain what that mysterious sight could be, which was making progress toward the shore.

By the distant appearance of the sails of the vessel our forefathers first concluded that it was some great water fowl, and as the vessel came nearer to fair open view, they concluded that it must be their God, coming to bring them some new kind of game. And when the vessel reached the shore, they saw the Captain of the Ship, and then concluded that he must be the almighty himself, as he had blue eyes. This was another great wonder, and by it they further concluded that he must certainly be the Great God.

Our forefathers highly respected the arrival of their Great Father, and did instantly spread white Beaver skins from the shore where the vessel landed to a certain tent where the wise men and counselors were assembled together, for the Captain to walk on. The kind disposition of the Captain induced him to tell our forefathers that he was not the almighty, but that he was their brother, that in ancient times he was with his brethren, and by the various changes that frequently occur in this life, he had some how got separated from his brethren, but he expressed great joy, that he had now arrived and found his brethren again, and hoped that he would never be again separated from his brethren.

He further told our forefathers that he had merely come in search of his red brethren and seeing that he had discovered his brethren He would then return to his people, and inform them how that he had discovered their brethren on the great Continent and which would cause great joy throughout the nations who were situated beyond the Deep Waters.

He gave our forefathers many presents such as hoes and axes and tin buckets and the next year he came again in company with a large number of his people in order to come and reside among their red brethren, at which time they saw our forefathers wearing hoes and axes and covers to the tin buckets about their necks. He then showed our forefathers the design of the hoes and axes. Handles were put into them, and large trees were cut down before them, which created a general time of laughing, to think how greatly they had been mistaken in regard to the design of the presents that had been given to them.

Father we do further beg leave to state, that when you first arrived onto our vast American continent, you was [*sic*] destitute of land, but your Munsee children were always liberal towards you in granting you their lands according to your necessity. You first requested your Munsee children to grant you as much land [as] what a Bullock Skin would cover, and which was cut into small cords, which was laid in the form of a circle on the land which you desired to have, and we your Munsee children directly complied to your request for said land.

Furthermore, your Excellency will please permit us to state further that at another time afterwards, you did that is figuratively speaking, your Nation applied to our Munsee Tribe again for more land, which was our Father then promised, that we should grant him as much land as a middling sized lad could travel around a tract of land in one day's journey, and again your Munsee children did likewise grant this earnest request for more land.

And now, Father, you have got all our land, and we at this time are very poor, have no land at all, not so much as to set one foot on, and you have plenty of land lying waste, and we think it would be better for us to have some of it than to have it lying useless as it presently does, and by our persevering industry, we think we may get our living on it.

We would further state in relation to our destitute [state] that the present amount of annuity allowed to us is nothing as it were in proportion to the annuities allowed to other tribes, because some of them now yearly receive from thirty to seventy and one hundred dollars a head, while we the poor Munsees receive something like dollar a piece, which is almost a trifle, and likewise these tribes never had no more land than us.

And again we would further humbly beg leave to remark in connection to what has already been said in regard to the Munsee Tribe being liberal toward their Great Father, when he first came to them on this our vast continent, and made applications to our forefathers for a sufficient quantity of land for his subsistence, that his earnest request was freely granted by our forefathers. And we would further say that we do rejoice with exceeding great joy to think that our forefathers were able to show kind favor to our Great Father on his arrival to this Continent, and not only this but we likewise rejoice that our Great and kind Creator has so highly favored him in prosperity, since he has come to this Continent and has rendered him to become a great Nation.

And now our Great Father, your Excellency will please permit us to say further in regard to this important subject, that we observe that your stature as it were (figuratively speaking) almost reaches the heavens, and your arms extending from the rising of the sun and to the going down of the same, and we are sensible that it is the Almighty who is now building you up, on the foundation where our forefathers once stood. Our forefathers first had this greatness granted to them by the good will of the Almighty, but he is now granting it to you. And now in all your splendor and greatness, we do entreat you most tenderly as our father that you will never forget your poor red children.

We the Munsees, were the first tribe that you came to on this continent, and we were the first ones that listened to your wants for land, and we were the first Indian nation that received you, our forefathers were then living on Manhattan Island where the City of New York now stands.

From these two distinctly different accounts, one can see that the Dutch and Munsee were literally from two different worlds. The Munsee clearly sensed something important was approaching. Their devotion to the Creator led them to believe it must be a great blessing, perhaps that they were about to meet the Creator Himself.[5] Many of those who gathered to hear and discuss these strange prophecies of 1608 did soon "meet their Creator" in the spirit world, and were then reunited with their ancestors. A small contingent of Canarsie warriors died almost immediately upon meeting this blue-eyed "God." In September 1609, a total of thirteen Lenape were shot by Hudson's men in various incidents.

Why the Munsee Treated the Dutch as Gods

The Munsee had an expanded interdimensional view of reality in 1608. Anything was possible, given the right conditions. They talked to the Creator, sought guidance from their ancestors, witnessed miracles, and predicted the future through signs.

In Munsee spirituality, there are no truly inanimate objects—not in the European sense of the word. Even rocks have a spirit and give up their life in the sweat lodge. The people looked for signs and they were all good. Gratitude is the first cardinal principle of Native American teaching, so they were prepared to be grateful, and showed their gratitude with furs and good meat.

SIGNS

Signs from spirit are called *Kee-gay-no-lay-woa-gan* in Munsee. Signs come in infinite varieties, and the elders know and can interpret signs, whether in dreams or in life, as if there were writings on the trees.

A comet is said to be a sign of war, and heads in the direction of the source of trouble. To point to a shooting or falling star will bring bad luck. However, the star is said to fall where an enemy is hiding. In Shawnee, the comet is *tecumseh,* "panther passing across the sky." When Tecumseh was born, a large comet streaked across the sky from north to south. That became his *unsoma,* an event worthy of notice that may become a good luck symbol through one's life. In light of the Delaware belief about comets mentioned above, it's interesting that all Tecumseh's early battles were to the immediate south of where he was born at Chillicothe, Ohio. In these battles along the Ohio River, he was very lucky indeed.[6] It was only when he fought in the north that he had difficulties.

Gladys Tantaquidgeon wrote about other types of signs in her book on the Delaware.[7] Both ends of a rainbow were said to point to water. It is said that when a wolf barks at a person, that person will live a long life. A snowfall late in the spring with the wind blowing toward the north means the spirit of winter and snow is returning to its abode in the north. An autumn with abundant nuts and berries indicates a severe winter coming. A ringing in the ears means impending bad news. Storms may indicate the local mountain spirits or manitouaks are not pleased. A hawk going left to right means to watch out for danger, and two wolves can be a warning to prepare for trouble. A crow chattering at us can signal danger, and a songbird might carry a message for us. A bear imparts strength, but can also offer spiritual protection. An eagle tells us of company coming, or may tell us one of our ancestors is trying to reach us. Any unusual event in nature is looked at as a possible sign, and is interpreted much the same way we interpret dreams. Traditional Lenape feel closely related to and are involved in a constant network of communication with every living thing.

PREPARING TO MEET GOD FACE TO FACE

With such deep beliefs in signs and the constant interaction between the world of spirit and this world, it is understandable that the Lenape had divine expectations of the Dutch. First of all, they came from the east, the direction of the sun—the closest thing to the Creator we can see with our own eyes—and from a direction where there was no known land, only endless ocean. The leader was obviously some kind of chief— Keeshaylummookawng is thought of as the chief of the spirit world. The very appearance of the chief confirmed their expectations to a tee—he had a white face and wore red, white being the color of the grandfather and grandmother spirit of each animal, and red being the sacred color, the blood of life. The chief had blue eyes, which may have reminded them of the blue spirit lights of the ancestors seen in the sweat lodge. His helpers carried intoxicating beverages that altered one's state of consciousness. These spirit helpers gave the Lenape tools that made work easier, and many objects that the Lenape could not explain. The visitors carried much copper, a metal associated with the high noble people of Alumette Island and Lake Superior, and spoke a strange language no one had heard before. Later visitors had a magic book through which God Himself spoke to them, in a voice only they could hear. These were certainly good signs. In addition, there had been continuous signs for at least one year, given in the form of visions to the grandfathers, foretelling of the coming of important visitors. The Lenape didn't know for sure if the visit would be good or bad, but it was obvious a year in advance that it was something very important, something that would change their lives.

The Algonquin say that death is part of life, just as winter is part of spring, and that death means change. We can't accept one gift from the Creator without accepting the other. We can't live forever, or prevent anything from changing. We can only prepare ourselves for change. Nevertheless, it is tragic that so many who had so much to share with the world died so quickly after the long-awaited meeting with the "gods" from the east.

Although there are no written records, the Lenape certainly would have increased their purification activity in preparation for such a great event. Sweat lodges would have been running on a regular basis. Charles Wolley, an Englishman visiting New York in 1678, noted, "Their general remedy for all diseases is sweating; Which is thus: when they find themselves in any way indisposed, they make a small wigwam or House, nigh a river-side, out of which in the extremity of the Sweat they plunge themselves into the Water."[8]

During the winter of 1683–1684, William Penn observed an Indian named Tenoughan undergoing such a cure in a "bagnio" ("sweat lodge"):

> I found him ill of a Fever, his Head and Limbs much affected with Pain, and at the same time his Wife preparing a Bagnio for him: The Bagnio resembled a large Oven, into which he crept, by a Door on the one side, while she put several red hot Stones in a small Door on the other side thereof, and then fastened the Doors as closely from the Air as she could. Now while he was Sweating in this Bagnio, his Wife (for they distain no Service) was, with an Ax, cutting her Husband a passage into the River in order to [assist him in] the Immersing [of] himself, after he should come out of

his Bath. In less than a half an Hour, he was in so great a Sweat, that when he came out he was as wet as if he had come out of a River, and the Reak [*sic*] or Steam of his Body so thick that it was hard to discern anybody's Face that stood near him. In this condition, stark naked his Breech-Clout excepted, he ran to the River, which was about twenty Paces, and duck'd himself twice or thrice therein, and so return'd (passing only through his Bagnio to mitigate the immediate stroak of the Cold) to his own House, perhaps twenty Paces further, and wrapping himself in his woolen Mantle, lay down as his length near a long (but gentle) Fire in the midst of his Wigwam, or House, turning himself several times, till he was dry, and then he rose, and fell to getting us our Dinner, seeming to be as easie, and well in Health as at any other time.[9]

Moravian Missionary David Zeisberger apparently observed similar sweat lodges among the Munsee in 1775, and recorded several words relating to the sweat-lodge experience. *Pee-moh* is sweating, *pee-mook* means going to the sweat lodge, *peemo-ahk'n* or *pimoacan* means sweat lodge in Munsee.

The sweat lodge, as still practiced by Algonquin peoples today, is much more than a sauna. It involves a pipe ceremony, much chanting and prayer, and the teachings of the elders, the most savory and powerful of which are saved for the lodge. In some lodges, berries and other ceremonial foods are shared, and a drinking gourd is passed around. Heart-opening songs are sung and in many cases, the members of the circle share their innermost thoughts and fears with their brothers in the lodge. There are few experiences that encourage as much bonding between people as the sweat lodge does; in fact, when thirty people crowd into a tiny wigwam and all the lights are turned off (the "doors" to the sweat lodge are closed, and no light comes through) and everyone is singing their hearts out while being "cooked," it's easy to imagine how the people might indeed "become one" as the old teachings suggest.

Sweat lodges became more and more scarce in New York City as the Dutch expansion pushed the Lenape west. It was a sacred ceremony, and not something done in crowded, noisy areas.

The Lenape were well advised to purify themselves, for they soon found out that the Dutch were all too human, and conflicts arose quickly. It wasn't long before the Lenape refused to discuss sacred or ceremonial matters with the Dutch, with the exception of a trusted few. The Dutch brought rapid change, but they were not divine messengers, merely businessmen.

QUEST FOR WAMPUM

The Dutch traders were not interested in understanding Lenape spirituality. It was too foreign to their whole way of life. They were interested in doing business with them, at first for their furs, and later for their wampum as part of the fur trade. How this trade network developed is a tribute to the marketing ingenuity and persistence of the Dutch, not without ample help from the industrious Lenape as they grew more dependent on Dutch metal goods and glass beads, and eventually, wampum as well.

Wampum beads have a long history dating back at least four thousand years. During the Strawberry Dance Festival, held in *kwtehimkicox,* June, loose wampum beads were scattered on the ground for the children to "peck," like a turkey gathering berries. This was to make them better berry pickers during strawberry season.[10] They were allowed to keep the beads not only to make things with but to trade with their friends. Many such beads were offered to Henry Hudson when he arrived in 1609. It was quite a compliment; the preparation time for each bead was considerable, given the tools available at the time.

When the disreputable Dutch trade secretary, Jacob Eelkins, captured a beloved sachem of the Pequot in 1622, he was offered fifty thousand beads for the sachem's release. It was then that he realized the value and extensive resources of wampum available in America, two important factors in developing a standard currency.[11] Overnight, Secretary Eelkins became the unofficial financial wizard of the New World by setting the value of the wampum exchange rate. Soon the Dutch, English, and French recognized wampum as legal tender.

New York City is the fiscal capital of the New World today, and some say of the rest of the world as well. So it is not surprising that it was a combination of the Lenape skill and speed in creating wampum and Dutch marketing ingenuity that created the basis for a "free world economy" near Wall Street. When Eelkins discovered that wampum (or *sea-wan*) could be used for "money" in the New World—at least as a substitute because it was something portable of consistent value—it became the first real currency used between the Dutch and the Native Americans. It also enabled Europeans to establish lucrative financial relations with the great trading center of the Lenape of New York for the first time.

Wampum belts are woven from white or purple shell beads. The white beads are made from three species of whelk—*busycon canaliculatum, busycon carica,* and *venus mercenaria*—most common on Cape Cod. The purple beads are shaped from the purple rims of the shells of the quohog (oyster) that thrive in shallow, sandy bays and harbors, so plentiful around Long Island. The quohog were twice as rare as the whelk, and so the purple beads were worth twice as much.[12] Three purple beads were worth an English penny or a Dutch Stuyver, whereas three white beads were worth only a halfpenny.

It had long been said that wampum belts, from *whap-pa bieel,* "white strings of beads," were "talking belts" or "talking beads" because they were used as visual aids in sacred story-telling ceremonies in which the history of the people was recounted in full. New Yorkers still use the term *wampum* to mean currency without realizing it is disrespectful, because its original purpose was a sacred one. "Wampum is our heart" is a common Native American expression.[13]

Without wampum, a message had less validity and authority. Father Jogues, a Jesuit missionary, said, "Whoever touches or accepts the present which is made to him is bound to fulfill what is asked of him through that present."[14]

The beads were hard to make and beautiful when woven together and the Algonquin were very particular about how the wampum was strung, indicating high reverence for it as an art form and ritual object.[15] Before the advent of printed money, most trade currencies were "art" in some sense, showing by some unique feature that a craftsman had put his individual stamp on it with his skill. Wampum beads were a dramatic example, often strung so as to depict scenes and indicate prophecies. They were more often used as gifts than as cold currency, although there is a fine line between gifts and currency in a communal society such as that of the Algonquin. The wampum were woven on looms like beadwork, usually in six-foot lengths, or the height of a man's body. A single "belt" of this length was referred to as a "fathom" by the Dutch, and later the English. A single fathom represented many days' work. [16]

Part of the value of the belts derived from the difficulty in crafting them. The shell blanks were cracked off of the shell and then ground against an abrasive rock until bead-shaped. Algonquins of the area used stone drills to create the clean holes through which the hemp or deer sinew was strung. The bead was held in place by a wooden device, a tiny Bagettaway or "lacrosse" stick, which served as a vice, held down with the foot. The hard, slender stone drill was "rubbed" between the hands, spinning it back and forth to make the holes. It was hard work.[17]

When the Dutch brought steel awls called "muxes" to trade, the stone drill became obsolete, and wampum became twice as easy to make. The Algonquin were smitten, and began the long, slow journey into trade deficit. The muxes worked many times faster and didn't break as often as stone drills, but they devalued the currency as well as the craft and made them dependent on Dutch metals forever. For the Lenape, it was a devil's bargain.

The Dutch quickly began to experiment in making wampum. If we create our own wampum today, it is called counterfeiting, but things were different then. When the new system was finally up and running, it placed New York ahead of other cities in the financial field. (Most of the shells came from New York.) It changed the local economy in a dramatic way, and wampum soon became legal tender in all of New York State and New England as well. It led gradually to the establishment of European money markets in New York, and there has seldom been a "fair trade" for the Native Americans since. The wampum exchange rate kept going down, while the Euro-dollar of the 1600s kept going up.

The coastal Algonquin depleted their moderate beaver population by 1618, but they still had abundant quohog. Between 1618 and 1619, thousands of beaver pelts were brought down from western Massachusetts alone, offered in exchange for wampum beads, which increased in value with distance from their source. A trade triangle developed, the Dutch providing European dry goods in exchange for wampum, and then offering that same wampum to inland Native trappers and hunters—to whom the wampum was more valuable—for their pelts, which were no longer available in the shoreside areas. These pelts were then sold in Holland for phenomenal sums to make felt hats. Everyone benefited, and although there were disputes from time to time over the value of goods, the triangle lasted over fifty years. It was a difficult process, with a long lag between investment and return, but the Dutch were cautious traders, and soon had large reliable supplies of wampum, more reliable even than those of the Lenape and Pequot, whose supply was affected by weather and seasonal shifts in the quohog population. The English became envious of the success of the Dutch and tried to undercut their operations, building trading posts upstream from the Dutch posts to intercept business.

"Wampum is the source and mother of the beaver trade, and for goods . . . without wampum we cannot obtain beavers."[18] This, from Peter Stuyvesant, whose name came to mean "penny man" as Stuyvers became the standard coin in New Amsterdam, with a value equivalent to one English penny.

By 1630, the Dutch were shipping ten thousand furs a year to the Netherlands, a level of production that was maintained until 1669, when the English took over the fur trade by force. The Dutch had been content to trade goods for beads, however the English almost immediately began demanding tribute in wampum and fining the Algonquin in wampum for the slightest infraction of English law,[19] running the last remaining Algonquin out of the very business they had created and maintained for thirty-six hundred years.

One curious footnote to history is that although the Dutch traded for years with the Lenape, according to the former's paper records, the archaeological record shows few Dutch-made trade items found in the ground in the New York area. Meanwhile, an abundance of such Dutch trade items were found buried in Iroquois sites to the west. My theory is that for much of the following period, the Lenape were under the protection of the Iroquois as a vassal state and had to make payments of tribute. They would have given up the Dutch goods first before anything of real value.

Politicians for Sale

The first politician in New Amsterdam[20] was Governor Willem Verhulst. He was appointed in January 1626. History tells us he was very irresponsible and not much liked. He was not the last New York politician to receive bad press and be ousted, just the first. He lasted only a few months, and was replaced on September 23 of the same year by the shrewd and hard-nosed Peter Minuit, a Walloon.

The year 1626 was an important year for the new colony. Minuit had just landed on May 4 with a new group of immigrants and needed to build thirty houses before winter. It was on May 26, 1626, only three weeks after setting foot on Manhattan, that he reputedly made his infamous deal with some Native American passers-by. He needed vacant lots for those thirty houses. According to historians, he probably did distribute axes and other goods, but he had no clear agreement, and whatever agreement he had wasn't with the proper individuals.[21] Many believe that the following day, he made up a document to look like a deed, and used it to convince the Werpoes to the north to leave as well.

The famous $24 figure was assessed in 1846.[22] With inflation, that figure would now be over $600. Even the generous Lenape would never have let fourteen thousand acres of downtown real estate go for $600. They clearly thought the arrangement temporary and local in nature, if indeed there was any agreement at all. To Algonquin people, the earth is our mother, quite literally. It is greater than us, it has been here millions of years, and it will be here long after we're gone. Without the earth no life could exist. Being grateful every day for the earth was the foundation of a spiritual life. The idea of selling the earth was as absurd as selling the air. And for $24! Obviously there must have been some misunderstanding when the Dutch "bought" the land from the Native Americans.

According to Charles A. Weslager, author of *The Delaware Indians: A History*, the United States later used the Native American philosophical statement "we cannot own the earth" to their own advantage, interpreting it to mean that *they,* the Native Americans, cannot own the earth, but *we,* the United States of America, can. The government claimed that Indians had only sold to the colonists and later the United States their own right of occupancy, and could only trade it for other occupancy in return. This meant that the government would retain ownership of reservation land it was "giving up" to displaced Indians as it took their original land and their right to occupy it from them. This was a cynical misconstruing of the Native American sentiment, "The earth does not belong to us, we belong to the earth."

SHARING THE LAND

Many of the first treaties and agreements between colonists and the Algonquin resulted in the two peoples living side by side. Algonquin sachems who had been asked to share their land had agreed: Squanto at Pawtuxet (Plymouth Rock) with Miles Standish and the Pilgrims; Tamanend at Shackamaxon (Philadelphia) with William Penn and the Quakers; the Tayack of the Piscataway at St. Clements Island in the Potomac with Father Andrew White and the Catholics of the Ark and the Dove. They agreed to share the plot of land they lived on, within sight of the colonists.

The same was true with the Lenape and the Dutch on Manhattan, but the arrangement didn't last long. The Dutch came asking only for enough land to grow a little bit of corn, not far from a spot where the Lenape grew their corn, and that was readily agreed to. They were to share the same land, and be neighbors, but it wasn't long before the Dutch had completely walled themselves in, blocking Lenape use of the island of Manhattan from Wall Street to the southern tip of the island. Their "fortress" contained the once-sacred Council Elm at Bowling Green, and prevented the Lenape from visiting or meeting there. It also cut off the end of the Great Mohican Trail, which was severed by a large wooden gate where it entered the colony.

The Lenape had the intention of sharing the land for one or two years for their mutual benefit. Such an arrangement was common practice, and it would have given them a chance to see if the Dutch knew how to care for the land they were sharing. The Lenape would have been happy to instruct them in the best use of the land, but as it turned out, the Dutch had other ideas

HUMAN BEINGS FOR SALE

On June 26 of that same year, 1626, just one month after Peter Minuit had evicted the Canarsie from lower Manhattan, a ship with eleven slaves from Africa arrived. They were immediately put to work clearing the land and building Fort Amsterdam, at the foot of the Mohican Trail. New York's race problems began shortly thereafter. Under British rule, the slave issue became more heated. In 1712, twenty-five black slaves revolted; they set fire to a building and ambushed the whites who came to put out the fire. They were captured and tortured to death, hung, or otherwise executed in full public view. By 1720, one out of five people living in New York was a slave.

POMP AND CIRCUMSTANCE FOR PETER MINUIT

At One Centre Street, near the location of the old lakeside Lenape village where Peter Minuit swindled the gentle Werpoes out of their beautiful land, there is a Roman colonnade made of marble. It is inscribed along a lintel twenty-five feet above the plebian masses. The Latin and English letters are each more than a foot high. The message reads, "MDCXXVI Manhattan 1664 NEW YORK." The choice of architecture speaks volumes: it is an imitation of both the façade at the Fountain of Trevi and the Arch of Septimius Severus in the Old Roman Forum. Severus was not only thought of as the King of Bad Architecture, he died in 211 C.E. in Eboracum, now York, England, after which the city of New York was named. The original arch stands within sight of the Palatine, where Severus built his palace and where, according to legend, Romulus marked out the boundary of his new square city with a plow circa 700 B.C.E., creating the foundation of the Roman Empire. However, Severus was the first emperor of Rome to live outside the Palatine, and he chose York, the Roman military center to the north.[23] The subliminal message of the colonnade in Manhattan is that Peter Minuit, who staked out New Amsterdam with his plow, was a reincarnation of the god Romulus, establishing an empire, and that Manhattan's emperors of commerce were entitled to their empires as much as Severus was to his.

Whenever I look up at that thing I wonder, "Which event from 1626 are they celebrating? The first ousting of a New York politico, the introduction of Negro slaves to Manhattan, the Werpoes' scandal, or Minuit's $24 sleight of hand?" It was such an eventful year, I can only guess the answer. Less than half a block away, on what is now the Surrogates Court Building, is a marble statue of a feisty Lenape warrior standing in a grotto next to the well-fed Peter Minuit in his expensive beaver hat, with the Goddess of Justice standing between them as if she were a boxing referee keeping them apart. It is as fine a depiction of a "Manhattan Indian" as you will ever see; the Werpoe character, however, looks a little perturbed by all the ballyhoo just to the east of him, right on top of their now-forgotten lake.

By 1623, all but two to three hundred Lenape had been driven from Manhattan. Many Lenape had lived along the East River, but they all either died of disease or had been driven off by Wappingers. The Dutch had a disruptive influence on every aspect of Lenape life. By 1624 Lenape drinking had already become a problem. It marked the beginning of a spiritual decline and the eventual removal of the Lenape from the area. They had been sold up the Hudson River.

8

THE TWO-COLORED SNAKE *A History of the Dutch Occupation of New York*

There are many stories about snakes among the Algonquin. One story tells of two Native American children, a boy and a girl, who find a harmless little snake, with blue and red (they could be blue and orange) stripes, wriggling in the forest. They take it home as a pet. They feed it leaves and other odds and ends, only to find that it grows at an amazing rate. The more they feed it, the more voracious the snake's appetite becomes. It eats the dog, then the cat, then all the surrounding squirrels and rabbits. It even tries to eat the baby, but is stopped in time. However, from that point on, the boy and girl are occupied every waking minute with finding meat for the snake so it won't eat them. The snake turns into a monster and begins devouring the land and everything on it. It is said that snake is still alive today, but no one will say what form it has taken. This is a children's story but it illustrates how the Lenape felt about the New Amsterdam settlement, which seemed so harmless in 1625.

ONE LITTLE SNAKE

The Dutch had been trading with the Lenape along the Hudson River since 1610. In 1613, the Dutch begged the Lenape to let them establish a small trading post on the south tip of Manhattan. The

Lenape agreed to "just one"—*guttah*. Prior to the tragic events of September 11, 2001, the World Trade Center, the world's largest trading post, stood just twenty blocks north of its seventeenth-century predecessor.

On June 3, 1621, the Dutch West India Company was founded in Holland, and lucrative trade with the Lenape became an essential goal of the new company. However, it wasn't until March 28, 1624, that the Dutch established a provisional order, a plan of government based on the *Artikelbrief*, a charter of rules governing life aboard ship.

On March 30, 1624, thirty families set sail from Amsterdam under Cornelius Jacobsen May, who became the first director of the colony, although Willem Verhulst is usually the one credited with this distinction. These colonists settled on little Pagganck, "Nut Island," later Governor's Island. In 1784, when New York City became the capital city of the state, the governors lived there.

The main newcomers were a group that neither spoke Dutch as a first language, nor originated in Holland. They were a Protestant group called the Walloons, and they came in large numbers: 110 men, women, and children were on the first ship of settlers in 1624. They were the Celtic population of the low country in the eastern regions of what is called Belgium, and they spoke Old French, a Romance language. A second ship soon followed. The Walloons survived a harsh first winter in the New World. By spring of 1625, there were a few bark cabins on the east side of the island, which was less windy, plus a stone counting house, literally the first bank of New York.

In Greenwich Village, a Dutch colonist tried growing tobacco on a burned Lenape-cultivated field and found the soil yielded amazing growth. Before long, planting in Lenape fields, burned or not, became a popular practice around the colony.

Soon there were two windmills west of Broadway, close to the *Noort* or Hudson River. One was near the tip of Manhattan, the other just a few blocks north. Another windmill, as well as a sawmill, was built on what is now Governor's Island.

Meanwhile the Mohican established a trading post in 1624 near their old great council fire at Fort Orange and did a good business with these traveling salesmen from Holland. The strangers bearing gifts kept asking the Lenape for more furs. By 1625, the Lenape found they had hunted all the available furs on Manhattan. The Mohican, who had a network that reached further into the wilderness, soon became the main suppliers of pelts. History records that the Mohawks wanted to take over the fur trading along the river, and it triggered the Mohican War, which was over by 1638. The winners, the Mohawk, made the Mohican pay tribute. A person acting as tax collector would take a canoe from Mohawk Castle, go east on the Mohawk River, then south on the Schoharie, portage to the top of the Esopus then downstream to Saugerties, collecting tribute along the way. He would then return up the Hudson River, turn left and go home. The English gave guns to the Mohawk, while the Dutch would not give guns to the Lenape, taking their furs in exchange for items that did nothing to protect them from the wrath of their long-standing rivals.

THE LOVABLE BEAVER

Sometimes white people who came to Manhattan were thought of as "beavers," and that wasn't necessarily a compliment. It was not an indication that they were close to nature; they were just busy. They cut down trees as fast as lightning and built things with the logs, blocked ancient trails and trade routes, and covered parts of streams. They dug holes. In other words, they were like beavers.

The Algonquin had very sophisticated ideas about animal husbandry and the ideal relationship of humans to the environment. Their view was a very interactive one. Part of our job as humans was to control certain animal populations and cultivate others. Any farmer can tell you that a bunch of beavers allowed to propagate for any amount of time will put you out of business—and under water—in a few months. It is good to remember that beavers are gigantic rodents with teeth that can cut your arm off. Like other rodents, they reproduce at an alarming rate. Although beavers in moderate numbers will have a positive impact on the environment, too many beavers soon become a threat to the entire ecosystem.

There is an old Algonquin story that has more than a kernel of truth to it. The story tells us that in the old days, the beavers were very large, the size of small bears, and that they were so industrious and busy and goal-oriented, they cut down all the trees. The ecosystem was ruined: The birds couldn't nest, there was no shade, and all the animals were unhappy. The Creator saw this and said, "These beaver are not good stewards of the land which I have given to them to have dominion over. I will strike them with lightning and make them smaller. That will punish them. Then the other animals, such as the bear, will be able to hunt them and eat them, and their numbers will be less."

The paleontological record shows that beavers indeed were much larger at one time. As the beaver were always pointed out as a nuisance, Algonquin hunters did not treat them with any particular respect. Their skins were useful, their teeth could be made into dice, and their tails were a delicacy, even if their meat was just so-so. There were so many beavers, the Algonquin never imagined a world without beavers, and never developed any custom of protecting them. It would be like going to a farmer and asking him not to kill field mice or rats. He'd say, "There are so many rats, there will always be enough. Why not kill them?"

When the Dutch said, "We want all the beaver pelts you can find, and we'll give you these neat little trinkets in exchange," the Lenape said, "Why not?" They didn't realize that the Dutch were making the same offer to everyone. Within a few years, Manhattan was without a single beaver. Soon the Hudson Valley was without beaver, and most of New Jersey as well. Once they were protected again in the mid-twentieth century, the beaver quickly returned, in moderate numbers. These industrious rodents play a powerful role in the ecosystem, controlling the water levels and the tree growth, as the Lenape knew and respected.

SMARTER NOT HARDER

The Lenape were as busy as the Dutch, but in a different way. The Lenape would look for signs, and try to make the best use of their energy by harmonizing it with the environment. Rather than fight nature, they would try to use it to their best advantage to leverage their efforts. All of the same needs that the Dutch inventions and constructions met, the Lenape had already accomplished using means existing in nature. One had only to be flexible and patient. While the Dutch developed sharper axes, the Lenape used fire in combination with stone axes to fell large trees. The Lenape were masters of using controlled fire to clear timber when necessary. The Dutch cut each tree individually. Rather than make immovable houses in places that flooded in the spring, the Lenape would build movable longhouses and wigwams that could be assembled in a day if necessary. Rather than weed their gardens, they planted crops like squash between the corn stalks to kill both bugs and weeds and shade the roots of other plants. In addition to carving wooden bowls, they cut off the tops of gourds, which made perfect cups and bowls with little or no effort. Rather than build paved roads, they used the rivers as highways. Rather than rely on surgery and complex medicines, they used preventative medicines, with herb teas as a regular beverage at every meal.

The Munsee and Unami had never seen horses before. It wasn't until 1624 that the first horses were brought by ship to Manhattan, and like other Algonquin around the continent, the Lenape were quite taken by their strength, grace, and beauty. The arrival of the horse would ultimately quicken the spread of European development as wagon production went into overtime. (Two hundred years later, the Lenape themselves would be master horsemen of the plains.)

HEADS WILL ROLL

There were only about 270 people in the Dutch settlement at the time Minuit took over the directorship in 1626. The Dutch role in the New World—whether they were primarily traders or settlers—was never clearly defined, and that was a stumbling block. Minuit mishandled things so badly that he was fired in 1631 and replaced by Bastiaen Jansean Krol in 1632. Krol lasted one year. Wouter Van Twiller became director in 1633. He began conducting extensive land deals with the Lenape. To his credit, the deeds were carefully handled. Between 1636 and 1638, Governor Van Twiller registered "purchases" from Lenape sachems, fifteen thousand acres in three locations in Brooklyn. This may have included the future site of the First Dutch Reformed Church of the Flatlands.

Still, in 1638 there were only four hundred Dutch residents in the borough. After two years under Van Twiller, due to gross mismanagement, New Amsterdam had still not grown in population, while other colonies were booming. There was a string of buildings along Pearl Street up to Broad Street, a few houses north of Maiden Lane,[1] and some on Vly Street nearby (*Vly* means "creek" in Dutch), but the colony hadn't expanded as they had hoped. They widened the ancient hunting trail that ran through the fort, and at first called it Heere Straat. Later it became known as Breedewegh. It wasn't called Broadway until 1664, when the English renamed everything.

Van Twiller was fired in 1638. The choice of his successor was an unfortunate one that would permanently mar the reputation of New Amsterdam: Willem Kieft (pronounced *keeft*). Some reports paint a picture of Kieft as alcoholic, spiteful, paranoid, and capricious—but that was his good side. The stolid writer E. M. Ruttenber's accounts in *The Indian Tribes of Hudson's River to 1700* are hair-raising enough. When angered, he could become positively bloodthirsty. He replaced Van Twiller, pledging to clean up the mess the former governor had left. Kieft started out as a great reformer, but then went overboard, becoming a dictator.

At first Kieft bought outright several large tracts of Lenape land in Kings, Queens, and Bronx Counties to expand the colony. He cleaned up the corruption of others but was soon corrupted himself. After that point, he was extremely hard on the Indians, hijacking their wagons of corn on the road and killing all who tried to stop him. His Indian name became "Corn Thief." Meanwhile, smallpox, diphtheria, typhus, and measles continued the process of reducing the Lenape population to 10 percent of its former size. The Dutch practice of clear-cutting forests for firewood and forts made life hard on the Lenapes. A narrow island like Manhattan could not supply the large number of trees needed for such a project, but the Dutch were determined to get a foothold in this rugged environment by any means necessary. The deer on which the Lenape depended for their survival were completely annihilated, while the unshepherded Dutch cows demolished the Lenape cornfields. Frustrated and hungry, the once-peaceful Lenape started to kill Dutch livestock and even a few settlers. Eventually Kieft's psychopathic side began to come to the foreground.

The Mohawk-Mohican war ended in 1638. Kieft demanded taxes of the Lenape in the form of wampum. He claimed this payment was due to the Dutch for protecting the Lenape from their enemies—but they had never done so. He overreached his influence with the Lenape, and became greedy and arrogant. If anything, it was they who had been protecting him, working as scouts for the Dutch cause. This arrogant act was the turning point in New York's early history, and it eventually brought about the downfall of both the Dutch and the Lenape of Manhattan.

It could be said that the first "Vietnam" fought by America was here in Manhattan, for the senseless demand for payment without exchange brought about a war that was to escalate out of control, with no clear winner. Just as Vietnam became "Johnson's War" for reasons fair and unfair, this war became "Kieft's War," and it was a bloodbath. The Lenapes, who had been fairly peaceful considering their predicament, now saw no choice but to turn their newly formed armies, or war parties, against the Dutch. Kieft, alcoholic and sadly out of touch with reality, tried to intimidate the Lenape, who still had a continent full of relatives to join them in war if necessary.

Kieft readied his troops, and in 1640, the war, which was to last five long years and cost hundreds of lives, began in earnest. According to reliable firsthand written reports from David de Vries, easily the most widely respected man in New Netherlands, Kieft had babies butchered before their parents. A total of eighty heads were brought back with Kieft's approval. What Kieft should have realized is that the Lenape practiced a strict form of capital punishment, even when chiefs were not involved, which amounted to "an eye for an eye." If someone was murdered, either the murderer or one of the family members had to pay, either in trade of considerable value, such as pelts, or with their lives. It was part of the old Lenape belief in balancing out accounts right away, not letting things go on too long or harboring resentment. This law could be waived at the request of the bereaved, as it often was. If someone pressed charges for murder, there was an extensive investigation, people were interviewed, and the penalties were severe. Keeping in mind they had no prisons, such a conviction often meant expulsion or death.

When Kieft started killing more Lenape than there were Dutch, he must have thought the Lenape would run in fear or be unable to exact punishment. In fact, the Lenape proved that they could wipe out the Dutch at any time, but it was against their humanitarian principles. Even with an opportunity to do so during the Kieft War, they refused. The Lenape may also have been lenient in order to insure that they could continue to trade with the Dutch in the future. The Dutch had shipments from Europe. The Mohican and Iroquois had little to trade that the Lenape didn't already have, but their mercy was not mercenary in nature; the Lenape still remembered when they were a peaceful people.

In 1643, "The Year of Blood," Kieft instigated numerous massacres all around Manhattan and the surrounding area, most notably against the Arresick of Hoboken and the Rechtank of the East Village south of Delancy. Both villages and all inhabitants were completely annihilated. In September 1643, in the most significant battle of the war, a party of 1,500 Lenape warriors appeared from the north, coming from Westchester and other predominantly Wappingers territories, and fell upon the little colony as if to annihilate it. They destroyed everything with the same weapon the Dutch had used, fire, leaving the city in ashes, but sparing the lives of the Dutch. The 1,500 were under the command of the Wappingers Chief Mayanes. The 250 unarmed Dutch were at his mercy, and the rules of engagement would have allowed him to do his worst, and yet he decided to spare them all.

Ruttenber commented on how easy it would have been for Mayanes to eliminate the entire population in that one well-planned surprise. The women and children were hiding in flammable straw huts while the men standing guard were easy targets for the bow and arrow. Instead, Mayanes's men, the most skilled warriors of the region, killed none,[2] thinking they had left a clear message: "We are compassionate. We spared your lives, but we will not be pushed around. Negotiate with us as equals."

Unable to understand or accept the message, Kieft was insane with rage. As he saw it, the Dutch had lost some of their material objects for no reason. He offered a phenomenal sum of 25,000 guilders to any army that would wipe out the Lenape. A mercenary militia of 150 British soldiers in New England were offered not only the money, but "as a further consideration that [the colony of] New Netherlands should be mortgaged to the English for the payment of the sum offered."[3]

The Dutch and English were not on good terms, and to offer to mortgage the entire colony to the enemy just to get revenge on someone who spared the lives of your people seems extraordinary, even treasonable. But that's what he did. Tellingly, no one would take the bait. No one trusted his word, and his colonial investment was a bad risk. He offered to sell his soul and no one wanted it.

After the smoke cleared, "Willem the Testy"[4] was thrown out of office, though he was kept on in various lesser positions, and John Underhill, an English Indian fighter, became governor. Whatever minor flaws in temperament Kieft had were soon forgotten. Underhill was worse. He organized a counter-retaliation force— whether they were mercenary militia or volunteers or both is not clear—and in the following months, destroyed over fifteen hundred men, women, and children, one by one. He took others to the fort and tortured them. Kieft once again was seen laughing out loud at the sick, demented tortures, like cutting off men's genitals and stuffing them in the victim's mouth until they choked, and then cutting off their heads on a millstone. The reliable David de Vries witnessed and recorded such atrocities, and witnessed Kieft's mother-in-law, the mother of his wife and of the secretary Van Tienhoven, kicking their heads around like soccer balls. It was said they actually played soccer with the heads, their jaws removed to make them rounder and better suited as soccer equipment. A Lenape woman captive who witnessed this exclaimed that there had never been such cruelty committed in all the wars in her people's history.

It was during the confusion of war that Lenape, either Siwanoy or Weckweesgeek, killed Anne Hutchinson from Rhode Island. Famed as a courageous woman, perhaps this time she was a little too courageous. The Dutch had given her a tract of land in the Bronx near the north foot of the Throgs Neck Bridge, but it was Lenape land they had no right to give. It's not clear how much the Hutchinsons realized they were in danger, or the seriousness of the war. Katherine Kirkpatrick's book, *Trouble's Daughter,* details the story quite well. Young Susanna Hutchinson was captured by the chief of the Siwanoy and named Fall Leaf because of her red hair, which the Siwanoy had never seen before. When the chief found that the woman he had killed, Anne Hutchinson, was a great orator among her people, he changed his name to Annehook, his way of pronouncing her name. This was a Lenape warrior's way of honoring a person he would otherwise respect, whom circumstances forced him to kill. He also took on the parentage of the Hutchinson's child and raised her as his own until her release.

The Kieft War ended in 1645, by treaty at Albany. It had been a long and deadly conflict. All told, at least sixteen hundred Algonquin were killed, and many Dutch from isolated incidents, mostly in scenarios the Lenape code judged to be capital punishments or self-defense. At the resolution of the war the Dutch said, according to Wassanaer's *Colonial History,* "All this through foolish hankering after war; for it is known to all right-thinking men here, that there Indians have lived as lambs among us until a few years ago, injuring noone, and affording every assistance to our nation."[5]

Kieft's own allies attributed the complete ruin of the Dutch colony to his Tribute Policy. Young Susanna Hutchinson was returned to the British against her will at the age of nine or ten—the question of her age has never been resolved. It was decreed in the truce of 1645 that all prisoners were to be returned, regardless of their wishes. Susanna Hutchinson, as she was once again known, did not wish to leave her Lenape family, but was forced to become a British subject once again, although she did not speak a word of English. Eventually she moved to New England, learned to speak English, married John Cole, and had several children. Her descendants include many names associated with New York City's history, and some of its greatest benefactors: the Harrimans, the Bushes, the Whitneys, not to mention John Singleton Copeley, the portrait painter whose work now hangs in the Metropolitan Museum of Art in New York.

In violation of the treaty, Underhill continued to massacre the Lenape people. There were three more major incidents, and several minor ones. With a force of one hundred and twenty, he attacked the Canarsie who were under Chief Penhawitz, driving them off the Canarsie homeland now known as Brooklyn. Later, with a force of eighty, he slaughtered one hundred and twenty of the Maspeth, a subtribe of the Rockaway living near what is now Newtown Creek. Then in 1647 Underhill personally commanded one of the greatest massacres in North American history at a place called Pound Ridge. Between five- and seven-hundred Algonquin were ambushed and killed as they were gathering for the important spiritual celebration *k'mo'hok ki'coy* or "hungry moon," often called Maple Sugar Dance.[6] Twenty-five of those killed were Wappingers, and Chief Katonah was among them, although there is reason to believe Underhill was looking for Mayanes.[7]

Arriving at midnight at Pound Ridge on foot, the white colonists (some say 200 of them, some 130) found three rows of well-constructed houses, each seventy paces long (some say eighty), made of square logs. One-hundred-eighty Lenape came outside to see what the noise was and were killed where they stood outside the houses. Others tried to escape but were driven back into the houses. General La Montagne gave the order to burn them inside the houses. Soon the many longhouses were torched. Eight men escaped. The people inside preferred to die by fire than be killed by whites, so they sat inside and didn't make a single sound. Not one Lenape among the many hundreds who were burned alive screamed. It was one of the greatest mass murders ever to take place on North American soil, and it was carried out with religious zeal. In defense of his actions, Underhill quoted scripture, saying "The Scripture declareth women and children must perish with their parents. We had sufficient light from the word of God for our proceedings!" For eastern woodlands Algonquin, this was their "Wounded Knee."[8]

A FATHER AND HIS CHILDREN

When Peter Stuyvesant arrived in 1647 the colony was in disarray. The Dutch colonists were cowering in makeshift huts around the fort, afraid to return to their farms. Kieft was sequestered, drinking himself to death, they said. Most of the others were drunk as well. In his first speech, Stuyvesant said the famous words, "I shall govern you as a father his children!"[9] It wasn't meant as an endearing compliment. He was calling them a bunch of three-year-olds.

Peter Stuyvesant had found religion after a brush with death in Brazil, but he was very bigoted. He ruled with an iron hand for seventeen years. He was intolerant of individual freedoms, ideas, and religions, and attempted to outlaw all denominations other than Dutch Reformed.

Although Stuyvesant saw Native Americans as a hindrance to progress and was once quoted as saying, "I value the blood of one Christian more than that of a hundred Indians," he made peace with the Lenape. He established the first police force on Manhattan. His first constabulary consisted of nine men. He imposed stiff fines for driving wagons too fast on Breedewegh (later Broadway).[10] Overall he made Manhattan a safe place to be again, and the more settlers came. Within ten years, there were fifteen hundred people living in New Amsterdam, with 340 new row houses.

In 1654, Kieft was sent back to Amsterdam to answer for his crimes. The Dutch wanted to make an example of him before their allies, who had heard about all the bloodshed he had caused. However, he didn't live to stand trial. His ship was caught in a storm off the coast of Wales and sank with all on board.[11]

Amid much protest from the Dutch, including impeachment hearings in 1648, Peter Stuyvesant held on to his position of power until 1664, when the British arrived. On August 27 of that year, four heavily armored English warships sailed into New York harbor and did to the Dutch what the Dutch had done to the Lenape and the Swedes,[12] using overwhelming force to make a point. On September 5, the British opened fire. Stuyvesant, who hated the British, climbed painfully to the top of the ramparts of Fort Amsterdam in spite of his wooden leg, and surveying the attack, said simply, "I'd rather die."

His timid business partners in the Dutch West India Company looked at the huge ships, and looked at him and said, "*We* don't want to die. Come down from there." They quickly got together a petition to surrender. Ninety-three Dutchmen signed it and handed it to Stuyvesant. Two days later, Stuyvesant begrudgingly surrendered without firing a shot. His men lowered the blue and orange colors, and New Amsterdam was a thing of the past.[13]

HOSTILE TAKEOVER

Two days later, the city was renamed New York, after the brother of King Charles II, to whom the entire colony had been promised as a birthday present. The thirty-one-year-old Duke of York and Albany was aboard one of the British ships, watching the proceedings. He later won the scramble for the English throne in 1685 and ruled the British Empire as James II. But his victory was a bitter one, as he was a terrible king and was overthrown in 1688 after only three years on the throne.

Stuyvesant purchased a modest fruit farm in the Bowery section of rural Greenwich Village and settled down to a quiet life. He died four years later, in February 1672, and his body was placed in a vault near his home in a chapel he himself had built. That chapel is now St. Mark's Church, on the corner of St. Mark's Place and Second Avenue in Manhattan. He is lying just inside the door in the front foyer, at about knee level. According to local legend, people still hear the sound of his restless "silver" peg leg tapping on the pavement as his ghost walks the night.[14]

THE GREAT SEAL

The Great Seal of the City of New York is divided equally between the Dutch and the Native American, a source of pride to the more than forty-thousand Native Americans now living in the great metropolis. The four-hundred-year-old struggle to maintain an identity as aboriginal people in this most intensely bargained-for island in North America is still alive, as long as this symbol remains, on subway cars, police stations, and city buildings. If anyone says, "Indians don't belong here anymore!" a Native American need only point to the Great Seal and say, "Yes we do!"

Marked "1625," the Great Seal commemorates the mutually beneficial trade relationship between the Dutch and the Lenape. The Indian holds a bow in his left hand, but no arrows, rendering him harmless, however the two feathers standing straight up behind his head actually mean "I'm on the warpath," although it is doubtful the engraver knew this fact. He is wearing moccasins, but no leggings, and only a breechcloth as clothing, although he wears a belt. The Indian man is in braids. In some versions, he wears a headband.

The Dutchman wears a cap of the time and has long hair. He is wearing shoes and hose and pantaloons, plus a vest and a belt. He is holding a plumb-bob in his right hand, an ancient stone-laying tool and mystical Masonic symbol representing balance and the secrets of the pendulum, used in divination. The Knights Templar, a secret Masonic society dating back to the 1300s, have been involved in every phase of New York's exploration and construction, up to and including the present day. The Dutch engraver who created this seal must have been a Mason.[15]

In the center is a Dutch coat of arms, with a windmill propeller in the center, a keg of rum on both sides, and beavers waiting patiently to be turned into beaver hats above and below. This coat of arms was on the flag of New Amsterdam, which was orange and blue, the colors of the modern-day flags of the Mets, Knicks, Islanders, and Jets. Equally prominent is the American (or Native American) eagle, with his wings spread over the heads of both men. Surrounding them all is an almost complete circle of laurel leaves, almost identical to that which is on the Lincoln "wheat" penny.

The banner encircling the bottom half of the seal is marked with the words: *"Sigillum Civitatis Novi Eboraci."* It means "Seal (or 'sign') of the City of New Eboraci." As mentioned in Chapter 1, Eboracum is the name the Romans gave to York in England when they conquered it.

A relief of the great seal is carved on the outside of the building of the Museum of the City of New York, with the human figures about ten feet tall.

"An Ancient Citie"

According to colonial records, the Charter of the English Governor Dongan in 1686 declared New York to be "an ancient citie." A hundred years later, the newly independent Americans of "New York" were so caught up in their future plans, they had already forgotten what was so ancient about it, and scoffed at the phrase. This was the New City of the World—the city of the future. It was to become perhaps the most European city in America, and the one most obsessed with progress, a word that has no translation in Lenape. Most New

Yorkers have never looked back. Perhaps if they did they'd be surprised to learn what a very ancient city they occupy, a metropolis thousands of years old. It's time we honored that history and came to an understanding of what New York really is and where it comes from.

9

THE WORLD
OF THE LENAPE

One reason the immigrants of the New Amsterdam colony had such a hard time adjusting to their new world was because they had a poor understanding of the original inhabitants and their culture. To the Lenape, their own way of life made perfect sense. There was an intuitive logic in everything they did. The Dutch found the Lenape language very difficult and misinterpreted much of what they were hearing, and like most tourists exploring an alien civilization, they misinterpreted everything they were seeing as well. Although the Dutch could find common ground in the shared struggle for survival, they could not understand the Lenape value system, which was not oriented toward dead objects, but viewed all objects as animate and spirit-led. The settlers of New Amsterdam were used to seeing everything in writing, with fixed points of reference, and Lenape was a fluid, oral culture.

What follows is the basic introduction to the world of the New York Lenape—how they traded, how and what they ate, how they dressed and sheltered themselves, their medicinal traditions, transportation, and recreation. This is information the Dutch settlers sorely lacked.

SHOPPING CAPITAL

Manhattan has always been a great shopping mecca, at least since the invention of the canoe. There were trading posts set up along the many trails where one could trade wampum or barter for furs, minks, pearls, and perhaps even copper imported from the Great Lakes. The southern tip of Manhattan in particular was a well-known trading spot. Goods were plentiful, and fur traders traveled from hundreds of miles around to make deals there.

LENAPE LIVING

Native craftswomen and -men made pottery, basketry, beadwork or birch bark crafts with great speed and skill.[1] Understanding the facility with which they produced their few necessary accessories helps us to understand the Lenape attitude of nonattachment to material possessions. A small *wikooum* or "wigwam" could be constructed in six hours, basketry in an hour, and pottery in several steps.

Throughout the early millennia of occupation, the winters were too windy and cold on Manhattan, and the Lenape left for more sheltered areas in November. The land was also too rocky to support a huge population. Later, with more advanced stone tools, they were able to adapt to the harsh conditions. The inhabitants moved from place to place, setting up their lodges where they wished. They typically moved their tents and wigwams two or three times a year, with the majority of time spent near their cornfields.

The Lenape built both longhouses and wigwams. Both were made from bent saplings, often hickory. They were covered with grass, bark, or with mats made of reeds. A hole in the top allowed smoke to escape. In the larger wigwams, a circular bench for family members to sleep on stretched around the inside of the dwelling. Some of these wigwams were thirty feet in circumference, or about ten feet across. On the whole, they were watertight and warm in the winter. The sachem's house would be set up so as to receive guests.

Notable sachems had clean, well-constructed wigwams with bark lining inside as well as out, wooden carvings hung around the walls, and even painted pictures such as portraits of important people.

The majestic community longhouses—often as much as sixty feet long and fifteen feet wide, with plenty of headroom—could contain six or seven families, or about twenty-two people at once, usually all related. The flooring was of packed earth, ideal for sweeping with a branch. The side and back of the structure was made of reeds, or the bark of chestnut, elm, or ash.[2] Large pieces of bark would be peeled off and placed at the bottom of a stream and then weighted down with large stones. After a week or so, retrieved and dried, they lay flat enough for easy use as siding.[3]

A bark lodge was constructed by pounding two rows of closely spaced holes in the earth with the rows about ten to twenty feet apart. Saplings were forced into the holes and bent over and lashed or wound together to form a dome-shaped trellis. This provided the framework on which chestnut, elm, linden, or other bark shingles or woven mats were attached.[4]

The ridge of the roof of the longhouse was designed with a half-foot opening from one end to the other. The front door was kept small for better insulation, thus everyone had to kneel upon entering. It was customary to say, "All my relations," or another blessing as one entered or exited. Once inside, a visitor might be smudged down with burning sage, tree fungus, or sweetgrass so that any unwelcome spirits would be removed. The doors were made of flat bark or reed mats. Some of these reed mats were remarkable works of art.[5] No iron, lead, or stone were used in the creation of the longhouse, even after such materials became readily available.[6]

A long pole was suspended horizontally from end to end of the big house or lodge, and objects and bags of food were suspended from it by strings of braided corn, not unlike the horizontal pole in the Midewiwin lodges, which holds sacred objects aloft during the gatherings. Bearskin blankets were used for sleeping.[7]

Minisink Indians to the northwest[8] preferred oval or round-ended longhouses with a single doorway located on the side, away from the prevailing winds. The Algonquin chose village sites with prevailing winds in mind.[9]

The Architecture of Peace

Defense was not generally an issue in building within Algonquin villages, except in rare cases when they were in proximity to Iroquois or other enemy settlements. There were rarely palisades, trenches, stockades, or other designs of war in precontact villages. Diplomacy was paramount to the Lenape, and the larger Algonquin nation. The lack of architectural defenses helped to insure the careful continuation of good statesmanship.[10] In more militant Native American societies, houses were larger and clustered together, with a double stockade fort surrounding them, set on a hill for strategic advantage. The fortresses were also in clusters, as allied villages tended to establish themselves on hills nearby. Such communities had to be highly organized, with a hierarchal pecking order and an unquestioning sense of duty to superiors, so that the moment the enemy was seen on the horizon, the entire village knew whether to attack or defend.

But that is not how life was in Lenape Hoking in 1609. Diplomatic means mediated relations between the eastern New York Algonquin and other peoples. Mediators, usually elders, held council with those who had a disagreement. One had always to respect one's elders, so their multi-tribal council decisions were usually honored.

Algonquin settlements were built near streams for convenient use, and on the sides of hills for better drainage and protection from wind. Strategic areas such as points or necks of land surrounded by water on three sides were favored for permanent settlement. Before 1300 c.e. most homes were still being built exclusively on the western banks of rivers. However after that time, homes began to be placed on either side. Homes were typically clustered together so that tools could be shared, but each family had adequate ground space near their wigwam for sports, children's games, and home industries. Gardening areas were usually only a few hundred feet away at most.

HOUSEHOLD MANAGEMENT

Throughout the Algonquin world, the men hunted and the women followed and cut up the meat with knives, placing it in baskets and carrying it back to the village. The women also skinned the animal and cleaned the hides. The elder women performed many useful tasks in helping to prepare meals. One might have seen women as old as eighty winters vigorously pounding "Turkish" beans out of their pods with a stick.[11] Women owned the lodges, and the new bride-groom usually moved in with the bride and her family.

TRANSPORTATION

The Lenape carved dugout canoes from a single tree, a labor-intensive process that took a minimum of ten days to complete. Some dugouts rivaled wood sculpture in their smoothness and the amount of skill demanded. They plied these canoes on a coast-to-coast highway system that used no fossil fuel and cost nothing to maintain, with no tolls, red lights, or bridge traffic. This pollution-free marvel was the North American river system, although it could have its inconveniences: for example, unexpected waterfalls, the need to carry one's boat two miles through snake-infested bogs or to paddle upstream against the wind, ice floes in the winter, and rocks that could rip open the bottom of the boat.

Manhattan itself had only the Werpoes' pond, the Canal Street stream, those at Broad and East Tenth Streets, plus the inlet at East 108th Street, but what it did offer was access to the ocean, affording the traveler free travel to any spot along the Atlantic Coast. In the early days you could get almost anywhere between Manhattan and the Rockies by canoe without having to carry your boat or walk too far, via the Hudson, Mohawk, and Oswego River route to the Great Lakes.

Entering the Hackensack, Raritan, or Passaic Rivers from the Mohicanituk (Hudson River), one encountered a network of streams that led to almost every settlement in northeast New Jersey as well. Natives coming to visit New York State could travel downstream from Calgary, Alberta, Canada, along the Missouri River and its tributaries, passing Cincinnati, Ohio, in a couple of weeks, followed by a jaunt up the Ohio-Allegheny River route, eventually reaching the placid Mohawk River and the Hudson beyond.

What made the system work were the trails all along the way, tracing alongside the streams, fording them, or connecting them together. The Minisink Trail did all three, connecting the Mohicanituk with the Lenape See-poo (Delaware River), tracing the route of the Esopus, Rondout, and Basher Kill, and fording a stream or two toward the south.

Many of the longer trails were within sight of water for most of the way, a remarkable feat. The Catskill Trail (now partly Route 23) ran along the Catskill Creek, the Mohican Trail (now Route 9/ Broadway) along the Mohicanituk, the Delaware Trail (Pennsylvania State Route 209) along the Delaware River, the Ramapo Trail along the Ramapo River, the Raritan Trails such as Routes 533 and 513, and so forth, along the Raritan's branches. Plus there were upland trails such as the old Pocono Road, Wyoming Trail, or Rockaway Trial.

HEALING

An old expression advises that "Your medicine is under your feet!" It's also been said, "Not one medicine has ever been found that was not known or used by some Native American group for hundreds of years."[12] The Lenape, the grandfathers of the Algonquin, had regular contact with other peoples from far away with access to herbal knowledge. They traded for quinine, iodine, or other tonics from the Deep South, and their knowledge of which plants to use for what ailment was extensive. The elder women talked to the plants to find out what they should be used for and what dosage. Through years of experience, and through a vast educational network of elderly ladies and some old men talking about their medical problems and what worked, they developed and handed down quite a retinue of herbs and cures. There were few common maladies for which the Lenape hadn't found a natural treatment.

One of the first things to understand is that an open field just a few hundred feet square may contain approximately one hundred *m'beysun* plants or "medicinal herbs"—"weeds" as you call them—growing wild. Dandelion, red clover, yellow dock, violet flowers, and burdock, for instance, all can help boost the immune system and prevent diseases such as cancer when prepared properly.[13]

PREVENTATIVE MEDICINE

The first rule of good health in 1609 was not to get sick in the first place. The Lenape drank fresh, clean water and herbal concoctions every day; they exercised and bathed regularly in streams and lakes. Native New Yorkers performed rites of fasting and purification several times a year. The Algonquin insist that the sweat lodge cleanses the skin so well that it prevents blemishes throughout life. In combination with herbs and fasting, the purification lodge cures or prevents a wide variety of diseases by preventing toxins and parasites from building up.[14]

If all else failed, the Lenape might consult their *kitzinaeka* or "medicine man/woman,"[15] making sure to offer tobacco for the spirits and a gift for the healer who acted as the tool of the Creator.

The Munsee and other Lenape also used crystals extensively, both for ritual and in their necklaces and other decorative ornaments. Some Algonquins to the north frowned upon this practice, but it was and is popular with the Cherokee and most southern Algonquin. Throughout the Native peoples of North America, there seems to be a tacit acknowledgment of a previous "great civilization" on an island in the Atlantic, and a general consensus that a great calamity occurred involving the misuse of crystals. It is for this reason alone, if not others, that there is a simultaneous fascination and repulsion where crystals are concerned among Algonquin people. The Lenape were very open to outside ideas, and from time to time, copied "crystal" fashion from the Cherokee or other Iroquoian people from the southwest.

THE WELL-DRESSED LENAPE

Far from being half-naked savages, the original Native New Yorkers were well dressed, but not by European standards. The New York expression "dressed to kill" had a more literal meaning in 1609: in the occasional times of war, Lenape warriors painted their faces red and black, with white or black circles around the eyes. These were not fashion statements, but very serious aspects of the profound ritual of preparing for battle. The Lenape claimed that when they were painted for battle in this way they were *Manitoo,* a word with no English equivalent.

Women of the region often tied up their long straight hair into a club at the back of the head skillfully woven into the shape of a beaver's tail—all without bobby pins.[16] Lenape men of the region often singed their hair off with a red-hot stone, leaving a cock's comb–like crown of hair that would then be dyed.[17] Tattoos were also popular, etched with porcupine needles.

A reasonably skilled artist among the earliest European arrivals drew portraits of Lenape men. The men are seen wearing light-colored leather skirts, with a feather placed jauntily in a checkered headband. They have bare chests crossed with a bandolier for bow quivers, and each is wearing a pendant. They look, healthy, happy, and friendly. Another source describes men with leather loincloths as well. [18]

The Lenape men of the Tappan and Weckweesgeek around Yonkers to the north wore beaverskin coats.[19] They wore the warm fur side inside next to their skin in the winter, reversing it to keep the fur outside in the summer to place the cool leather next to their bodies in the hot sweaty months. They also used bear hide, wildcat hide, and raccoon hide in the same manner.

Early visitors described the remarkable "turkey feather mantles" or coats the Lenape men wore. The turkey feathers were attached to a netlike cloth underneath and woven in tightly to repel rain and appear iridescent.[20]

Children were permitted to be naked outdoors until their thirteenth year. At that time, women as part of their coming-of-age ceremony would begin to wear wrap-around skirts and robes; however, they still went bare-breasted in the summertime.[21]

"The women wore aprons front and rear, and in winter, a skin or hemp robe. Bags, suspended by thongs from the neck, served as pockets."[22] Skin moccasins, leggings, and a belt were worn by men and women alike. Sometimes the Lenape women might wrap themselves in a deerskin shawl with fringe. In cooler weather, they wore a long fur robe attached at the right shoulder by a knot and at the waist by a girdle. Wampum made from quahog shells was worn in strings and stitched to their garments. It was also made into bracelets, armlets, and earrings and worn around the neck, arms, and waist.[23] They also wore girdles made of whale fins, as whales were abundant in the surrounding waters, and wove animal hair into cloth, as well as hemp.

Quillworking was a great art, involving large quantities of time and patience. The quills would be plucked or boiled from the porcupine, then dyed in various vats or pots, then sorted by color. Then the artisan flattened the quills by drawing them through his or her clenched teeth. Then the quills were wrapped around a solid object and carefully tied together underneath.[24]

It was fashionable to wear leggings and moccasins of elk hide, although some shoes were made from straw. The moccasins were softened by continually working them with the hands. Harder-soled moccasins were worn by people further west, but the Lenape were known for soft-soled shoes. There was also a kind of ankle boot moccasin for rainy weather, waterproof and very comfortable, usually without decoration of any kind. Each boot was made out of a single oval of buckskin sewn together at the front of the ankle for a tighter fit; a drawstring gathered the boot at the ankle. The boot would be well oiled with bear grease and other oils until it possessed a dull shine, rendering it completely waterproof.

The first traders brought with them "tinkle cones," small music-making ornaments. Lenape women sewed these into their clothing. No such tinkle cones have been found in the Lake Superior region, the source of most North American precontact copper. The Dutch cones were made out of old copper pots and cut in triangles. The famous Jingle Dance came to an Ojibway healer in a vision many years ago. In that vision, she saw that a sacred dance performed in the dark around the body of a sickly chief, with jingles on the women's dresses, would bring the old man back to health. It worked, and the Jingle Dance as we know it was born.[25]

Deerskin for clothing was brain tanned while wet, then stretched on a frame and rubbed with a bone. Many women wore a curious squarish cap made of leather. After trade with Europeans began, the same cap was also made of cloth.[26] At that time, more glass beads replaced the labor-intensive wampum beads.

Both men and women wore pendants of stone around their necks. Many also wore knives, tobacco pouches, and pipes on tethers around their necks. Women sometimes wore pearl necklaces, but they did not consider them precious as the Dutch did.[27] Copper was also worn as jewelry, more so with the Dutch trade. An artisan could make a lot of bracelets from one copper kettle.

Cosmetics

It was customary for women to smear bear fat on their skin and hair, or perhaps a lotion made of bear grease, sunflower oil, and nut oil. The grease helped to keep mosquitos away. This also functioned as suntan lotion, if not the first in the world, then certainly the first used at Rockaway Beach and Coney Island. It prevented the bright red sunburns Lenape are prone to, which may be the real reason Europeans perceived them as "redskins." In the old days, the people were proud of their reddish skin from being out in the sun, since it was a little like the color of the sacred ochre. One visitor wrote of the Native women of Manhattan, "In complexion [they are] of a clayish colour, the hair of their heads generally black, lank, and long hanging down. Their hair being naturally black, they make it more so by oyling [sic], dyeing, and daily dressing, yet though they be very careful about the hair of their heads yet they will not endure any upon their chins, where it no sooner grows than they take it out by the roots or scrape it off with a kind of razor made of bone."[28]

One of the mates on Henry Hudson's *Half Moon* in 1609 recorded in his journal: "They go in deer skins, well dressed. They grease their bodies and hair very often and paint their faces with several colours, as black, white, red, yellow, etc., which they take great pride in, everyone being painted in a different manner." Van der Donck described how Lenape women made themselves irresistible by adding "black spots of paint on their faces, here and there."[29]

Manhattan Cuisine, c. 1609

The people of Lenape Hoking roamed freely in search of food, and lived as self-sufficiently as possible, considering the lack of abundant farming land in the region. They relied heavily on the sea for food and were fond of sturgeon, a very large, heavily scaled fish then abundant in the waters of the Mohicanituk River, using their scales as scraping tools. They harpooned large fish and shot medium-sized fish in shallow streams with a bow and arrow; they also caught fish in weirs, and with seines and gill nets. Netting parties regularly went out to sea; others used bird-bone or copper fishhooks in the beautiful rivers on the mainland.

People ate alone or together whenever they were hungry, using whatever was available to create a meal for themselves. The exception was ceremonial feast times, when everyone would have been expected to bring delicacies and eat together.[30]

In the longhouse, it was customary to sit or lie on the ground, or on fur mats, usually on one's left side, with feet toward the fire. People drank from turtle shell bowls, used utensils made from calabash gourds, and picked roasted ears of corn from their *notassen*, baskets made of split ash.

The Lenape women boiled food by dropping hot stones in a pot or sack of plants, meat, or liquid. This same method was practiced in Europe around 3000 B.C.E., and in other parts of the world. They would chop up animal bones and boil them to extract the broth and oils to use later in soups, then extract the bones and pick out every ounce of marrow with a marrow pick and eat it, or suck it out of the bone.

Here are two classic Native recipes, one surely known to the Native New Yorkers. First, a recipe for corn cake: Scrape the corn off the cob with a deer's jawbone, then pound or grind the kernels with a foot-long pounding stone or pestle made of hewn granite. Smash the kernels into the mortar stone until the kernels turn into cornmeal. Sift the cornmeal through a "sifting basket," or *notassen*, made of split white ash, but woven loosely at the bottom, and collect the siftings in a tortoise shell or calabash gourd bowl.[31] Mix the sifted cornmeal with water from the stream and pat it into little cakes. Then wrap the cakes in cornhusks or plant leaves, and then bake under the hot ashes in your central fire until it smells right. Then remove them with a pair of deer antlers. Let cool and serve.

Here's another delicious recipe to try, one that has been popular since at least 1000 B.C.E., for acorn pudding. Making bread, cakes, or pudding from acorns is a tricky process, since the *segabun,* or ground nuts, contain much tannic acid, which is very, very bitter and can make you vomit, become ill, or go mad. Therefore you have to soak them a long time. First, you extract the meat from the nut with a fish bone or other kitchen utensil, then pound it thoroughly all morning with a mortar and pestle; again hewn granite is recommended. Then let the acorn mush soak for a while in water, drain, and place the mush in a basket made of tightly woven split ash. Then go down to the creek and wash it thoroughly several times. Now dry the mush in the sun until it turns to powder. Only then is it palatable.[32] From this *sapsis,* or "mush," you can make soup, pudding, or bread, or pad it into a veggie burger. It helps to add maple syrup so that it will bind together and look more like a meal. Add other flavors according to taste. Fish brains are a Lenape favorite.[33]

Eat as much of your acorn pudding as you can; the Lenape never, ever threw away food. That would be considered not only wasteful, but disrespectful to the spirit of life itself, which the food embodied. This belief was and remains widespread among Algonquin people from all over Turtle Island.

POTTERY

Algonquin pots were rounded at the bottom. Being of lighter weight, they were more fragile than their Iroquoian counterparts, a reflection of the Algonquin's highly mobile way of life. It was often easier to make new pots upon arriving in a new locale than to lug the old pots around. Algonquin pottery was characterized by its use of the distinctive ladder design. Many pots were castled at the mouth by pushing the rim into four square corners and then upward to represent the four directions.

The pots were used to cook food or carry and store water. They could also be tied and suspended over a fire, the rounded ballistic shape allowing the heat to distribute itself with perfect equanimity throughout the inside of the pot, cooking all the food evenly, with no cold spots.

No Word for Trash

It is said there is no word in Algonquin for garbage. Everything has a use and a reuse, and its name reflects that function. Once you name something trash, you rob it of its identity and its usefulness. Trash implies uselessness, and this concept is a laughable one, only expressed as part of a wry joke or teasing. Micmac Indians use the word for "potato peelings" to describe something pretty nearly useless; however, they actually use potato peelings for many purposes, including composting the garden. If the lightweight pot cracked in the fire, or was damaged when the tripod fell over, the shards were used for other purposes—as scrapers, for example. Shells were piled in middens, while bones and all organic materials were placed in open pits and periodically covered with thin layers of dirt, grass, plants, and other organic material—composting. When the pit was full, it would be covered over well with dirt, and a new pit started. This soil would later be used to grow corn.[34]

Recreation

Contrary to what many presume, life among the Lenape was easier most of the time, at least in terms of work hours, than it was for Europeans. Most Lenape had to work at trading, planting, hunting, and gathering only three or four days out of the week to be comfortable. Although winters could be hard and famine was always a possibility, there was plenty of time for recreation under normal circumstances. The Lenape played a form of football that was like soccer. The people of Lenape Hoking also played a form of cards involving gambling with pieces of reeds. They made dice out of sawed-off beaver's teeth perforated with dots, and gambled with those as well.[35]

The Lenape believed in psychic ability and telekinetic powers. They also understood the rather complex combinations of chance that are at work in the natural world, and games of chance gave them a way of participating, and also testing their own power. Many stories tell how the change of the seasons is caused by gambling between the grandmothers and grandfathers of the four directions; thus they knew that the exact time of the appearance of spring, summer, fall, and winter was subject to chance, and many random or complex factors. Like many things in Lenape culture, an everyday activity was representative of a much larger principle.[36]

The game of "Hubbub" was played with five round disks, white on one side, black on the other, with designs often etched or drawn upon them. The five disks were placed in a bowl. A contestant then tossed the disks upwards and caught them with the bowl. The player was awarded two points when all five disks landed on the same color, and one point if four disks landed on the same color. The player received one stick for each point earned. When he or she failed to earn any points, the bowl passed clockwise to the next person. The game was completed when one player obtained all the sticks.[37] Furs and carvings and other objects of value were wagered on the victory, and it was customary for players to shout "Hubbub hubbub!" and make noise, apparently either out of excitement, or in order to distract the contestant so that they would fail to catch all the disks.[38]

Leisure hours might be spent smoking a pipe, sitting around talking or telling tales, or just reflecting on things. Old men performed the more time-consuming chores of making fishing nets and carving wooden bowls and ladles.[39]

This has been a brief description of life in the Lenape world at the time the Dutch arrived. Many of these practices still continue today, but in modern forms and settings not always recognizable to outsiders. To really understand the Lenape people, one must have some understanding of the nature of their ancient languages— Munsee, Unami, Renneiu, and the old Mohican—which are discussed in the following chapter.

10

SWEET AND FULL
OF MEANING

The Languages of Manhattan

It is easy to blame the Dutch businessmen working out of Manhattan for failing to learn the language of the land, and instead forcing the Natives to learn their foreign tongue. If they had learned to speak Lenape as respectful visitors would, much of the fighting would have been prevented, and the philosophically and ecologically superior culture of the Lenape would have been better preserved, regardless of the outcome of wars. How the preservation of this language would have changed the course of history is hard to say, but one can easily imagine that its preservation as part of our folk culture would have enriched our cultural diversity and understanding of our relationship to the land.

The fact is that European arrivals encountered a bewildering conflux of Lenape-related languages in and around Manhattan from the time of Henry Hudson onward. In 1609 there were four major Algonquin languages in the area, each with its own dialects, some of which were in transition at the time. These four are each among the most difficult languages in the world to learn.[1] They are Munsee, Unami, Renneiu, and Mohican.

Mohican is the oldest form of the four, dating back to at least 1000 B.C.E. if not earlier; Munsee is next oldest, dating to 1000 C.E., Unami is third oldest, dating back to 1100 or 1200 C.E. and Renneiu is newest, dating back to 1300 C.E. Each of these distinct languages was born from the one before it, mixed with the influences of not just the Mississippian mound-building civilization, which has Mayan roots, but the Caribbean as well, adopting fragments of words from the Taino. The Renneiu language is a mixture of these four, plus the *r* substitution, which originated with the Incas of Peru perhaps two thousand years ago, and reached Manhattan only a few hundred years before the arrival of the Dutch. The *r* replaces *l* in words of Munsee or Unami origin, and replaces *n* in words of Mohican or Massachusetts origin. This new conglomerate language was emerging as the language of choice when the Dutch arrived, and was spreading to other Long Island nations in1609. The language was even spreading throughout the Hudson Valley among the Esopus Munsee at the time of contact. Renneiu dialects in New York State included Canarsie, Rockaway, Matinecock, Wappingers, Siwanoy, and Manhattan. With so many languages and dialects, it is no wonder the Dutch were bewildered.

In order to address this problem, albeit belatedly, I wish to offer an introductory guide to the languages of the Native New Yorkers. A brief Munsee vocabulary appears in Appendix I. Here then are my observations.

THE SOUND OF THE OCEAN

One early Dutch observer described the sounds of Lenape language as "sweet and full of meaning." William Penn wrote, "Their language is lofty yet narrow . . . in signification full; one word serveth in the place of three."[2] My own experience with the Algonquin way of speaking certainly confirms these observations. There is nothing in the English language to compare it with. Sometimes it is hypnotic, like the sound of the ocean. At other times it is rapid-fire like the call of the thrush. Only a few Englishmen can make their language sing like that, but most fluent Algonquin speakers can.

A Complex Grammar

With all the forms of respect to be shown to each type of person we might meet, all of which are built into the language, the grammar is so complex that it can't be dealt with here except in a simplistic way. In John Eliot's book of 1666, *The Indian Grammar Begun*, he examines grammar in the Mohican-related Massachusetts language. In his "grammar" he conjugates the verb *koowac*, "to keep" for example, 440 times, producing over 75 variations on the root word. In *America*, a book written and published by John Ogilby in 1671, one unattributed account said that the occupants of the region (New England) "have no grammar whatsoever." In fact, the grammar was so complex that it seemed to be nonexistent.

Hand Signing

Much of Lenape communication is nonverbal. Facial expressions, gestures, and body language are deliberate parts of Lenape communication, and range from the obvious and simple to the highly elaborate and complex. These visual cues are considered a great art form and are part of the vanishing heritage of the Munsee nation. In the right circumstances, these gestures can speak volumes, either with or without accompanying audible speech.

It is therefore not surprising that Lenape were and still are masters of Native American Sign Language, a codified nonverbal language system that allowed those from unrelated nations to make treaties together. As premiere scouts and translators of the old West, the Delaware descendants of the Native New Yorkers made constant use of Native American Sign Language.

Native Americans were the only people to develop a continent-wide hand-signing language. It was so logical and effective that it, along with the French system, was adopted as a basis for today's American Sign Language.[3]

Let's take for example an expression today's New Yorkers say all the time, "Thanks, you made my day!" This can be expressed in Native American Sign Language as follows: "Thanks" is shown with the right hand sweeping upward and out toward your friend until the palm faces him. The hand bounces slightly at the top. To indicate "you," point to the person you are speaking to. To indicate "make," hold your right wrist with your left hand and make chopping motions. "My" is shown by pointing to your heart. "Day" is shown with the right hand making the sign for "sun" with the circular "okay" sign (thumb and forefinger in a circle) and then sweeping from right to left in an arc that reaches from the shoulder to a point just above the head. In any such signs involving the passage of a day, the right shoulder is dawn, the head is apparent noon, and the left shoulder is dusk. The moon is represented by a large letter **c**, the thumb and forefinger far apart, sweeping also in an arc. This can be used to show the time of night, or a month's time.

Now you know how to say, "Thanks, you made my day" to any Native American signer. However, a Native signer would be more likely to say, "Thank you, you make sunshine in my heart" (since only the Creator can "make" a day). The same signs are used as in "you make my day," only reversing "my" and "day." Day becomes "sunshine" and "my" becomes "my heart."[4]

In Native American Sign Language, "I love you" is both hands crossed over the heart. However, if the situation is not so good, and you want to say, "Don't rat on me" or "Don't talk about me like that," point to your mouth with the forefinger and middle finger of the right hand, then point to the left in sharp, jabbing motions, then in pantomime, throw something to the ground with that same hand. This will send a clear message that the words are bad and should be discarded.[5]

EVERYDAY EXPRESSIONS

The most common everyday expression in most languages is "hello," but Munsee does not have such a word. Zeisberger translates "I salute you" as *Quan-go-mael,* but this has been given a variety of interpretations. The most common greeting is *"Koo-la-mool-see?"* (or *koolamoolthee*), which means "How are you feeling?" The Micmac, Algonquin of the northern variety, have no hello either but say *"May-dah-lain?",* which also means, "How are you feeling?" The more emphatic Micmac expression *"Maydaleeoolain?"* implies many such questions, such as "How has the world been treating you?" but no one I know seems to know the Munsee equivalent. Again, as with the Micmac, there is a different suffix to this greeting depending on whom you are talking to and how many people are in the room. For simplification, you can add "Hutch!" to the end to refer to the second person singular in Munsee.

When it is time to go, there is no word for good-bye. The Munsee say *"Xu-la-pitch-k'naew-wooxlth!"* (The *l* is soft as in Welsh.) It means, "See you again!" As with the expression *"Upnamooltess"* among my people, the Micmac, there is no final parting, even in death. We are all part of a great and endless circle of life, and there is no good-bye. In a world without time, there is no final separation. And again, there is always a different suffix to *"Xu-la-pitch-k'naew-wooxlth!"* depending on who you are talking to. The proper response is a hearty "Yuh!"

The next most common expression in most languages is "Thank you," and the Munsee has many forms of this. The easiest and most common is the ancient form, which has derived from the Mohican *"oo-nee-weh."* The Munsee substitute the *n* with an *l* as usual, and say *"oo-lee-weh!"* There are many ways to say thank you as there is much to be grateful for in this life. However, there is no word for please, at least in Munsee or Unami as it is spoken today, and I would say, rarely used in English by people with an Algonquin first language. If you need something, you ask for it, without shame and without lowering yourself before another person.

SPIRITUAL WORDS IN MUNSEE

The Munsee had a rich spiritual life, and it is still reflected in their ancient language today. The correct pronunciation of the often-used word for the Creator is *Mun-ih-toh* (the stressed letter *i* is like that in *fix*). When speaking to the Munsee, the missionaries would use the word *Mun-ih-to* as the word for the devil, and insist they translate it as such in their own speech. This divided the people as it turned all traditional Munsee into devil-worshipers and caused a lot of confusion, which remains to the present day.

For centuries, the people of Manhattan and all of Lenape Hoking *meel-lelx* "gave" *k'shah'taeo* "tobacco," *woounj(w)tea-hu(n)g* "from the heart" to the *keek-ess*, "elders," for them to share their *Le-na-pay wap-see-q'n*, "Indian medicine." They would ask them to share their *ex-la-tcheen-wing-suk*, "many stories," both *whuss-ka* and *xo-wee-aeoh*, "new and old." They thought of them as *xspo-waeo*, "wisdom keepers" (someone with wisdom) and listened carefully to them as they were *a-kxun-dja-lee-te-haeo*, "thinking their big thoughts," to try to understand. They were taught that it was good to possess the *mask-ka-neh-so* or "personal strength" of *ma-xo-mis maxk(w)* "grandfather bear," tempered with the patience of *ma-xo-mis tal-le-ga*, grandfather crane, and *ma-xo-mis t'kxwaqx*, "grandfather turtle."

The Munsee *keek-ess*, "elders," taught that *Mun-ih-toh*, "Creator" was *no-la-lee-huk* "good," and that all life was *tay-tee-owq(w)*, "a circle," that included all *wes-suk* "creatures," all *no-la-lee-huk*, "good!" They called this way of life the "red road," which could be said *mox-kaeoh aan-esh*. But the missionary's *max-pom-beel*, "black book," said that the ways of the forest, *ko-pee*, were evil. The missionized Munsee no longer *gkunt-ta-kaeo* "danced" in the *wax-aeo* "moonlight" around a big fire, *a-kxun-dja tun-daeoh* wearing the *may-sing-gwaeoh,* "Tree Spirit Mask," one of the faces of *Mun-ih-toh*. Other unconverted Munsee continued with their *a-kxun-dja-wee-kee-wam,* "Big House Ceremony," which made their Christian friends very *men-no(n)k-suk,* or angry.

Today a majority of the Munsee in Canada are church-going Christians, however there is a growing feeling that one can be Christian and yet still be proud of the great Munsee spiritual tradition that has been preserved from thousands of years ago. However, the use of the word *Man-ih-toh* still causes confusion. These traditional words were taught to me by Beulah Timothy (nee Snake) of Moraviantown, Ontario, who is a church-going Munsee Delaware woman.

New York Slang and Street Expressions That May Have Munsee/Algonquin Roots

New York City may be the slang capital of the world. One hears every type of expression sooner or later, and they come from all over the world—from Italy, Israel, England, Africa, the American South, and Puerto Rico. It shouldn't be surprising then that some of these expressions may have come from pre-Columbian New York—in fact, they may never have left.

A lot of our street expressions are strikingly similar to literal translations of Munsee lingo. Others may come from the closely related tribes of the Algonquin, especially in the South. As Americans, our first reaction is to suppose that the Algonquin heard these Americanisms and copied them, translating them into their own language. However, these same expressions, as translated here, show up in Algonquin tongues in the most remote areas of northern Canada where French is the only European tongue spoken, and sparsely if at all. It therefore stands to reason that some "American" slang comes from the First Americans, rather than the other way around.

Sure Thing

For example, the expression, "for sure," (or "fer sure," as is often heard west of the Rockies) with an upward nod of the head, is found in Munsee as "*keh-la-wak!*" *Keh-la* means "for," *wak* means "sure." The quizzical expression, "You sure?" with shoulders hunched up, would be stated, "*Keh-la-hon-eh?*" in Munsee. The famous New York expression "Fu'geddaboutit!", said with a brush-off gesture, is a direct translation of the Munsee slang expression, "*Wun-ess-ee-il!*", which literally means "Forget about it!" As with the English equivalent, it can be used in two or three different senses: the literal, "Don't even think about it"; the warning, "Don't try anything"; or the generous, "No need to repay me."

All Shook Up

Another expression that is understood perfectly among the Munsee is "he has cold feet"—about getting married, or about taking an unpopular position in politics, for example. "*Saa-see-te-pok*" in Munsee means "he has cold feet." The slang term "all shook up" was made famous by a Cherokee singer, Elvis Presley, who came to New York City once or twice,. This may be a Native American expression. "*Nun-geeh-loh!*" in Munsee means "I'm all shaken," or "I'm all shook up!" over something.

Family Ties

A lot of people in New York today refer to their wives as "my ol' lady," and their husbands as "my ol' man," never stopping to think where that turn of phrase came from. Those are both common Algonquin "slang" terms. In Munsee "*Kee-tox-kwee-sum*" is literally "your old lady," and "*K-meeh-loh-sum*" means "your old man," both referring to your spouse. Street people say "li'l ol' man," to refer to an elderly fellow, usually with affection, or a mixture of affection and derision. In Munsee there is the expression, "*Loo-shish*," a "little old man."

When the preacher intones, "My brothers and sisters…" hand out, palms angled up, there is some Biblical precedent of course. However, some country preachers may be unknowingly passing along a customary Native American greeting, which in Munsee is "*Neem-tes-suk!*" or "My brothers and sisters…" which is how any good oration begins. "*The* brothers and sisters" is also a street expression used in New York City, referring to the community, in the same manner as it is used by the Algonquin.

Youse Guys

In Algonquin's complex grammatical system there are several forms of the second person: you singular, you plural, and apparently others. "I give to you" and "you give to me," might use different forms of "you" or "*kee*." In Old English, the translation of the second person plural was easier, as "ye" was plural and "you" singular. In Munsee, the word for you singular is *kee*, whereas the plural form of you (youse) is *kee-loo-wa*. Today, when speaking English, the Munsee in Ontario say youse consistently when speaking to more than one person, whereas the Munsee and Unami in Oklahoma consistently say you-all (yawl) in the same situation, perpetuating their conscientious and precisely diplomatic sense of language into whatever tongue they are made to speak. I can't help but believe that this particular "trademark" of New York City speech, the notorious "youse guys," has at least some of its roots in Native American speaking habits.[6]

I Swear

Many slang expressions are designed to help us deal with anger or frustration. The expression "I swear!" is a common Munsee expression of frustration as well, "*N'mat-town-he.*" This might be said, as in English, with one hand in a fist, though not threateningly. When someone is confusing us, we say, "Wait a minute. You lost me!" The ancient Munsee had no word for minute, but say "*Ktaan-hee!*" "You lost me!" with a brushoff from the forehead, nonetheless. When someone tells us something we don't believe, we express our incredulousness with "Oh really?" said with a contortion of the face. In Munsee it is "*Kehl-ah-ha?*" "*Ah-ha!*" means "really!" To tell a "yarn" in English is to tell a long story. In Munsee they say "*Aay-laa-tchee-mu-moh*," telling a "yarn" too. If the yarn is meant to deceive, we might say "He's faking! He's making it all up!" The Munsee expression "*Noh-lee-ton*" is translated as "He's faking. He's making it all up!" The expression "I flattened that guy," means you hit him and he either fell down or was "flattened" in some metaphorical way. In Munsee, the same expression exists: "*Pak-hee-tae-how,*" (the *p* is soft) or "I hit/flattened him!"

When someone is being foolish, we often say they're "crazy," or "going crazy." In Munsee these two terms are linked in the single word "*K'petch-eh!*", or "he is crazy/foolish." The term "nuthouse" in American slang is found in Munsee as "crazy-house," or "*K'petch-e-hoo-wee-kan,*" although this would have been from later times, since the Native Americans did not believe in shutting up and jailing those who were troubled, or needed help. The word for "he's in jail" is "*K'paa-haa-so,*" or "he is behind closed doors," or "he is shut up." The reference to the "shut door" as jailer is indicative of the Algonquin distaste for being indoors altogether. It is also reminiscent of the door-related slang terms we have for jail: "slammer," "lock-up," or "behind bars."

BAD MEDICINE

Americans use the metaphor "spoiled rotten" to refer to a child who is "snotty." The Munsee use the expression "*Match-ee-leh-oo,*" which means "He is spoiled rotten [like a bad apple]." When we get frustrated with someone, we may say a four-letter word referring to what a cow or dog leaves behind. This expression is surprisingly universal. The Munsee say "*moy,*" and when peeved might employ the expression *"K'moy-end!"* which implies, "Oh, poop on you!" or something to that effect. We might say about this person, "He's a whiner!" The Munsee say *"Nee-**laaw**-soo!"* This means "one who is whining [like a dog] all the time." That person might say about us, "He is a gossip. He spreads 'the dirt' around!" The Munsee (and many Algonquin peoples) honor the earth, but employ this same use of the word "dirty," not in regard to sex, but to someone who spreads "bad medicine." In Munsee, the expression is *"Neesk-**toon**-hey-oh"* or "He talks dirty, he spreads dirt." The word for "dirt" as in "What's the dirt on so and so?" is *"Neesk-ay-oh."* "He's no good!" (or "up to no good") is *"Maa-tchee-**meen**"* in Munsee. The colloquial term "He is useless" translates into Munsee as *"Mak-wek-laoo-tay-oo."*

The term "not right in the head" is probably of Native American origin, spoken *"Waa-**laant**-peh-oh!"* in Munsee. Another similar term is "He has a big head!" This is an ancient Native American teaching about vanity and pride. *"**Waant**-peh-oh!"* means "He has a big head," a "swelled head," or "he has a big ego." I have heard the nickname "Walking Eagle" to refer to someone who is "full of themselves," so burdened they can't fly. Sometimes such a person will be addressed in street slang as "big guy," "Mr. Big," "big shot," or "Big man." In Munsee, the word is *"**Wat**-tchee-len-no,"* "big man," although it could be a compliment, depending on the inflection, referring to someone of importance.

An Essential Phrase for Travelers

When visitors to New York are trying to be delicate, they might say "and where's your little room?" or "where's your outhouse?" (Some refer to it as "the smallest room in the house.") Women might say, "I have to go to the little room and powder my nose," all of which are meant to suggest that the call of nature is imminent. During colonial times, the Munsee imitated the politeness of the whites and developed the expression "little house" to refer to the "outhouse" in a flowery way. This term is still used today in Munsee country to refer to a bathroom: "*Week-waam-ush,*" "the little wigwam." As with the English equivalent, it can be spoken with the knees together, the universally understood nonverbal gesture of urgency.[7]

TIMELESS EXPRESSIONS

A few Lenape words are still in use today in New York, but their meanings have changed. A geek is someone who is not very *with it* today, but the Lenape used *geek* to mean "him." Perhaps when the first Dutch appeared with their pale white faces, their quill pens and pantaloons, the Lenape pointed at them and said "*Leenkway geek!*" ("Look at him!") and a New York phrase was coined.[8]

The word *wonk* is a very trendy word in New York these days. It is generally used to refer to a giant in any particular field. Donald Trump is referred to as a real estate wonk. Betty Ballantine is referred to as a publishing wonk. Frank Cashen is a baseball wonk, and so forth. The Upper East Side was called *Rechgawonk* in Lenape times, That's where all the rich "wonks" live.[9]

Another similar word that has survived in New York is the suffix for he, she, or it is, *ay-yoo.* It appears at the end of any Unami word where "it is" or "it is like" is appropriate, such as *tan-ghann-ay-yoo*—"it is a little creek," *ap-ton-ay-yoo*—"he is speaking," or *ho-bo-ay-yoo*—"he is smoking the pipe," which is where Hoboken, New Jersey gets its name. The Munsee ending *-aeoh* means the same thing.

All four directions have this suffix, for example *lo-wan-ay-yoo* means "it is to the north" and *shaw-wan-ay-yoo,* "it is to the south." If there were Lenape weather report shows, the suffix would appear a lot. *Mech-a-tay-yoo* means "it is deep snow," *pee-mok-way-yoo* means "it is raining," *was-san-day-oo* means "it is a clear day," *woa-pa-nay-yoo,* "it is morning" or possibly "it is first light" (*woa-pa* is light, *nay* is first, and *ay-yoo,* it is). *Wal-un-day-yoo* is "a warm day," probably an imitation of the English "warm day."[10] Passamaquoddy uses the same ending in some words, for example, in the words for the seasons: *Niponeeoo,* "It is summer"; *Siqoneeoo,* "It is spring"; and *Pooneeoo,* "It is winter."

The names of animals are usually descriptive, and therefore include a lot of "it is": *Met-tum-may-yoo,* "it is a wolf"; *mo-ay-can-ay-yoo,* "dog" (or "it is like a wolf"); *mon-ach-gay-yoo,* "it is a ground hog" (or probably a picture word describing the groundhog).

When you give directions on how to find a certain trail in the woods, you can use this suffix: *Schachachgeu,* "it is straight"; *schindee-kay-yoo,* "it is plentiful with spruce"; *see-hee-lay-yoo,* "it is falling water" (probably another picture-word describing the scene); *wees-a-way-yoo,* "it is yellow" or "it is the color of [a flower?]."

So next time you're in Manhattan and a New Yorker storms up to you and says, *"Ay, you!"* you can answer sweetly, "Why yes it is!"[11]

RULES FOR STORYTELLING

Storytelling is an important part of life in Manhattan. People tell stories about great moments in sports, where they were when the lights went out, what they were doing when John F. Kennedy died, and especially all the trials and tribulations they had getting to work this morning.

The old Munsee storytellers spoke directly to the person listening, and spontaneously changed the story to impart some bit of wisdom to the listener. They seldom told a story the same way twice. Traditional Algonquin stories circle around slowly like distant eagles seen through the trees. You sometimes have to strain your ears to keep track of the story line. The story line might dwell on one idea or image and repeat it several times, and then jump to a different subject entirely. It's been said that much of the old-time storytelling styles have more to do with modern hypnosis than modern fiction. The old yarn-weavers were skilled at setting a mood, taking you into another world, sometimes the world of their own irrational dreams, then snapping you back to reality with a surprise ending.

In his introduction to *The White Deer and Other Stories Told by the Lenape*, John Bierhorst goes into detail about the rules of Lenape storytelling. He writes:

> Generally the time for telling was after dark and almost always during the coldest months. That stories must be told only in winter is a very old rule, widespread in native America. Delaware used to say that if tales were told out of season, "the bugs would chase you" or "all the worms would take after you." Some said the ground had to be frozen: if it were not, and if stories were told, snakes and lizards would crawl into bed with you. As explained by others, there should be stories only "when things around cannot hear" never in summer, when "everything is awake." According to one source, if you do tell stories in summer, you need to announce beforehand, "I'm sitting on twelve skunk skins." This is sufficient to ward off the harmful creatures, so they will not crawl all over you.
>
> It is said, however, that there are two kinds of stories, real and fictional. The fictional tale, or (in the Unami language) *athiluhakan,* is the one that must be told only in the winter. Stories about real people or real events can be told any time. . . . In the view of one knowledgable traditionalist, tales about the trickster *Wehixamukes* are "winter stories." But another authority, equally knowledgeable, when asked point blank if a Wehixamukes story is an *athiluhakan,* replies, cautiously, "Well now, wasn't there really a *Wehixamukes?*" [12]

The absence of rigid boundaries between fictional events and real ones, dreams and reality, exaggeration and fact, makes it difficult to make or keep rules in Lenape traditional life. However it is from within that gray area that the Lenape draw their power, and it makes their stories powerful. Here is a story about the creation of the human race, which explains how evil came into existence. Like most Lenape stories, it has a teaching and a surprise ending.

> Sky Woman had a daughter. She told her daughter, "Whatever you do, don't go toward the setting sun!" but she went west anyway.

The West Wind was meant to be her husband at a future time, but she was still too small and it knocked her down, and in doing so, made her pregnant. She had two sons, one bad and one good. The daughter died giving birth, and became Tobacco Woman. The evil son claimed that the other son killed the daughter. Grandmother had never heard a lie before. The world was so new, that no one had thought of it before. Sky Woman was so upset, she left the earth, rose up into the sky and became Grandmother Moon.

The good son told the bad one that he had said something untrue. The bad son lied again and said that he didn't. The argument went on, and they agreed to play the peach pit game, a form of gambling, to decide who was right. Split peach pits were painted black on one side and white on the other. They were placed in a bowl and tossed, just as in Hubbub, which uses shell disks. A combination of three or four of the same color would win. The evil son was sure he would win and take over the world. The good son prayed to the Great Spirit for help. If he lost, life on earth would have ended, just as soon as it had begun. When it came his turn, he tossed the peach pits way up in the air. As it turns out, the chickadees had made their heads the peach pits, and rose up singing, flying away so that he would win. And that is why the world still exists today, and why there are still liars.[13]

NUMBERS

Numbers have mystical significance in Algonquin life, especially the numbers one through twelve. There are twelve levels to the spirit world, twelve layers of clouds in the Lenape sky, twelve posts in the Big House (a larger longhouse used for important ceremonies), twelve days in the great ceremony. The number seven is of equal importance to twelve because there are seven directions in Algonquin spirituality, the four cardinal points on the horizon, up and down, plus the journey to the center.

But the other numbers each have great significance too. Seeing three deer carries a different message than seeing nine, although that meaning will shift from place to place and person to person. Numbers one through ten are most important, as it is the number of fingers on both hands. A complete number chart appears at the end of this section. Here are my own insights into each of the numbers one through seven and how they tend to enter into pan-Algonquin spiritual teachings. They will be stated in Munsee/Unami. (Again, the Munsee pronounciation is based on Beulah Timothy's.) This is only an introduction, as deeper levels of teachings should remain unwritten.

The number one, *goh-tah/goo-tee*, represents the oneness of all life, and that we all came from one original source, the sun. This oneness is embodied by the Native expression, "All my relations." The stone people, the tree people, the plant people, the birds, fish, and mammals, all are one family and we are a part of it. That is the core teaching. Another way to say it in Unami is *mai-auch-so-woa-gan,* "unity." We walk the higher road, *po-kway-way-chen,* to find that original spiritual source, and in doing so, walk close with the Creator. The expression *Mun-ih-to-woa-gan* refers to "spiritual strength" or the power of one who walks close with the Creator.

The number two, *neesh-shaw/neesh-schee* represents the male and female, father sky and "mother earth" *gahowes hakee,* in Unami. All nature celebrates the male-female polarity in a great variety of ways. The spirit of all males and fathers is represented by the sky and the color blue. The spirit of all females and mothers is represented by the earth and the color green. The yin-yang teachings of China are very much in spirit with the Algonquin teachings of polarity.

The number three, *n'xah (or n'xo(n))/na-tcha,* has to do with the trinity of life, which is father sky, mother earth, and ourselves as the baby. We are the child of the universe, and when we are in a sacred space, such as in the sweat lodge or fasting in ceremony, dwelling in our *oo-tchee-tchan,* "soul" or "spirit," we are the third part of the Algonquin trinity. We are the sons and daughters of God. That spark of the Creator of love and peace of heart is in all of us, and it makes us holy and sacred. What we do with that determines the course of our lives and of history. It all comes down to us. This relationship we have with father sky and mother earth is expressed in the saying, "We are created for some great purpose or design," or in Unami, *gay-mooch-wee-lay-lay-mook-hoom-men-nah.*

The number four, *naeo-wa/nay-woo* is embodied by the four directions, going clockwise: east, south, west, and north. There is a fourness to everything, if one has the eyes to see it. There are four parts to the self—the body, heart, mind, and spirit, and each one is linked to a direction and a color. The four colors are usually red, white, yellow, and black, in a variety of orders and attributions. There are four ways of seeing the world—through the five senses, or through emotion, reason, and intuition. There are four phases of the wheel of life, childhood 0–15 years, youth 15–30 years, middle age 30–45 years, and elder 45–60 years.[14] Before pollution and disease, people often took another turn around the wheel, living to 120, but even then no one ever began the third hoop—it was easier to stop at 120 winters and start over in another lifetime. The meaning of the number four is endless in this world. When the Lenape perform ceremony, they will often thank the four directions in turn, standing at the center. When you stand in a circle it is called *woch-a-ga-po-ae* in Unami. When you honor all four directions, you are honoring the intricate balance of all life.

The number five, *noa-lin/pa-le-nach,* makes us remember that we are in the center of the four directions. In ancient times the young Algonquin men would go on a long walkabout[15] journey to the four directions of the world, represented by the colors red, white, yellow, and black. According to story, they would make a great circle all over Turtle Island, bringing back a passport or signature stone from a far-away place to prove they were there. The number five is the journey back home to the invisible center for which there is no color.

The number six, *gut-tash/goot-tash* is the universe in all its splendor. It is the six colors (red, white, yellow, black, green, and blue), the six directions of the spheres within spheres in which we live. We could spend an entire lifetime exploring the beauty of the six directions and never be finished, such is its variety. The Unami expression *Ay-dja-djan wah-nee-shee* is appropriate, because it means, "Wherever you go, may the way be beautiful for you."

The number seven, *neesh-shash /nisch-ash* the most sacred number of all, represents the whole circle of the Medicine Wheel, the entire visible universe, plus the return to the invisible at the core center where everything comes together, *mah-way-nay-men*. It represents not only the journey out into the world, but the journey inside to find the self. It includes the same six colors of the six outward directions, but it is invisible. We know white light contains all the colors of the rainbow, which is the bridge to the other world and the bond between all nations in peace. The Medicine Wheel is a compass designed to help us find our self. I have often said that the compasses of the white explorers led them out to the four horizons, away from themselves and their true center, whereas the Medicine Wheel guides the people on their journey back to themselves. The word *gee-tchee-toon* means "one's final destination" and expresses the completeness of the number seven.

No Word for *The*

The Lenape of the seventeenth century had a very different way of seeing the world than most Americans and Canadians do today. The best method of knowing this for certain is to study the language. Lenape is a very experiential and relational language. Their way of using words reinforces a more ecological or holistic way of looking at the world. Algonquin city builders avoided walls wherever possible. They cut off the viewer from seeing the world in its fullness. It has often been speculated by archaeologists, not philosophers, that the

lack of fortifications in Algonquin settlements indicates the importance of diplomacy, communication, and language. Study of the
language confirms this. Some of the basic barrier words we use today
to form walls around our concepts are missing as well. Take for
example, one of the most important and often-used words in the
English language, *the.*

There is no word for *the* in Lenape, nor does it appear in other
Algonquin languages. The article *a* appears, just as it does in French
and other European languages as the number one. In French, when
you say "a boy" you say *un garcon,* in other words "one boy." The same
is true in Lenape. You'd say, "*Nay-ta len-no-teet.*" However if you
wanted to say "the boy" in French, you would say "le garcon," whereas
you can't say that in Lenape.

The Lenape language wants to know: "Which boy?" "Who is his
father and mother?" "How old is he?" "How is he related to the
speaker?" The word *the,* if heard through the ears of a Lenape speaker
of hundreds of years ago, would probably sound rather odd. This
word acts as a conceptual barrier. It answers all those questions
emphatically without actually telling you anything.[16]

When you can't use *the,* it forces you to answer the questions that
are so important to human relationships: what, where, when, how,
and who? These are pieces of information that open our hearts and
minds. They pique our interest. Aspiring writers would do well to
think hard before using *the* in a sentence. "*The* vase" is flat and col-
orless, whereas "*my* favorite," "*your* old," "*this* remarkable," or "*that*
beautiful," vase sounds much more inspired.

Many early missionaries had a difficult time trying to tell the
Algonquins that the church had "*the* way, *the* truth, *the* light." They
couldn't say it in Lenape. They would have had to say, "a way, a truth,
a light" or even more equanimical, "my way, my truth, my light."
When these same missionaries went to talk to the Lenape about "*the*
Son of God," the Lenape probably heard, "*a* son," or literally "*one* son

of God" and probably agreed to join up so that they could learn how to be one too.

Most of all, *the* prevents intimacy and blocks emotion. Doctors know this, and when talking to a cancer patient, will often use *the* to refer to the patient's body, organs, and disease. They will say, "The cancer in the body is no longer in remission. The survival rate for *the* type of cancer involved is, say 60 percent over ten years." What they are trying to say is, "You have cancer and you're probably going to die if you don't do something." That's probably how an old Lenape sweat doctor would have said it. The word *the* makes it all sound like a math problem and nothing to worry about.

Likewise the media talks about "*the* environment," "*the* pollution in the air," "*the* chemicals in the water," when what they are talking about is *your* environment, *your* children's air and water. People talk about *the* weather, but we really mean *our* weather, as the climate is different on the other side of the continent.

Lenape is an oral language, not a literate one, therefore, the speaker and the spoken-to are always both present in the room. Instead of "open the window," a Lenape can say, "open window" and then point to which one. This would be correct and would help engage the listener with visual cues. If they said "Open one window," it would indicate that it didn't matter which one.

The is also used to indicate superiority and exclusivity. New York City's jargon is full of them. People say "The City," "The Big Apple," "The Mayor," "The Village," "The Neighborhood," "The Lower East Side," "The Upper East Side," "The Ferry," or "The Garden." When seen anthropologically, such nomenclature exposes a shocking degree of ethnocentricity, as most of these designations have counterparts across "The River" and elsewhere.

What makes this teaching of relativity so emphatic in the language is that the root word may change slightly as you switch from his/her/its to my/your/our as a suffix. Root words are really little sentences filled with verbs and adjectives, and they can change. In fact, there are few if any nouns in Algonquin languages, a fact that dwarfs the *the* problem in its implications. Not only do these words not exist except in relation to other things, they don't really exist period. They act in relationship to other things. Tracking down the core reality behind Lenape language is like trying to pinpoint the concrete center of an atomic particle in quantum physics. Everything is in relationship to everything else. You can't find *the* center, *the* origin, because there's no *the* there. Without *the*, there is no way to see the world without being part of that which you are looking at. Lenape and other Algonquin languages revel in this fact, and force you to take part in the drama of life around you, to get your hands dirty.

FEELING WORDS

Trying to bridge the gap of understanding between two very different cultures is never easy. Some things translate directly, like "to eat" (*gemeze* in Mohican), but most Algonquin-English translations require explanation. Translating emotion words is tricky; some feelings are universal, some specific to the culture. It is said that during war times, when Algonquin men and women were tortured by enemies in battle, they would not cry out; to do so would allow the enemy to capture their spirit, or to truly defeat them and their emotions. This does not indicate a lack of feeling but rather the importance of feeling in Algonquin culture. Only by living and working with Algonquin people can this gap be bridged, but language can be a starting place. The root word for feeling in Unami is *len-dam*. These two syllables show up in almost every word describing emotion.

Ach-kee-len-dam means "to feel melancholy." Gan-schay-len-dam is used to express wonder, "to feel amazement," while la-chaoo-way-len-dam means "to feel concerned." Mee-way-len-dam-mau-weel means "forgive me," while Mee-way-len-dam-moa-ga indicates "forgiveness."

N'ha-chay-way-len-dam-men means "I feel hope." *Nee-poos-gay-len-da-men* means "to feel glad, merry," and *noh-lay-len-dam* means "I rejoice." *Pach-gay-len-dam* means "to feel angry."

LENAPE FAREWELL

Shortly after 1782, almost immediately after the Americans won the revolution against Britain that the Lenape had helped them fight, the Americans declared that all Lenapes and Mohicans were to be removed from the New York region. Most had left New York City by then, but this new removal pertained to the entire area as far north as Albany. Land was set aside in the new territory of Missouri, and the Lenape were expected to walk the entire distance. Most Lenape made other plans, but all had to leave. Only those who could pass for white and assimilate into the culture and economic system of the white world could stay as unwelcome guests in their own home.

As a monologue to be read with music as part of a dance scene in a play by Eileen Charbonneau, I created a poem in Unami Delaware and English to capture the sorrow of that final moment when the Lenape gathered to say farewell to all their friends and relatives, and even their enemies. Now that all were without land, such disputes must have seemed irrelevant and hollow to them. I hope the following poem will help convey the emotional experience of a removal treaty that the history books have made to sound so reasonable.

YOU AND I ARE LIKE WATER

(In Unami and English)

Ni woch ki alinaquat m'bi (umpee)
You and I are like water.
Ni woch ki alinaquat m'bi.
Coos tchupik tekenuk
achsuanl tchupik ni-wachtschuk

The pines are rooted in our forests
the stones are rooted in our mountains
the corn is rooted in our soil
chasquaysem tchupik nihakki
ees nee woch ki
but you and I
ailnaquat m'bit!
are like water!

Gilunoo matta'tschupik hakki
We have no earthly roots
woch achtchin messochwi!
and must keep running!
ejajan
whereever you go
ejajan
mamschali, mamschali
remember me! remember me!

Ni woch ki, alinaquat m'bi
You and I are like water
ni woch ki, alinaquat m'bi
alinaquat sheepoos
our lives like tiny streams
messachwe
running downhill
mogowoa gitchitoon!
no one knows where we end up!

Lill!
Tell me!
Delli tchanindewogan

What's the difference
between you and me . . . and the water?
ni woch ki . . . woch m'bi?
Mochwa!
Nothing!

Luewak achtchin aan
They say that we must leave
achtchin aan, aan woole-hakki
that we must leave, leave this sacred land!

Al pepetelaan,
Like a shower of rain,
pimuchquayu wachtschuk
pee-etchookw
we are turned from these mountains
by changing winds
and can't return
mo-ma-tschil
mamschali!

Ni woch ki tchanind seepoo
You and I are from different rivers
ees ootchitchan giluna liniquat!
but inside we are the same!
Our hearts split like wood!
Ktehena pachat tachan!
We cut our hair in mourning!
Gisch kschummen milach
Giluna pomsi aney metelen
We walk a humble path
ees geesquey machtapeek
but this is the hardest day of all!

Delli aan?
Where will we go?
Ni woch ki mochwa wikooum!
You and I have no home!
Ejajan!
Wherever you go
Mamschali! Mamschali!
Remember me! Remember me!
Mamschali! Mamschali!

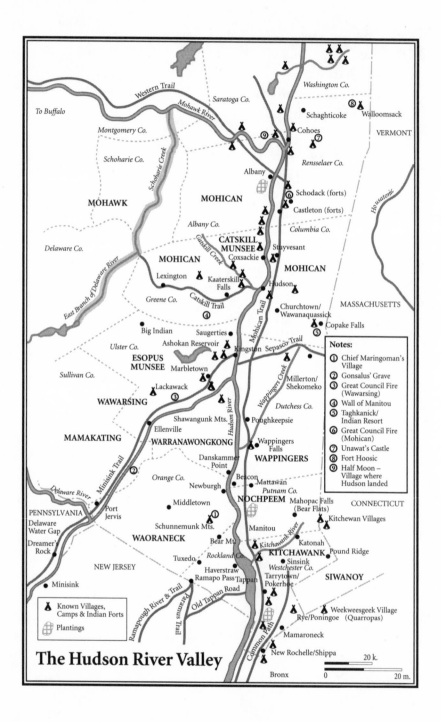

The Hudson River Valley

11

NATIVE NEW YORKERS EAST OF THE HUDSON RIVER

A Trip through Westchester, Putnam, and Dutchess Counties

There are many stories about the Hudson Valley, with its lush landscape of great rivers, waterfalls, mountains, and sheer cliffs. One of the most remarkable movements in American art began when an artist from New York discovered Kaaterskill Falls along an old Indian trail[1] and painted it. The Hudson River School was born from that one painting, as thousands of artists flocked to the Catskills to see for themselves if such beauty could be real. The great-grandchildren of those artists, and of some of those Indians, are still living in the Catskills today.

With their spectacular vistas, there is something very healing about these mountains. This visual beauty was greatly appreciated by even the most stalwart Munsee warrior or sachem. Often choosing stony silence while living and working in the village, an Algonquin man might become dramatically eloquent upon encountering a magnificent valley or waterfall. Even these "stony" types cultivated an emotional relationship with Mother Earth, and felt a strong connection, especially with the land of their birth. The Munsee often located and maintained permanent village sites for the sake of a suberb view as much as for defensibility and proximity of resources.[2] For many Munsee, this majestic view from the open flap of the wigwam was not one of the Delaware Valley, but of the Hudson Valley, or the land in between.

These two great rivers, the Delaware and the Hudson, were both central to the life and ways of the Munsee. They occupied, navigated, and revered the Delaware River from the Raritan, in the south, to Binghamton in the north where it forks east and west as one travels upriver. They likewise utilized and revered the Hudson River, from the Sapohannikan landing at Fourteenth Street in Manhattan to Rhinebeck, New York, on the east bank, and from Staten Island to Catskill Creek in the west, sometimes traveling north through friendly Mohican country to find its headwaters near Mount Marcy,[3] at 5,344 feet above sea level the highest point in New York State, in what is now Essex County.[4]

To the Munsee, both the Hudson and Delaware Rivers represented the waters of life, and the journey back toward their place of origin, the headwaters, was considered parallel to the spiritual journey back to the Creator. Even though the headwaters of the Hudson were in Iroquois territory, as were those of both the eastern branch of the Delaware, near Roxbury, New York, and the western branch, near Stanford, New York, it was such a sacred journey that if you met your enemy at that headwaters you would not strike or criticize him, but treat him as your brother.[5]

WESTCHESTER

Let's imagine we are traveling northward on the Mohican Trail, called the Albany Post Road in colonial times, later the Old North Road, and today Route 9. This trail passes through the Hudson Valley all the way to the Canadian border. Leaving the Bronx, we cross the outer boundary of the city and see the Weckweesgeek village called Napekamak, "Our People's Field,"[6] the future Yonkers. Here we would see fields with scattered wigwams and gardens on both sides of the dirt path. A little further is another small village of wigwams, now Hastings-on-Hudson, and just beyond, the Weckweesgeek village that will become Dobbs Ferry. Yet further north, we find the Alipconck village at future south Tarrytown. The trail continues north to Hokohongus village, then, a half mile further, to Sintsink, which means "Stony Place." Part of this beautiful landscape became Sing Sing Prison and the town called Ossining. As we head north we see the villages of Kestaubuic and Kitchewan.[7] The Croton River was first called the Kitchwonk or "Big Rapid River," and the Kitchewan were the people of that river, which was later named after their Chief Croton. Here, the Mohican trail veers inland before offering a place to ford.[8]

On our left we pass the Senasqua village that later travelers will call Teller's Point. One of the best-known tales of Westchester folklore concerns "the walking sachems of Teller's Point." At the confluence of the Croton and the Hudson River now known as Croton Point, there was a palisaded fort, from which the Kitchewan made their last stand against English invaders. According to legend Chief Croton himself stood at the top of that wall of timbers, showered by bullets and arrows as he led the resistance. The English broke through the Kitchewan lines and set fire to the fort. As the last of his men died, Chief Croton jumped into the flames so as not to hear the English shouts of victory. As he fell to his death, he pronounced a terrible curse on the British, that they be driven from the land.

A Kitchewan burial ground was located nearby at Teller's Point. Some whites had buried their dead alongside the bodies of the Kitchewan, upsetting the remaining members of the tribe, descendents of the ancestors whose spirits were disturbed. After an Englishman built a proper British manor house right on top of the site of the palisaded fort at Croton Point, the manor became haunted, and the Kitchewan began to rise from their graves and walk the night, protesting the wrongs that had been done and confronting all who would or could listen. The ghost of Chief Croton walks among them, and his spirit can still be seen from time to time around the village of Croton. According to legend, the sachem appeared to the colonist who owned the manor in 1776 and, repeating his curse that the British should be driven from the land, urged him to join the American Revolution, which he did. Some say Croton's Curse helped the fledgling United States win the war.

Next we pass the Meahagh village that today is the town of Cortlandt, with a village of Oscawana to our left. Finally, we reach the Sachoes village at the north end of Westchester,[9] now Peekskill, named for Dutchman Jan Peek. The trail veers to the east, along what is now Division Street, and heads across Peekskill Hollow Creek, and into Putnam County.

As most of Westchester's early inhabitants lived to the east of the Mohican Trail, there are many other trails branching off to the east from the main trunk along the river. The Succabonk Trail heads east by northeast along present Pines Bridge Road. The Putiticus Path runs from the Mohican Trail to the Bedford settlement; and the Muscatow[10] Trail, meaning "it is marshy, with rushes," runs to the north by northeast.

The Common Path, a wide, well-worn trail, runs parallel to the Mohican Trail, along the eastern bank of the Bronx River.[11] The Bronx River is the dividing line between the Wappingers to the west and the Siwanoy to the east, and the path is "common" to both populations.[12] Today that path is White Plains Post Road, which passes through cities like Mount Vernon, Tuckahoe, Scarsdale, and White Plains. There were many secondary trails branching off from this route and several navigable streams.[13]

Along these trails and streams were at least fifty-two Lenape villages (in Westchester County, as recorded in the last half of the

1600s), mostly speaking Wappingers, Siwanoy, or Weckweesgeek dialects of the Renneiu language.[14] These people were descendants of the original Clason Point people, a day's journey to the south, who developed new ways of living about 1300 c.e., including the new R dialects.[15]

Let's look at these cities alphabetically:[16] Ardsley was once a Lenape village, but its name and character have not been preserved in any known records. It has been erased from history. Armonk apparently derived from Warramaug or "Good Fishing Place."[17] There were four villages at Bedford, including the Cantitoe village. There was one village at Briarcliff Manor, and three villages at Cortlandt.

Chappaqua is translated as "a separate place,"[18] which is interesting because there was no village there. There were two villages at Croton, one of which was the headquarters of the respected Kitchewan, and the other of which was a stockaded fort or "castle," which served as the chieftaincy or capital of the Kestaubuic, a smaller, lesser known group. The Kitchewan, or "Croton" Indians were a subgroup of the Wappingers, who were also called "Hoogland" or "Highland Indians." The Wappingers were a large, newer, "progressive" group that stretched from Poughkeepsie to Manhattan along the east bank of the Hudson. Their subtribes included the various ones around southern Dutchess County, the Nochpeem east of Garrison, New York, the Kitchewan, Ammawalk, Sintsink, and Sachoe subtribes, plus several in what is now Connecticut.[19] All in all, there were twenty known "Wappingers" tribes, although the term does not appear until 1762 in a deed from Chief Daniel Nimham.[20]

There were two villages at what is now Dobbs Ferry, one of Weckweesgeek, who had come from White Plains originally. In Munsee, the word means "people of the birch bark," as *weekwee* is "birch" and *geek* means "him."[21] They were centered in what is now White Plains, but were scattered to various locations early during

Dutch settlement. It is known that there were conflicts between the Weekweesgeek and the Munsee that may have contributed to their disruption.[22]

There were two villages at what is now Greenburgh, one at Indian Hill, which was probably the location of a great council fire, and another unidentified settlement nearby. There was a prospering Siwanoy village in a low-lying area at Harrison, New York. The Siwanoy were very lively and industrious people centered in what is now western Connecticut, speaking a dialect of the Renneiu language. This village of ghosts at Harrison now lies submerged beneath the man-made Rye Lake.

There were villages at Hastings and Lewisboro, and a fully stockaded Siwanoy village was situated at Mamaroneck. Mamaroneck was named after a sachem of the Kitchewan of that name,[23] possibly meaning "stripes on his arms," although some say it refers to where salt and freshwater meet on the Mamaroneck River. The nearby Mianus River was named after the great Chief Mayanes.[24] There were two villages at Mt. Vernon, just to the west of the Common Path, but their names have been lost.

There were three villages at New Castle; the villages of the Kisco Indians, or the Sintsink, who were related to the Wappinger, and one other, which is forgotten. There is also a rock shelter in the area, which was used in early times as a hunting camp and perhaps a dwelling for a related group of people.

Located at New Rochelle, there was once a busy village of the Shippa, closely related to those at Clason Point in the Bronx, if not the same. The word *shippa* in Munsee means "a long reach" of land.[25] The Shippa were major players in the wampum manufacturing trade and had control of a long stretch of land overlooking the corner of Long Island Sound on both sides of what became Pelham Road in New Rochelle. They took the shells they collected to the *laaphawaching* ("wampum factory" or "place of stringing beads") at what is now the foot of the bridge to City Island, the Bronx, to have them made into wampum.[26] There was one other unidentified village within the city limits of New Rochelle, further inland.

At North Castle there were three villages, plus a Lenape stockaded "castle" which inspired the present name. Also in that area are three rock shelters: Nebo, Rinch, and Riverside Rock Shelters.[27] At North Salem there were two Lenape villages, one called the Pequenahunc village[28]and one of the villages of the Kitchewan.

There were two villages in North Tarrytown, the village of Pokerhoe, and the Hokohongus village of the Sintsink tribe. Philipse Manor had two villages, one of the Sintsink sachem and one other, plus a camp and shell midden dating back to the time of the mastodon, 6000 B.C.E.

Besides the village of Sachoes, a subtribe of the Wappingers, in Peekskill, there was also a village of Hoseco in Port Chester. A town of the Toquam, a subtribe of the Kitchewan, was situated by Pound Ridge, which is now home of the Pound Ridge Reservation. Here one can still visit the "bear rock" petroglyph, a silhouette of a bear carved on a bear-head-shaped boulder probably dating to at least 1400 C.E.[29] The other major petroglyph at Pound Ridge is Spy Rock, which is a large slanted rock escarpment with extensive peck-and-groove markings on its surface that are generally believed to be astronomical markings. Although badly weathered, it seems possible that the markings depict constellations, with lengthy grooved lines pointing to the sky. Theoretically, on a given night of the year, one could lay down facing a given design and see the matching constellation or star rising above it, along the groove.

The town of Katonah was named after Wappingers Chief Katonah, who was killed in the great Pound Ridge massacre led by John Underhill in 1647.

There were two villages at Rye, one of which was the village of Poningoe on Manursing Island, which served as the seat of the chief of the Shonanocke. There were three villages at Somers, including the village of Nanichkestawac, also known as Petuquepaen.

At Tarrytown was the Weckweesgeek village of Alipconck. There were large and ancient shell heaps from Spuyten Duyvil, Dutch for "to spite the devil," to Tarrytown along the east bank of the Hudson, indicating many centuries, or even millennia of occupation by aboriginal people. This stretch of Route 9 was called The Weckweesgeek Trail by the Dutch and The North River Road north of Tarrytown.

Tuckahoe means "a root that is good to eat," such as a turnip, in Mataponi, which is a language spoken in Virginia. But it also means "cradleboard" in the R and Y dialects to the east. Both refer to the jack-in-the-pulpit. This remarkable plant looks like a baby in an Indian cradleboard, but has a root that is good to eat. That is why it was called "Indian turnip" by the early settlers who were dependent on Native Americans for help in identifying what could be eaten and what was poisonous. They soon learned that the root of this plant should be carefully prepared, and that one should never eat the red berry that comes in the autumn, which burns the mouth like fire.

The Algonquin processed the root carefully by drying, heating, or soaking it in water. Its northern Algonquin name is *sig-a-bun,* similar to the word for "ground nut." Tuckahoe was not a village in Lenape times, but a place where many jack-in-the-pulpits were "wildcrafted," or cultivated in the wild, ready to be harvested. They were located just off the Common Path where the Bronx River divides into the Tuckahoe and Aquehung Rivers, in the moist, rich soil of the thickets, available to all hungry travelers and to future generations as well. Today the town of Tuckahoe has a population of 6,300, but only a few jack-in-the-pulpits growing wild here and there, mostly down the embankment at the river.[30]

The Siwanoy village of Quarropas was located at what is now White Plains. This was the home of the powerful Weckweesgeek sachems. As whites moved in, the Weckweesgeek sachems moved to a place called Napekamak, probably "field near that river," on the Hudson River Highlands, now the bustling urban city of Yonkers.

Finally, there were at least four Algonquin villages at Yorktown, New York, one of which is now submerged by the reservoir. The others are buried beneath suburban lawns and condos.

PUTNAM AND LOWER DUTCHESS COUNTY

Putnam and Dutchess were once a single county, called Dutchess, founded in 1683. In 1697, the lower section was awarded to Adolph Philipse, and called the Philipse Patent. In 1719, Dutchess County was split into three "wards," Philipse to the south, lower Dutchess in the middle, and upper Dutchess—the Mohican area—to the north. Putnam was then created as a separate county in 1812, roughly retaining the same boundaries as the original Philipse Patent.[31] Some locals say the entire Philipse Patent was a Wappingers "reservation" until 1697. A patent is not a deed, and so, if true, Philipse would still have had to purchase the land from the Wappingers, piece by piece if necessary.

If we follow the Mohican Trail through the short stretch that crosses Putnam County, we come upon a place called Manitou, which is a slight mispronounciation of one of the Unami words for Great Spirit, *Man'toh*, similar to the Munsee *Munihto*. Ancient campsites have been found around Lake Mahopac, which means "bear-flats" lake, to the east of here. At one time these camps would have encircled the lake's perimeter.[32]

A story is told about the time in 1665 when the English had conquered New Amsterdam and were moving up the Hudson River Valley, making deals, buying land, and shooing Natives off. They wanted Lake Mahopac most of all, but it was so beloved by the Wappingers that they refused to sell. Finally the British found a young subchief named Omoyao, but he too refused to make a deal for Mahopac. He was arrested on false charges and tied to a tree. The

British set the forest around him on fire and left him there to die. His sweetheart Maya heard of this and went to untie him. They ran home only to find a huge battle going on. Thinking he'd betrayed them, the Mahopac scorned him and escaped into the woods. Omoyao was cut off by soldiers of the crown in every direction. He and Maya climbed the high rock towering over the lake. As redcoats charged up the rocks to capture them, the two young lovers held hands and jumped to their deaths together, and Mahopac was lost to the Wappingers cause.

In Garrison, burials were excavated south of what's now the train station, along with an Indian planting field and village site. A copper knife was found nearby at the mouth of Indian Brook.

The main trail veers to the east here. There were many Nochpeem villages off in the woods. The Nochpeem ("a misty place") were a Wappingers subtribe that shows up on early maps of the New World in the general area of Fahnstock State Park and the Wiccopee region. Their land is still some of the most beautiful in the area.

Travis Corners was an early settlement or trading post, situated along the future Old Albany Post Road, a picturesque remnant of this beautiful Mohican Trail. This road stretches ten miles from Division Street in Peekskill to north of Nelson Corners near Cold Spring, where it rejoins Route 9.[33]

Entering Dutchess County at Breakneck Ridge, which is the foot of the Fishkill chain of mountains, the trail passes through Mattawan (Fishkill Creek), which means "where two waters meet." The area is now known as Beacon, New York. In 1663, Mattawan and the land across the Hudson was the home of the Waoranecks, a subtribe of the Esopus,[34] their southern boundary stretching from Bannerman's Island east through Putnam County to Connecticut.[35] The Wappingers lived here also, along the Fishkill Creek and east to the Taghkanick ("forest") Mountains. The Wiccopees lived above the highlands. Villages exist at Fishkill Hook, the flatland near Fishkill, and at Denning's Point in Beacon, at the Mattewan, where early fireplaces and graves, including ancient stone implements, have been found.

Beacon, New York, was established in 1913 as a combination of Fishkill Landing and Mattewan. According to Patricia Clyne, author of *Hudson Valley Tales and Trails,* in 1683 some Wappingers sold Francis Rombout, a new patentee, "all the land that Rombout could see." They meant to add, "at ground level." Working with Jacobus Kipp and Guilian Van der Plank, Rombout and the others led the Wappingers Indians to the top of South Mount Beacon, 1600 feet up, not an easy climb. Rombout claimed all the land he could see, amounting to 85,000 acres, a vast area that included the future Beacon, New York, and parts of Fishkill.[36]

The Wappingers were so upset with the deal, a delegation was sent all the way to London to see if anything could be done to break the agreement, or have it renegotiated, but their pleas fell on deaf ears.[37] Chief Nimhammau, who lived in Dutchess County between 1712 and 1744, was one of a long series of sachems in the Nimham lineage (see Appendix III). The first one, Nimham I, was from Mericocke, near Hempstead on western Long Island. He moved to Raritan, New Jersey, and became a sachem. The sachem we know as Chief Nimhammau, who moved from Raritan to Fishkill and Wappingers, New York, is either the elder one, or his son. Assuming it was his son, Nimhammau fathered Nimham II, known as "One Shake." One Shake's son in turn was most likely the famed Daniel Nimham, who fought many fraudulent land deeds in the 1700s. There is a Mount Nimham today near Carmel, New York.

There was a Wappingers village at New Hamburg, New York. An early quarry site, including chert in limestone worked by Indians, was found above the Metro North railroad tunnel there. Another ancient chert quarry worked by Native Americans centuries before Henry Hudson's autumn excursion up the river exists four miles northeast of New Hamburg along the same limestone ridge.[38] The ancient

inhabitants of Dutchess County used chert for knife blades and projectile points.

The Mohican Trail passed to the right of Wappingers Falls, the
site of an old Wappingers village. In the old days, villages were not set
right up against waterfalls. Although the scenery is beautiful, the
sound of the crashing water dulls one's hearing and blocks out the
sound of approaching enemies. Common sense dictates that the
Wappingers lived on the east side of Wappingers Falls, at the top of
the steep embankment and halfway up the long half-mile slope to the
Mohican Trail. In fact, one of their burial sites lies next to the
Episcopal church on the side trail later to become Route 9D, at the
edge of the plateau. Others lived all along Wappingers Lake, which
crosses the trail a mile to the north, and along the eastern branch of
the creek upstream from the lake, into what is now New Hackensack.
Mohicans would come and live among the Wappingers along
Wappingers Creek from time to time, although it was not considered
their territory.[39] In the Native languages of the Hudson Valley the
word for "friend" means "one I am at peace with." In Unami, the
word is *laan-go-maat. Laan* is peace.

A few miles to the north is Poughkeepsie, a word that has been
spelled forty-two different ways and which means "the safe, sheltered
spring" or "the safe, pleasant harbor" in Mohican.[40] The harbor,
which lies between Call Rock and Adder Cliff, is very shallow and
only good for canoes and rowboats.

When "the long reach" along the Hudson's Poughkeepsie shoreline was deeded to whites, the Wappingers invited sachems from
neighboring nations to cosign on the contract. This preferred custom
became increasingly difficult to manage as time went on, as traditional Algonquin neighbors scattered to the four directions and
became harder to find at treaty time. That deed was cosigned by
Mohican sachems from Schodack (M'skatak) and at least one leader
from the Westenhoek Mohicans on the Housatonic straddling the

New York–Massachusetts border.[41] Wappingers cosigned on Mohican deeds as well.

The nearby Nine Partners Patent of 1697 came into dispute in 1730 when Nimhammau discovered that what was by original treaty a "two mile" strip between the Connecticut and the Hudson Rivers had been stretched into one *twenty miles* wide! Nimhammaw, a Native person who was quite adroit with legal footwork, and others sued and won, and the nine partners' heirs had to come up with additional payment for the well over 130,000 acres they had stolen.[42]

Burials from ancient times were found at Fox Point in Poughkeepsie, and also to the east of the Metro North railroad tracks as they were being laid in 1882. A mass burial, as if from a prehistoric massacre, was discovered in La Grange, a suburb of Poughkeepsie, on Sprout Creek.[43]

At Staatsburg, a remnant of the Mohican Trail is preserved as the Old Post Road. The route then goes north into the Mohican region itself. Their territory started at the middle of the Beekman Land Purchase, which is now Red Hook, New York.[44] However, the Esopus were involved in deeding the land before 1683.

In 1680, the Dutch colonized Ryn Beck, which was still inhabited by Sepasco Indians. Beyond that point, one would have almost immediately encountered Mohicans. In 1766, the Beekman family started an inn at Rhinebeck, just south of Red Hook and south of the Mohicans, to assist travelers on their way north to Albany. That tavern, the Traphagen, has been in continuous operation ever since. It was located right at the crossroads of King's Highway and the old Sepasco Trail, now approximated by Route 308.[45] It was built of stone in order to withstand possible Indian attacks. There were none, as it turned out, but it was a refuge in times of war with Britain. This inn became the Beekman Arms, which has been continually open for business since. Colonel Henry Beekman's grandson, Robert Livingston, was a signer of the Declaration of Independence, as well as some other documents that affected the Munsee, Mohican, and other Natives of New York.

Further north in Dutchess County, the Moravians came and settled in the Mohican village of Shekomeko in 1742, now Pine Plains, and Wachquadnach shortly thereafter. It was the first place in what is now the United States where Indians and white missionaries lived together. A minority of converts were Wappingers, Minnisink, or Esopus. Most were Mohican, then called Wompanosch. The presiding Mohican elder there was Schawash. The land around Wachquadnach on the Connecticut border was deeded by Metoxon of the Mohicans, and others.[46]

The local white population was very disturbed by the Moravian missionaries actually living and working with "wild Indians." It was decided that the Moravians would have to appear in court and take an oath in order to stay. This was a ruse since they knew that it was against the Moravians' belief to take an oath of any kind, since one could be forced to say words to God against one's will. Unable to take the oath, the Moravians had to leave the county. Many of the natives stayed, however, or fled into the woods, and later mixed with runaway slaves. The remains of that mission house were still visible in the 1920s at the north end of Indian Lake.[47]

12

THE HEAD OF
THE WOLF
Orange and Ulster Counties

At one time the utter and exclusive domain of the wolf totem state of the Lenape, the Munsee Nation, Orange County is shaped remarkably like the head of a wolf, his ears at Pine Bush in the Shawangunks, his eyes at Wallkill, and his nose at Cahoonzie. It looked even more like a wolf before the neck was cut off to make Rockland County. This, of course, is coincidence, but it helps us visualize the geography very clearly. The most important area to the Munsees in Orange County was the area of Port Jervis, at the wolf's mouth. But let's first look at other areas. It will help us understand the importance of Port Jervis to the Munsee.

THE WAORANECKS

The Waoranecks, a Renneiu word that I interpret to mean "they are good, peaceful people,"[1] were a major force in the Hudson Valley. However, it should be clarified that there were two branches of this Esopus group, north and south. The old southern group extended from Bear Mountain to Danskammer Point just north of Newburgh, along the Hudson. The eastern boundary of Orange County today was originally defined by the southern Waoraneck's whereabouts during the 1600s, with the exception of a small settlement across the Hudson around what is now Beacon. There was also a second group of Waoranecks in New Paltz, extending from that highly populated area down to Danskammer Point, although this second territory was shared with their Esopus relatives the Warranawongkong, or "The Good People Near the Mountains."[2] Given that the southern section has long been "prime waterfront real estate" from the Algonquin perspective, it is likely that the Waoranecks settled there early on, and as they became overcrowded, their second-born moved north, subleasing less valuable land in the north from their cousins the Warranawongkong.

The point of convergence of these two subtribes was Danskammer Point, called Cedar Cliff (*quaotuk watchu* in Renneiu, *ka-ho-see watchuk* in old Algonquin) before the Dutch. The place name Cedar Cliff or Cedar Point appears throughout Algonquin territory, especially at sacred places. Algonquin people planted particular trees for special purposes so that their children could enjoy the benefits years after they themselves had passed away. Cliffs were appropriate spots for meditation and prayer; the Algonquin generally burned cedar branches in their prayer fires for smudging purposes. When settlers arrived, they found many places called Cedar Cliff, often overlooking water, or with a "superb view,"[3] all of them sacred to at least one clan or family.

Danskammer Point,[4] on the banks of the Hudson River just north of Newburgh, became a spot where Natives would gather to celebrate all night with drumming and dancing rituals. From the Dutch accounts, these revelries got pretty wild. The Dutch had been warned many times not to go near these sacred rituals by the Algonquin, who felt that they wouldn't understand, or would be offended by some rituals, or that they would scare the spirits away and ruin the ceremony. *Kintekoy* or "sacred dance gathering" ceremonies, could be fairly polite affairs but often could involve somersaulting or jumping through fire, screaming, self-torture, and other shamanic trance practices, especially just before a war. Those who did intrude were often captured. A Dutchman from Fort Orange and his wife were captured at Danskammer Point. The Dutchman stabbed his captor and killed him, only to be burned on the rocks by the man's friends. The wife was captured and ransomed. Couwenhoven, a Dutch military leader during the Second Esopus War,[5] went to the point regularly to meet with Munsee leaders by prior agreement, and reported that the Indians "who lay there about on the river side made a great uproar every night, firing guns and kinte-kaying, so that the woods rang again."[6] Dutch stories claim that if a harmless animal appeared during the ceremony it meant everything would be fine, but if a predator appeared, there would be trouble.[7] A Munsee translator, Kit Davits, slept one night with the Indians there, who had four captives with them. One of the captives, a woman, told him of a plan to attack the whites' Great Plot at Kingston, then Wiltwyck.[8]

To the immediate west of the Ramapo mountains is Tuxedo, New York, the name of which is derived from *P'tuxito*, which means "they are the round-footed ones," a nickname for the Munsees. In the Wanaque, the graphic symbol of the Lenape Confederacy, the Unami are represented by the outline of a turtle, the Unalatchtigo by the wild turkey footprint, and the Munsee by a rounded wolf paw print, hence the name P'tuxito.[9] It was here that the first tuxedo suit was invented and marketed, with great success, by a local tailor. Hence, the plain and simple Munsee gave the world one of its most elegant terms, the tuxedo, or "tux," as most people refer to it. Tuxedo lies on "the wolf's collar," the southern border of Orange County.

The Mamakating,[10] "place where they gather at the river," centered on the border between present-day Ulster and Sullivan Counties, also frequented Orange County and may have lived at Middletown and Goshen, New York, from time to time—probably seasonally.[11]

Route 13, the scenic King's Highway, which connects Warwick to Chester, was once a Munsee trail. It leads past Schunnemunk Mountain, which means "tall place, extending upward." The *unk* ending, like *kong*, means "place near a mountain." The "k" means "this" place. Not far from Schunnemunk, Woodcock Mountain, whose name derives from the Munsee Winegtekonk,[12] which means "good fire place near a mountain" can be seen. Colonial records indicate a Native American burial site off to the side of the King's Highway, and near the "good fire place near the mountain," which was thought to be Schunnemunk Mountain by the non-Algonquin-speaking colonists. They were wrong, and their accidental reversal of the mountains' names concealed the exact location of the sacred site from prying eyes for over three hundred years.

King's Highway shortcuts a bend in present Route 94, which otherwise approximates one of the old trails. Chief Maringoman was a notable sachem, identified as Waoraneck in the Dutch records, whose village stood between Washingtonville and Blooming Grove along the Route 94 trail. The palisaded fort there was referred to as a "castle" by the British in 1726, at the incorporation of Blooming Grove.[13]

This Route 94 trail stretches to the northeast from Chester, where it follows along Moodna Creek, before ending in Newburgh. This route was of some importance during British occupation. The legend behind the name Moodna is tragic and fascinating. An early settler named Murdock, his wife, two sons, and a daughter, lived in a cabin near the creek. A young and fearless Munsee named Naoman, who also lived nearby, was not afraid to stand up to corruption. The new chief in his village was cruel and corrupt, a harsh leader, who preached death to all whites on his land. Naoman warned the Murdock family that his tribesmen were about to attack them by surprise. Murdock grabbed his wife and children and ran to the banks of the Hudson where he found his rowboat waiting. They were halfway across the Hudson when a dozen angry Natives—the particular subtribe has never been identified—launched their several canoes and gave chase. Murdock shot six times and killed six, but the rest captured him and his family near the Fishkill Landing, and took them back to the village. The chief twisted Mrs. Murdock's golden hair in his hand and holding a knife to her throat said, "Tell us what Indian warned you and betrayed his tribe, or you shall see husband and children bleed before your eyes." Before she could speak, Naoman stepped forward saying, "It was I," and kneeled for execution, which was swift. Matters got out of hand after that, and the Murdock family was killed except for the wife, who was held for ransom, and lived to tell the story. The stream was then named Murderer's Creek, and so it remained, until the 1850s, when the name was changed to the more respectable Moodna, from the Dutch word *Moordenaar*. My suggestion is to rename it Naoman's Creek after the Native American hero who cared about human rights and stood up to the powers that be.[14]

Washington's troops later set up camp near Murderer's Creek, near the old Indian trail. That trail also stretches far to the southwest, directly through New Jersey to the ancient Minisink site at the Delaware Water Gap where the Wyoming Trail passes west.

Today, there is a sprawling forestland township called Minisink (not to be confused with the one in Pennsylvania) at the "wolf's chin" of Orange County. Both were once part of the eighty-mile-long Minisink territory along the Delaware. One of the first white settlements in the region was built at Orange County's Minisink, but was burned before the Revolutionary War by Joseph Brant on his long raid up the Minisink Trail.[15] This trail is one of the most fascinating and mysterious features of New York's geographical history.

MYSTERY OF THE MINISINK TRAIL

Mistakenly called the Old Mine Road, even on road signs today, Route 209 has a long and winding history. Legend had it that it was built by Ponce de Leon in the 1500s while he was looking for silver and copper mines, the fountain of youth, and eternal life. Unfortunately the historical evidence doesn't run in his favor. Originally called the Minisink or Mamakating Trail by the Munsee, it traced an old Munsee water route stretching from the Delaware to the Hudson.[16] In 1664 it became a British trade route, unofficially called the Queen's Highway, then became the King's Highway in 1670. It was called by various nicknames at least to 1745, always retaining the generic King's Highway as it was a major cross-country route. Over the next ten years it was renovated and made smoother and wider to prepare the way for the high-speed stagecoaches and fast wagons that were on the rise. In 1756 it was officially reopened as the King's Highway, but with a different look. By taking a trip along the many side routes of what is now pragmatically called Route 209, many of which are still called King's Highway, one can still see these stagecoach roads much as they were in 1756, but with asphalt added. Those winding country roads still possess some of the charm and beauty and much of the illustrious past of the Minisink Trail.

Driving southwest on Route 209 today, one can see literally dozens and dozens of stone mansions in the old style. Mile markers 6, 7, 8, 9, and 12 (as measured from the Kingston Court House in the 1700s) are still visible from the road. The "6 miles to Kingfton" stone is at the old Bevier house, now the Ulster County Historical Society. The stone that reads "7 miles to Kingfton" is in the front yard of Darryl Britten's colonial farmhouse. The grassy path that runs through his fields is the original route of the Minisink Trail and later the King's Highway. An eight-mile marker stands at the old planta-tion stone house set back off the road now; a "9 miles to Kingfton" marker stands sixty paces south of the corner of Duck Pond Road and Route 209, up on an embankment; and the "12 miles to Kingfton" marker is found in the town of Rochester on today's King's Highway under a low-lying apple tree, one hundred yards from the

Rest Plaus Road intersection, several miles east of Route 209. These relics from the past help us locate—in space, time, and spirit—the course and fate of the old Minisink Trail itself.

The original trail connected the northern Munsee capital of Esopus, now Kingston, with the central capital, Minisink, near present-day Port Jervis. As to whether it continued south along the New Jersey side of the Delaware River, as does Route 521, or on the Pennsylvania side, is a matter of controversy, as huge masses of rock blocked the way on the New Jersey side. There are old lead and copper mines located at the southern end of the Minisink Valley, however historians generally agree that the Munsee didn't possess the means to perform the repeated smelting this type of low-grade copper required. They had to acquire the softer, malleable copper from the eastern shore of Lake Superior. Therefore it is considered unlikely that they dug the so-called Pahaquarry Mines, or used the Old Mine Road to get to them.[17]

Some Munsee today claim their oral heritage preserves the memory of a certain place in the mountains near Ellenville where the wind was so fierce that a fire could be made to reach the 2,000 degrees needed to smelt copper ore, and that they did so.[18] However, the feat has not been reproduced in modern times. Local historian Marc Fried writes about the stories and legends of "the lost silver mines" of the Shawangunks, but the hard proof still lies somewhere deep in the rock of the mountains.[19]

Known for centuries only by the Lenape legends that surrounded it, the Old Spanish Mine supposedly lay somewhere between Napanoch and Ellenville, both situated on the Old Mine Road. Much to everyone's surprise, the mine was finally discovered deep in the mountains in 1906. The cave is over five hundred feet long, six feet high, four feet wide, and "straight as an arrow." In 1906, Professor Mather, then state geologist of Ohio, investigated it and concluded that it was built by the men of Ponce de Leon, some of whom came north to seek their fortune after failing to find the Fountain of Youth.[20] A stream of water now flows out of it. This has fed the belief that the Old Mine Road was built by Spaniards in the 1500s. Even Herbert Kraft, foremost critic of the Old Mine Road legend, agreed that this was a lead mine and that the Minisink Trail could have connected Kingston to Napanoch for mining purposes.[21]

One of the most fantastic legends of the Old Mine Road is passed down to us from a Dutch character named Benny Depue. He claimed that an aging Indian friend of his "Old Ninety-Nine," a "chief" and last remaining member of "The Ninety-Ninth Tribe"—brought Benny blindfolded to a place deep in the Shawangunk Mountains. He eventually guided Benny into a cave and undid his blindfold. The old chief lit a candle, and Billy saw before him endless chests of treasure—gold, silver, and diamonds. According to the story, this was the secret hideout of New York's own Captain Kidd. The entrance was once again blocked with a large stone, and Benny was blindfolded for the journey home. Needless to say, he was not allowed to take away any souvenirs. The chief died within a few years, and it wasn't long before Benny was trying to find his way back to Captain Kidd's hideout. Unfortunately for Benny, the paths were designed to fool the unwary and cause them to be lost forever in the wilderness. He reconsidered and returned home empty-handed but with a good story. Years later, around 1890, the *Ellenville Journal* reported that Captain Kidd did indeed cheat an investor out of a half share of loot and hid it somewhere in the Catskills, and that one local adventurer went out in search of the treasure and was never found again.[22]

Such stories about the Catskills abound, and most are probably completely fiction. In any case, we do know that the Munsee blazed the original trail, which was laid out to border as many rivers and streams as possible, so that travelers had access to fresh water whenever they wished. Even with modern maps and aerial photography, it would be hard to find a better water route than that outlined by the

Minisink Trail. That is why the Delaware and Hudson Canal (D & H Canal) was built along this same corridor in 1826. The Munsee therefore were the original "surveyors" of the canal, one of the most financially successful in American history.

The War of 1812 blocked shipments of soft coal from England. This inspired several forward-thinking American industrialists to devise a plan for mining and distributing American coal that would make the United States energy-self-sufficient in times of war. In the end it bolstered the American economy as well. The D & H Canal carried the bulk of the coal bound for New York City. The canal provided transportation between the coalfields of Pennsylvania and New York ports along the Hudson. It was the first private enterprise to cost over one million dollars. The canal was 108 miles long with 108 locks, 22 aquaducts, 136 bridges, 22 reservoirs, 16 dams, and 14 feeders. The first canal was three feet deep, but was increased to six to accommodate bigger boats. Unlike the Esopus, the Rondout, and the Basher Kill, all waterways of the Munsee, the D & H didn't last. The first railroads, put in to feed the canal, gradually took over, and the D & H was abandoned in 1899. Later the railroads were abandoned as well, and cars and trucks took over, driving on a road that followed the course of the Munsee-engineered Minisink Trail.

ULSTER COUNTY

The northern half of the Minisink Trail lies within what became Ulster County, and the development of the trial and the growth of Ulster County go hand in hand.

In the Second Esopus War of 1663, which took place in the vicinity of the Ulster County seat, which is now Kingston, the Esopus Indians were "humbled" by the Dutch; their elder Peace Chief Preuwamackan was slain along with the War Chief Papequanaehen.

A heavily armed Dutch expedition set out on September 3, 1663, from Wiltwyck and headed down the Wallkill Valley looking for the

Indians. On the 5th of that month, they came to the first maize field and found two Munsee women and a Dutch woman peacefully gathering corn together.[23] The days of such casual cooperation were about to end. Two hours later they found the almost completed Munsee fort, a perfect square "castle" on a lofty plain on the eastern slope of the Shawangunks at Shawangunk Kill. This site, near the present-day Shawangunk Valley Firehouse, is one of the most important in Munsee history, but it is now on private property slated for development.

The posts of the castle were fifteen feet above ground, and three feet below, and the palisades were as thick as a man's body, with two rows of port holes. The Dutch prepared for a surprise attack, but a Munsee woman saw them and "sent forth a terrible scream." The warriors inside were alerted. They ran for their houses to gather their arms and then ran to the cornfields. The defenders gained a good position, but suffered heavy losses; Chief Papequanaehen, fourteen warriors, four women, and three children died. In addition, the Dutch took thirteen prisoners, men and women both, plus an old man. The ancient elder walked a half an hour then could go no further. The Dutch gave him "his last meal," and left him there in the wild, presumably to die.

The Dutch also recovered twenty of their own, who had been living as captives, plus much ammunition,[24] furs, and hides. Of some eighty within the fort (counting the rescued captives) only about twenty-seven of the warriors and a handful of the women and children survived the Dutch attack,[25] a decisive turning point in the history of Ulster County. For the Esopus Munsee it was "the shot heard round the world." Kieft's War had been far away, but this was in their own backyard.

There is a humorous story that came out of this episode, however. Catherine, the wife of the French Huguenot, Louis Du Bois, had been among those living in captivity. When he came to rescue her, she took one look at him and ran with the Indians. Noticing her reluctance to be rescued (and her eagerness to escape his company), he called out "Stop, T'rene, or I'll shoot you!" Apparently she didn't like being married to a man who'd shoot his own wife, and kept running.[26]

After the destruction of the new Munsee fort, the Minisink Trail was opened up for white travel. The Munsee fell on hard times, but the Dutch prospered. White settlements sprang up all along the road, often on old Munsee sites. Many houses were built, not far from Wiltmeet,[27] the site of an old Esopus fort. The two populations learned to get along. A peace treaty of 1669 clearly outlines the territories of the "five Esopus sachemdoms of the Munsee," which were still holding strong in the territories of their ancestors who had lived on both sides of the Hudson River for centuries. The first were the Waoranecks, whose land stretched from modern-day Beacon on the east bank of the Hudson River, Newburgh on the west, and possibly Middletown, on down to Danskammer Point on the west bank. Second were the Warranawongkong, whose territory stretched from Danskammer to the Catskill Mountains near Saugerties. Their center was at the Shawangunks, but they had a major village at Wiltmeet, near the Minisink Trail.[28] They have also been called the "Wampings," or "from the place of white rocks."[29] The Warranawongkong territory matches very closely the borders of modern-day Ulster County, west to the Shawangunks. The third listed were the Mamakating, who were centered west of the Shawangunks in the Mamakating Valley, through which the old Minisink Trail passes as it leaves the boundaries of modern Ulster County and enters Sullivan County. The fourth listed were the Wawarsing, who occupied the area surrounding the present town of Wawarsing, also along the old road, in the southwest corner of Ulster County. Their council fire was at the junction of the Wawarsing and Thopackock Creeks.[30] The fifth group were the Catskill, who lived in Greene County along a trail (now Route 32) that extended north from the Old Mine Road from today's Saugerties to Catskill Creek, according to Ruttenber.[31] This same territory was apparently also occupied by the Mohicans,[32] and so it is not clear who the "very loving people and very old men" were that Henry Hudson noted in his diary when he met them in that location in 1609. The Catskill Munsee had control over the flint mines at Coxsackie, well within Mohican territory. It is known that, north of Saugerties, lived a woman sachem named Nipapoa, which apparently means "Hidden Moon" in Munsee. It therefore seems possible that hers was a Munsee village, not a Mohican one, regardless of the location.[33] In 1609, when the "loving people" saw that Henry Hudson was leaving, they broke their arrows and threw them in the fire. This was a way of asking him to stay, and showing him he would be safe there. They supposed he was afraid of these weapons and wanted to reassure him. Ruttenber believed these were the Catskill Esopus, however today the "loving people" are claimed by the Mohicans as their ancestors.

There was a steep, rocky Indian trail up what is now the Plattekill Cove to Tannersville to the west, which the Esopus Munsee would take to gather spruce sap for medicine to put on cancers and also for glue. By tapping the maple sap on that high plateau they could extend the maple sugar season by ten days, since the sap stops rising ten days later at the higher altitude (2,000 to 2,200 feet above sea level, as opposed to 800), just as spring weather comes to the high Plattekill Pass ten days later in the following moon cycle. The seasons are very much a matter of altitude, something always expressed in Lenape thought. Most herbs that disappear in July by the banks of the Hudson could still be found on the high ridge into August. After several wars with the Dutch, the local Indians were not quite as friendly as at first, and brought prisoners of war up the steep Plattekill Trail. However, the Esopus did not live up there under normal circumstances.

KINGSTON

Kingston was home to many groups of Native people, as a gardening party in 1906 at the Old Senate house revealed; buckets of arrowheads and spear points were dug up without much effort, and an Iroquois bowl was found in a stream bank nearby.[34] The Redoubt area was named after an Indian fort that stood there during Stuyvesant's time.

When Ulster County was formed in 1683, it stretched from Murderer's Creek, now Moodna Creek, to Sawyer's Creek in Saugerties, embracing much of the old Minisink road and still including among its population a large number of Munsee people. Like New York City and Albany, Ulster County was named after James Stuart, the Duke of York and Albany, who was also the Earl of Ulster.

The Esopus held out for quite a while at Kingston. The Esopus Chief Ankerop lived in Rosendale until 1680, and continued to hold forth in the area until at least 1700, probably living in the mountains further south. On Stephen and Robin Larsen's forestland at the Center for Symbolic Studies south of Rosendale, there is what appears to be the foundation of an ancient cabin, nestled in the crook of a bending stream, which was considered prime location to the Lenape. A now-vanished ridge-top trail once connected it to the Rosendale area. Perhaps this was where Ankerop lived out the last years of his life. We don't know.

BIG INDIAN

There is a town in the back hills of the Catskill Mountains called Big Indian. The story behind the name, whether completely factual or not, is representative of the personal tragedies endured by both the Munsee and those who loved them during the early contact period. It seemed that nothing ever came to a happy ending for the beleaguered Munsee. Winneesook was a seven-foot-tall Munsee living in the Esopus Valley near Marbletown. Winneesook means "snowfall,"[35] but the white people called him "big Indian." He fell in love with Miss Gertrude Molyneux, a proper lady of the town. At first she was embarrassed by his dramatic overtures, for he lived in the woods, but after a while it was clear that she was getting very interested. Her parents became hostile and forced her to marry a Mister Joseph Bundy, a man of means capable of protecting her from the "savage." But Gertrude had a mind of her own, and did not find Joseph to her liking. She eloped one night with the "big Indian," and they escaped into the woods together and settled down to raise a family in the wilderness. Gertrude's parents continued to complain of the captive state of their daughter, but to no avail.

Several years passed, and when someone's cow disappeared, certain people spread rumors that it was "that big Indian!" Joseph Bundy, still seeking revenge for the loss of his wife, led the charge. They found Winneesook and chased him for miles until they reached what is now Big Indian, New York. According to the story, Joseph called out, panting, "I think . . . the best way to civilize . . . that yellow serpent . . . is to let daylight into his heart!"

Joseph raised his rifle and fired. Big Indian staggered to the hollow of an old pine tree where he hid for a while. Gertrude found him there and held him upright in her arms until he died, as her ex-husband looked on without remorse. Gertrude and her children moved to that spot to tend his grave, and they formed the nucleus for the future town of Big Indian. It is handed down that the tree remained standing as a local landmark and was often pointed out to visitors to Big Indian until the 1880s, when it was cut down to make a railroad embankment. On the way from Marbletown to Big Indian is the town that bears a variation on his Munsee name, Winnisook.

The Hudson Valley is full of such legends about the Munsee, and the struggles between the two societies as the Dutch and later the English tried to get a foothold in what they called the New World. Few aspects of Munsee culture, however, are the subject of more stories and legends than the Minisink Trail. In the following chapter we will follow this trail back to its earliest days.

13
A WALK DOWN THE MINISINK TRAIL

As we have seen, the ancient Minisink Trial stretched from the Hudson River at Kingston, to the Delaware River at Port Jervis, approximately sixty miles. Its route is now approximated by Route 209, although many of the side roads are actual segments of the trail, paved over, but still surrounded by beautiful landscape. In this chapter, we'll trace the Minisink Trail as it was when both Dutch and Munsee walked it together in the early to mid-seventeenth century.

We begin in Esopus, the name of which was a "Greek" mnemonic, after the famed Asopus River in Boetia, for Sheepoos, meaning "a small river." The name was changed from Esopus to Wiltwyck by Peter Stuyvesant in 1661. Wiltwyck, generally interpreted to mean "the place of savages [wild men],"[1] was at one time home to at least one thousand Warranawongkong Munsee.

Seventeenth-century Wiltwyck encompassed one of the most fertile areas left behind by the glacier, with 215 acres of Native cornfields and over 100 pits full of beans and corn.[2] Wiltmeet, a large area nearby now approximated by the towns of Esopus and Kingston, was considered special because the Munsee could get two corn harvests in one year from the field below the ridge, instead of the typical one.[3]

There was a Munsee Bagettaway or lacrosse field on a small plateau at what is presently the corner of Hoyt and Pierpont Streets in Kingston.[4] This favorite game of the Lenape often went on for days. At the end of the day, a player would jab a stick in the ground to mark the place the ball was, and play would pick up the next day where it left off. The game was considered sacred and they didn't like the Dutch watching. Today the area is completely built over.

The Minisink Trail started somewhere near the Hudson River, passed the present-day courthouse, and became Hurley Avenue, not far from Lucas Avenue, now one of the busiest streets in Kingston. Lucas Avenue was originally called the Neversink Turnpike Road, after the Neversink Munsee tribe at the other end. People say the Neversink were so named because they were such skilled makers of canoes, but the word means "a promontory." The turnpike was renamed Lucas after Judge Lucas Elmendorf of Kingston, who founded the newer road in the 1600s. The Lucas Turnpike, now county Route 1, travels parallel to the Minisink Trail for many miles, providing a fine view of the Shawangunks from the west, particularly Castle Point, before joining up with the Minisink Trail at Accord.

Several roads in Kingston still have native names, such as Ponck-hockie Street, site of an old Lenape burial ground, and which traces the Ponckhockie Path, mentioned in early deeds. In Lenape that would mean the "land where there are lots of annoying bugs," or sand flies, although this fact has escaped everyone's notice.[5] Here again is the tricky practice I call "double Dutch," whereby the settlers would come up with a whimsical Dutch place-name that sounded like the original Munsee name. It would help them remember the Munsee name whenever they were talking to Munsee, and helped them to name it in Dutch. The custom, however, confuses historians, who may think Ponckhockie comes from "*Punt-houk-ee*," Dutch for "point, or hook, of land." Actually the location is inland from the Roundout Landing.

There is a small outcropping of rock off Delaware Avenue at Hasbroucke with the carved likeness of an Indian chief locals call "Chief Ponckhokie." How it got there isn't really known.[6]

Broadway was also an aboriginal path, and Albany Avenue is very old, though it's not clear if it was indeed built over Lenape pathways. Foxhall Avenue was part of a path leading west from the Hudson River that was made over into a roadway to the Thomas Chambers estate, which still stands. This trail was referred to as early as 1652.[7]

Many Dutch place-names have prevailed in Kingston, notably the Rondout and the Strand. The Rondout, now full of tourist shops, was the site of an Esopus Indian trading post and perhaps a small fort, at a spot where several important trails came together. Clovis people, the early ancestors of the Algonquins, once lived there.[8]

The town of Esopus was formed out of Kingston in 1811. Today it is a quiet suburb and home of the Black Bear Trading Post on Route 9W, run by Roy Black Bear, a Mohawk. The Iroquois first settled here in 1300, but most left after a few generations. The trading post includes an Iroquois museum with many Native American cultural artifacts. The Algonquin settled here around 3000 B.C.E., mostly along the Hudson at Connelly Cove on the Rondout Creek, and in the Parsells Street section of Sleightsburgh. By 1500 B.C.E. there were dugout canoes and soapstone pottery being traded. Maize didn't come until 100 C.E. There was a settlement called Nescatuck, which in Munsee means "muddy tidal river." It was renamed Libertyville by patriotic people in 1880. Ulster Park is an offshoot of Esopus that has been the site of Native villages since at least 1000 B.C.E.

The trail in this region is called Hurley Avenue, which enters the town of Hurley and becomes Main Street. The Dutch called it Nieu Dorp, or the "new village" on the Esopus. It was settled by Dutchmen who were unhappy at Beaverwyck (now Albany) near Fort Orange. It was formerly a Munsee village and fort called Atharhakton or, as some say, Atkarkarton, meaning "fields that are ready to plow,"[9] possibly an extension of the Esopus settlement. Skirmishes between the Esopus Indians and the Huguenots were numerous there.[10] A prominent Esopus leader in this area was Sunksquaw, whose name the patriarchal Dutch were told meant "top sachem," but in fact means "woman sachem." It wouldn't be the first time the Dutch erroneously presumed a Lenape chief to be a man.[11]

There were two caves nearby, west of what is now Connelly Cove. A large cavern and a smaller cave provided shelter for thousands of years to Native people during the long winter months. In the mid-1900s, those shelters were destroyed by a quarry company.

The town of Connelly, at the northern tip of the town of Esopus, on the Rondout Creek across from Kingston, witnessed what may be the longest cohabitation between whites and traditional Native people in the entire Hudson Valley. This mutual sharing of the land lasted 215 years, from 1610, when the first Dutch traders came after Henry Hudson, to 1825, when Munsee Hank Paul and his mother still lived in a hut beside a spring near where the Connelly Road joins Millbrook Road today, just south of the Rondout Creek bridge. His elderly mother died that winter, and not long after Hank gave up his home and disappeared into the hinterlands, never to return.[12]

Three-quarters of the way between the six-mile marker and the seven-mile marker from Kingston, in today's Marbletown, once stood a chestnut tree that was said to be at least five hundred years of age. It is memorable in that a white elm grew out of its base, mostly surrounded by the trunk of the older tree. This had great symbolic significance to the Munsee, who have an almost religious reverence for "the tree people." The chestnut represents the ancestors, as its ground nuts provided a main staple for the old ones thousands of years ago. The white tree could represent the great spirit, or the grandfather spirit of elm trees. It could also be viewed much as a Catholic person might behold a "mother and child" sculpture, a symbol of new life. This was a great gathering place long ago. It is at the intersection of two foot trails and one water route, a shortcut trail to the Shawangunks to the southeast[13] and the Minisink trail itself. As it was accessible by canoe, it also connected to the Esopus River to the west, which comes closest to the old road at that point, and then disappears as we go south. Louis Bevier, one of the first settlers in the area, bought the land. His stone mansion now houses the Ulster County Historical Society. The Wiltmeet village site in present-day Marbletown is on top of a razorback ridge north of Tongore Road. Tongore Road was formerly Mill Dam Road, an old King's Highway that went by the Munsee village along the north bank of the Esopus.

The Esopus ran much higher in spring three hundred years ago than it does now, thanks to the Ashokan Dam, so the trails used to run higher upland than the roads do today. The King's Highway was made to avoid cutting through private farmland, and it varied at places from the original trail, but many of the milestone markers are still in place.

An Indian trail, overgrown in places and much of it streambed, runs from near the Ulster County Historical Society along a ravine eastward till it splits. Then the path follows to the right and to the Indian caves beyond. Walking along the old rocky trail to the town of High Falls we find a dry streambed along the trail. In the old days, it only dried up in summer, revealing a hole in the ground that leads downward to a secret underground cave. A river runs through the cave, directly under the streambed, and the rock shelf allows only a short walk for those without hip waders. Locals have called it Pompey's Cave for over four hundred years; some say it was the name of the slave who found it. In Munsee, *pom'pey-leew* means "it is a stream," with similar words referring to traveling along a streambed. The Munsee traveled along the stream bed in both directions to get to the cave entrance. It lies 150 steps from the Lucas Turnpike, and from the Benton-Barr Graveyard, the site of a forgotten Munsee village.

An old Munsee story says the original people lived in the earth under a lake. One man emerged through a hole and saw a deer that had just been killed by a wolf. He brought the deer back and shared the meat with his people. They enjoyed the meat so much that they emerged as a group, and began spreading throughout the land. Those were the first *sketambowg*, or "surface beings,"[14] as we call them in Algonquin.[15]

The Great Captain Pipe of Sandusky said that the Delaware are descendants of the Wyandot (Huron) who sprang from the hole, which can still be seen near Lake Huron. One of the women who emerged, a virgin, gave birth to twins who spoke a different language than Wyandot, presumably Munsee and Unami. In another version, she is not a virgin, but a headstrong Wyandot girl who disobeys her father and runs away with a lover of her own choosing and is exiled.[16]

Down the road a bit we see the impressive Shawangunk Mountains rising to the east. The name Shawangunk dates back at least as far as the Second Esopus War (1663). The fanciful Henry R. Schoolcraft, who took a great interest in Native American place-names, was the originator of the translation "white rocks," however it clearly means "the mountains where you go south" in plain "baby talk" Lenape.[17] The Shawangunk range does indeed "go south"— there is a wide ridge along the top, which can take you as far south as Georgia, along a winding route. Others say it was originally the name of the valley and the Minisink Trail, which do go south as well.[18]

The steep Shawangunks divide Ulster County in eastern and western halves starting at Rosendale. The Warranawongkongs were the people of the eastern half, whose natural boundaries set the boundaries of Ulster County's eastern shoreline. North of the mountains, the Warranawongkongs spread to the west as far as the ridge of the Catskills at Lexington, near the headwaters of the east branch of the Delaware, with the Mohawk people on the other side. The Wawarsing occupied the remaining area of Ulster County to the south and west. The old, "lost Wawarsing Trail" led from present-day Wawarsing, eastward over the mountain between Mud Pond and Lake Awosting, and then down to the site of a seventeenth-century Munsee fort in present-day Gardiner. *Awosting* means "on the other side." The name of nearby Lake Minnewaska may not be Munsee, but if it is, it means "drinking water on the other side."

Some believe that the name of Lake Mohonk, which lies on the other side of the mountain to the east, means "A Great Tree," but it is generally thought to be derived from *Maggeanapogh*, or "Great Rock."[19] No one is sure if it is even Lenape.[20]

During the Second Esopus War, two large palisaded Warrana-wongkong Munsee "castles" were destroyed near New Paltz, the new fort at Shawangunk Creek and an older fort at Port Ben on the other side of the mountain in Wawarsing.[21] According to local tradition, nearly a century later the Munsee of New Paltz eventually befriended certain Dutch and not others. In the summer of 1755, the sachem of the time gruffly showed the three grandsons of Isaac DuBois, an original patentee of New Paltz, three places where he would allow them to build their homes along the trail that is now Springtown Road, in "Indian country," west of the Wallkill. They were instructed to build only where they were told.

The following spring, the three brothers found themselves sitting snugly in their new houses while all the other land along the trail—now appropriately called Springtown Road—was flooded by the Wallkill River. The roads were waist deep in water, but their three stone houses stood high and dry. Those three houses still stand today, thanks to the advice of the Warranawongkong sachem, and the three that did as they were told. One can still see the 15-inch wide floor-planks, the wavy window glass, and huge ceiling beams of another time inside those stone houses.[22]

Beavers probably abetted the flooding. Beaver trade was an important activity before the 1630s when the beavers were wiped out by poorly organized trapping enterprises. Today these industrious creatures have returned, and they can now be found well inside the city limits of New Paltz, especially in the waters along the Wallkill Rail Trail and in and around the Wallkill River to the west.

Near the crest of the Shawangunks is the place the Munsee called Coxing, or Koghksohsing, "near a high place." The Cedar Ridge Road that leads to it may be the remnants of the trail that "goes south" ultimately to Georgia, although the area is covered with trails. Coxing today is still very beautiful and primitive looking, with a stunning waterfall that possesses the aura of a more rustic time. A Coxing road lies near Route 209, and leads to a location still called Coxing in the Alligerville area.

Parallel to the old "streambed" or Pom'pee-leew Trail is Wuchite Road (a word that implies "it is new," *wuskitay* in Munsee), which runs between the Minisink Trail in Marbletown and High Falls. One wonders how new a road could be, named in a language not generally spoken in the area since the day in 1710 when the Munsee elder Hirriam Hecka of what is now Ellenville passed away.

Stone Ridge, formerly Butter Fields near the Shawangunk Mountains to the east, is next on our journey. Like the name Munsee implies (from *minsi,* for "stony country") in Lenape "it is very stony country." The Munsee trail that is now Route 213 begins here,[23] surrounded closely by ancient colonial buildings, and follows the path of the rolling waters of the Esopus River. This road takes us to West Shokan at the foot of Peekamoose Mountain with its grand peaks climbing 3,875 feet into the sky, and then on to Ashokan. Some say this hamlet is named after Chief Ashokan, who was supposedly killed in a fight over a woman by Chief Tongore on Dancing Rock in West Hurley,[24] but there is no evidence for this, or even that Dancing Rock was even used for drumming and dancing ritual by the Esopus Indians. Tongore was actually a Dutchman, a wealthy property owner named Gizbart Krum Van Tongoren.[25] He was no Indian chief, but the town of Olive Bridge was originally the town of Tongore, in honor of the mythical chief. In fact, the word Ashokan means "where waters converge"[26] or "outlet of a stream,"[27] which was somewhat accurate, although the Ashokan Reservoir has drastically altered the land. (The Ashokan Reservoir came in between 1907 and 1913, inundating not only Davis Corners, but Glenford, West Hurley, Ashton, Olive Bridge, Olive, and Ashokan as well.) There *is* record of a Chief Moonhaw in the area. His name translates as "a burrowing dog"[28] (or other animal) in Munsee, but no tall tales exist about him, perhaps because he was a real person. Nearby Shandanken means "place of hemlock trees,"[29] of which there are many. It is also the name of a chief who lived at Catskill Mountain House for a while.[30] Blossom Falls is supposedly named after the mythical Indian woman Spring Blossom who leaped with her lover to their deaths at the falls. This waterfall is near Tears of a Cloud Falls.[31] Such fictional stories abound in the legendary Catskills.

To the right of Route 213, now under water, is the former town of Davis Corners. There are several Davis families in the region, some of whom are descendants of the Munsee, some of whom are not. The Reverend James Davis, a Munsee of the region, recently told me that his ancestral homeland, and the house of his father and his father's father, lies at the bottom of the great reservoir, along with many of the artifacts and landmarks of the Munsee people, many of which were originally from New York City area, and driven into the mountains. He claims descent from Kit Davits, an interpreter who traded with the Lenape. Ironically the Ashokan Reservoir is considered part of New York City, for all means and purposes, and is clearly marked so, even though New York lies eighty miles away as the crow flies.

There are many eagles in the mountains over by the Ashokan Reservoir. Young Lenape men used to go look for feathers for their hair, "for good luck" they'd say. Eagles are respected like elders, and to find one of their feathers is akin to finding treasure. Here is a Munsee tale about the getting of eagle feathers.

One day, a certain Munsee boy—I'll call him Xwa-tchee-len-oo, which means "Big Eagle," or "Big Shot" depending on the inflection—climbed to the top of Peekamoose Mountain with his bow and arrow, laid out some wolf meat, and hid in the bushes, waiting for an eagle. He made a prayer to the eagles, saying "Come and let me hunt you down so I can possess one of your tail feathers."

A small eagle came to taste the meat, but the boy ran out and shooed it away, saying, "You're too small! Don't eat all the meat! I'm saving it for a bigger eagle!" The bird flew away, and the boy went into hiding again. Soon a second eagle came, bigger than the first, and it began to eat the meat. Again Big Eagle ran out, yelling, "Stop! Stop! Don't eat the meat! I'm waiting for a *really* big eagle to come!"

The bird flew away. Finally, he made another prayer and asked for the biggest eagle in the world to show up. Suddenly behind him he heard this loud rush of wind, and a noise that sounded like when his mother cleaned a mat by shaking it in the wind. Suddenly a great pair of talons grabbed his shoulders and picked him up in the air. He looked down and he was flying over the Esopus River. He looked up and there was the biggest eagle he'd ever seen. He yelled, "Put me down!"

The eagle answered, "I sent you my youngest son, then my next youngest, but you shooed them all away because they were too small, and now I am insulted. I think you are very vain and greedy! I'm going to teach you a lesson, big shot. I'll give you a choice; I can either drop you and we'll see if you can fly as well as my two sons, or you can come to my nest and help raise my eaglets as your own, and feed them until they are big enough to suit you!"

Xwa-tchee-len-oo answered, "Well, I certainly don't want you to drop me. Uuuh, let's go to the nest!"

For the next three turnings of the moon, the boy lived high in a tree, living in the nest with the eaglets. It was his job to take the worms that were brought and drop them down the eaglets' throats.

After a while, they would start to spend more and more time away from the nest, until they were hardly there at all. The boy called to the big eagle and said, "I am lonely. I miss my family. Can I go home now? Your children have already left the nest!"

The eagle took him back to the top of Peekamoose Mountain, and left him there, saying, as he flew away, "I hope you have learned your lesson!" The boy turned around. There on the rock was one large tail feather from the eagle. He said, "That's good enough for me! I am grateful for this beautiful gift from the eagles!" And the funny thing was, that feather brought him lots of good luck in the months to come.

Returning to the Minisink Trail, we leave the Esopus River, heading south. In Accord, the Rondout comes to within our view to the east, and runs alongside us until Phillipsport. Thereafter, the Basher Kill Creek accompanies us to the Delaware. Basher Kill may sound like a violent warrior, but the name memorializes a female sachem named Basha, a common girl's name.[32] Just as Queen Weetamu of the Wampanoag area of Cape Cod was a great warrior, Basha may have been as well. We don't have that piece of information, but a Lenape sachem was a pillar of strength, regardless of gender.

The name of Rondout Creek refers to a small fort or "redoubt," specifically a Munsee "castle" along the path into Kingston. The rustic hamlet of Alligerville lies on that creek today. Algonquin palisade walls were built with a "berm" at the bottom, made from dirt thrown up from digging the trench, which was usually eighteen inches wide. The long posts were placed upright in the trench, then filled in, packing the berm up around the base at least six inches. There is a "Berme" Road at High Falls, thought to be named after the remains of the fort.

At High Falls, the Rondout is joined by the Wallkill River as it ends its long journey from Mohawk Lake in faraway Sparta, New Jersey.

The next town along the trail is Kerhonkson, which some say means "near a place of shallow water."[33] It also means "the place where the geese go in for honking," in "double Dutch." Today the goose is a symbol of the town and the Kerhonkson High School athletic teams as well.

Now the trail climbs up the mountain to Mombaccus where until recently an old corn mill remained standing at Mombaccus Kill. The earliest settlers found a sacred Maysingway face carved in a sycamore tree near the junction of the Mombaccus and Rondout Kills—a Dr. Westbrook reported having seen it with his own eyes— and found it remarkable enough to name the area after it. However, what was a sacred invocation of the Master of the Hunt to the Lenape, was a grotesque face to the Dutch.[34]

Oral tradition explains the phenomenon. Lenape ancestors were traveling in their home country between the Delaware and the Hudson Rivers, and were miserable from not following the ways of the Creator, Keeshaylumookawng. They were crossing a mountainous region, when they saw a great stone face in the wall of rock before them, and felt that it was a sign from "he who creates us with his thoughts" (presumably the "Indian face" seen from Lucas Turnpike in the cliffs of Castle Point Rock, in the high Shawangunks).[35] Believing it was the face of the Creator himself, they carved many images of this face in wood and placed them in the Big House. It became customary to carve the face in each of the twelve posts of the Big House. Soon they started the practice of carving the face in a living tree. It was one of these faces, the face of the Creator, which the Dutch called "Mum-Bacchus," "*mum,*" to wear a mask; *Bacchus,* as in bacchanal, the pagan worship of Bacchus, a Roman god of nature.[36]

A Wawarsing fort stood along the west side of the trail, now Samsonville Road, halfway toward Pataukunk, which means "prayer retreat near a mountain."[37] It was destroyed during the Second Esopus War in 1663.[38]

Wawarsing, New York, is our next stop. According to the latest census, its current population is eight hundred, but it has consistently been a population center since ancient times. Generally thought to mean "it is a place where the stream bends or winds," or possibly "a very good place," Wawarsing was also called Socconessing, or "water hole." Early settlers said Wawarsing meant "Blackbird's Nest," which was somewhat in jest, as the name has the word "sing" in it.[39] There was an Esopus fort at the foot of a great bluff called "Indian Hill" in Wawarsing that was destroyed on August 31, 1663, by Captain Kreiger, during the second Esopus War. This was the capital and location of the great council fire of the Wawarsing band or sachemdom of Esopus Indians at the confluence of the Ver Nooy Kill and Rondout Creek.

The area is also called Port Clinton and Port Ben. By 1695 to 1705, the Minisink Trail was a wagon road at least as far as the old fort. The Old Stone Church of Wawarsing, referred to as "the Old Meeting House" in 1742, was built along the trail that passes the old fort site in the 1600s, and was the site of a colorful confrontation between whites and Natives. During the last Indian Raid on August 12, 1781, several unidentified Indian warriors entered the church and "amused themselves by throwing tomahawks at the panels of the pulpit, leaving gashes which were never repaired."[40] Two white marksmen tried to shoot the Native American intruders, but missed and ran away. Their bullet holes also became part of the church interior. When the church burned down in 1843, all evidence if this incident was erased, although some say the scarred pulpit was saved for a time, till it was accidentally used as firewood by a young janitor

The Munsee called the fort Ankerops, which the Dutch translated in 1699 as "A Great Wigwam," although the *s* ending indicates it was "lesser in size." This would suggest the fort at Shawangunk on the other side of the mountains was even larger than this one; they were similar structures in many respects, both destroyed during the Esopus Wars. The fort at Warranawongkong was certainly a great wigwam. But was the other larger fort then named "Ankerop?" We don't know. The name "Great Wigwam," or Ankerop, was a title given to Chief Kawatch-hikan, who lived closer to the other fort, which hypothetically could have borne that name as well, unknown to the Dutch. Chief Ankerop signed the deed for Esopus (later Kingston) in 1652, and lived at Rosendale before retiring in old age to the mountains. The fort called Ankerops was also the council house where the Esopus and leaders from other tribes met. The historical marker is at the corner of Route 209 and Geary Lane. The hill begins a hundred or so yards down the lane.

Next we come to Napanoch, which means "that land overflowed by water." There is an old stone icehouse in town that was built as a first home by the Bevier brothers, the first white settlers in the area, in the 1600s. Abram Bevier had a cannon, a device the Lenape reportedly feared, in his home situated right at the edge of the Minisink Trail. His house was fashioned into an American fort in 1781 by the colonial army, to make use of his cannon. The house of politician Andreas De Witt, who summoned one hundred Delaware from Pennsylvania for a peace conference on November 16, 1761, has been rebuilt upon the same foundation at least once, but is still standing. Chief Michtagh Monolap was the presiding sachem on the Native side of the table. The Delaware had sided with the French during previous wars, but when the French surrendered at the Plains of Abraham in Ottawa in 1759, the Delaware had been left to face their former enemies, the British colonists, all over North America. Chiefs such as Monolap had to change their policy toward their former enemies or face an overwhelming threat of attack, without help from the French.

At the peace conference, Monolap, holding a wampum belt, said, "Many years ago there was a treaty made between the Governor of New York and our ancestors, and we was settled at Minissing [along the Delaware] and there was fire kindled for us, and the smoke of that fire was to ascend straight up into the air, it was not to be driven by the wind neither one way nor the other. It is our desire now to live according to our former covenant as long as Sun and Moon shines."

Upon saying this, he offered a gift of a beautiful wampum belt. Monolap continued, "We desire that you dry your tears and wipe your eyes open so that you see clearly out of your eyes, and cleanse your hearts so that you no longer feel enmity."[41] This is also the wording of the Condolence Speech of the Mohawk, a people to whom they were now subject. This ceremonial oath or speech is part of the peace making process of the Hodenosuannee, and usually delivered by the Condole Chief. It was taught by the Peacemaker to Iatwenta, or "Hiawatha," and has been handed down ever since. It is meant to honor the hurt feelings of those who have lost loved ones.[42] It was a highly dramatic speech, and appropriate for the situation Monolap faced, having led the fight for his people against the British for so many years. That day, November 16, 1761, was a pivotal moment in Munsee history, for it began the long process of reconciliation with the British. Many Munsee kept that allegiance through the Revolutionary War, which was their undoing, and contributed greatly to their disappearance from American history.

The English knew that the moral of the story of the smoke was that the Munsee were to side neither with the French nor the English, and now they pointed out that by siding with the French, the Munsee had broken their promise. The British asked that all war captives be returned, and the Munsee said it would be done.

A second meeting in Kingston was arranged. Major Levi Pawling, speaking on behalf of the English Crown, said, "We look to you as Brethren and we bid you welcome here. You told [us] ten weeks ago when we met you at Rochester [the old village of Rochester on Route 209, not the city on Route 90] that you was earnestly desirous to live [in] peace." Not to be outdone in the art of oratory, the silver-tongued Major Pawling added, with more than a touch of his acerbic wit, "According to your desire, we have dried up our tears and wiped our eyes open, so that we may see clear, but cannot *see* any of His Majesty's subjects who have been captivated by some of *your* people...."[43]

The Munsee explained that their "uncles," the Mohawk, had instructed them to release the prisoners at East Town, Pennsylvania, five moons hence, and that is what happened. After that, peace reigned on the frontier for many years.

Continuing down the trail we come to Ellenville, which dates back at least to the early 1700s. To the east and straight up the side of a mountain we find the Ice Caves. These were certainly known to the Wawarsing Indians, and probably considered a place of reverence, as by all indications their ancestors had lived in the caves. In 1779, the people of Napanoch, and Fantine Hill, now part of Ellenville, were attacked by hostile Indians and hid in the caves, which they were led to by a mysterious Indian figure who helped them survive the ordeal. Local legend has it that he appeared among them again as an old man many years later, trading furs and hides, never revealing if he was the same person or not.[44]

There are two sets of ice caves, the more spectacular ones a mile or so to the north of Sam's Point, which are considered the "largest of their kind in the East."[45] The lesser caves are on the western slope of the mountains, near Ellenville, two miles from Sam's Point. It may have been near the northern caves that copper could have been smelted, with the numerous copperhead snakes serving as guardians of the precious metal, while timber rattlers guarded the trees from lumbermen. Sam's Point, the southwest terminus of the "high Shawangunks," is named after legendary pioneer and Mamakating resident Samuel Gonsalus, whose father Manuel Gonsalez II,[46] was the first resident of what is now Sullivan County. In 1758, during the French and Indian War, Sam was pursued by a "scalping party" of Delaware from the Minisink region who had already killed three settlers. He evaded capture by jumping off the point and, landing in some soft bushes below, lived to tell the tale.[47] The story was reported in great detail in the *New Paltz Times* of March 10, 1865. Flying Sam died of natural causes in 1821 at the age of eighty-eight.[48] The cliff from which he made his famous leap was finally named Sam's Point in the late 1800s.

The Mamakating Indians called Sam's Point Aioskawosting, and the settlers called the jutting point of rock "the nose of Aioskawosting." This presents an interesting puzzle: *Aioska* in Munsee indicates a buck's horns,[49] and *awosting* means "on the other side of," or "across from." The rock escarpment is best viewed from "across the way" at Indian Springs Road in Wallkill, but no modern feature of the rock looks like buck's horns,[50] so we have to assume either that "Buckhorns" was the name of a prominent chief and that the rock was named after him, or that the point itself "wore the buckhorns" among all the mountains of the Shawangunk; in other words, it was "the chief" of the Shawangunks, as it is indeed the highest point in the entire Shawangunk Range. This corresponds with an ancient Algonquin tradition of recognizing "chiefs" among groupings in nature, usually the largest of that group: the moose is chief of the land animals, the whale the chief of the water animals, the eagle the chief of the raptors.

We enter the Mamakating Valley at Summitville, where rows of oak trees line both sides of the trail, and eventually we come to Shawanoesberg or "Shawnee Town," now called Wurtsboro, after the Wurts family, merchants from Philadelphia who financed the canal. It is the site of Council Hill, which in old times was the location of a great lodge for council meetings of the Munsee and the Shawnee, occasionally with leaders or representatives of other tribes as well. Lead was mined in Wurtsboro. Some lead is soft enough in its natural state to be extracted with everyday tools, and such was the case here. The father of Ramapough Lenape elder Talking Leaves often spoke of such a lead vein, and mined it himself. However, he never had a chance to show his son the location before he passed away. Sadly, many Munsee traditions were lost in the twentieth century in this way. Nearby, to the west, was the village of Lackawack, now lost beneath the Rondout Reservoir.

Honk Lake, which stands to the right of what is now Route 209, is created by Hunk Falls, which are seventy feet high. *Gunk* or *honk* as a suffix means "a place (or spot) on (or near) a mountain."

Further down the Old Mine Road we pass through the heart of the Mamakating Valley. The only Europeans to settle in Mamakating were French Protestants. Later these French migrated to Peenpack, which in "double Dutch" means "low, soft land," but in Munsee means "looks flat," or "flat water." At the junction of the Peenpack Trail and Route 209 (formerly the Minisink Trail) is the home of Philip Swarthout. He and his two sons were scalped by Mohawk Chief Joseph Brant's men in the raid of October 16, 1778. It was along Route 209 that the New Jersey militia pursued Colonel Joseph Brant of the Mohawk after his raid on Port Jervis (then "Minisink") on July 21, 1779. Wendy Harris of the Cragsmore Institute has found military documents confirming that Joseph Brant was accompanied by none other than "Flying" Sam Gonsalus. Apparently Sam was part Indian.[51]

As we move to the south, the towns become further apart. Homowack means "where the water runs out," referring to a cave that runs with water.[52] The local name *Topatcoke* may refer to "a pot" of water, as the spring there boils but does not seem to overflow its banks. Next we come to the Westbrook Fort and house, built in 1750 by Tjerck Van Keuren Westbrook. The village of Westbrookville was named in his honor. It was Dr. Westbrook who saw the Maysingway mask on a tree and called it "Mum-Bacchus," after which the town of Mombaccus, New York, was named.

Passing through the beautiful Peenpack Valley, at the village of the Huguenots, we see to our left the Peenpack Trail that leads to Cahoonzie. Cahoonzie means "the old elm tree." (The first settler of Huguenot New York was William Tietsoort in 1690. He set up a blacksmith shop along the Minisink Trail, deep in Lenape territory, at the request of the Lenape themselves, who gave him the land west of their village.) Crossing the Neversink River and heading south, we approach Port Jervis, once part of the great Minisink capital area and a highly populated region known as a center for Munsee culture and handicrafts. Just a mile or two further, we reach the great river known by many names: the Delaware, the Lenape Seepoo or Lenape Wihittuck, "River of the Lenape," or Keht-hanne, "The Greatest Stream." In the Lenape world, the more legendary a place or person, the more nicknames it collects over countless generations. As late as 1792, this part of the Delaware Valley was wild, and Munsee roamed free. No white settlements could be found for forty miles in either direction along the river.

The Minisink region extends forty more miles southward to the Delaware Water Gap, Dreamer's Rock, and the Wyoming Trail. Fowler Street in Port Jervis was once a trail to a canoe launch. If we took that path, and followed along the shoreline, we would arrive at Maghhackamack, or "pumpkin field." It is also called Schaikackamick, or "in an elbow," in reference to a branch of the Neversink River, which runs into the Delaware at this point. In 1789, Neversink was renamed Nahant by the new white settlers, but the Machackamech Cemetery, circa 1743, with its puzzling Munsee name and the graves of many pioneers and half-breed Indians, remains.[53]

14

NATIVE NEW YORKERS OF STONY COUNTRY
Rockland County

If Orange County is a wolf's head, it is a wolf that has been tamed, for the line that now separates Orange from Rockland County, angled to the northeast, forms a collar around his neck. This "collar" was placed there on February 23, 1798, during the administration of John Adams, creating two counties out of one.[1] Rockland County is the wolf's neck. In itself it is in the triangular shape of a simple arrowhead pointing westward, with the Tappan at the lower back corner, the Haverstraw at the upper half, and the Ramapough at the point, stretching back at least halfway to the Hudson River. As its name implies, Rockland too was the exclusive home of the "Minsis," the People of Stony Country. Let's get a closer look at these three important Munsee nations.

THE TAPPAN

At the lowest tip of New York State west of the Hudson is the town of Tappan, named after the Tappan, or Top-paun, Indians,[2] a prominent Munsee tribe. Their territory stretched from Nyack, which means "point of land," down the Palisades shoreline of New Jersey as far south as Manhattan's north tip. They were close kin to the Hackensack Munsees to the south of that point, most likely divided by the great Wyoming Trail now approximated by Route 80.[3] The Old Tappan Road leads west into New Jersey from the Hudson to Lake Tappan, which crosses the border between New York and New Jersey.

Chief Willem, sachem of Tappan, signed the Treaty of 1645, which helped to bring Kieft's War to a close. Sessekemick was sachem in 1645, followed in 1659 by Chief Taghkospemo, who was involved in the treaty selling Staten Island to the Dutch. The town of Nanuet was named for another sachem, Chief Nanawitt. Chief Towachkack of Tappan changed his name to Jan Claes, or Claus, and Rockland County's Clausland Inlet was named after him. A Munsee elder who used a bird totem as his mark also took a Dutch name, Johannis Hys.[4]

From treaty signatures we know that Keghtakaan was sachem of the Tappan in 1657, and Assowaka and Towachkack were both sachem in 1671. In 1701, many of those Munsee near the growing city had left the area, but the Tappan were holding firm, with 150 young warriors under the command of the great Tappan chief Mem-shee. (The population ratio between warriors and "civilians" is usually 4 to 1, so there must have been at least six hundred Tappans at that late date.) Several Natives tried to sell the Tappan land using various titles, but Mem-shee stopped them all.[5]

Tappan Zee, or the Bay of the Tappans, which, with Haverstraw Bay is the widest section of the Hudson River, was named during Dutch times in honor of this large group of people. The Tappan are known to most New Yorkers today because of the Tappen Zee Bridge, an impressive span that bears an erroneous *e* and almost three miles of the New York State Thruway, from Tarrytown to Nyack. It is the only bridge across the Hudson from Westchester County, and is a local landmark, like its misspelled sister bridge to the south, the Verrazano Narrows Bridge, which is short a *z*.

THE HAVERSTRAW

North of the Tappan were the Haverstroo, or "Haverstraw" Munsee. This is a Dutch term; the Native term is lost, although the name Reweghnome was applied to at least a subtribe of this group.[6] Their territory extended north along the Hudson to Bear Mountain. Sessegehout was the sachem during the Second Esopus War of 1663. The town of Haverstraw bears their name today.

The Haverstraw's northernmost landings faced a rock formation now called Anthony's Nose across the Hudson and beyond that, a town still called Manitou, or "Great Spirit," today. In 1683, the Haverstraw sachem Sackagkemeck deeded what is now Bear Mountain State Park to Stephen van Cortlandt.[7] North of this point are the five Esopus and later Wappingers tribes. The oral heritage of the New Paltz area, among others, preserves the story that signal fires were relayed by Natives along the Hudson long before the American colonists used them during the British invasion. The signal went from Manhattan's north end, to Tallman Mountain, to Bear Mountain, to Mount Beacon, to Poughkeepsie, to Springtown, to Kingston.[8] By giving up Bear Mountain, Sackagkemeck broke the most important link in that chain. From Bear Mountain you can see from the tip of Manhattan to Kingston on a clear day, where the entire chain of signal fires would have been visible. These fires were a symbol of hope, pride, and safety to the Munsee and related tribes of the Hudson Valley.

Haverstraw Bay, the site of large shell heaps dated to the Haverstraw ancestors of 5000 B.C.E., constitutes the tribe's eastern boundary. Their western boundary is unclear, but it probably extended past Rockland County to the end of present-day Harriman State Park. The Haverstraw were absorbed into the Tappans after the English conquest of 1664, and eventually disappeared as a political entity.

THE RAMAPOUGH, KEEPERS OF THE PASS

The Ramapough, or "mountaineer Munsee," on the other hand,

never disappeared. Their people still occupy the southwest portion of the point of that projectile which is Rockland County, on all sides of Ramapo Mountain. Ramapough means "slanting rock."[9] (I will be using the more common non-Native "Ramapo" for geographical terms here.) They are of particular historical importance because, though only twenty miles from the northern tip of Manhattan, they continue to survive. In a four-hundred-year struggle against their ultimate Goliath, New York City, the continued defiance of this small band represents one of the most protracted and hotly debated real estate battles in U.S. history.

The Ramapo Mountains form an impenetrable wall of green intersecting New York's lower border, stretching through Harriman State Park from north of Pomona to south of Ramapo Lakes, fifteen miles into New Jersey. There is only one westward pass through the Ramapo Mountains, at Hillburn and Suffern, New York, and Hillburn "belongs" to the Ramapough Munsee.[10]

Naturally such a pass has always been a bottleneck for every type of transportation since the mammoth hunters of 5000 B.C.E. wandered down from Canada. New Jersey Routes 507 and 202 are both old trails that converge there, as does the Nyack Turnpike. Route 202 is the old Ramapo Trail, which runs along the entire length of the Ramapo River[11] and stretches from Route 80 (once the Wyoming Trail) to the Haverstraw Road in the northeast, which is actually part of the same trail. Ramapough have lived along this path for centuries, and many still do. There was a Ramapough tribe in Connecticut in early colonial times. As they were driven west, they held together as a unit until reaching Yonkers, New York. When the Weckweesgeek moved to Yonkers as well, that band of Ramapough were pushed out, and their trail vanishes. It is probable that some of these scattered and joined the Munsee who were already at the pass that now bears their name.

New York State's southern border was drawn right through that pass as well. When a railroad was built to the northwest, it too was built roughly along the old Route 507 trail site now called Orange Avenue. The tracks had to take that route so that the long freight trains didn't have to climb too steep a grade. At some point, Route 17 was built as the main route through the pass. When the mighty New York State Thruway was constructed, it had to be detoured fifteen miles out of its way so as to enter through the pass. Now Route 287 links to Hillburn as well.[12] There are two hills on either side of the pass surrounding the Ramapo River in Suffern, New York, the Noorde Kop, or "North Head" in Dutch, and the Hooghe Kop, or Hoven Kaupf ("Grower's Head"), which are east and west of the gap of level land in between.

The Ramapough people lived around the Ramapo River and fished for pickerel, bass, sunfish, and trout in its grass-filled waters, and collected the mussels that continued to be plentiful in the area until the 1950s.[13] They also hunted the raccoons that lived off the mussels, but they wouldn't eat the opossum, as they were said to be grave robbers.[14]

They hunted on slopes of the mountains, and still do. Talking Leaves, the Fire Keeper for the Ramapough Nation, told me that when he was growing up his Ramapough family ate squirrel pie, pigeon, rabbit stew, and of course, venison. He hunted deer with a bow and arrow. "My uncle taught me how to do it," he said. He made the bow and arrows himself, and he told me how to split the feather of a goose and attach three, possibly four sides to the shaft, about a quarter-inch from the notch, to get the best grip and flight. "If one feather touches the bowstring, it could throw the arrow off course," he said.

When the white people came, the Ramapough would vanish into the steep mountains, almost inaccessible to those who didn't know the way, where they would be left alone.[15] Today the real Ramapo River has been dammed up above and below the pass, some of it built over, some cemented in, and the intact section is directed along a man-made route. There are now mainly stocked trout in the river, and no mussels have been seen in the area for at least fifty years.[16] One of the Ramapough Indians' chief concerns is for the welfare of the environment of the pass: their ancestors made a covenant with the Creator to keep it beautiful and in good health.

The Ramapough are beset with the strictest housing codes on both sides of the state line, with unusual restrictions for building on slopes, considering they live on a steep mountain. The Ramapough own land collectively and are state recognized, but they are seeking federal recognition, which would give them legal status as a separate nation with more autonomy. They applied for this recognition in Washington, D.C., as recently as 1994, and at first believed they would be recognized. The Supreme Court, however, rejected the 1994 application in a surprise decision, based on (1) the claim that they could not document their roots back past 1776 (the Algonquin is an oral culture, and they don't write things down), (2) that their native ancestors who identified themselves as "natives" on the colonial muster roles failed to identify exactly which local tribe they were from (many census reports didn't ask for that type of information), and (3) their chiefs in past centuries had shown insufficient leadership, giving the people too much autonomy to be recognized as a tribe under the federal government. (The Algonquin pride themselves on maximum freedom for individuals to govern themselves, one of the founding principles of the United States. Nevertheless, they signed treaties and negotiated for the valuable land that lay in the area surrounding the pass, identifying themselves at first as Iandagagh, and later as Ramapough Lenape Indians.)[17] Their appeals are now being drafted and may again reach the Supreme Court.

SPOOK ROCK

In addition to the Ramapo Trail, one of the most important old trails north from Manhattan was the Paramus Trail. It wandered through what is now New Jersey along the Saddle River, called the Peramp-seapus River by the Munsee. The town that grew up on its banks became known as Paramus, New Jersey. The trail then makes its way into the heart of Rockland County, New York. It too links with the old Wyoming Trail, which is now Route 80, to the south.[18] Where the Paramus Trail crosses a smaller trail—now Highview Road, from Monsey, New York, (pronounced Munsee) to Suffern, New York—there is a great council rock now called Spook Rock. It was a spiritual gathering place not only for Munsees, but for Native Americans from all over the eastern seaboard.[19] When the Dutch witnessed these pilgrimages to what appeared to be an ordinary rock, they called it Spuke Rock, or the "Rock of Spirit," or "The Breath of Life," in Dutch. This crucial spot too lies within the territory of the Ramapo Mountain Lenape.[20] Talking Leaves took me there one rainy day. It is a large rock sitting on top of other rocks, about fifteen feet above the street, perched on a high embankment that once afforded a clear view of the sloping mountain below. I could see that the two streets below had been trails, and that this was once a great crossroads, but further than that, I had to turn to the history books.[21]

According to Julian Harris Salomon,[22] it is perhaps the most important authentic Indian landmark remaining in the entire New York metropolitan area. It was once on top of a high mound. Old accounts tell us "it was in the form of a huge rounded fireplace, below which there was a cave, now filled with stone." It was a holy place, a shrine, "the abode of the spirit force, which for them was to be found in plants, trees, animals, and in all manifestations of nature."[23] As with other sacred shrines around the world, the Spook Rock tradition was probably initiated when a Native person saw a vision at the rock, perhaps foretelling the future, told everyone, and it came to pass. The Ramapough have always looked for signs, tokens, and omens, and have watched the animals, to help them and guide them, as did Crazy Horse of the Lakota, who also went to sacred caves to help find his answers in visions.[24] After one person had a remarkable vision, seekers and holy men and women would come and leave offerings, tobacco, pieces of buckskin, special plants, hemp cloth, and the like, asking for wisdom and guidance.[25]

Spook Rock Road leads to another ancient meeting place, called John Wood's Tree, onetime site of a gigantic oak of untold years that was accidentally destroyed in 1810 by a party of hunters who built a fire in its hollow base. It most certainly sprouted from an acorn before the arrival of Verrazzano in 1524. Spook Rock Road ends at Harriman State Park. In a direct line beyond the tree is Horsetable Rock, an ancient shelter used by the ancestors of the Ramapough, now in the heart of Harriman State Park, above Seven Lakes Road.[26]

BLOODLINES

Whites have always tried, and continue to try to portray the Ramapough as foreigners: Dutch, blacks, Tuscarora, Gypsies, or Hessians. However, they are the only actual nonforeigners to be found still living in community in and around New York's metropolitan region. According to Salomon, "Similar groups existed and still exist in Ulster, Schoharie, Greene, Columbia, Dutchess, and Orange Counties in New York. In all these the Indian element is predominantly Munsee and Mohican, but there has been so much intermarriage with whites and blacks that today few have a high proportion of Indian blood."[27, 28]

These prejudices about the Ramapough still exist today, sometimes quite openly. Ramapough parents often feel that their children do not get a fair shake in school because their family names—de Groote, de Groat, de Vries, Van Dunk—give them away as Ramapough. Life is especially hard for the black-skinned Ramapough children.[29]

In 1911, Frank G. Speck described three distinct regions of Ramapough Indians. In the eastern hills near the Hudson the population was sparser, with a predominantly white strain. Ten miles further into the Rampough range, the "mountaineers" were much more numerous, running well into the hundreds, with more Negro features and traits predominant, though the Native American genealogy was still clearly evident. Westward, toward the Delaware watershed, "the Negro strain is less apparent and the white families boast of their Indian blood."[30]

The main Ramapough Lenape villages in New York were Johnsontown, Furmanville, Sherwoodville, Bulsontown, Willowgrove, Sandyfields, and Ladentown. Better known, however, as Native American strongholds, are the towns just south of the border, namely Hillburn, Stagg Hill, and Ringwood.

There's a story that tells of a news reporter who was looking to do a story on Johnsontown. He wandered all over but couldn't find it. He met a woodsman in a wild valley, "Where's Johnsontown?" he asked. "Here!" replied the woodsman. "You're in the middle of it now!"[31]

Ramapough switched from living in wigwams to log cabins in the mid 1600s and some still live in them. The last true Ramapough log cabin was built in 1932, however some that were built long ago are still in use. One cabin occupied by the Youmans family in 1924 was only eight feet wide and ten feet long, with a height of ten feet at the peak of the roof. It had a pounded earth floor and only a few pieces of furniture. Three of the Youmans children slept in the loft spaces in the triangular space between the ceiling and roof.[32] In the 1930s, a Ramapough cabin that had been in continuous use since 1779 was demolished, marking the beginning of the end for the log legacy of the Ramapough people.

15

NATIVE NEW YORKERS OF THE NORTH— THE MOHICAN

Dutchess, Columbia, Rensselaer, Washington, Saratoga, Schenectady, Albany, and Greene Counties

In our exploration of the Hudson Valley, we have so far visited the Wappingers and Siwanoy east of the Hudson River and other Renneiu-speaking peoples of the Clason Point culture.[1] But to the north lies a different group of people—the Mohican, a people who were speaking an ancient language at the time of contact. They lived on both sides of the Hudson River, which they knew as the Mohicanituk. They were called "The People of the River That Flows Both Ways," or Mohicannau, as some say it. According to Daniel G. Brinton and James Hammond Trumbull, the two best-known authorities on Mohican history, *maugh* means "large," and *hikan* means "ocean" or "sea." The suffix *ituk*, "a river that flows both ways" was first recorded as part of the name by author Electa Jones in 1854, but today it is often added.[2] If the Mohican are the direct descendants of the Orient Point people who originated at the far tip of Long Island before 1000 B.C.E. and spread inland as far west as the Shawangunks[3] and even the Delaware, this definition makes sense. Virtually all of the territories occupied by Orient Point people in 1000 B.C.E. were speaking Mohican-derived languages in 1626. Orient Point people were sea people who lived halfway up an estuary or inlet, where they could enjoy both fresh and saltwater plants and fish. The Mohican lived halfway up the Hudson.

Although far from Manhattan, which lies at the heart of our story, the Mohican are probably the most famous of all Native New Yorkers, and their language is very similar to the one spoken in Manhattan three thousand years ago.[4] It is a parent language to the Munsee, the Unami, the Renneiu languages, and those of eastern New England. At contact, there were three dialects of Mohican spoken: the Stockbridge dialect, spoken in western Massachusetts; the Albany, or Schodack dialect, spoken on the upper Hudson; and the Dutchess County dialect, spoken at Shekomeko, near present-day Pine Plains, New York, upper Dutchess County. There is a modern town of Shekomeko, New York, on County Road 83, but the Native mission settlement started in 1740 wound up eventually at Indian Lake, five miles to the east, often referred to as "Millerton."[5]

The Hudson River at Poughkeepsie flows upstream twice a day, due to the ocean tides coming sixty or so miles up the river. Even at those times, it actually flows two directions at once, upstream on the shoreline and downstream in the center. This can best be seen from the grounds of the Beacon Sloop Club at the Beacon train station. This is why the Mohicanituk, "The River That Flows Both Ways," is so named, and the Mohican or Mohicannau, are its children.

In September 1609, Henry Hudson arrived in a brightly painted boat called *The Half Moon*. He waited for four days, and then a few Mohican canoes came forth to greet the fantastic ship with offerings of food and pelts. Friendly gestures were exchanged on both sides. Hudson, whom the Mohican noted as more finely dressed than the other sailors, came forth to greet the Mohican from the deck of the ship, and a canoe was lowered to the water. The food was accepted and sent to the ship's galley for preparation. Hudson was very careful, and the first visit went well.

Five ships, including *The Tiger* whose captain was Adriaen Block and *The Fortune* whose captain was Hendrick Christiaensen, returned in 1613 intent on establishing trade and making maps. Soon there was a Dutch stockade called Fort Nassau on Castle Island, situated in the Hudson River just south of Albany. It was fifty-eight-feet square, surrounded by a moat, with two large cannons and a total of eleven swivel guns. The Dutch fort on Castle Island prospered until the spring of 1618, when a great flood rushed down the river, breaking up the ice and hurling it against the stockade. The waters broke through and swirled around the building, but the traders escaped and abandoned the post. The next Dutch stockade was built on the west bank of the Hudson near the mouth of Norman's Kill, on Mohican maize fields.

Six years later, in May 1624, Cornelius Jacobsen landed near Norman's Kill with a group of eighteen Walloon families and began laying down the rules of a new colony. The families were given a six-year contract to work the land, taking on a six-year debt to pay for the right to the land, though the land did not necessarily belong to the Dutch and therefore they had no right to give it away. The Walloons could only sell land to other colonists and could only grow approved crops, with surpluses sold only to the colony. In return they would get whatever supplies they needed from Holland for two years.

The Mohican had outgrown the banks of the northern Hudson and expanded eastward into Connecticut centuries before the Dutch ships arrived. They prospered along the Housatonic ("Place of Stones") River, developing a strong presence through western

Massachusetts and Connecticut. Their language is more closely related to their Massachusetts nephews than it is to that of the Delaware.

The Mohican traditional culture as first observed by the Dutch must have been a fascinating mixture of beliefs, stories, and ways of speaking from their old northern Wabanaki roots,[6] mixed with influences from the more recently introduced southern corn culture. It is not clear which of these influences came from the Munsee to the south, and which seeped in from their traditional rivals the Hodenosuannee to the west. In any case, the Dutch took poor notes, if at all. As the Mohican were pushed off, converted, sent into war, married off, and otherwise decimated by disease and trouble following the Dutch occupation, much of their culture was lost.

MOHICAN CLOTHING

In *The House of Peace*, Louisa A. Dyer describes the Mohican as being "long, not broad-headed, with high cheekbones and aquiline noses, with deep-set eyes." She describes their wigwams as similar to the Iroquoian longhouses, often twenty feet wide and up to a hundred feet long. They did not have corners, but were rounded like an elongated wigwam. There was a long pole down the center as in the Munsee longhouses, and shelves and benches on the sides. The Mohican were a prosperous nation, and had the highest standard of living anywhere in the New England/New York territory. Hides and furs lined the insides of their longhouses for extra warmth and comfort.[7] The Mohican wore two kinds of deer hides, the tough buckskin made from the male deer, and the softer doeskin, made from the female deer. They would hunt and kill the deer, tan the hide with the animals' brains, which they rubbed in, then wash the hide with ashes and water to loosen the hair. They'd wash it again and then dry it, repeating the process several times until it was soft and pliable. The fur was scraped off with a scraping tool, and the undersides of the skin were smoked to help preserve the leather. Usually it was the women who sewed the pieces into clothing, using hemp thread and bone needles. They were cleaned by rubbing with yellow ochre.

The men wore breech clouts with fur robes tied and knotted at the shoulder. These robes were used at night as blankets. Their moccasins were decorated with colored porcupine quills, colored hairs, or later after the Dutch traders arrived, dyed beads. Moccasins have been called "the most serviceable foot covering ever made by any people."[8]

The whale-fin girdle-pieces so popular among the Lenape did find their way up the Hudson to Schodack from time to time, but they were rare. Intricate hair combs were carved from moose antlers. Women wore beautiful necklaces of rounded antler and bone, strung together on hemp string, or a strand made from the outer husk of the butterfly weed.

Children wore no clothes in the warmer months as it was thought that that their muscles would develop more correctly without the interference of clothing. It was also believed that the children would grow up more vigorous and illness-free if they relied on developing thicker blood and better circulation to stay warm. The lack of clothing may have helped the body throw off toxins as well.[9] Later on, as they grew to young adulthood, fashion became a higher priority.

As with the Lenape, the hair was greased to prevent it from becoming dull and brittle in the hot sun. Mohican women never wore feathers in traditional times, but wore their hair in two braids, one on each side of the head, with a beaded headband. Most men wore two braids of shoulder length, but left free at the top a "scalplock" of hair that was dyed and decorated with feathers for special occasions. The headband would often be dyed red in the old style with soft red fiber, decorated with strips of deer fur.[10] Occasionally warriors would singe off all their hair except for the scalplock, which they would decorate with hawk or eagle feathers.

Their eating habits differed little from those of the Lenape to the south, although moose and elk meat were much more readily available. Dyer also indicates they added wild plums and mushrooms to their diet.

Mohican Spiritual Life

One of the areas of Mohican tradition hit the hardest by contact with white culture was their spirituality. It must have been a unique mixture of old northern Algonquin "shamanic"[11] mysticism and the Big House traditions and moral teachings of the Lenape. There were also more than a few traces of Mohawk spirituality and mysticism blended in. It is known that the Peacemaker of the Hodenosuanee dwelt among the Mohican near the Cohoes ("Shipwrecked Canoe") Castle. This powerful teacher, whose words of forgiveness, condolence, compassion, and unity have resonated through the ages, must have had a tremendous impact on their sense of ethics and goodness.

The Mohican, like Algonquin everywhere, believed that all men were brothers, and that we are all children of the Mother Earth. Each person said "Thank you" before putting aside his bowl. As Dyer puts it, "The hospitality which never turned either friend or foe away from the wigwam hungry was another way of showing gratitude for the abundance of food furnished by the great spirit for all."[12] Singing and dancing were clearly an essential part of Mohican ceremonies, and were considered primary forms of worship. Dyer asserts that they took the place of prayer, for the Mohicans seldom asked Gitchee-Manitou (the Great Spirit) for anything, certainly not for wealth—wisdom perhaps. Dance was a way of becoming one with the Creator, as motion is synonymous with the dance of life.[13]

Those experiencing sickness or other misfortunes might attribute the trouble to bad spirits. The troubled person would then leave gifts out at places where such spirits were known to have lived. Of course, gifts and offerings were made to the Creator as well, usually tobacco, but other objects of value to the bearer could be added to the exchange in order to establish a deeper link with the universe. Like their northern ancestors, at least some of the elders must have practiced elk scapula reading, a process of burning the scapula bone of an elk in the fire, and interpreting the lines that form from the cracks as "writing" from the Creator. This technique is found among almost all ancient subarctic and shamanic cultures. They also most certainly looked for signs in the actions of birds and animals. If a bird dropped an object such as a berry or fish from the sky and it landed at one's feet, it would be taken as an omen or message, just as if it had been seen in a dream. This is part of the meaning of "dreamtime," as people refer to it today—the conviction that the earth is not only alive but also conscious; that we are all inside the dream of Manitou and even the appearance of inanimate objects has meaning.

SPIRITUAL WORDS IN MOHICAN

The Mohican language, a wellspring of Algonquin culture and a transition between archaic and modern Algonquin, is currently dormant. There are no fluent speakers, but work is underway to revive it—in the Stockbridge area with Lion Miles, the Albany area with Steve Comer, and in Stockbridge, Wisconsin, with Matt and Sheila Powless, and many others. Many of the words now being heard again after two hundred years have to do with expressing spiritual concepts. These words played an important role in the long spiritual history of New York State and help convey the spiritual outlook of the Mohican.

One of the most important terms to learn in any language is "thank you." In Mohican it is *ooneeweh*, the pre-L equivalent of the Unami *oo-lee-way*. The Mohican thank the Creator for everything that life gives them, and thank the Mother Earth for all that she provides. There is an old saying in Algonquin that in the beginning there was only one teaching and it was "be thankful." The people said, "Is that all? Just one? Aren't there more teachings?" and the Creator said,

"Okay, you don't like that one, I'll give you hundreds of rules to follow instead." After that, life got complicated.

As with most Algonquin languages, the Mohican have no word for good-bye. You just say, "See you again," *kumpanaxen*. This reminds us that life is a circle: even when we die, we will see each other again in the spirit world.

That which is sacred and holy is called *kausekhoiyek*. Things that relate to the spirit world and come from the Creator's love—visions and songs—are *kausekhoiyek*. In the ancient languages of the north, there is not always a clear distinction between "visions" and "dreams" as in the English language. The Mohican word for dreams is *onoquaam*, the pre-L equivalent of *oolonquam* in Unami—however it could be used in reference to a vision as well. The only Algonquin language I have come across with a separate word for "vision," which is not a dream, is in the Natick dialect of Massachusetts; the word is *monomansuonk*.[14] Massachusetts language is like Mohican, but much altered by missionaries such as John Eliot and others, who may have influenced their thinking. I have been also told that the Natick developed a word for "time," which was an alien concept to the Algonquin before 1620. "Time" is still untranslatable into many Algonquin tongues, other than the popular "what does your clock say?" However, much of what the missionaries preached was already obvious to the people of Turtle Island, as the following quotation illustrates:

> A Mohican of the 1700s whose name was Tschoop said, "Once a preacher came and began to explain to us that there was a God. We answered—'Dost thou think us so ignorant as not to know that? Go back to the place from whence thou camest.' Then again another preacher came and began to teach us, and to say—'You must not steal, nor lie, nor get drunk, etc.' We answered—'Thou fool, dost thou think that we don't know that? Learn first thyself, and then teach the people to whom thou

belongest, to leave off these things. For who steals, or lies, or is more drunken than thine own people?'"[15]

One word for God in Mohican is *Pohtommauwaus,* "that to which we pray." There are many more. The supreme being or Great Spirit is without gender, as women are as much a part of "it" as men are. There is no linguistic problem in speaking of "it" because he, she, and it can all be expressed with one word. It does not mean that God is a "thing" or that the Mohican worshiped objects.

The word for the soul, spirit, or "ghost," is *m'chuch-cheek,* which is related to *tchee-chan,* the word for "spirit" in Lenape. The Mohican also have the word *kchich-chuhq-nauk,* meaning "his spirit." In Algonquin, the thing we call the soul is really a vessel like a clay pot, which is filled up with the universal spirit like water. When we immerse ourselves in the spiritual life, it is like dipping a clay pot into a river. The distinction between the water inside and the water outside the pot is not definite, but there is a difference. That's what the Algonquin paradoxical vision of life is like; we are all separate yet we are one spirit. Regardless of whether we can "see" it or not, it is *wnau-mau-wauk-un,* "truth."

TOBACCO

The Mohican believed that cured tobacco soothed the mind and made the thoughts sober. It is much safer to smoke tobacco in its pure state, and less addictive, although not without its problems. It was considered a form of medicine, and one that should not be over-used or abused. Many people in the twenty-first century "smoke to calm their nerves," which is a way of saying it "soothes the mind." (However the tobacco they use is sprayed and dosed and poisoned with over a hundred chemicals.) This sense of calm or peace is called *manow* in Mohican, but only through thinking deep thoughts, praying as one with the Creator, and doing good, *waunehk,* do we find *makowa-manow,* which means "true peace."[16]

RITUALS ARE NOT GOD

One reason Mohican spirituality seemed to vanish is that it was such an integral part of every aspect of their life; it could not be isolated into a "thing" or artifact of culture. It transcended culture. When their lifestyle was forcibly changed, the spirit remained, but in a formless state. In the most ancient and revered Algonquin mysticism, the Great Spirit is infinitely intelligent and powerful, and if we can tap into it as a wholeness within, all things will be made clear to us and anything that is not right with us will be made right, even if it takes "supernatural" means to accomplish it. Whether it is something ordinary, like a message from a friend, or what the Europeans call a "miracle," it all comes from the hand of the Creator. There are many roads to this inner wholeness, one for each person born. There were no priests or clergy. Everyone had the road to the Creator within them. No one prayer, no matter how eloquent, could get you into that state of connectedness, timelessness, and openness; no one type of burnt offering, no matter how precious, could earn you that right; no one deed, no matter how beneficial, could make you worthy of that understanding and wisdom. Either you got it or you didn't, and all the sweat lodges and vision quests won't make a difference if your heart is not open to the heart of the Creator. All the scapula augeries in the world can't guide you if your ears are closed to the words of the Creator.

THE GREAT BEAR IN THE SKY

The Mohican had some phenomenal rituals, in which the miraculous was an essential part of the process. Some, such as the ancient bear ritual, are not for the weak of heart. Clues to Mohican ritual can be found in Frank G. Speck's *The Celestial Bear Comes Down to Earth*, written in collaboration with Nekatcit, Josiah Montour, and Jesse M. Moses, Jr., an elderly man of Mohican and Munsee descent. Moses describes five ceremonial "seasons" or feasts; the Bear Feast in January, the Maple Sugar Feast in March, the Planting Feast in May, the Strawberry Feast in June, and the Corn Feast in September.

He describes bear rituals that were not typical of the Munsee, but were performed in the context of the Munsee Big House Ceremony by those of mixed descent. Some time before what is now known as Groundhog Day—which was a variation developed by the Delaware of Punxsutawney, Pennsylvania—was the time the bear came out of hibernation to see his shadow. At the new moon, a woman of the tribe would dream of the whereabouts of the bear to be sacrificed, and the men would hunt him, making offerings and prayers, and asking him to come to the Big House to be eaten. This marked the start of the bear-hunting season. They would not hunt "the smooth bear," one with very little hair, as that was the one the boy lived with in the story and song "The Boy and the Bear," often sung in the sweat lodges of the Wabanaki.

As Speck points out, many aspects of these "Mohican" rituals are held in common with the Wabanaki, the Algonquin of Maine, and the Maritimes. They are also linked to the Midewiwin ceremonies of the longhouse practiced by their Ojibway cousins. He also suggests that the two "halves" of the Big House itself represent the joining of the Mohican "house" with the Munsee. The two halves are aligned with Mohican to the east and Munsee to the west, but the Mohican are clearly part of the northern "bear cult" traditions of the old Algonquin, and the Lenape part of the southern "corn cult" traditions of the south. The Big House is a double longhouse, and at least in its earliest inception, was part of both ceremonies, the corn in September, the bear in January.

In the bear ceremony, the floor of the Big House becomes the sky, and the stars of the constellation Ursa Major, or Big Dipper, are marked on the floor in some subtle way. Each of the dancers would stand in a spot representing one of the stars and dance that star. The four stars of the dipper represent the bear, whereas the three handle stars are three hunters. The faint star, or *anaksook,* standing beside the middle of the three is "the little hunting dog." Always visible at night, this constellation was used by the Mohican and Delaware for orienting and navigation. In one story known throughout the eastern woodlands, three boys and their dog were hunting a certain bear for years. The bear climbed the sky and became a group of stars, and the boys followed right after him, becoming stars themselves.

At the start of the ritual, the chief went out with twelve helpers to find the bear. They summoned him from his lair, and told him to walk to the Big House to be killed. The bear took the lead and the men followed. The bear was expected to walk in through the eastern door, where the chief would say, "We will all meet later, in the sky," and slay him. If the bear lay down or refused to cross a creek or stopped along the way, the chief told the bear, "Right here we will have to kill you. We want your body for the Big House."[17] If the bear lowered his head and closed his eyes, he was killed and skinned in a manner the reverse of that for game animals, starting at the head. Then the pelt was given to the chief.[18] The "naked" bear was carried inside the Big House and set down on the floor. The bear hide was then wrapped around the center post, just below the Maysingway faces, masks placed upon or carved into the twelve posts of the Big House. Then the bear was cut up and cooked by the women for the feast. Each night for five nights, the chief would give teachings to the men outside the Big House until the moon came up. The bear meat had to be completely eaten by the rising of the fifth moon, although Speck is not sure how that was managed. As the moon waxed more fully, the nights were filled with dancing and celebration. The entire ritual took twelve days, the sacred number of the Big House.

After the fifth moon, the spiritual powers were strong, and the Recitation of Dreams began. The twelve men who had hunted the bear sat in a circle. The chief would hand the sacred turtle shell rattle, *cuxweni-kan,* made from a painted turtle,[19] to one of the four drummers sitting on red benches, whose job was to sing or repeat the dreams of the twelve hunters. The first drummer would carry the shaker across the room to the first of the hunters and lay it on the floor in front of him. As each hunter recited or sung his dream, he'd shake the painted turtle rattle and then slide it to the next man on his left, until the turtle had gone all around the circle. It would then be returned to the place between the chief and the center post representing the star the white men call Alcor (close to Mizar) in the Great Bear Constellation Ursa Major, or Big Dipper, representing the little hunting dog in the story. The chief's seat was apparently in the place of the last hunter at the end of the Big Dipper's handle. The turtle has thirteen scale plates around the edge, twelve dorsal and one vertebral, representing the months or moons of the year in Mohican cosmology. There are twelve days and nights to the ceremony, twelve hunters, twelve prayer sticks and prayer cries, twelve posts in the Big House, twelve Maysingway masks, and twelve levels of clouds in the sky representing the twelve levels of the spirit world. On the twelfth night, the moon was full, and the people would dance until sunrise under its glowing light.

TEACHINGS FOR THE CHILDREN

The Mohican children were taught to listen to their elders, and to learn the lessons of the teaching tales and stories. In *The House of Peace,* Dyer states that the "rules" or teachings the Mohican children had to learn were simple but were not always easy to keep. There were nine teachings, as listed in her work, set down in the mid 1950s: (1) Help those in trouble. (2) Feed those who are hungry. (3) Care for the aged. (4) Be kind to strangers. (5) Tell the truth. (6) Be honest and do not steal. (7) Be industrious. (8) Do not take life of any kind needlessly. (9) Give obedience to the sachems and the chiefs.[20] As a cautionary note, such utterances were teachings, not rules, and were taught by repetition, not punishment. The Algonquin considered it futile to try to force children to do anything they did not understand, and would try reason as a first line of enforcement.

MOHICAN GOVERNMENT

The smallest unit of government was always the family. The mother ruled the roost and disciplined the children. The children took their mother's clan name, which would have been either bear, wolf, or tortoise. When the family was on the trail, the father was the supreme power, with absolute authority as to what was dangerous or inappropriate. Boys used small toy-sized bows and arrows when young. When they were old enough to use real ones, the uncles would take over in raising and training them, making rules and giving them instruction. When they became grown men, they became part of the government of the people—a government of noninterference.[21] The people valued their freedom over all else. Mohican philosophy placed a greater priority on the quality of life, at least from an intrinsic standpoint, than mere survival, and often proved it. The mottoes of their two neighboring states—"Don't tread on me" and "Live free or die"—are attributed to whites, but I have always believed they were "borrowed" from the mouths of sachems of the neighboring Abenaki whose culture is closely related to that of the Mohican. It is no secret that the pioneers and early colonists were profoundly inspired by the fiery spirit of independence that the Native people possessed and the tolerance they demanded from their governmental leaders. King George III certainly felt the impact of that new sense of "independence."

Each sachem possessed the *minoti*, or "peace bag," of the tribe. It contained wampum belts and tokens used in sending messages and making treaties. Each sachem had a council of subchiefs, plus a war chief. He had one person called an "owl," or orator, who would speak to the people, or to visiting dignitaries, like today's presidential "press secretary." He would also have at least one messenger, who could run very fast over long distances. The nearby Mohawk Trail was designed with this in mind. Other trails had similar purposes. War was declared by the peace chief, or local sachem, and then all power was shifted to the war chief. However, it was the peace chief who had the sole right to declare the end to war. The women chose the candidate, who was then nominated by the grand council. If the council rejected him, the women would have to come up with a second choice. Once one of these figures had been nominated and elected, there would be a great ceremony. The induction ceremony for the grand sachem, who presided over all Mohican chiefs, was held at Scotiak, or Schodack, a name derived from a Mohican term for an "ever-burning fire place." The central council fire of the Mohicans located there was considered to have been taken from the original fire of Creation at Oka, preserved by the first ancestor for hundreds of years and then kept ablaze by the Mohican people for thousands more.[22]

MOHICAN BUILDING TECHNIQUES

The Mohican marked trees and rocks with totem signs to define their territory and hunting grounds. They painted, carved, or blazed the totem signs, depending on the surface. Wigwam coverings were made of elm bark, or if elm was not available, basswood bark. They would make deep, long vertical cuts in the elm tree with a stone knife, then cut around. Wedges of wood or stone would be hammered in to split the bark in one piece off from the tree.[23]

Cutting down a tree to build a fortress, or "castle," as the whites referred to them, was not easy with stone tools. The Mohican would often burn fires at the base of a tree to weaken the trunk for easier cutting.

Most known castles were built on a hill near a river or stream. A fence was made of long, thick, pointed logs driven into the ground. This fence might be sixteen to thirty feet high. Sometimes the stockade was three rows deep. Longhouses and smaller dwellings would be set up around the outside of the stockade, some say as many as twenty to thirty dwellings of various sizes. When attacked, the people of the village would grab their prized tools and furs and a few other possessions, and dash through the gate of the stockade to safety. Each castle housed a war chief. The exact number of Mohican castles that have ever been built has been long debated; estimates range from four to forty. There was one on the west bank of the Hudson near the mouth of Norman's Kill, one at "the ever-burning fire place" near Castleton, one on the east bank of the Hudson at a place called Panhoosic, "waterfall,"[24] where Troy now stands. Another castle was called Monemius, beside the Mohawk River near Cohoes. Another was called Aepjin's castle,[25] below Albany, near the village of Schodack, where the grand sachem lived.[26] Aepjin sold the land of Schodack to the whites in 1680. The Dutch had once come to Schodack professing friendship and tolerance. It is sad to note that within fifty-six years of the Walloon landing, the eternal fire had either been extinguished or moved into hiding, the land abandoned to the Dutch for shell beads. By 1750, the political influence of the once-powerful Mohican was extinguished in the Hudson Valley, though not their people, who still live today in Stockbridge, Wisconsin.

The Land of the Mohican: Northern Dutchess County

Let's examine the territory of the Mohican lying within New York's present boundaries, county by county, starting where we left off, in northern Dutchess County.

The Mohican and Wappingers[27] were such great allies at the end of the sixteenth century that their marked territories appear intermingled like building blocks of different colors when viewed on a map of old Dutchess County.[28]

At Rhinebeck, there was an old Mohican village called Sepasco, possibly on the flat area on the southeast corner of Sepasco Lake, an area covered with oak trees and their numerous acorns. The word *Sepasco* could be from "a small river place," or the old Algonquin for

"ground nuts."[29] The Sepasco Trail ran westward from the lake, crossing the Mohican Trail (Route 9) at what is now Rhinebeck, and
ending at the banks of the Hudson River at a Mohican village that is
now Rhinecliff. The exact route of this trail is debated, but quaint
side roads off of today's Route 308, which travels directly northeast
from Rhinecliff to the lake, attest to its former location. Near the lake,
the trail connects with the one that is now Route 199, leading to
Shekomeko. The entire Sepasco Trail may have been a northern spur
of an ancient trail that ran from Rhinecliff to Cornwall, Connecticut.
From Rhinecliff one could see the smoke from the fires of the
Warranawongkong, the largest and most powerful of the Esopus
tribes at present-day Kingston, across the water.

The eastern part of Rhinebeck remains a rural area even today,
and it is said that Mohican held out for years in the woods, resisting
assimilation. Rhinebecker Janet Jappen tells the following story: Ms.
Jappen's grandfather had bought an ancient farmhouse from a
woman whose family had built the plain clapboard structure, typical
of Rhinebeck Dutch design, centuries earlier. After signing the
papers, he asked if there were any interesting stories about the place.
The woman revealed that in the 1880s, when she was a girl, an old
Mohican Indian who had been living in the woods had become fragile with age, and started to spend the winters in the house with them.
He would sit on the wide planked floor beside the fire all day, just
looking at the flames, never speaking. He would now and then pick
up a tiny stone or pebble from a crevice in the floor and roll it toward
the kitchen door, apparently to see how close to the door he could get
the stone to rest without actually touching it. Bemused by his "sport,"
his eyes would turn back to the flames, and his thoughts would turn
back to his private reveries once again.

The unnamed Mohican soon passed away and was buried in the
yard. A pile of stones was placed on top of his grave as a memorial to
this remarkable man.

Jappen described an Indian well on the farm property, which apparently had already been there when the original Dutch ancestors of the old woman came to Rhinebeck, and which is still there today. Ms. Jappen showed me the trail that passed through virgin, uncut forest where they say the old Mohican lived, in his wigwam, right up to the advent of the twentieth century.

COLUMBIA COUNTY

North of Dutchess is Columbia County, where the Mohican were known to live until at least 1855. Though most were relocated to Stockbridge, Wisconsin, some surely remained in the woods for years afterward. Here the Mohican trail is most closely approximated by the four-lane highway called Route 9.

Long ago, to our east, there was a place the Natives called Wa-wanaquassick, "where the heaps of stones lie," near the banks of the Nanapenahakan ("the stream that runs through our land") Creek. Today the site is Churchtown, named after a church built there by white settlers. But the spot was once a shrine, which the Natives honored by piling stones. The Mohican approaching the site would pick up a suitable rock and carry it with them, and then place it on the pile. Sometimes such piles were shrines to a great person who had died, sometimes they were simple shrines intended to inspire those who passed by. This was an ancient custom among the Algonquin people; everyone made an offering.

A Mohican village existed at what is now Catskill Station, but most of the people lived at campsites and moved from place to place. Traces of camps have been found at the bay southeast of Hudson, New York; near Linlithgo; north of the mouth of Kinderhook Creek; west of Columbiaville; on the east side of Claverack Creek south of Stockport; on Kinderhook Lake; and on the north shore of Copake Lake. A Mohican campsite at the north end of the county later became the town of Stuyvesant, New York.

Copake, New York, the name of which derives from *coo-peck*, variously translated "snake water," and "pine pond,"[30] is a town on the eastern side of the county. It was once the site of an Indian "resort," a place where aboriginal people went to relax and socialize. The actual site is at a spring on the side of a mountain that is now called Tom's Mountain. The original name was Taghkanick,[31] or "in the forest," which is now the name of a nearby town, Taconic, New York. The well-known Taconic Parkway's name was derived from this otherwise forgotten resort location.

RENSSELAER COUNTY

Rensselaer County was a stronghold of the Mohican people, but today much of its precolonial history is buried beneath towns and roadways. Most of what is known about its aboriginal past has been surmised from the few fragmented clues that have been extracted from that vast archaeological record.

There were Mohican villages at Schodack Landing and further on at South Schodack. There was a fortified "castle" at what is now Castleton. Schodack Center is where the legendary Mohican council fire was located, home of the Mohican grand council. Further on there was a Mohican village at East Greenbush. On the banks of the Hudson is the town of Rensselaer itself, the site of the Moenemies' castle. When Van Rensselaer bought the land on both sides of the river in 1630, he got the castle in the bargain.

Not far away was a place called Walloomsack. This is a Munsee term meaning a "red rock," or a rock that has been dyed red. This spot is now part of the town of Hoosic, New York, near Bennington, Vermont.

There was a huge village at South Troy, and several at Lansingburg, including the site of Unawat's Castle, opposite Van Schaick Island. There was also a major village north of Waterford Bridge along the Hudson where a large quantity of tools and relics have been found.

At the north end of Rensselaer County is the town of Schaghticoke, which has a long Native history. The Hoosic River empties into the Hudson here. An ancient village site has been found at this spot that yields "Eskimoan" implements, probably from the proto-Algonquins. Also within the township of Schaghticoke is the town of Reynolds, home of the Knickerbocker Estate, where a council fire and a great council oak existed for centuries. The main site at the Knickerbocker Estate lay where two small streams converge. Trudy Richmond of today's Schaghticoke people says the name means "where two rivers converge." There are two places by this name, and two rivers or streams converge at both places, one in north Rensselaer County and one in Saratoga County. These Schaghticokes were removed to Stockbridge, Massachusetts, around 1750, but a large party of their people continued to visit the original tree once a year until 1850. They were always accompanied by an elderly woman, probably Eunice Mahwee, who lived to a vigorous old age of 104.[32] This tree at the Knickerbocker Estate was planted in the early 1700s to commemorate the Covenant Chain Treaty between the English and the Schaghticoke. It died and was cut down in the 1980s, and pieces of it remain in the hands of many Schaghticoke people today. The Schaghticoke had wigwams and continued to conduct yearly pow-wows at the Nook (at the Old Cline Farm) in South Amenia, New York, until the 1800s.[33] The Schaghticoke Tribal Nation today is centered in Kent, Connecticut. Their original land was an oblong shape that stretched across the New York/Connecticut state border, encompassing what is now Dover Plains, Amenia, and Rensselaer, New York (including the Knickerbocker Estate), and Milton, Connecticut. The Schaghticoke Tribal Nation has been locally recognized since statehood. They have been seeking federal recognition since 1936. It is thought that they were originally an offshoot of the Pocumtuck of western Massachussetts, an L or Delaware-type dialect, although I suspect them to have Mohican origins, if only ancient ones.

There were numerous castles or fortresses throughout the region, some say only two or three really large ones, but they were legendary throughout the infant colonies of North America. There was a castle at Fort Hoosic, two and a half miles from Eagle Bridge, at the northeast corner of the county, not far from two separate village sites.[34]

TRAIL TO THE SOURCE

The Mohican Trail, today Route 9, continues north into Washington County, through Glens Falls, New York, to the southern point of Lake George. There the trail splits, the eastern spur running alongside Lake George, now State Route 9N, the western spur continuing along the Hudson, winding to the left and right of it, as the river is but a modest one. This is now State Route 9. The two trails converge again at Keene, New York, and continue on through Abenaki country all the way to Canada where Interstate 87 merges with Route 9 and becomes Canadian Route 15. The trail site runs along today's Route 15, and along the east banks of the St. Lawrence River. In ancient times, one would ferry across at various points, one of them where the Peace Bridge now stands, the birthplace of the Native American ironworking industry. One would cross here to a great island in the middle of the St. Lawrence River, covered with trees and Native villages, similar to Manhattan in many ways, but slightly rounder in shape, and more mountainous.

In the center of the island is a sacred mountain and near the sacred mountain is an ancient sacred area where the Algonquin say their ancestors originated thousands of years ago. The sacred mountain is now Mount Royal, a tourist attraction, and Oka ("pickerel") is now the city of Montreal. There is still a township of Oka within the city limits, and it was here that some Algonquin say the first human was created. When a golf course was proposed for this area, Native Americans from all over North America came to defend their Garden of Eden. The media in general were mystified why these Indians were fighting to the death over a golf course. They were told it was a sacred burial ground, which only added to the confusion. In fact, it was the site of the first eternal fire of Creation.

A spark of this Creation fire was taken southward down the Mohican Trail to Schodack and placed there several thousand years ago, where it existed at least from 1000 B.C.E., possibly earlier.

It is my belief that the members of the main branch of the Mohican family tree literally walked down the Mohican Trail from Oka to Schodack (and the much smaller island, Castle Island), and from there all the way to Bowling Green, Manhattan Island, where they set up a secondary council fire. From these fires, their descendants spread throughout the Hudson Valley and Long Island, setting up secondary fires along their way. They were joined by Algonquin from Alumette Island in the Ottawa River to the northwest who also recognized in Manhattan a familiar terrain. It is also likely that the Mohican of 1000 B.C.E. set up camp and council fire at Minisink Island in the Delaware River, a location that later gave birth to the Munsee culture as we know it.

All the trails we have been exploring would have developed over time, branching off from that Mohican Trail and from those first council fires. The Great Council Fire south of Detroit, in what is now Brownsville, Michigan, was moved there either from Oka or from Schodack, and from there to the Midwest after the War of 1812, by the Potowatomi. Thus, the region of New York State has always been a seat of power and tradition for Native Americans, both Algonquin and Iroquois, as it is now for the people of the United States.

WASHINGTON COUNTY

Washington County was a mining and hunting area for the Mohican, more than a place of residence, so there were fewer Mohican settlements than in Saratoga and Albany Counties, which were quite populous.

A Mohican village stood on Woods Creek where Fort Ann, Kingsbury, and Hartford meet, with another village site almost directly south, on the east slope of the creek, near Smith Basin, right off Route 4. There was a village on the south border of Savannah township, plus an earthworks and another village nearby. A Mohican village lay on the west bank of the Seneca River and others existed at Cambridge and Walcott, near the New York Central train tracks. There was a Mohican village at Sodus ("silvery waters")[35] Point on Sodus Bay, and four more Mohican villages in and around Marion, New York, though none were castles or fortresses.

There was a popular Mohican campground in the township of Whitehall, a few miles south of Lake Champlain between Metawee and Woods Creek.

SARATOGA COUNTY

Saratoga County is to the west of the Hudson, although at Glens Falls in Washington County the great river takes a sudden turn to the southwest, creating a puzzle-piece-like northern border for Saratoga County. There are many settlements all over the county, though in many cases they are Mohawk (rather than Mohican), or hard to distinguish. There is a village site in Schuylerville and a burial site discovered during excavation for the opera house. A small village was found below Mechanicville, opposite the town of Schaghticoke. A large village covering an extensive area has been found on Round Lake, apparently quite old, plus a smaller village on the inlet to the lake. Remains of the fortress described as Unawat's Castle were found on Poebles Island, near the mouth of the Mohawk River. There was a village site near Vischers Ferry that was destroyed to build a portion of the Erie Canal, and another at Half Moon, New York, east of Clifton Park.

SCHENECTADY COUNTY

Not much is known about the Algonquin of this area, except that the town of Schenectady itself was a prosperous village with clearly marked tracts of land when the Dutch arrived. There were about ten campsites discovered before 1922, and several burial areas. There were also village sites at Rexford and south of Glenville.

ALBANY COUNTY

There were many Mohican trails in and around Albany County before the Dutch, but not as many villages as one would expect for an area so close to the ever-burning fire place of the Mohican at Schodack. It was clearly, however, Mohican land, with small numbers of Schaghticokes. One of these settlements was at Oniskethau, named after the wife of a great chief, now called Coneyman Creek, Dutch for "rabbit hunter." There was a trail from Cohoes at the corner where the Mohawk empties into the Hudson, down to South Bethlehem, and campsites were set up all along the way. A train track now runs parallel to it, about six miles to the east. The trail passed over an escarpment at what is still called Indian Ladder Road, one mile from Meadowdale Station. In a niche where the rocks were twenty feet high, a tree was felled against them, and the branches lopped off to make steps. It was still in use in 1820. Indian Ladder Road now grants travelers access to the higher ground, however there had been a ladder of some sort placed there by locals well into the twentieth century. A trail known as "the bear path" leads around the cliff as well.[36] Burials have been found in Washington Park and Bethlehem, and there is evidence of Mohican occupation there, up to recent times. There was also a trail that followed Western Avenue in Albany along what is now Route 20, leading to Schenectady County and westward on to Buffalo, New York. There were camps at Dunnsville (Dunn is a common Mohican family name) and Fuller's Station, Guilderland, McKownville, and the sand flats of west Albany. There were hunting camps along a trail going from northwest to southeast, from Schoharie County through Altamont, Meadowvale, Voorhees-ville, and Clarksville, to Coeyman's Hollow and on to Coxsackie in Greene County.

Steamboat Square, a central landmark in Albany, was a large agricultural area when the Dutch arrived. Continuing to the south, we come to Greene County, beyond which lies the land of the Munsee.

GREENE COUNTY

In the early days of Dutch settlement, there were apparently some Wappingers living on the west bank of the Hudson near Albany, from Catskill Creek north through Albany County region, to the edge of Mohawk country. During the Dutch and Indian wars of 1643 and 1663, Aepjin and Wapperonk were two important Wappingers chiefs. In 1680 Aepjin sold to the whites an area near Albany which stretched from Beeren Island to Smack Island up to Van Rensselaer's castle.[37]

Most of the village sites are located along the Hudson River on the eastern side of the county or in the valley of Catskill Creek, at least to South Cairo. The Mohican didn't live in the mountains to the west, though a few rock shelters and hunting camps, such as the one at Windham, have been found. It was in the Catskill region that a "Squaw sachem" (as the colonials called them) named Nipapoa lived. In Munsee, Nipapoa means "Hidden Moon." Shirley Dunn writes, "A woman sachem of Catskill, Nipapoa was a signer of a deed for an island in the Hudson River below Albany. The same Indian signed deeds for land in the Catskill area and in present-day Columbia County across the river." Two things intrigue me about Nipapoa: first, she was a woman sachem whom the Dutch recognized—most Native women of authority were not recognized by the Dutch, and second, she was a Catskill Indian with a Munsee name. There are names that make sense both in Mohican and Munsee, since Munsee evolved out of the older Mohican, and Nipapoa may be one of them.[38]

Heading south along the banks of the Hudson, we come to Coxsackie, where there was once a village, a major flint quarry, and several camps along the river. Coxsackie means "land of the honking geese."[39]

Athens, New York, was the site of the village of Mackawaic, or "Black Rock." You can see the black rock itself on the river. Near here, around Sleepy Hollow Lake, a long necklace of copper beads was excavated. It may have come from the great old copper culture at Alumette Island, where many Lenape ancestors came from. This necklace, with exactly three hundred small, uniform copper beads and a notched pendant, has been dated to well before the arrival of Columbus. It was not found near any colonial artifacts or even other Native artifacts.[40]

The following story that relates to the southern part of this region concerning the plant known as Indian plume, bee balm, or "Oswego tea," which is quite plentiful in the Catskills.[41]

A great plague (possibly smallpox) was among the people, and cutting down the lives of half the population or more, like so many trees. The maiden Lenawee was engaged to be married to a Saranac ("river that flows under rocks") Indian from up north. He was called "The Arrow." He came down to the Esopus area for the wedding. Suddenly, he caught the disease and he died as well. Lenawee offered herself as a sacrifice. She prayed to the Great Spirit that she could offer her life in exchange for her people, and bring an end to the plague. She stood beside his dead body on the ground, held a knife to her chest and said, "Lay me with The Arrow. I am but a blighted flower!" Upon saying this, she killed herself, and her blood lay all over the ground where she fell.

The next morning when the people returned, both of their bodies had disappeared and her blood had vanished, but in its place, was the bright red Indian plume, also called bee balm. The families decided to hold a great feast, and to honor the unlucky couple they decked their hair and garments with the bright red flower. Then they made tea out of the plant, and it cured the disease that had been plaguing them.

A trail ran along Catskill Creek, later the Old King's Road. It turned north and arrived at the old village of Wachachkeek, "hill country," on the banks of the Catskill Creek, west of Leeds, New York. This site is near the intersection of King's Road and Old State Route 23, formerly the Catskill Trail, the first of five great flats that will became part of the Catskill Patent. To the north was the village of Quichtok, or "high place." Just up the hill and further to the northwest were the Mohican villages of Wichquamhtekak, Potuck, ("swampy brook") and Pachqueack, also along the creek. There was yet another major village on the flatlands, to the south of the joining of Catskill and Kaaterskill Creeks.

Moving west along the Catskill Trail we would come to an area called Tagpohkight near South Cairo. This is the edge of the Mohican settlement area where many were brought to be buried. Beyond this point is hunting area only, though the trail continued west, following the path of modern Route 23 from Cairo to Windham.

The trail brings us to Harpersfeld, then we turn left on what is now Rural Route 33 to Route 12, then take Route 10, which is still called the Old Catskill Turnpike, one of the most picturesque routes in the Catskills. At Meridale, we turn right onto Route 28 and pick up the Catskill Turnpike/Catskill Trail again at Route 357. Along Route 357 the modern traveler will see signs and plaques marking the locations of Indian council elms and pioneer homes, clues that this was a prominent trail west in the mid 1700s. Route 357, also an endless string of scenic splendors even today, becomes Route 7 in Unadilla and meets its final destination where the Unadilla River converges with the Susquehanna in the heart of Delaware County.

Back toward the river, there was once a village and Mohican stockade inside the question-mark bend in the creek just outside of Catskill, New York. Both Lenape and the Mohican liked to build forts inside such hairpin turns with the natural moats they provided. This castle was on the southwest corner of Jefferson Flats, now called

Castle Heights. There was a small village at the foot of Hop-O-Nose Hill.[42] Another called Quat-a-wich-nach ("place of the great over-flow of the stream," i.e., boggy land[43]) lay on the west side of the Kaaterskill Creek on the high land opposite Temmerman Hill. Today the New York State Thruway passes through here.

According to Washington Irving, the Natives considered the "Kattsberg" or Catskill Mountains to be the dwelling place of Manitowak, spirit beings who created the weather, ruled over by a "squaw spirit," as he put it, said to be their mother, who dwelt on the highest peak of the Catskills, possibly Hunter Mountain, which is 4,050 feet high. Irving writes of this "old woman," in his *Sketch Book:*

> She dwelt on the highest peak of the Catskills, and had charge of the doors of day and night to open and shut them at the proper hour. She hung up the new moons in the skies, and cut up the old ones into stars. In times of drought, if properly propitiated, she would spin light summer clouds out of cobwebs and morning dew, and send them off from the crest of the mountain, flake after flake, like flakes of carded cotton, to float in the air; until dissolved by the heat of the sun, they would fall in gentle showers, causing the grass to spring, the fruits to ripen, the tobacco to sprout, and the corn to grow an inch an hour. If displeased, however, she would brew up clouds black as ink, sitting in the midst of them like a bottled-bellied spider in the midst of its web; and when these clouds broke, woe betide the valleys! [44]

Along the river to the south near today's Route 9W were three large villages at Green Point, a land mass surrounded by lily pads that extends well out into the Hudson River. Further south was the Mohican riverside town of Pes-squaw-nach-qua ("a woman's breast") now Dewitt Point. The small island that inspired the color-ful name is still there, but the St. Lawrence Cement Company has bought up the entire shoreline to Smith Point so you cannot see it.

Parallel to this is Route 32, which approximates an old trail connecting the Algonquin towns of Cairo, Saugerties, Kingston, New Paltz, and Newburgh. Route 32 crosses a side branch of the Old Catskill Trail, now Route 23A, near Kaaterskill Falls, the name of which is thought to be derived from the Dutch word for "cataract." However, there was also a Mohican Chief Kaankat, mentioned by the Dutch in 1626.[45] Thus, Kaaterskill may be another example of "double Dutch," one from which the name of the entire Catskill region derived.

At Saugerties the main trail south—along the Esopus at the river's most navigable stretch—was what is now County Road 31. Several historic stone houses are found along Route 31, notably the Brinck House. Dr. Joe Diamond, archaeologist at SUNY, New Paltz, confirms that Country Road 31 was an important native trail, hence one of the first to be turned into a road by the Dutch.

Saugerties was sold to Governor Andros of the Dutch on April 27, 1677—for a blanket, a piece of cloth, a shirt, a loaf of bread, and some coarse fiber to make socks—by Kaelcop (or Kaelcoptl), the Esopus Indian and chief of the Amorgarikakan family. Like many sachem names in the Renneiu language, it is distinctly South American in flavor, possibly dating back to the Hispaniola period during Christopher Columbus's era, or from the time of the original "slave trade triangle" between Hispaniola, New York, and London, shortly thereafter.

The northern boundary of the deeded area was the Sawyer's Kill where a Dutchman named Barent Cornelius Volge operated at least one sawmill between 1652 and 1663. The Indians called Volge "The Little Sawyer," which in Dutch translates as "Saugerties." A partial reconstruction of his mill stands today at the north end of Seaman's Park.

THE SACRED MOUNTAIN

As with many ancient cultures around the world, the Lenape and Mohican of the Hudson Valley reserved the mountains for fearless hunters of game, and also fearless seekers for God. As Manitou is found at the highest of twelve levels of heaven, parallel to the levels of clouds in the sky, so one ascends to God by climbing the mountain, not just symbolically, but in fact. It is said that the power of spirit increases as you climb higher, and that most people are not pure enough to withstand that power for very long, and come back down to the valley sooner or later. Some Algonquin thought says such an ascent can make you crazy if you're not ready for it. The stereotype of a "crazy" hermit living in the mountains has its historical roots in such ancient beliefs.

There is a wall of majestic mountains over three thousand feet high and stretching over fifteen miles along the Hudson River from Overlook Mountain to Catskill Mountain. This range was sacred to the Mohican and Esopus Munsee whose territories overlapped here, and so people call it the Wall of Manitou, although there is no hard evidence to prove the name originated with the Mohican. These mountains are perceived by many as sacred. Overlook Mountain, the southern terminus with its expansive view, was chosen by the Kargu School of Tibetan Buddhism as the North American seat of the Karmapa, the spiritual head of the Kargyu. To the south is the Zen monastery on Meade Mountain. To the north is Indian Head Mountain, a hikers' paradise. There is a large yoga retreat at Haines Falls on the other side of High Peak, north of Plattekill Cove. Nestled in the mountains to the north are North Lake and South Lake, direct translations of their aboriginal names, used as fishing camps by the Natives. Beyond Stoppel Point and Round Top is Catskill Creek, the official borderline of Mohican territory and a main Mohican travel route.

The Wall of Manitou is so tall it was said to reach halfway to heaven. No one lived up there in the old days, and few live there today. But the Munsee and Mohican would go up to that top berth, halfway to heaven, to get a taste for the afterlife and to do a four-day fast alone, with no one near but God.

THE SLEEPING MAIDEN

High above the spot where Rip Van Winkle slept, and much earlier in Catskill history, there was another sleeper, an Indian maiden.[46] Her secret spot was called Garden Rock, where Kaaterskill Falls now stands against the sky. She was not just any maiden, however, she was a Manitoueeskwa, a female Manitowak, and something of a shapeshifter. She had many magical powers. She separated the night from the day, made the stars and moon, and wove the clouds for the Great Spirit to rest his head upon.

One day, a young traveling man, probably a Munsee, but we're not sure, was snooping around her private lair, and saw many great gourds hanging from the trees. As he grabbed one of the pendulous gourds, it broke, and water poured out of the gourd in a great torrent. The waves of water washed him over the edge of a great cliff and he fell two-hundred-sixty feet into a great pool of water, where he drowned. The maiden had been very vexed when the young man tried to come upon her unannounced and had sent the magic, but after she realized what had happened, she had second thoughts. She went down to the pool to take a look at the face of the mortal man she had killed. Upon seeing his face she fell in love with him, but could not bring him back to life. She floated back up the cliff and stays now at Garden Rock forever in hiding, crying her tears in gushing torrents.

That cliff today is the three-hundred-foot multitiered waterfall, Kaaterskill Falls, and sometimes you can see a rainbow around the pool at the base. That's the Manitoueeskwa's love shining over and protecting the spirit of that unwary traveler until she can figure out a way to make him immortal. If you climb to the base of Kaaterskill Falls on a sunny day, you might see the rainbow with your own eyes.

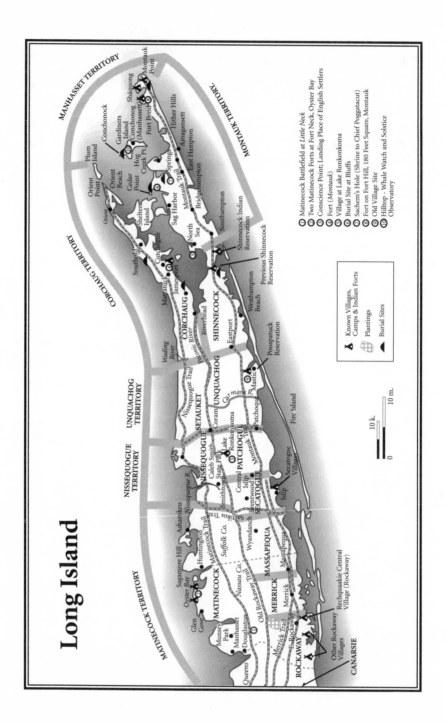

Long Island

MATINECOCK TERRITORY

MANHASSET TERRITORY

CORCHAUG TERRITORY

MONTAUK TERRITORY

NISSEQUOGUE TERRITORY

UNQUACHOG TERRITORY

Montauk Point
Shagwong
Conchonog (Manhasset)
Conchonock
Fort Pond
Gardiners Island
Hither Hills
Plum Island
Hog Creek Pt.
Amagansett
East Hampton
Springs
Orient Point
Orient Beach
Cedar Point
Bridgehampton
Orient
Shelter Island
Sag Harbor
Montauk Trail
Southfold
North Sea
Cutchogue
Mattituck
Jamesport
Southampton
Shinnecock Indian Reservation
Previous Shinnecock Reservation
Peconic River
Wading River
Riverhead
Eastport
Westhampton Beach
Poospatuck Reservation
Oxmans R.
Mastic
Fire Island
Secatogue Villages
Islip
Central Islip
Brentwood
Patchogue
Montauk Trail
Coram
Ronkonkoma
Lake Ronkonkoma
Caleb Smith State Park
Smithtown
Nissequogue Trail
Nissequogue R.
Suffolk Co.
Nassau Co.
Huntington Trail
Matinecock Trail
Asharoken
Sagamore Hill
Oyster Bay
Glen Cove
Manhasset
Munsey Park
Douglaston
Queens
Old Rockaway Trail
Merrick Trail
E. Rockaway
Massapequa
Wyandanch
Setauket Trail
Merrick
Massapequa

CORCHAUG
SHINNECOCK
SETAUKET
UNQUACHOG
NISSEQUOGUE
PATCHOGUE
SECATOGUE
MATINECOCK
MASSAPEQUA
MERRICK
ROCKAWAY
CANARSIE

Reechquaakie Central Village (Rockaway)
Other Rockaway Villages

① Matinecock Battlefield at *Little Neck*
② Two Matinecock Forts at Fort Neck, Oyster Bay
③ Conscience Point; Landing Place of English Settlers
④ Fort (*Montauk*)
⑤ Village at Lake Ronkonkoma
⑥ Burial Site at Bluffs
⑦ Sachem's Hole (Shrine to Chief Poggatacut)
⑧ Fort on Fort Hill, 180 Feet Square, Montauk
⑨ Old Village Site
⑩ Hilltop - Whale Watch and Solstice Observatory

Known Villages, Camps & Indian Forts
Plantings
Burial Sites

10 k.
0   10 m.

16

THE MYSTERIES
OF LONG ISLAND

In ancient times, Long Island was called Matouac by some, Paumanok by others. Matouac means a "young man," or "the young warriors," referring to the younger tribes of the western half of the island. *Paumanok* is a term in the Renneiu language indicating "land of tribute," in reference to Long Island's role as a main source for the quohog and conch shells used in the manufacture of sewan or wampum, often used to pay tribute or taxes to another tribe.[1] The people of Paumanok often had to pay tribute to the militarily superior people of the mainland.

Long Island has a long and significant role in the unwritten history of the Algonquin people. Just as North America is seen by Native Americans as a big turtle, with Mexico as its tail, Florida as its rear right leg, and Baja as its rear left leg, many Native people around Long Island today see Matouac as a big fish or whale, with its tail pointing east and its jaw at Rockaway Point in the west, ready to devour Staten Island. If that is true, Manhattan Island seems to be a worm on a hook just above its head, ready to snare it. That describes the odd relationship between the two islands: the vastly larger of the two always trying to avoid being overwhelmed by the smaller.

Although Manhattan Island and Long Island are clearly separated by an ocean channel called the East River, their political and cultural boundaries have long overlapped. The Canarsie were a prominent tribe on Long Island, but also on Manhattan, their territory stretching all the way to the Hudson River and the eastern shore of Staten Island to the west. In recent centuries, the boundaries of New York City and Long Island have overlapped extensively. According to recent census data 4,259,500 of New York City's seven million residents actually live on Long Island, approximately 60 percent. That is because at the turn of the twentieth century half of Queens County and all of Kings County (also called Brooklyn), which are the two Long Island counties closest to Manhattan, became incorporated as part of New York City, greatly increasing its size. The eastern half of Queens then became Nassau County, one of the state's newest counties, which currently has a population of 1,304,300.[2] East of Nassau is Suffolk County, one of the oldest counties in the state, stretching across Long Island to its tip. In spite of its distance from New York City, Suffolk is home to 1,364,700 people, thanks to the development fueled by the Long Island Railroad.[3]

RAILROAD TO THE PAST

How many Algonquin villages were on Long Island? Let's take a present-day conveyance—the Long Island Railroad, with its 352 miles of track along the 117-mile length between Manhattan and Montauk,[4] to get an idea of how many place names on Matouac Island (Long Island) still bear the names of Algonquin villages or refer to precolonial times in some way.

First we board the Ronkonkoma train. People translate Lake Ronkonkoma as "Bottomless Lake," which is fitting, but the word *Ronkonkoma* probably means "Peaceful Lake" in Nissequogue (a Matouac language that is still spoken). We start out at Penn Station, indirectly named after William Penn, who was much loved by the Lenape. The train departs and soon we pass Woodside and Forest Hills, both of which were wooded areas during Matinecock times, but they are no longer. Then we pass Kew Gardens and Hunter's Point, which reflects one meaning of the name Matinecock, "Good Hunting Place."

Soon we arrive at Flatbush Station, site of an ancient hub of pathways converging from all over the island, including of course the Flatbush Trail of the Canarsie that became Flatbush Avenue. Then we come to the Nostrand Avenue and East New York stops—both in Brooklyn. Next is Jamaica Station, back in Queens, one of the largest rail hubs in the world. The name Jamaica derives from either a Lenape word for beaver, *tamaqua,* or the old Algonquin *yau-may-ko,* "Place of the Beaver." We pass Mineola, Hicksville, Bethpage, and Farmingdale, then enter into Suffolk County and stop briefly at Pinelawn, and then the conductor calls out, "Next is Wy-an-danch, Wy-an-danch!"

Wyandanch was named after the Montauk Sagamore Wyandanqx, who was also grand sachem of all Long Island—with the exception of the Canarsie territory, now known as Brooklyn. The Canarsie were spread over parts of three islands: Long Island, Staten Island, and Manhattan, but also lived on many smaller islands throughout the region. Wyandanqx played an important role in Long Island history and probably visited here at some point in his long life.

THE STORY OF HEATHER FLOWER

A story has come down to us about the beautiful daughter of Wyandanqx, Heather Flower, of whom he was terribly fond. Wyandanqx had granted her permission to marry a young brave who had been heroic in a war against their enemies, the fierce Narragansetts. The grand sachem was presiding over the wedding ceremony at Montauk, when a group of Narragansett warriors under Chief Ninigrate swooped in and killed the hapless groom, along with a few Montauk braves, and carried Heather Flower off as a screaming captive. The British nobleman Lion Gardiner, whose descendants still live on Gardiners Island, became involved. He went to Rhode Island and negotiated effectively with Ninigrate, persuading him to give up the girl and send her back to Montauk. It was a difficult task and Gardiner pulled it off with aplomb. When he returned with the girl, Wyandanqx was so grateful that he offered Gardiner a large plot of land on the Nissequogue River, which Gardiner accepted. When the Welshman Richard "Bull" Smith arrived, Gardiner, a businessman, did not hesitate to sell the land for good money. Richard Smith's progeny intermarried with the Nissequogue and are still thriving to this day at Smithtown, proud of their Nissequogue/Welsh heritage.

Some Natives may hold a grudge against Lion Gardiner because he designed and built the English fort at Old Saybrook that helped repel the Pequot in 1636. The English destroyed the Pequot as a nation in 1637 at Mystic, Connecticut, and Gardiner, a British nobleman, did play a role. Wyandanqx was clearly not unhappy about the fate of the Pequot, since he too was at war with them. Wyandanqx sold Lion Gardiner the island that now bears his name for the price of "one black dog, a gun, some powder and shot, and a few Dutch blankets," a very generous offer on the sachem's part. That island was a sacred place, so the two men must have already developed a deep friendship even then.[5]

In spite of the Narragansett attack, Wyandanqx had many grandchildren and great-grandchildren, including Montauk Chief David Pharaoh. In Philadelphia today hangs a painting called *King of the Montauks*, which is a portrait of Chief David Pharaoh (1838–78).[6] In the picture, he is riding in an open wagon drawn by an old tired horse between the dunes, followed by a faithful black dog. In spite of the central character's simplicity and station in life, the very fact that he survived with dignity as a Native American until 1878 is a matter of pride to the Algonquin of the eastern seaboard.

Heather Flower remarried many years later, but chose to live a quiet life of solitude. Wyandanqx's sister, however, married the famous Montauk surveyor Cockenoe. He had been captured by the Pequot as a youth and sold to Richard Calicott of Dorchester,

Connecticut. There he soon met the Reverend John Eliot and helped him translate the Bible into the Massachusett language. He finally made it back to Montauk in 1646, now an educated man, and began working with Chief Wyandanqx as his translator. Cockenoe died in 1702 and is buried on Montauk.[7] An island off Connecticut's north shore is named after him.

Heather Flower's burial place is not certain, but today's Hither Hills cemetery is named after her. It was formerly known as Massacre Valley, in memory of a war between the Shinnecock and Montauk. It is an ancient burial site aligned with the lower arm of Gardiners Island. She may be buried at Fort Hill Cemetery at the place of her former home with Wyandanqx. There is a great council rock there, which has great historical significance according to Montauk tribal historian Robert Redfeather Stevenson. In ancient times, a fire would blaze at the base of the rock, which could be seen like a beacon by sailors on the ocean. Many councils were held there, and it is considered a spiritual vortex, a place of spiritual power where the ancestors dwell. Other such vortices are acknowledged to exist at Block Island near Rhode Island and at Lake Ronkonkoma, "The Peaceful Lake."

THE PEACEFUL LAKE

Up ahead is Deer Park. In the 1900s deer were almost extinct in the area, but now they are back. Deer Park is where you'll find the trail that went from Long Island Sound to the ocean in ancient times. That trail is Route 231 today. Right next to it is the Sagtikos State Parkway. *Sagatakoos* means "rattlesnake" or "snake with the hissing throat," according to some. It is more likely related to the tribal name Secatogue, which means "black or colored land."

After passing Brentwood, our train comes to Central Islip, the heart of the Secatogue territory. Islip was purchased from Sachem Winnequaheagh of the Connetquot on November 28, 1683. The expansive Connetquot State Park preserves at least part of this beautiful land as Winnequaheagh knew it. A Secatogue village lay a mile southwest of here along the Champlin Creek, near Olympic, New York.

Reaching Ronkonkoma, which is at the southern edge of the Nissequogue Nation's border, we take to the trails. The lake is still there, further east, its crystal-clear waters shining in the sun as they did five hundred years ago. This powerful gathering place, Lake Ronkonkoma, looks like a volcanic lake when viewed from an airplane. Its white sandy beach, now a tourist spot, was once a highly sacred place of religious ritual. Since the time of Orient Point culture and before, Natives would travel a hundred miles or more in pilgrimage to its shores, to undergo ordeals and vision quests, similar to activities at Dreamer's Rock in the Delaware Water Gap. The lake was so sacred to Long Island Natives that they didn't eat the fish from its waters out of respect, and perhaps for fear of desecrating it. The lake is so deep that its bottom has yet to be successfully sounded. According to Robert Redfeather Stevenson, there is no other like it in appearance or shape.

THE PATH TO THE NISSEQUOGUE

There was a large Ronkonkoma village along the eastern shore of the lake. Their hunters were good stoneworkers who used quartz for arrowheads. These people were ancestors of the Nissequogue. Past the lake to the west is an old brick church beside a stream, Saint Joseph's Roman Catholic Church of Ronkonkoma. There is a story the Natives of this area tell about the Nymph of the Nissequogue. A vision of a young Native Nissequogue girl—some assume she is a chieftain's daughter—appears on the Nissequogue River in a canoe. Riding with her are two large dogs, the size of Saint Bernards, but more of a wolf-like, Native type of dog. She has no paddles and seems adrift. People who view her are stricken with the belief that she is in great danger. They panic, and feeling compelled to try to rescue her, they leap into the water and usually drown in the effort.

According to the Nissequogue, there were four appearances of the "nymph" or Indian maiden in the twentieth century alone. One was in the 1930s, two in the 1940s, and one in 1953. In each case, the viewer of the apparition reportedly died almost immediately thereafter. The apparition is usually only seen by the person who drowns. In the incident of 1953, the nymph was seen only by the individual, although over seventy people attending a picnic at the church were present. The victim didn't drown like the others, but died in a fire forty-eight hours later.

Walking north we come to the Nissequogue River at Smithtown, and Caleb Smith State Park, which is still very wild. The Nissequogue people have always gathered plants in this area, and still do today.

The Smith family, a group of short, stocky people, arrived in 1697 and made alliances with the family of Chief Mayhong. Apparently Mayhong had grown up as a Mohawk in his youth, but had left to go shell fishing and eeling along the north shore of Long Island, and may have shown up not long before the Smiths did. There may have been a feud or political problem up north, and when Mayhong's Mohawk people discovered the river, they chose to stay. Apparently they were somewhat belligerent toward the neighbors at first, but things settled down eventually, and they learned the local language, but spoke it with a Mohawk accent. Mayhong's family shows up in the 1690 census as "free men, non-white."

As the stubby Smiths intermarried with the towering Nissequogue over the generations, they came to a more average height, although the extremes still show up once in a while. In 1802, Mayhong's family suddenly became listed in the census records as "white men," and part of the Caleb Smith family. That Smith family still runs Smithtown, although the cattle ranches under the Smith name are now gone. Richard "Bull" Smith, a big beefy Welshman who shows up time and time again in colonial records, was the patriarch of the family. He had to negotiate with the Nissequogue as well for the piece of land he bought from Lion Gardiner. According to family oral tradition, the Natives first said something like, "You whites are soft and weak. Why should we listen to you?" (They were six foot seven, remember.) Smith probably answered with words to the effect of, "What do you mean? I'm as strong as a bull!" They retorted,[8] "That's a lot of land you want from us. If you can carry a bull on your back the entire perimeter of that land, you can have it!"

Smith really wanted the land to farm, so he got down underneath a bull and lifted it up carefully. Placing the forelegs over his shoulders, he actually carried the small bull on his back. His face was red as a beet, but he got more than halfway around the rectangle of the property in question. With only a hundred or two feet to go, he collapsed under the great weight of the bull. As he lay on the ground gasping for breath, the Nissequogue laughed and cheered and said something to the effect of, "You can have that land for your farm. You've earned it, even though you didn't make it all the way. You're OK with us!"

They lifted him up and carried him to the shade of a tree to rest. Little did they know that their grandchildren would be marrying one another some day and telling the story of how "Bull" Smith got his colorful name, as they diligently farmed that same plot of land. The current Nissaquogue chief, Raymond C. Wheeler, is a direct descendant of Bull Smith and Mayhan both.

Exploring the South Shore

Aboard the train once again, we head back toward Jamaica in order to explore the stops along the south shore route. We pass through Syosset (another old village site) and Mineola, which is really part of Garden City. Garden City is named after an Algonquin planting field that went on for miles, one of the largest on the eastern seaboard.[9] There was a smaller one in nearby Hempstead. Wyandanqx had a whole network of cornfields connected by large trails. He distributed the corn equitably, so that no one ever had to go hungry. Dutch

Governor Kieft's men used to steal the Native corn. A Montauk delegation is recorded as saying to the Europeans, "Are you our friends? You are only corn-thieves."[10]

Following along the southern branch of the Long Island Railroad, south of Jamaica we pass through Rockville Center, the old capital of the far-flung Rockaway domain and home to the Rockaway sachems. Further along we arrive in Merrick, a town named after a Matouac tribe of the same name—one of the thirteen principal tribes of Long Island. Eventually we come to Massapequa, a town that was once the capital of the Massapequa Nation. The word means "shallow pond." After this comes Amityville and then Copiague, part of the Secatogue Nation. Then we pass Lindenhurst, and arrive in Babylon, which lies just east of the ancient north-south Indian path that is now Route 231.

THE PLACE WHERE THE SUN COMES UP

Next tracing the Montauk rail route, we pass Islip, former home of the Connetquot, then pass into Patchogue land at Oakdale, and arriving in the town of Patchogue, named after the nation known by that name. This rail travels along the same general route as the old Montauk Trail, probably three thousand years old, which is now Route 80, and in some places Route 80/27.

Mastic-Shirley is the site of the Poospatuck Reserve today. It is only 3.2 acres in size but filled with history, and located on the old Unquachaug land. Then comes Speonk, an Algonquin word, then Hampton Bays, where the Shinnecock's reserve used to be located. Then we pass Southampton, where the Shinnecock are now located, East Hampton, and eventually Amagansett, which is the name of a Montauk subtribe. Here we disembark and begin walking again.

The native Algonquin of Long Island were generally a peaceful people, protected by the distances both by land and water from other dissimilar tribes. During the 1500s and early 1600s, however, the

Pequot were able to wreak considerable havoc on those of the north shore. The people of eastern Long Island were peaceful amongst each other because they were there for a reason; it was the place chosen by their ancestors for sunrise ceremonies and burials.

The term "sacred land" has been used in a variety of ways to mean different things. Paumanok, however, was clearly set apart from other areas of Turtle Island as especially sacred to the Algonquin from at least 1000 B.C.E., the dawning of Orient Point culture, onward. During this time, virtually everyone of the Orient/Mohican culture chose to be buried in this one place where the sun rose. In some cases, bodies were transported hundreds of miles by canoe so that they could be buried here in high ceremony.

Their burials were highly magical and shamanic in every sense, with abundant use of red ochre to bless everything. Red ochre is a kind of paint made from red clay with high iron-ore content. Anything that was ceremonially painted with the red ochre was "made stronger" and protected from misfortune or bad medicine. The paint became an expression of the power of the medicine man as a tool of the creator to cover or protect the object spiritually. The body was painted as were the mortuary gifts. Some of these gifts were pottery, objects used by the deceased in this life, or new ones made for the occasion. As each pot had a pot spirit within it, the departed spirit could not use the vessel in the afterworld unless the pot spirit was released by its own death. Therefore the pots were ceremonially "killed" at the burial site, smashed to pieces in view of everyone, so that the pot spirit would rise to the spirit world and become useful to the deceased.

The term Wabanaki, the "People of the Dawn" or "People of the East, Where the Sun Comes Up," defines not only the red-ochre cultures still thriving in Maine and the Maritimes, but it is a term used in various forms throughout the Lenape domain. In the Renneiu language, the term is Wampano, the "People of the East." Among the speakers of the Nemi type of language, the word is Wampanoag, a people who are closely linked to this same sacred place. Among the Lenape languages, Unami, Munsee, and Shawnee, the term *Wabanaki* still exists as a place-name and surname. The culture of solar ceremonies was very ancient, very widespread, and unified from this very location. Remnants of it still exist today, but it was very strong at the time of first European contact.

These proto-Mohican speakers were the grandfathers of the Lenape, and in some sense the grandfathers of all the Algonquin east of the Mississippi. In 1000 B.C.E. their territory extended north to what is now Boston, south at least to Maryland, and west at least as far as the Delaware River. Manhattan was, as usual, centrally located as a transportation hub during this time. However, no matter how far away they were based, these ancient people would ask that their bodies be brought to Montauk, Orient Point, or one of the sacred burial sites on eastern Long Island to be buried or cremated.

We walk eastward from Amagansett and ascend a hill. Standing here on the morning of winter solstice, you can see the sun come up right at the point of Napeague Bay, and beyond that, the point at Montauk Downs. These three points are in alignment with that sunrise. In the evening, you could turn to look in the other direction and see the sun set over East Hampton, another old sacred site, and also see it in alignment with the south shore for five or six miles past that.

We walk on about four miles until we reach the town of Springs. From here the summer solstice sun rises exactly in alignment with the long point of Gardiners Island to the northeast. Then in the evening it would appear to set right over Bridgehampton, then Water Mill, then Southampton, then in alignment with the Shinnecock Reserve and Westhampton Beach beyond that, each site with their circle of drummers moving the sun along to the next village to the west.

Many famous sacred sites in Egypt—the Great Pyramid of Giza, the Sphinx, the temples, most of which were constructed about 2000

B.C.E.—were aligned to the rising and setting of the sun, at both summer and winter solstice, and also aligned with each other. From any
given site, you would see the solstice rise and set directly over the
neighboring site. These formed a grid or complex of sites up and
down the Nile River Valley. There are similar complexes all over the
world. But what the Lenape ancestors did on Long Island is in some
ways more incredible.

Next we head to the shore at Hog Creek, near Sebonac Harbor.
Sebonac was the name given to the descendants of the Orient Point
culture after they were decimated by a disaster about 763 B.C.E. The
word means "Place of Ground Nuts," or "Acorns." The oak was very
sacred to Native peoples because it sheltered and fed the ancestors
when other food was scarce. The ground nuts are honored all over
Algonquin North America in place names and in ancient customs.

Across the choppy bay, on Gardiners Island, we climb to Whale
Hill, where the Natives used to go to spot whales, and to be the first
to drum up the sun. This was the first of the sacred sites.

The western crest of Whale Hill is 110 feet up, the highest point
on the island. Imagine for a moment that you are a medicine chief in
the year 1000 B.C.E., walking on foot, perhaps thousands of miles, to
find not only the place where the sun comes up first, but also to find
the perfect solar observatory, where the entire horizon is flat and visible, but with rock outcroppings against which to measure the sun's
movement through the solar year.

From this windswept point you see nothing but water around you,
nothing to obstruct your view of the horizon, except that three-
quarters of the way around the horizon there are rock outcroppings
rising above the bay. The ancient astronomers of the Algonquin people
could have seen the sun take its full journey across the sky without
obstructions, yet had natural stone markers to chart its movements by.

Just on the horizon to the northwest is a great notch of sea that
sits between the rocks at Orient Point and the rocks at Plum Island.

That is where, as the Algonquin would have observed, that the sun "goes to die" at summer solstice, at least from the perspective of those standing here. That is where it sets on June 21 each year. The large red ball of light would have been funneled through that narrow channel on the most sacred day of the year, creating a "red road" of sparkling light across the crest of the waves. That is why they began burying their loved ones there, to be close to the sun, at least in a metaphoric sense. The medicine chief could have performed the burial at dawn at Orient Point, with the sun sitting at the long shore of Plum Island to the northeast. Then at sunset the people could have gathered here on Whale Hill to watch Grandfather sun descend on the burial plot, bathing the loved one in red light, purifying the body with its sacred fire.

Back then, Gardiners Island was Conchonock, "The Place of Many Dead." Not only did the Lenape wish to be buried at Orient Point, but right here where we are standing. People from hundreds of miles around wanted the same honor and, of course, soon there was no more room. So someone had an inspired thought. They located the exact spot where the winter solstice sun rose, looking from where we now stand. That became the village of Montauk, and a sacred burial place. Then they found the exact spot where the winter solstice sun set, again looking from this spot. That became Sag Harbor.

Sag Harbor at first was exclusively a sacred burial site. As was their custom, people planted acorns in the mouths of the dead, and soon there were oak trees everywhere. When Sag Harbor became too crowded, they found by simple observation the exact location where the summer solstice sun set when viewed from Sag Harbor. They chose the spot that was also in alignment with Orient Point to the northeast. That point became the ancient Corchaug village now known as Southold, named in the early 1600s in honor of its antiquity by the English. Corchaug are the people who watch over Orient Point, Southold, Peconic, and Mattatuck—all those sacred sites along the north shore. Their name Corchaug means "Ancient Ones." They are direct descendants of those solar-searching medicine chiefs who charted the universe without ever leaving earth, all by marking the movements of the sun.

All together there were at least forty natural alignment sites in a near-perfect grid covering about eight-hundred square miles, developed over a three-hundred-year period, each one near or directly on the horizon of the site next to it. These are just the ones you can detect on a map today, based on Algonquin place-names and other clues. There may have been many more.

The Early Dutch traders claimed that Lenape medicine men knew the movements of the sun, moon, and stars intimately.[11] The ancient Algonquin were especially interested in the Pleiades, the Seven Sisters. Their whole nature-based mysticism made it almost mandatory to find a way to do things that involved nature as it is given, without changing it. If nature was the body of God, then any such alignments or conveniences were gifts from the divine and should be utilized, but they should not be created artificially with pyramids and stone temples. The Corchaug "sun worship" phenomenon may have arisen out of the simple fact that, here in this place, the land formed a natural observatory like nowhere else. They had prayed to the Creator to show them the mysteries of the universe, to give them understanding, and He brought them here. It was an answer to their prayers.

However, there was a five-hundred-year period, from about 730 B.C.E. to 200 B.C.E., during which life was very harsh and unbearable and the Lenape lost all knowledge of this aspect of their past. Apparently wars had already broken out between the Long Islanders and the mainland even then. This is now called the Sebonac Period. In those generations, many of their old ways were forgotten. But we know that they maintained the old villages and sacred spots even through hardship, because over time they evolved into dozens of Long Island's modern cities.

17

THE THIRTEEN TRIBES OF LONG ISLAND

Long Island is covered with the names of ancient Algonquin peoples and places, but what do we know of these people and what are their stories? What were their trails and boundaries? What do the place-names mean?

One of the most widely quoted "facts" about the Native New Yorkers of Long Island is that there were thirteen "tribes." Originally they were all one peaceful people who gradually split into subnations or tribes. The number thirteen has long been debated; there are in fact as many as twenty of these subtribes on Long Island. In this chapter, however, I will categorize them into thirteen groups, based on the most common grouping by Natives and scholars alike.[1]

The fact that Long Island was home to a hoop of thirteen tribes has great significance for a people who had an in-depth understanding of solar, lunar, and stellar movements. The parallels between the pattern of the turtle shell and the tribal geography of the island are clear, with its thirteen squares surrounding a neutral central area, each square representing one of the thirteen moons in a year.

In the case of Long Island, the terminal moraine of the Wisconsin Glacier and the areas to the north and south of it constitute the neutral middle territory. However, many villages and trails existed in this neutral territory, and in fact that parcel of hilly land was generally considered part of the land of the tribe on the nearest shore.

When English settlers arrived on Long Island in 1640, during the reign of Grand Sachem Wyandanqx, the territories were by no means equal. The Matinecock territory was vast while the Merrick territory to the south was tiny. No Native American confederacy ever consisted of nations of equal size or population, and Long Island was no exception. In fact there were five distinct principal nations along the north shore, all north of the Rockaway Trail/terminal moraine line, and eight to the south of that line. That central line is now partly covered by Grand Central Parkway, and the Long Island Expressway further east. The climate, flora, and fauna of the north side are distinctly different than that of the south.

As in most Algonquin territories, the hunting grounds are divided up—one family or clan to each tributary, the same arrangement as one would find among members of the Algonquin Nation of the Ottawa River Valley (one of the eighty-four Algonquin-speaking nations), or even in parts of the Delaware Valley. In Long Island there are only five true rivers, and none are over ten miles long: the Nissequogue, the Peconic River, Carmans River, the Connetquot near Islip, and the Sumpwamp. (These original Algonquin names are all in use today.) The thirteen principal nations, each with its own numerous communities, are (going clockwise from the east): (1) Montauk, (2) Shinnecock, (3) Unquachaug, (4) Secatogues (Patchogues are a sub-tribe) (5) Massapequa, (6) Merrick, (7) Rockaway, (8) Canarsie, (9) Matinecock, (10) Nissequogue, (11) Setauket, (12) Corchaug, and (13) Manhanset. Circling clockwise from the east has become standard practice in the Medicine Wheel ceremonies of certain eastern Algonquin.[2] Perhaps it originated in the council circles of Long Island, but more likely the Medicine Wheel existed for thousands of years and the Long Islanders formed their nations in its likeness. The numbers by no means indicate rank of importance; it is only a device to help the reader keep track of the various names and groups.

MONTAUK

The Montauk ("Fortified Place") lived on the land stretching from Bridgehampton to Montauk Point, including Gardiners Island by some accounts. It is a sandy area, much exposed to the wind and rain and squalls from the ocean. There are no natural inlets. Nevertheless, Native people have lived there for thousands of years. As we saw in the last chapter, it is one of the areas where the people who used red ochre ceremonially—thus sometimes referred to as the Red Ochre People—traveled to bury their dead. The eastern-most point of land was generally the home of the grand chief, and here that was Montauk Point.[3] Montauk sachems generally held the title of grand chief of Long Island, although the Montauk, Shinnecock, Manhanset, and Corchaug, all bordering on Great Peconic Bay, maintained a protective league of their own during times of attack from Connecticut's Natives. The location of the sachem's longhouse was at Konk-hong-anok, or "Fort Pond," at Montauk Point,[4] named for a Native fort on the northeast side of the pond—in the late nineteenth century Fort Wycoff was built right over the site of this old Montauk fortress—and another on Fort Hill. The Montauk used large monolithic headstones of granite to mark the burials of great leaders. Robert Redfeather Stevenson says that most of these, some of which are the headstones of his great-grandfathers, are now being used by the wealthy to decorate their expansive lawns. Each one weighs many tons.

There was a workshop at Fort Pond, just south of Montauk, a place where bows, arrows, sharp tools, and other everyday stone tools were knapped. A village site with a wampum manufacturing center stood near Three Mile Harbor north of East Hampton. There was a Montauk fort erected in 1661 on Moninick Hill near Nespuague.

The Dutch were the first Europeans to settle Montauk. English colonists from Lynn, Massachusetts, landed at Southampton in 1640, and immediately removed a Dutch insignia attached to a tree, which was considered to be a valid boundary marker in those days. This wooden plaque, complete with a Dutch coat of arms, constituted legal claim to land ownership. Showing more than a little contempt for the Dutch, the English threw it on the ground and replaced it with a fool's head carved in wood, and began building their homes.

The Dutch learned of this from members of the Montauk delegation and descended upon the transgressors, arresting a few. They took them to New Amsterdam, tried and convicted them of wrongdoing, sentenced them, and then released them after they promised never to set foot on Long Island again. As soon as the sloop returned from New Haven to retrieve them, a few went right back to the Montauk area and continued to build their homes on Home's Hill on the north shore of what is now South Hampton.

The English settlers bartered with the Natives for eight square miles of land that cut across the south branch of Long Island, offering twenty coats, twenty-four looking glasses, twenty-four knives, and one hundred muxes for use in making wampum. Mandush, sachem of a Shinnecock group, deferred to Chief Wyandanqx, who closed the deal. Huntington village was established in this new territory under the name Ketanomocke, meaning "Principal Inside Place" or "Back of the Bay." They were attacked in 1653 by the Narragansett, and many Montauks lost their lives.[5]

When Long Island was split in half between the English and Dutch in 1650, English to the east, Dutch to the west, Wyandanqx's power was diminished. His brother Tackapousha was elected sachem of the Dutch side of the island. In 1658, smallpox wiped out half the Montauk population and Wyandanqx was poisoned by enemies of the tribe. His young son Wycombone became chief, sharing responsibility with his mother, a "squaw sachem." Wyandanqx's dying request was that the Gardiner family act as guardians for the boy, which they did. John Lyon Gardiner, whose ancestor Lion Gardiner reputedly purchased what is now Gardiners Island in 1639, considered the family to be closely linked to the Montauk Nation and recorded a short list of Montauk words during the Revolutionary War.

THE SACRED WHALE

Whales have always beached themselves on Long Island's shores. We still don't know why the whales do so, but the Native people of Matouac have always relied on these gifts from the sea for their tools and food. Early in their history, perhaps even six to seven thousand years ago, the people of Long Island decided it wasn't enough to wait around for good fortune; they'd go and bring good fortune to themselves by becoming expert whalers.

Their oceans were home to right whales[6] in the winter months, the best time to go whaling in the north Atlantic. They never used less than two dugout canoes at once. They would corral the whale far offshore and then drive it ashore where men, women, and children would beat the creature with spears, hatchets, and knives, and then leave it to succumb to its wounds.[7]

According to William Commanda, Wisdom Keeper of the Algonquin People, the whale was often killed offshore, and devices made of nets with flotation devices made of inflated livers and other organs attached, were used to float them to shore.

Whales are sacred to the Montauk and other Long Island Natives who have always recognized them as highly intelligent beings. It should be noted that a beached whale could feed thirty Montauk families for an entire winter, and this "generosity" was greatly appreciated. Part of Montauk spirituality involves the fins from a whale, and whale-fin rights were a major treaty issue during the early contact period. The Long Islanders would cook and then dry the fin and crumble the material into a powder and use it in ceremony similar to the way other Algonquin use tobacco, as an offering or medium of exchange with spirit. There are several narrow, reedlike bones inside the fin—similar to the fingers of other mammals only, of course, concealed—which were extracted and used as writing pens. The tip was generally dipped in red berry juice or other red ink, and used to draw sacred glyphs or designs. Later, as whalebone scrimshaw became more popular, the fin bones were used to "paint" or color the scrimshaw designs. Similar designs were also made on hides.

Native American whalers were among the best in the world, and the Montauk played a major role in the early development of New England's whaling industry. The early colonists learned the rudiments of whaling from them and, with improved methods such as light cedar boats and iron harpoons, became America's first white offshore whalers. For some generations, however, they continued to recognize their Algonquin neighbors as the more skillful, and employed them when possible to hurl the harpoon and to wield the lance.[8]

The fictional character Tashtego in Herman Melville's *Moby Dick* represents not one but hundreds of Algonquin whaling men who were expert in every aspect of the chase, and were considered mentors and bringers of good fortune throughout the long history of whaling.

The Montauk region is home to the great whaling port of Sag Harbor. The name also derives from an Algonquin word, *Saggabonac,* "The Place of Ground Nuts," also spelled *Sagaponac,* both names of two towns nearby. As a whaling port, Sag Harbor was second only to New Bedford in Massachusetts. In the winter of 1845–46, Sag Harbor weighed in over a million dollars in whale oil and bone from a fleet of sixty big ships manned by Shinnecock, Montauk, Nissequogues, and Wampanoags. They were paid handsomely. In the streets of Sag Harbor, Long Island Indians flush with cash could be seen spending and giving away their money lavishly, some of them under the influence of rum. Others could be found exhibiting their whale-ivory scrimshaw work.

In 1871, the last whaling ship to go out from Sag Harbor, *The Myrna,* never returned, and the era had come to an end. Many men lost their lives at sea; one ship grounded right off shore and sank, losing all hands. It was a dangerous operation, and most families of Long Island lost more than one son or cousin to the whales.

Montauk Spiritual Practice

Montauk spiritual practice involves the use of eel grass, which is similar to the well-known medicine plant of the northern Algonquin known as sweetgrass. It is said that the eel grass feeds the sacred goose and is considered "help from Creator" for humans as well. The word for "goose" is *galoosa-hee-ho(n).* The goose is the helper. If one needs help, one makes an offering of tobacco or the whale-fin mixture to the Great Goose. The Great Goose receives it and circles around the earth. At the dawning of the following day, the sound of the crying goose would be heard bringing the message, and the person would have an answer. The mainland Lenape have similar traditions about Tellega, the blue heron, who brings messages for them. The blue heron feather is exchanged at peace councils and peace gatherings. The heron is the peacemaker among birds; the Penobscot of Maine still speak of the path of the peacemaker as The Way of the Heron. In New England, it is the eagle who brings the message the next morning at dawn. This Eagle Prayer is an important part of Micmac spirituality. According to Raymundo Rodriguez, the name of the spirit helper on Long Island is Galoosawabi, "White Feather," which I believe to be this goose-entity, due to the similarity of names. His name is always uttered outside, usually in the morning. It is possible that the great spiritual teacher of the New England Algonquin, Glooskabe (Glooskap in Micmac), may be derived from the word *galoosawabi,* "white feather." It could be said that the Micmac/Abenaki teacher Glooskabe is a peacemaker, as there are many stories of the thousand or so Glooskabe stories still told, in which he brings peace and justice to the people. If so, it could point to a common origin of the peaceful Way of the Heron, the Eagle Prayer, the Glooskabe stories, the Lenape blue heron tradition, and the white goose lore of Long Island.[9]

~

The Montauk language was a Nemi type in 1600, similar to Mohican, however it gradually switched to a Pequot (Yenni type) language by 1700, and was still being spoken in 1900. On November 17, 1910, railroad heiress Jane Benson won a land case in the State Supreme Court by convincing the judge and jury that the Montauk Indians no longer existed and therefore had no treaty rights, even though a tribal roll with 506 adult names on it was submitted on behalf of the Montauk. Benson argued that "to be so recognized, the Montauks must be governed by a leader whose orders must be obeyed; consist of members who have turned their backs on civilized society; be able to make war or peace on their own; administer civil justice among themselves; and have a continuous history of regularly scheduled meetings for tribal business."[10] Accepted by Judge Blackmar at the time, this set a landmark precedent in New York State law that has been used to deny recognition of the state's Algonquin nations who are morally opposed to autocratic leadership, specifically the Ramapough Indians of Suffern, New York.

Shinnecock

The Shinnecock ("At the Level Land") territory stretched from Eastport to Bridgehampton. The Shinnecock Reservation, now between Southampton Beach and Montauk Highway, is one of the oldest in America, although it was moved across the inlet in 1848. It is famed for its great powwows, which attract people from hundreds of miles around. The Shinnecock are the primary remnant of the Sebonac culture of 700 B.C.E. that followed the great Orient Point cultural epoch, similar in habits, but not in scope or affluence.[11] Their language was different from that of the Orient Point Corchaug (which would have been an older form of Mohican than their own) or the Matouac R-speaking nations on all sides. The last fluent Shinnecock speaker died about 1930.

The first Shinnecock reservation was near Canoe Place. The great Paul Cuffee, depicted in *Uncle Tom's Cabin,* was the son of the full-blooded Shinnecock Peter Cuffee, and is buried at Canoe Place. In 1848, the Shinnecock gave up their claim to Canoe Place and settled across Shinnecock Bay, on the eastern shore.

This move must have been full of symbolic significance for the Shinnecock; their ancestors, the Sebonac, had always made their settlements on the west shore of a body of water. The newer R-dialect Algonquin, who had fled from the mainland and from Brooklyn and Queens to join the Shinnecock, had the habit of settling on the east bank or shore of a body of water. On Long Island, the prevailing winds strongly favor the settlement of a western bank. The move may indicate a loss of control over the region to the whites; however it may also simply be an indication that the R-speaking Algonquin refugees didn't mind the wind, as they were accustomed to it. If it is true that some of their ancestors were sailors of the trade winds from the Caribbean, it might help to explain their lack of concern for the wind, which earlier Algonquin peoples shunned.

The Shinnecock was one of the largest of the thirteen tribes of Long Island. Its population in 1900 was still six hundred strong. Sag Harbor is built on a sacred site in their original territory, which also includes the south shore of Peconic Bay. One of their many famous sachems was Wyandanqx's brother Nowedonah, "The Seeker," who was active in 1648. Another was Quaquasho, "The Hunter," who was known to be sachem in 1691.

There were ancient Shinnecock villages at Sag Harbor, near Long Pond, and at Hog's Neck, which is a punning adaptation of

Hogonock. Some of their burial areas were on the bluffs overlooking Sag Harbor Bay. There was a village near what is now North Sea, New York, and one near Weecop Bay. An early village was at Sebonic Neck near Cold Spring Pond,[12] one along Sebonac Creek, and another along the road from Canoe Place to the Shinnecock Reservation.

There's an interesting story about the Shinnecock that describes Algonquin independence perfectly. During World War II, they objected to the draft on the grounds that they were not beholden to the United States, but were a sovereign nation, like the Seneca and Mohawk, within New York State. The tribe fought long and hard for this recognition, and finally won. As soon as they had won and were not under any obligation to fight, most of the males of eligible age immediately joined in the war effort as allies of the United States, and were valorous in combat.

The Shinnecock grazed cattle on three thousand hilly acres, near what is now the Shinnecock Canal, until the railroad came through in 1859. Today their reservation is seven hundred acres, however many Long Island Natives live off reserve. The Shinnecock-Sewanaka Society works to unite off-reserve Natives of Long Island.

There is a rock at the town of North Sea, a few miles north of Southampton, Long Island, on Route 38, that bears a brass marker with this inscription: "Near this spot in June 1640, landed the colonists from Lynn, Massachusetts who founded Southampton, the first English settlement in the State of New York." It stands near the Conscience Point National Wildlife Refuge, which got its name as the first English colonist stepped on firm soil. Chief Nowedonah, "The Seeker," first saw the sloop as it approached. Upon landing, the first woman to step ashore said, "For conscience's sake, we are on dry land at last!"

The sachem and the white visitors attempted a conversation. Nowedonah's brother Wyandanqx, sachem of the Montauk, had already become friends with the Englishman Lion Gardiner. A third brother, Poggatacut, who was sachem of the Manhansetts, had met with the Corchaug leader Momoweton to arrange an agreement with the English to protect them from attacks from the Pequot, and so he was inclined to let them stay.

The English didn't waste time asking for merely a piece of land the size of a bull's hide, as the Dutch had done. They said something to the effect of, "Why not give us a strip of land stretching across the entire southern branch of the island, from sea to sea? You have plenty to spare!"

That request was granted, cutting the Montauks off from the rest of the Matouac Confederacy. That settlement was later called "Olde Towne" in Southampton. For the sum of three-score bushels of corn to be paid after the first harvest in the fall of 1641, and sixteen "coates," the Shinnecocks happily gave the English eight square miles of Native sand. The Shinnecock further stipulated that "the English were to defend the sayed [*sic*] Indians from the unjust violence of whatever Indians shall illegally assail us."[13] At the same time, Charles I had already issued letters patent to William Alexander for the whole of Lange Eylandt (Long Island).

Like the Montauk, the Shinnecock gradually switched, between 1600 and 1900, from a unique isolate form of the Nemi, or Mohican-type language, to a dialect of the Pequot type.

UNQUACHAUG

The Unquachaug ("Land Beyond the Hill") lived on a stretch of land from Bayport to Eastport. The Poospatucks, who still exist as a distinct cultural group today with a reservation fifty acres in size near the old village site at Moriches, are a subgroup of the Unquachaugs. Many of the Canarsie bands closer to the city moved east and joined the Poospatuck settlement during hard times. Thomas Jefferson and James Madison visited General William Floyd at the ancient Unquachaug village of Mastic, along the Forge River, in 1791 and collected a list of 162 Unquachaug words from the people of this nation. Jefferson's preamble to the *Vocabulary of the Language of the Unquachaug Indians* (1791) states that "this language is a dialect differing a little from that of the Indians settled near Southampton called Shinnecock, and also from those of Montauk or Montock, called Montock; the three tribes can barely understand each other" and notes that only three people could speak Unquachaug at that time.

The Unquachaug are connected with the Connetquot from the north and are not originally of Long Island. Yaphank is a contemporary Algonquin place-name in their region. Their main estuary was the Carmans River, known for its fishing, but they also had access to the Mastic Inlet. I believe the language is of the Pequot type, as they migrated from Connecticut centuries ago. Some consider the Patchogue to be a part of the Unquachaug family. The Patchogue villages were at Patchogue, Fire Place, Mastic, Moriches, and Westhampton. Their sachem in 1666 was Tobaccus.[14]

SECATOGUE

The Secatogue ("Black or Colored Land") lived on the south shore from Copiague to Bayport. Copiague was the location of a subtribe or community of the Secatogue, the name of a neck of land. They probably referred to themselves simply as Secatogue, not "the Copiague."

The Secatogue had access to the Great River inlet. The Eastern Path to the South, now Route 231 and its companion, the Sagtikos Parkway—ended here. At its southern end, it crosses Sagtikos Neck at present-day Bay Shore. Their main village was at Islip. They were hit early by both war and disease; however, they survived well into the British occupation. Their sachem was Winnequaheagh, who signed the deed for Islip in 1683. King George granted Sagtikos Manor, located on the south shore of Long Island near Jones Beach, to Stephen Van Cortlandt in 1697, who then purchased it from the

Secatogue Indians on October 1st of the same year, the deed of which is preserved in the state archives.

The large Patchogue tribe is shown on some maps as stretching from Great River to Bellport. They are considered part of either the Secatogue family of tribes, or of the Unquachaugs.

The Secatogue language switched gradually from the old Nemi type, a dialect of Mohican, to a dialect of the Renneiu or R language.

MASSAPEQUA

The Massapequa ("Large Shallow Pond") lived along the south shore of Long Island from Seaford to Copiague. The well-known town of Massapequa lies within this region, on the southern shore of the island. This tribe suffered heavy losses during Kieft's War. Then the fierce English warrior John Underhill defeated the Massapequa in battle at Fort Neck, near Mill Neck, in 1653 or 1654. This was the only major battle between the English and the Native Americans on Long Island. There is a rather expansive monument in marble commemorating the battle at Mill Neck, near Massapequa. (The mercenary Captain John Underhill later fought the Canarsie under the Dutch, going by the name of Jan Van der Hyl.) Two of the palisaded Indian forts from this war remained standing near the Massapequa's eastern border on South Oyster Bay for years,[15] giving Fort Neck its name. It was their chief, Tackapousha who, allied with the Dutch, became sachem of western Long Island after 1656. Massapequa speech was a dialect of the Renneiu language.

MERRICK

The Merrick ("Plains Country"), or Merikikes,[16] tribe lived on a square of land on the south shore from Baldwin to Seaford and a considerable part of the Hempstead Plains.[17] They are known mostly for their trails. Merrick Avenue makes their name a household word, at least among Long Islanders, but their language and peaceful culture

have been destroyed. The old Merrick Trail started in what is now
Jamaica, Queens, at Hillside Avenue, also a trail in those days. This
section is still called Merrick Boulevard. When it enters Nassau
County, all of which used to be part of Queens before 1899, it
becomes Merrick Road and goes to the south shore where it meets the
Montauk Highway, also an old Matouac trail. It may also have
extended north of Hillside Avenue into the rocky half of Long Island,
following the Old Post Avenue, then the Old Post Road, before cross-
ing under the Long Island Expressway. Their sachem in 1647 was
Wantagh[18] and there is a town just a mile or two north of Merrick,
New York, named after him. Their main village was at Hicks Neck.
They were Renneiu speakers.

ROCKAWAY

The Rockaway ("Sandy Land") lived from Maspeth in the west along
the south shore to Baldwin on what is now the Far Rockaway
Peninsula[19] and a narrow strip extending to the north shore through
Hempstead town, flanked by the Matinecock territory to the east.
R. P. Bolton, in his book *New York in Indian Possession,* shows this
northern block occupying the region from the Van Wyck Expressway,
site of an old trail, westward to the East River, along the north shore.
This would make sense, for the Rockaways are "east bank" Renneiu-
speaking people of the Clason Point type. Their capital city was at
Rockville Center, Rechquaakie in the Algonquin, the eastern-most
point of their territory, sometimes described as Near Rockaway,
where their principal sachems lived. Their sachem at first contact was
named Chegonoe, who was succeeded by Eskmoppas in 1670 and
Parnau in 1685,[20] after which time the Rockaways were expelled by
the British. A village and main burial place of the Rockaways was at
Cedarhurst, New York. There was a large Rockaway settlement on
Hog Island in Rockaway Bay, another at Hempstead, and another at
the head of Maspeth Creek in the north.

CANARSIE

The Canarsie ("At the Fenced-in Place") were located within Kings County and a small part of Jamaica in Queens. There are many sub-tribes, including the Marechkawick, Nyack, Pagganck, Massabarkem, and Mannahaning, to name a few. The Canarsies, led by Chief Penhawitz, were the principal traders with the Dutch among Long Island tribes in 1643, and it made them a powerful nation.[21] Sometime before the English conquest of New Netherlands in 1664, a large number of Canarsies migrated en masse to Staten Island. They had met John Underhill decades earlier, and knew what a British invasion would mean. A few went east and joined the Poospatuck at Mastic. The Marechkawick, also known as the Gawanus Indians, moved in with their relatives the Merricks near Hempstead. In 1670, the Canarsie signed Brooklyn over to the British. The Canarsie chiefs at that time were Peter, Elmohar, Job, Makagiquas, and Shamese.[22]

MATINECOCK

The Matinecock ("Place to Hunt" or "Broken-Up Ground") con-trolled a huge area of land encompassing most of Queens and the northern part of Nassau County, from the Nissequague River west to Flushing Bay at the west end of the Island.[23] Their main villages were at Flushing, Glen Cove, Cold Spring, Huntington, and Cow Harbor. The Matinecocks were split during Kieft's War in 1643. While many fought the Dutch in battle, Chief Whiteneymen (also called "One Eye") maintained diplomatic ties with the Dutch and negotiated for peace. The peace was continued by his successor Assiapam after 1653.

Some of the Matinecock place names in this region include Kissena Park (generally translated as "Cold Place"), Manhasset, Syosset, Asharoken, Fort Salonga, and Commac.

The town of Locust Valley is also known as the town of Matinecock, and the surrounding area—the neck of land that includes Sagamore Hill—was known in ancient times as The Stronghold. There were extensive populations there. Two forts stood at Fort Neck in Oyster Bay, the one in the south was a square earthworks fort, the other was a palisade on the meadow. The one stormed by white colonists in 1653 measured thirty by fifty yards. It had stood for four years. There was a large village and planting field at Oyster Bay, which was abandoned in 1650 due to political upheaval between the Dutch and English.

Council Rock at Oyster Bay was a Matinecock meeting ground, and the location of a sacred council fire. In 1672, George Fox, the founder of the Society of Friends (Quakers), gave a sermon there during his visit to America. Other villages stood at Glen Cove and Douglaston.

In the graveyard at Zion Episcopal Church in Douglaston is a remarkable sight for those interested in Long Island's real history: a tree bisects a huge split rock resembling a huge human skull. The rock is engraved with the words "THE LAST MATINECOCK" in large letters. The tree growing from the stone suggests the Lenape custom of burying the dead with an acorn in the mouth so that years later the oak would split the skull, bearing new life.[24] The epitaph is premature in the eyes of Chief Little Fox of Suffolk County, a Native American who is very much alive, known to the public as chief of the Matinecock. Chief Little Fox claims that his nation deeded the property to the church on a temporary basis and still has clear title to the land. One of the main goals of his people is to reclaim the Fort Totten area near Bayside, Queens, part of which includes a sacred burial ground, apparently in continuous use up to recent times. This campaign has been partly successful and cultural reeducation programs are already underway. There are now two Native American museums at the site.

There is a Munsey Park in Matinecock territory, just east of the modern Queens border, and just minutes from Manhasset. It seems that the Munsee people who evacuated Manhattan and headed east settled there in the 1700s, which means their descendants are probably still dwelling there, only an hour's drive from Manhattan.

MORE THAN A FISH STORY

The young Teddy Roosevelt used to visit Oyster Bay on Long Island Sound, in what is was then part of Queens, but is now Nassau County. He had uncles there to visit, and later while Teddy was still a teenager, his father rented a house there. At some point in his impressionable youth, in the 1870s, the delicate city kid sought out the company of a fisherman down by the seashore. Seeing an eager target for his colorful tales of local history, the seafarer pointed to a hill rising up over the former Stronghold of the Matinecock, and said, "See that hilltop over there? That used to be the place where the wigwam of the great sagamore Mohannes was set. He was a renowned chief among the Matinecock people, and his tribe was called the Mohannes tribe, after him. From that spot he could see all that was going on for miles, and all ships at sea. That's why they call it Sagamore Hill. A Sagamore is sort of like a president, or chief." Roosevelt's diaries are at Harvard, and include references to this pivotal incident.[25] Later, as president, he set up his summer White House on Sagamore Hill overlooking the harbor.

NISSEQUOGUE

The heart of Nissequogue ("Clay Country") territory was from Stony Brook to the Nissequogue River in Smithtown, although it stretched from Port Jefferson in the east to well past the Nissequague. The sachem in 1656 was named Coginiquant, and he lived at what is now the town of Nesaquake.[26]

Nesconset is another Algonquin place-name in the region. In the Renneiu language it would mean "place where clay is in the water." The present-day Nissequogue are extremely tall people, the men standing between six foot and six foot seven, the women no shorter than five foot seven. This most likely reflects their Mohawk ancestry, not their Matouac.

Life for the Nissequogue still centers around their river. Both the Nissequogue and the Peconic Rivers are so shallow that they can be waded across.[27] The elders refer to the place and river as Nissequaq, "this location where the clay is good," and the area as Neskwakee, "clay country." The river's source is a crystal-clear artesian spring of fresh frigid water, seven miles inland on the southeast corner of town. The spring is apparently still pristine and a source of pride for the Nissequogue. They still dig a small pit around the spring to collect the water so that pot-dipping is more convenient.

The Nissequogue, along with the Shinnecock and the Montauk, were much sought-after as whalers. Their sheer size and strength gave them an advantage in harpooning and hauling whales. Historians have often mixed them in with the Shinnecock, but they were rivals from at least the early 1600s when the Mohawk took over the Nissequogue shortly before the English arrived in 1640.

Perhaps the best known Nissequogue during the mid-twentieth century was a woman named Red Feather. Her Catholic name was Mary Frances Wheeler.[28] This braided elder was a fluent speaker of Nissequogue until her death in 1997 at the age of ninety-one. One of her sons has a partial grasp of the language today. One of her prosperous relatives on the Caleb Smith side of her family (see chapter 16) built a frame house for Red Feather to live in, with an elegant door facing the road. One of the first things she did was have her brother get an ax and chop a doorway through the back wall of the house. The elegant front door to the road was never used again. The reason was simple—the new door faced the Nissaquogue River. Three thousand years ago all Long Island Indians built their wigwams on the west bank halfway up a river that flowed both ways. The doors faced east so they could watch the sun come up, and also so they could see who might paddle up on the river, which was the main highway in those days. Like Red Feather's new house, their wigwams were built twenty to thirty feet up the bank of the river. When I explained this to her grandson Ray, he commented that virtually all the houses built by his family were unconsciously laid out facing the Nissequogue River on the western bank, in the same configuration. Red Feather's was the only one with the door built in the "wrong direction," facing the street, hence the need for the hasty reconstruction.

The Nissequogues gradually switched from the old Mohican to the Renneiu language spoken by a few today.

SETAUKETS

The Setauket, also called Seatalcats ("Land at the Mouth of the River"), territory stretched along the north shore from the mouth of the Wading River, west to Stony Brook and possibly to Port Jefferson. Their principal village was at Little Neck. There is a town of Setauket today in the area. Their most prominent sachems were Warrawakin in 1655, and Gil in 1675. All along the north shore of Long Island, one can find a great quantity of boulders and stones (left in the path of the terminal moraine), and limonite[29] "Indian paint pots," as well as occasional artifacts from the archaic and early woodland period.

CORCHAUG

The Corchaug ("Principal Place" or "Ancient Ones"), who were "a numerous and powerful tribe,"[30] are the direct descendants of the Orient Point people whose innovative culture flourished about 1000 B.C.E. The present name Corchaug is in the Renneiu language, common on Long Island after the mid-1600s. It has, however, also been pronounced "Conchaug," which is the proto-Mohican version associated with Orient Point culture. The name of the famous vacation spot Cutchogue is a Native Long Island variation on the same word. These ancient, highly shamanistic people, preservers of a great mystical heritage, are often considered to be the first recognizable Lenape group— hence the name "Ancient Ones."

The Corchaug territory in 1640, extending forty miles along the north coast of eastern Long Island, ran from Orient Point (and Plum Island) west to Wading River, and south to the Peconic River. Peconic, which means "small place," was also the name of the bay at the mouth of the river. There is a grandfather chestnut tree, which is beloved to many Algonquin on Long Island, still standing at Southold. Unlike many of the new blight-resistant hybrids, this chestnut actually grows nuts.

The island paradise of the Corchaug was called Yennicock, a beautiful area by all accounts. Yenni is the Pequot word for "Indians," "men," or "people," depending on how you translate it, but the Corchaug were not part of the nearby Pequot. Their greatest sachem in historical times was Chief Momoweton in 1648, but much of their history has yet to be reconstructed.

In 1636, the British colonists from New Haven landed at Yennicock at Conscience Point and settled in the territory of the Corchaug, just south of the region known by the Indians as "the old village." When an English plantation was established there in 1640, it was named South Old to describe its location, and was soon changed to Southold. The First Presybterian Church of Southold established by John Youngs on October 31, 1640, lays claim to being the oldest congregation of any kind in New York State.

There was a fortress, its enclosure embracing three-quarters of an acre, south of Cutchogue on the east side of Fort Neck. Ancient village sites have been excavated near the shore east of Cutchogue, a half mile east of Southold Village, on the opposite shore of the bay, along Greenport Harbor, and east of Greenport Village.

There are Native American museums at Southold on Mainview Road and at Greenport on Main Street. In 1933, a now famous memorial to the Corchaug people was carved into the living rock at Orient Point. Elliot A. Brooks, the carver, depicted a Corchaug chief's face and a Long Island "sunbear" or shrub bear, a small bear now rare on Long Island, beloved of the Natives. In many ways, the Corchaugs were the founders—or at least the direct descendants—of the post-archaic Algonquin civilization. They rightly can be considered part of the transition in Algonquin history from the archaic to woodland periods. They are the Ancient Ones. Having a face carved on stone gazing eastward over the sea to the rising sun appropriately symbolizes their enduring influence as the bedrock of Lenape culture and their love of the sunrise over the sea.

The south part of the area is famous among the Native peoples for its walking dunes. These sandy land formations actually travel up and down the island, carrying trees and plants and other features with them on their "stroll." If one places a marker post deep into the ground, the phenomenon can be seen. Orient Point to the north is part of bedrock and does not shift at all, as is true with the whole north shore. The south half of Long Island is very sandy south of the terminal moraine, whereas the north half is covered with rocks from all over New England. It is on the north shore of eastern Long Island that the contrast in wind—and therefore flora and fauna—between east and west bank settlements is most prominent. It is also here that the most varied food sources are found, halfway inland along estuaries or rivers that flow both ways. These factors became tremendous shaping forces in Mohican and then Lenape culture as it spread throughout the northeast. It was along the elevated north side of the Schuykill River, in what is now Philadelphia, that the descendants of these people first intermarried with the Mississippian people then living on the lower south bank.[31] There had been a long history of conflict between the tall, narrow-faced Corchaug people on the plateau and the round-faced, round-chinned Mississippians living on the flat plain. When they finally joined forces, they intermarried and shared their technologies, becoming what we now think of as Lenape people.

The Peconic River, so essential to the Corchaug's native landscape on eastern Long Island, is a salty estuary for about two miles. It has more of an east-west orientation than other rivers on Long Island, but the northwest bank is still more "protected" than the southeastern, and was therefore settled first. The Corchaug homes were mainly to the northwest, where the plant life was more vigorous. The eastern shore is also prone to flooding. On the eastern shore of most Long Island estuaries, only low shrubs can grow due to the harsh briny wind that comes in off the ocean. This is true more in the north than the south, where the ocean air blasts away everything more democratically than along the north shore. Fortunately blueberries, bayberries, and cranberries can grow on the east bank, and all the Long Island Natives loved to cross the river and gather them.

One of the newer developments in the Corchaug region is the planned excavation of a giant log fort built by the Corchaug people around the time of first European contact. Dated to about 1630 by historians, it lies on the west side of Downs Creek, still untrampled, but the logs rotted away to nothing. At one time the huge log walls enclosed an area of about three acres. Archaeologists and historians who have visited the site have already found many trade goods, indicating it might have been part of a vast wampum transport and trade chain that brought wampum beads into New Amsterdam. An old well was found nearby with numerous arrowheads over one thousand years old. There is a difference of opinion among historians concerning the Lenape adaptation of log construction at first contact with white settlers. Excavation of this site could provide some evidence as to how this transition occurred, and how much previous log construction had already been in use by the Lenape.

MANHANSET

The people of the Manhanset ("Island Sheltered by Other Islands") group lived on Shelter Island, Ram Island, Hog Island, and other islands in the region. Their main settlement was on Shelter Island, an ancient sacred site aligned with the solstices. The fort on the island dates from 1639. Large mounds of shells still visible there indicate the site. The area called Sachem's Neck today actually was the traditional home of Manhasset sachems such as the courageous Poygratasuck, Wyandanqx's brother who was sachem in 1648.[32] He fought the Pequot, Narragansett, and Mohican, and was finally killed in 1651, his head cut off by his enemies. Midway between Sag Harbor and East Hampton is a spot called Sachems Hole where there supposedly was a hole about eighteen inches deep in which the Manhanset sachem's head was buried, or rested temporarily.[33]

Robin's Island, right in the fork of the fish "flukes" of eastern Long Island, was originally called Ancannock, "Place of Fallen Timber." It is covered with clay deposits, excellent for making pottery. There were a number of Manhansets living on Ancannock when Europeans first arrived. Gardiners Island, named after the man who rescued Heather Flower, was occupied by Manhanset Indians at one time. There was a village on the west side of Gardiners Island and many shell middens. The contract for its sale, approved by Sachem Poygratasuck, included a rider stipulating that Gardiner would report any beached whales and save for the Natives "all the fins and tails," which were to be used in sacred rituals. Gardiner and his family were able to maintain the island as an independent barony until 1788, when it was annexed to the state of New York by a legislative act. It is known that Captain Kidd buried his plunder there, some of which was later found. Some of that treasure still lies beneath the sand under Gardiners Island, along with the deepest secrets of Algonquin history, those of the red-ochre people.

18

LENAPE EXODUS

In Lenape belief, our souls walk towards the west when we die, traveling along the "Spirit Road," which can be seen reflected in the Milky Way at night, each footprint a shimmering star. To many Algonquin people, the act of exiting a western door face-forward is a metaphor for death itself. This was one more reason for the Lenape to feel badly about leaving their homes and land to travel west into the unknown mysteries of the frontier. We can imagine that before departing, many purified themselves in ritual, fasting and praying to Munihtoh for guidance and protection.

In the Midewiwin Lodge of the Ojibway, at the completion of the four-day gathering, the participants exit the lodgehouse through the western door at the end of the structure. One must turn one's back to the west and back out the door, uttering a blessing. This is to acknowledge that one is still going to continue in this world and not enter the next.

Some northern Algonquin such as the Wabanaki of the Northeast believe we go full circle in life and pass on through the "eastern gate" when we die. Either way, there is a widespread Algonquin practice of "walking one's death," meaning to consciously live as if one could die at any time. This outlook can be practiced by anyone of any culture; it puts materialistic concerns in perspective, forcing us to live in the moment. The Algonquin are masters of this practice. The spiritually strong elder commits every action with full attention, as if this moment now were the most important moment of his or her life—as if it were the last. It is the practice of "walking one's death" that keeps us on the hard edge of reality, where our egos are held the most at bay, our minds are alert and lucid, and our hearts are open and infinitely giving. Putting ourselves in the "I could die at any moment" frame of mind may also help us understand the Lenape and Algonquin tendency to be highly emotive about things of the spirit but totally unmoved by the pains and losses of physical life.

The Great Disappearance

The disappearance of the Munsee from New York State was nothing new; they'd been disappearing ever since Giovanni da Verrazzano landed his ship, *The Dauphine,* on their lush shores. They had lost thousands to disease; thousands to wars with other Native Americans; hundreds, if not thousands, to battles with the Dutch; and a few to the slave trade. By the 1640s there were only a few hundred or so Lenape on Manhattan. By 1740, one hundred years later, there were probably only a few thousand Munsee in the whole state of New York, and most of them were invisible to white settlers. By the Revolutionary War the poverty level of those remaining in New York was so great that hundreds of Munsee people were dying of malnutrition. Many of the Munsee bones being repatriated from Orange County, New York, which date from the time of the Revolutionary War, appear to show signs of severe malnutrition; neck vertebrae in some cases appear to have deteriorated due to a lack of calcium and other nutrients.[1] We know why so many Munsee left the state to seek greener pastures; they were being starved out by a society that had no use or patience for their ancient ways. What is still unclear is how they left. Surprisingly not all Munsee went west.

They Went East

Many of the Algonquin of New York City did not immediately move west after removal—they headed east. Muncey Park in Nassau County,

Long Island, mentioned in the previous chapter, was settled by Munsee refugees from Manhattan in the early to mid-1700s. The Canarsie, who were apparently multilingual, had many allies throughout the region and many options. Thus they may have been inclined to make individual decisions as to their escape route. Some went east to Long Island to join the Poospatuck, Matinecock, and Shinnecock. Other Canarsie moved west to what is now New Jersey and settled with the Unami. Some may have gone to the east into the woods of western Connecticut. Some of the Wappingers of the Hudson Valley migrated east with their Mohican and Munsee cousins to Stockbridge, Massachusetts. Later they headed to western New York at the invitation of the Oneida to found the towns of New Stockbridge, New York, and later still, Stockbridge, Wisconsin, together with their newfound Oneida compatriots.

The northernmost Munsee, the Esopus Indians, were already scattered to the four directions by 1709. In 1680, Esopus Chief Ankerop left what later became Rosendale, and died about 1700. However, a few individuals, such as Hank Paul, remained in the area until 1825. The majority went to the Minisink region, a wide strip of land encompassing both sides of the Delaware River from Minisink Ford, New York—about fifteen miles north of today's Port Jervis—to about Minisink Hills, Pennsylvania. The region was named after the island of Minisink, which is situated near today's tri-state rock where three borders meet. Minisink has been translated as "Place of the Munsee" or "Island of the Munsee." It was on that island that the Munsee capital and central fire were located. This area remained a stronghold until the 1750s.

Survivors of the town of Schaghticoke on the east bank of the Hudson River went east into the mountains where Connecticut, Massachusetts, and New York meet. Some of the Rockaway people of Queens went further east on Long Island; most, however, moved to northern New Jersey, settling Rockaway, New Jersey.[2] Ultimately they joined with the general Lenape population in the Delaware River valley by around 1709 and started heading west shortly thereafter.

The Exodus through Pennsylvania

In the first phase of the Lenape Removal, the majority of Munsee, Unami, and their cousins moved directly west into Pennsylvania from New York and New Jersey, moving along a wide corridor in Pennsylvania, splitting up, joining forces, and blending with various cousins of other nations, officially amalgamating into a new Delaware nation about 1755.[3] However, to the north, south, east, and west, smaller groups of Munsee and Unami remained distinct as they continued their search for a new homeland. Theirs was a hard road, but if they had not persevered, we would not know the Munsee culture or their language today.

Underground Roots

Some Native New Yorkers stayed right where they were and went underground, intermarrying and opening inns and taverns along the old trail routes, some of which are still in business today or were so within recent memory. Davis Tavern, in Ulster County, the powwow grounds in Barryville in Orange County, the basket shops along the Tappan Road in Rockland County, and possibly Eddy Farm Resort, formerly of Sparrowbush, all have or have had Munsee associations that link back to the past.

Going underground was a tradeoff that allowed the Munsee to stay on the land and keep the families together, but it robbed them of their cultural identity and eventually their language. Those who intermarried found it a challenge to raise their children in a traditional manner, because interracial marriage was illegal until 1967. Saying too much could place the children in danger, so the Munsee spoke about such things in a sort of code, arguing for the logic of those traditional views without being able to give examples or terms. That was too painful a prospect for some, and they chose to move.

The Lenape had two beloved and well-worn trails to follow westward at the turn of the eighteenth century. These were ancient sacred trails, and so the journey west must have been bittersweet for them, a last pilgrimage.

As in Europe, Asia, and elsewhere in the world, great trails often start out not as trade routes but as paths of pilgrimage. This seems to be the case with the Great Westward Trail of the Lenape, very roughly approximated today by Interstate Route 80. It connected two of the most ancient vision quest sites in their region, the rock shelter at Inwood in Manhattan and Dreamer's Rock at the Delaware Water Gap in Pennsylvania.

To the south was another pilgrimage trail, or a chain of shorter trails, approximated today by New Jersey State Routes 78 and 22, connecting Communipaw (later called Pavonia, then Jersey City) with Easton and Allentown. I will call Route 80 the Pocono Road as it was sometimes called, and Route 78 the Tulpehocken Trail, in order to distinguish them. The more southerly path, roughly approximated by New Jersey's Routes 78 and 22, does not correspond closely with any modern road or roads, and traces are harder to find as we approach Pennsylvania to the west, near the Pohatcong Mountains. Towns like Watchung, Pluckemin, and possibly Potterstown, New Jersey, remain as possible clues to the old trail's original locations. The Pocono and Tulpehocken Trails were connected by north-south trails approximated by New Jersey State Routes 24[4] and 206, which cross Route 80 at Budd Lake (NJ). They continued toward Wyoming, now Wilkes-Barre, Pennsylvania. The Lenape used to camp at Budd Lake on their way down to the Jersey shores, along what's now Route 206 in New Jersey. This practice ended in 1710 when they sold the property to the whites and moved west.[5] There was also a trail that headed due south from Millburn (NJ), to the mouth of the Raritan at Sayreville (NJ), according to Herbert Kraft.[6] Many of those evacuating from Staten Island would have taken that route.

THE POCONO ROAD AND OTHER PILGRIM TRAILS

Interstate Route 80 as it is today begins in Fort Lee (NJ), an ancient village of the peaceful Hackensack, that some early maps name *Metch-kent-a-woom*. The original trail, however, would have started at the Hudson River, which had equal if not superior status as a transportation route. Fort Lee is the northernmost point one could easily land a canoe from Manhattan, for beyond that is Englewood Cliffs and the Palisades. The practical value of having a trail begin at that spot is obvious enough, for all southbound river traffic would see that as the first exit west.

The entire shoreline region of Manhattan from Spuyten Duyvil down to Fort Washington Park is scattered with a few of the most ancient settlement sites in North America, and is known to be highly sacred. For this reason, it is likely that in its earliest form, the Pocono Road was a path of pilgrimage from the Spuyten Duyvil/Inwood/Cloisters chain of shelters in Manhattan to Dreamer's Rock at the Minisink site and the Poconos beyond. Pocono is from the Munsee word *puxkwatul*, meaning "high up," or possibly from the Unami *pok-way-nay-oo*, "it is high up." This Pocono Road was apparently not made into a major paved roadway before the Revolutionary War. There are a remarkable number of Munsee place-names along the course of the old route.

Most Lenape moved directly to the Susquehanna Valley, a vast expansive region that follows the course of the Susquehanna River as it zigzags from north to south, from New York, across the State of Pennsylvania, and into the Chesapeake Bay in Maryland, 447 miles from beginning to end. This migration of Lenape took place between 1709 and 1742. It was perhaps the clearest and best-defined migration in their history, a hike westward of under a hundred miles over the two well-known pathways, to the Wyoming settlement, now Wilkes-Barre (PA), on the Susquehanna River.

If you were one of those Lenape migrating west in 1742, you

might go to the Minisink Hills, then move on to what is now Tannersville (PA) along the Pechoquealin Trail (a leg of the Wyoming Trail), which follows Interstate Route 80 to Big Boulder Mountain (PA). Then the trail route heads northwest to Bear Creek along today's Pennsylvania State Route 115 to Wyoming, now Wilkes-Barre.

Pennsylvania Route 209 along the Delaware was the site of the Delaware River Trail, which was the central corridor of the Lenape stronghold of the Minisink, off-limits to whites until the French and Indian War in 1754. At Milford (PA), a route called the Minisink Trail headed due west along Pennsylvania Route 84, crossing Lackawaxen Creek to Lord's Valley, an old mission settlement, then to Scranton (PA), connecting there with the Warrior's Trail, which ran along the Susquehanna.

Those who were migrating west would have filled other roads as well, such as the Lehigh Trail, part of which stretched along Pennsylvania State Route 145 from Easton (Lechauwekink), where the Lehigh and Delaware meet, to Lehightown (previously Fort Allen) and Jim Thorpe (PA), named after the great Sac and Fox athlete who was a football star at the Carlisle School. Nearby is the town of Nesquehoning, a Lenape word meaning "the place where clay is found."

Pennsylvania State Route 93 from Jim Thorpe and through Hazelton to Neskopeck, was called the Neskopeck Trail, which was the name of one of the Munsee prophets from the 1760s. At Hazelton, the westward traveler crosses the Nanticoke Trail, which leads to Tamaqua, Pennsylvania, to the south. Tamaqua, which means "beaver" was named after one of the greatest Lenape chiefs.

On the eastern-most spot along the Susquehanna River, and therefore the first spot they came upon as they trudged west, the Lenape founded the town of Wyoming, which is the Lenape translation of Susquehanna. The word *mee-chay-wee-ah-mee-ing* (which we shorten to "Wyoming") with a hard *g* or *k* at the end, in Munsee dialect means "where water crosses the big plain." The Susquehanna

River ("where water crosses the big plain" in Iroquois) was obviously named for its lower portion, which crosses a large plain as it empties into the Chesapeake at Perryville (MD). In 1709, the first one hundred to one-hundred-fifty Delaware settled into their new home along a new river. This town today is named Wilkes-Barre (PA); to the west is Wyoming county, named after this early settlement.

Further to the southwest, Shamokin, which we now call Sunbury, Pennsylvania, was the second most important settlement on the Susquehanna.[7] Nearby to the west are the Muncy Hills, named for the Munsee Indians who lived there, and also the town of Nanticoke (PA), named for the closest relatives of the Lenape. Past the Muncy Hills to the west is Montour County and Montoursville (PA), presumably named after the Lenape's friend Andrew Montour, a French/Seneca trader and interpreter of the time who was well liked by both government and indigenous leaders. Josiah Montour, a Munsee/Mohican, and one of Andrew's descendants born in 1872, coauthored, with Frank G. Speck and Jesse Moses, *The Celestial Bear Comes Down to Earth*, a valuable source of spiritual and cultural knowledge about the Mohican.

The third of the great Munsee-Lenape settlements on the Susquehanna was called Paxtang, which means "town at a flat place." Lenape trails connected these three towns—Wyoming, Shamokin, and Paxtang—along the river. Pennsylvania State Route 11 today hugs the contours of the Susquehanna River's west bank from Wilkes-Barre south to Sunbury, following the old Warrior's Trail. Then on the east bank, Route 147 continues south, following the Paxtang Path to Benvenue, a quaint misspelling of the French word for "welcome." Pennsylvania State Route 22 goes yet further south, by the old route to where Paxtang once stood. The entire journey, from Wyoming in the north to Paxtang in the south, would encompass a distance of over 140 miles. As you drive along these roads today, you will see historical markers recording the "Wyoming" migration story.

The Lenape loved their new "river civilization," and wanted to live there permanently. They had a beautiful river to fish in, places to plant corn and expand villages, and miles of true wilderness with few whites. The French and Indian War, which came in 1754, would change everything.

In 1720, Paxtang was still nothing but a ragtag encampment in the wilderness, but it grew steadily. By 1740 it was a Lenape population center, and the lower Delaware Valley was virtually abandoned. Paxtang soon far outgrew the two other towns; today what began as a tiny Lenape camp is the city of Harrisburg, the state capital of Pennsylvania.

If you were to walk northward along the river from Harrisburg today, you would pass Buffalo Mountain, Bear Mountain, Mahantango Mountain, Beavertown, Paxton (after Paxtang), Shamokin Dam, Buckhorn, Catawissa, Mocanaqua, Shickshinny, Penobscot Mountain, Wanamie, and Nanticoke (PA), all words familiar to the Lenape of 1709. Past Wyoming, the Warrior's Path reaches Scranton via Pennsylvania State Route 11, where it connects with the Minisink Trail.

Waves across the River

In 1718, the Delaware ceded many tracts of their old homeland in several treaties with Pennsylvania, causing more Lenape to settle along the Susquehanna. At this time, although Paxtang was still small, the population of the upper two cities of Wyoming and Shamokin and the surrounding areas along the trails must have been considerable— perhaps reminiscent of the prominence they had once had on the Delaware. But this reunion of the great nation was fated to be brief. Two years later, in 1720, a war with the Iroquois made their otherwise quiet life on the river more difficult. In two more years the Iroquois would drive some Delaware south into Paxtang, and force many others to cross the Alleghenies to the well-forested westerly-sloping plain between the mountains and the rivers. Most of those uprooted settled at Kittanning ("Place on the Great River"), a few miles north of what is now Pittsburgh, along the Allegheny River, but a long way from home for the people of the Delaware River. Kittanning is almost the same name they gave the mountains of their homeland on the Delaware River—Kittatinny Mountains—three hundred miles away. Kittanning and Kittatinny have similar meanings.

In 1732, the Lenape back home ceded yet more land to the Pennsylvania colony in the east, and moved west. This caused yet more Wyoming Valley people to go further west in search of elbow room, a cascade effect.

A New Generation

From this point in the migration history onward, I will use the non-Algonquin word "Delaware" to refer to the descendants of the people of New York who are not purely Munsee or Stockbridge Munsee-Mohican. After being removed, split up, and merged so many times, and in so many combinations, most of the descendants of the Canarsie, Rockaway, Matinecock, Siwanoy, Weckweesgeek, and various Munsee groups that had occupied the great and "ancient city" had thoroughly intermarried with one another, and were virtually blended in with the Unami, formerly of New Jersey. Some family lines of Nanticokes, Powhatans, Piscataways, Conoys, and even Hatteras Algonquins from the south were also mixed in. Add to these the closely related Wapanoes of Connecticut, speaking the Renneiu language, and others who had escaped from Long Island, as well as individuals from the Mohican nation, their ancient allies, and it became clear that a single collective term was necessary.

The term "Delaware" had been used for all Indians living along the "Delaware" River since 1610, albeit incorrectly. At this point, it must have seemed like a small inconvenience to adopt the name that everyone knew and used anyway. So many Lenape did, first in Pennsylvania, possibly in the late 1740s, and then in New York, some time before the Revolutionary War. It was widely acknowledged that the Delaware were still a potent political entity to be dealt with. According to Internet folklorist Lee Sultzman, "A common tradition shared by most Algonquin maintains that the Lenape, Nanticoke, Powhatan, and Shawnee were, at some point in the past, a single tribe which lived in the Lenape homeland. Linguistic evidence and migration patterns tend to support this, leaving only the question of when." [8]

In 1742, the last band of Lenape living at the confluence of the Lehigh and Delaware Rivers, now Easton (PA), left to join their western brothers. This was directly and indirectly due to the infamous "Walking Purchase" of 1737, foisted upon the Lenape by William Penn's own sons, but it was also at the request of Governor George Thomas, who could see that conflict was coming over land rights in the area. Since there was no waterway that connected the Delaware watershed with the Susquehanna, the Lenape used the two major trails, the Tulpehocken and the Wyoming Path, which was the western extension of the Pocono Road.

Alumapees, also known as Sassoonan, was the first "king" of the Delaware, who had been appointed by the English, for their own convenience. They had hoped to control and bribe Sassoonan into submission, and set up a central office for him at Wyoming. It was a very successful town, and soon the Delaware were joined by Shawnee, Nanticoke, Conoy (a western Piscataway group), Conestoga (an Iroquoian-speaking group), and southern Tutelo, (a Siouian-speaking group). The earlier Lenape practice of welcoming stray Shawnee in various parts east turned out to be significant. Just thirty years later in the Ohio Valley of 1770, the once-again homeless Delaware were welcomed into the many Shawnee villages all over Ohio with open arms because the Shawnee remembered the hospitality shown to them at Wyoming. Together the Delaware and Shawnee built up those villages into great Algonquin population centers.

The Treaty of Lancaster, signed in 1744 with Pennsylvania, demanded that all remaining Unami along the lower Delaware were to "leave the waters of their river" and move to Shamokin, where Sassoonan lived,[9] or to Wyoming, greatly increasing the importance of the upper Wyoming settlements.

Just west of Harrisburg along the Tulpehocken Path is the city of Carlisle (PA), the site of an early frontier fort where white soldiers could keep an eye on the burgeoning populations of Paxtang. That site is now part of the famous Carlisle Indian Residential School that produced great Native American athletes like Jim Thorpe. During the French and Indian War, many Delaware felt it necessary to leave their kin and head over the Allegheny Mountains to western Pennsylvania to join those who had already fled. They crossed the mountains on foot, or canoed along the Juniata River then left their boats and took trails over the Alleghenies. These trails were later widened by pack trains, and then wagons, as far west as Pittsburgh.

Sassoonan died in Shamokin in 1747. His oldest nephew Pisquetomen was too anti-English for everyone's comfort, so the English, under Sir William Johnson (1715–74) asked the Iroquois to pick the Lenape chief, ignoring the fact that the Lenape had broken free of Iroquois rule. The Iroquois, hardly tea-sipping British subjects, picked the warlike Shingas, which means "Swamp Thing."[10] Shingas had already left his brother Sassoonan at Shamokin, to live in the Ohio River Valley around Pittsburgh, and had to come back east to take office. Footnotes to history include a mention of Chief Shingas meeting with a young white warrior named George Washington in October of 1753, long before he became commander in chief of the Continental Army and later the United States.[11]

Not surprisingly, Shingas allied with the Shawnee, who happened to have over seven hundred warriors amassed on the other side of the Ohio River. At the time the French established Fort Duquesne at Pittsburgh, there were also two hundred Delaware warriors on the Susquehanna. They found their leader in the former war chief Teedyuskung ("He Who Makes the Earth Tremble"), who had become a man of peace. Born in the year 1700, and of mixed Munsee, Unalatchtgo, and Unami origins, he was already almost fifty years old and Sir William Johnson's senior by fifteen years. Teedyuskung was not a hereditary chief, and indeed, had once made his living as a broommaker, but he won his position through the admiration of his countrymen. The English called him "King of the Delaware." Teedyuskung was neutral in the French and Indian War, one of the few chiefs to accomplish this. The Iroquois tried to persuade him to join the English, while Shingas egged him on to attack the English. Finally he did attack, but only participated in one war foray himself, directing others from a distance. According to author Charles Weslager, these Delaware took so many "scalps, prisoners and [so much] plunder," that the English built six new forts in New Jersey's Delaware Valley to protect the colonists.[12]

Teedyuskung's departure from peacemaking may have been ill advised, as things got worse for the Delaware. The three main attacks made under his authority were met by divided opinion and dispute among his own people, and by overwhelming retaliation on the part of the colonists. In a sense, the storm of controversy has never subsided; the Delaware were never forgiven and the chain of events proceeding from that year contributed to the fugitive status of the Delaware, their exile in Canada, their endless land disputes, and the resultant distortions of popular history. Teedyuskung is quoted as saying, "As to me, I assure you . . . contrary winds may blow strong in my face, yet I will go forward and never turn back." The crosswinds of controversy were very strong in 1750.

In 1751, Unami and Munsee bands, still intact as small tribal units fleeing growing troubles with the Pennsylvania colony, finally reached what is now eastern Ohio. What sorrow and consternation William Penn would have felt if he had seen what had become of his settlement in the New World and had seen what his own sons did to his old friends the Lenape, who'd never harmed any true Quaker.

Between 1754 and 1763 the most famous chapter of the endless French and Indian War saga was written. It involved many characters and many colonies. It was called "the French and Indian War" by the English, although wars between the three rivals had been going on for years. This was to be the decisive chapter in the conflict between New France and New England and other British interests over the New World, at least in the region now encompassed by the United States. Many more Delaware of the Susquehanna and elsewhere moved west; less than a thousand stayed in New Jersey.

On April 14, 1756, Pennsylvania Governor Robert Morris declared war on the Delaware. In June of the same year, Governor Jonathan Belcher of New Jersey declared the Delaware enemies, and both governors offered a handsome price for Delaware scalps, following the past example of New York Governor Benjamin Fletcher, who had offered bounties for Munsee scalps in July of 1693.[13] The Lenape held onto and defended their villages in the Susquehanna Valley until 1768, when they moved on, continuing their painful exodus.

On September 8, 1756, three hundred colonial soldiers under Colonel John Armstrong burned down the burgeoning Delaware town of Kittanning. It is interesting that the modern town of Kittanning, with its busy truck and bus stop and souvenir shops full of "Indian stuff," is now in Armstrong County, named after the very man who destroyed the original town. Armstrong tried to rescue white captives and Europeans living with the Delaware, but they evaded capture, reportedly preferring the company of the Delaware and the freedom of Algonquin life to the social constrictions of the English.

It sounds a little surprising at first, but cases of white captives evading rescue can be found in every decade in the records of the conflict between the Lenape and the whites, from the Esopus wars to the conflicts of the early 1800s. When the treaty with General Henry Bouquet was signed in 1764, over half of the some six hundred white captives adamantly refused repatriation, preferring to live the rest of their lives as Delaware or Shawnee rather than go back to their families.[14] It was not even unexpected. Usually within a year or so of capture, whites taken by the Lenape were ready and willing to fight and die for their true freedom. This, more than any artifact of Algonquin culture, hints at the valuable way of life the Algonquin people were to preserve. It also lends credence to the position that the wars between the Algonquin and Europeans were not just land wars but ideological wars as well.

Most of those who escaped Armstrong's men moved westward to Shenango, near Sharon, Pennsylvania, and what is now the Shenango River Lake area. Some may have helped settle what is now Youngstown, Ohio, just over the border, since anything west of the Ohio was considered Indian land, and the Youngstown region was beyond the jurisdiction of the colony of Pennsylvania. It was about this time that the Munsee stronghold along the Delaware River began to crumble. After six thousand or more years of continuous occupation, the leaders and citizens of Minisink had to leave.

Sir William Johnson (1715–74) was appointed superintendent of Indian affairs for the English government, a position he held from 1755 till his death. Married to Molly Brant, sister of Mohawk Chief Joseph Brant and a woman of high esteem among Iroquois, Johnson was incredibly persuasive with the Hodenosuannee ("People of the Longhouse"). He persuaded them to ally with England.

In 1756, Teedyuskung, or "Honest John" as he was also called, pushed for a council with Sir William Johnson at the former's home in Lancaster, Pennsylvania, and it was granted. Speaking on behalf of all Delaware, Munsee, Mohican, Shawnee, and Nanticoke, and "fully empowered by them," he confronted the English with their numerous land frauds and firmly insisted on compensation, all without resorting to further warfare. He also represented each of the Iroquois nations of the confederacy. He demanded a pro-Indian secretary familiar with Unami to write down everything he said. After much resistance, "the sagacious twenty-seven-year-old Charles Thomson, master of the Quaker School in Philadelphia,"[15] was appointed to record his words. Thompson became an honorary Delaware and later helped Jefferson, another student of Lenape languages, frame the Declaration of Independence and the Constitution. Charles Weslager describes Teedyuskung himself as "resplendent in a gold-laced coat, riding boots with silver shoe buckles, checkered cloth breeches, and stockings with scarlet gartering. . . ."[16] According to E. M. Ruttenber in *Indian Tribes of Hudson's River:*

> The Lenape king stated his complaint boldly and plainly. To the governor's inquiry for specifications in regard to alleged wrongs in the sale of lands, he replied, "I have not far to go for an instance [of wrongdoing]! This very ground under me (striking it with his foot) was my land by inheritance, and it is taken from me by fraud. When I say 'this' ground, I mean all the land lying between Tohiccon Creek and Wyoming, on the river Susquehanna! I have not only been served so in this government, but the same thing has been done to me as to several tracts in New Jersey, over the river!" When asked what he meant by "fraud," he gave instances of forged deeds, under which lands were claimed which were never sold. "This," said he, "is fraud!"[17]

The next year Teedyuskung negotiated peacefully with the British, adding Wappingers, Conoy (a branch of the Piscataway, some of whom later moved up the Kanahwa River in West Virginia), Tutelos, Chugnuts, and Susquehannas to the growing list of his constituents, which continued to expand until his death.

The Delaware went to Easton, Pennsylvania, in 1757 and in 1758 to negotiate and sign what became the Treaty of Easton, embodying what the Munsee considered their ultimate commitment to peace. Receiving only a modest sum for their disputed lands, now covered with settlers' cabins, they dispersed to Ontario, Wisconsin, and Kansas, enduring much hardship.

In April 1763, Chief Teedyuskung was burned to death in a fire that leveled his entire village. It was probably arson; the site was resettled and rebuilt within two weeks by a group of whites. In that same year, France formalized its defeat in the Seven Years' War at the Treaty of Paris, losing Louisiana to Spain and New France to England. The English at last were in control of America. The Delaware, who had sided with the French, had nowhere to turn. Fortunately King George III declared in a proclamation that no Indians should be dispersed without crown consent. However, in that the Lenape had used their alliance with the French to threaten the English for decades, they were suddenly in a fragile position and were watched carefully. The English victors now had every advantage, including a long-standing alliance with most Iroquoian nations, whom they'd been supplying with guns, and who could crush the Lenape at any time. There was a renewed attempt at keeping all white settlers east of the Continental Divide of the Appalachians, and the proclamation protected the Indian country to the west of the mountains. It looked very promising for the British, and tenuous peace accords were struck in various regions.

Part of what some Americans considered the "madness" of King George III was his containment policy and his desire to protect the rights of Indians. This rather enlightened policy of giving the Algonquin at least some of their own land was considered an outrage by many colonists. In a dozen years, George Washington, a high-initiate Mason, would supposedly have a dream while camped at Valley Forge, a dream of "manifest destiny" in which higher beings were showing him that the future of the new American nation would spread "coast to coast."

In that same eventful year, 1763, inspired by the teachings of the Delaware prophet Neolin, the Ottawa Chief Pontiac surely must have had the opposite dream, because, with the help of Delaware warriors, he took nine out of eleven British forts in the lake region within a few days of each other. It was called Pontiac's Rebellion, but as he was not a citizen of Britain or the American colonies, it could only be considered an act of war.

One of the main events that triggered Pontiac's Rebellion was the death of Delaware Chief Teedyuskung. His son, the warrior Captain Bull, decided to take revenge on the settlers from Connecticut, whom he blamed for his father's death. In October 1763, Captain Bull and the Munsee war leader known as Squash Cutter led ferocious raids on the new Connecticut settlements in the Wyoming Valley and the upper Delaware Valley. They also attacked farms in the Minisink region of New York and New Jersey. As the retaliations of the white farmers and soldiers escalated toward war, Captain Bull joined Pontiac further west. The war began in earnest in May 1763.

For the moment, the Delaware were in the midst of a heady revival, marked by considerable spiritual and military success. It was not to last. The subsequent failure of Pontiac's Rebellion in 1764,[18] and the loss of the Pittsburgh region was to lead indirectly to their darkest hour, and to their fragmentation as a people in the promised land of Ohio, which many believe to have been the homeland of at least one branch of the Lenape family tree.

Pittsburgh is one of the largest cities of which the Delaware were cofounders, but its debt to Native America is not always recognized, due to the complexity of its early development. The existence of Pittsburgh was made possible by the Shawnee and Delaware affection for a white trader named George Croghan, and later by the kindness of Tecumseh's Shawnee father, Pucksinwah.

In 1763, the Miami gave the Shawnee permanent claim to land west of the Ohio River, which many believed to be ancient Shawnee land, so that these great warriors could reunite as the Shawnee Nation. Understandably the Shawnee drifted away from Logstown near Pittsburgh, and settled along the river on the west/north side, and also at Chillicothe, Ohio. Countless Delaware who had already been restless enough to leave the Susquehanna Valley went with them.

The Shawnee had not been united in many generations. The governor of Pennsylvania was worried about keeping friendly ties with this new military presence. He sent George Croghan, the most popular trader among the Shawnee, who called him Aquewelene, or "Blanket Man," to secure good relations with the Shawnee, Delaware, and Wyandot at the Muskingum River in Ohio. Croghan was accompanied by Andrew Montour, who was French/Seneca, as interpreter.

The plan was highly successful. The Shawnee brought the English into the central Miami village far to the west at Pickawillany, Ohio, and they secured an agreement to build a fortified trading post at the site now known as Pittsburgh. Croghan went back east with the good news, and immediately returned to Logstown. (Logstown now had proportionately more Delaware than Shawnee, and was gaining in Delaware population month by month.) Croghan brought a request to build a major fort twenty-two miles down the path at Forks of the Ohio—the confluence of three rivers: the Ohio, the Monongahela, and the Allegheny—to protect Indian interests as well as white. The request was granted. The French asked for the same and were blatantly refused.

The British began building a strong fort at the site four years later. In April 1754, the French swept in and captured it, finished the construction and renamed it Fort Duquesne. The Virginians under Colonel George Washington marched to recapture it for the British. Due to many miscalculations and mistakes, Washington was defeated by the French at Fort Necessity, now near Farmington on Pennsylvania State Route 40, which was called the Mingo Path originally, but which was then renamed Braddock's Road. Over one hundred of Washington's soldiers were killed. His men were allowed to return east, and marched rather dejectedly along Braddock's Road to Frederick, Maryland. That marked the beginning of the French and Indian War.

Feeling undermanned at Fort Duquesne, the French convinced the Shawnee (and Delaware) to fight on their side in the coming battle. A combined force went all out to help their new allies, and smashed the British troops decisively.[19] Shawnee Chief Pucksinwah was the brains behind the victory.

Croghan and Johnson were working on patching up the old alliances when the new governor of Pennsylvania, Robert Hunter Morris, unilaterally declared war on the Delaware and Shawnee and offered bounties for their scalps. New Jersey followed suit.

In 1759, the British finally retook Fort Duquesne under Colonel Forbes, ancestor of *Forbes* magazine founder Malcolm Forbes and his son Steve. The French retreated without a fight, burning their own fort. They could no longer protect the Lenape. At this point, the Lenape realized that they had to make peace with the English. Forbes began work on rebuilding the fort, which the British named after William Pitt. The village, or collection of shacks, as some described them, outside the fort was laughingly called "Pitts-burgh." At that time it was a ramshackle shantytown, but one in violation of the British treaty disallowing all white settlements between the Allegheny Mountains and the Allegheny and Monongahela Rivers, a seventy-mile-wide stretch of Pennsylvania reserved for the Delaware and Shawnee.[20]

In 1758, a major council was held by Croghan a few hundred yards up the Allegheny River from Fort Pitt. The Shawnee, Delaware, Miami, Ottawa, Cayuga, Seneca, Susquehannock, and Wyandot (a splinter group of the Huron) were there. As a symbol for lasting peace, the Shawnee and Delaware chiefs buried a hatchet under a tree where no one would find it. While some felt they were being too lenient about what was obviously a violation of international treaty and a possible threat to their security, the Delaware also recognized the ancient tradition of peacemaking as a path of honor, and the Shawnee Pucksinwah was among the greatest of peacemakers when circumstances allowed. It was only then that the much-trusted Croghan announced that Sir Jeffrey Amherst was the new British commander in chief.

It was a moment of shock and disbelief for the Delaware. It was well known that Amherst considered all Indians to be subhuman savages and discouraged any trade with the Indians, whom he considered to be unruly children of the Crown. Just when there seemed to be a glimmer of hope for the "grandfathers," that hope was shattered. The French were defeated all over the Great Lakes region, and with the fall of Quebec in September 1759, the English were in control. Amherst used the situation to starve out the Indians with high prices and restricted trade on essential items. The Indians had been led to believe that after the French were defeated, the English would abandon Fort Pitt and retreat eastward past the Alleghenies, but instead they poured into the region in greater and greater numbers.

Unbeknownst to "Blanketman" Croghan, based on a plan laid out in a letter from Lord General Jeffrey Amherst to Colonel Henry Bouquet, the blankets that were being sent as gifts to the Delaware and Shawnee were infected with smallpox and other diseases.[21] It was very effective in the short run, killing hundreds of Delaware and Shawnee without wasting a single British bullet. But the blatant lack of gratitude for Pucksinwah's generosity caused Pucksinwah's son to devote his life to holding the whites back behind the rivers, or driving them back if necessary. At the age of thirty-four, Pucksinwah became grand chief of the Shawnee in 1759, the youngest ever by far. Eventually his second son would rise to glory even more quickly. He named the boy Panther Passing Across the Sky, or in the Shawnee language, Tecumseh (1768–1813). For over fifty years, father and son together or separately, always in the company of the Delaware, were able to discourage illegal white encroachments on what is now the state of Ohio.

The night Tecumseh learned that his younger brother Tunskwatawa had lost the crucial battle of Tippecanoe, Indiana, to General Harrison was the night of the New Madrid earthquake of 1811, perhaps the greatest earthquake in U.S. history. A quake of its size and location today would split the United States in half, severing all ground transportation across the Mississippi and destroying thousands of homes. Parts of Kentucky today are still west of the Mississippi, so twisted was the course of the great river. For the followers of Tecumseh, the timing could not have been more portentious. Early on the morning of November 7, 1811, while Tecumseh was near New Madrid (now in Missouri), the battle of Tippecanoe was lost quickly due to his brother's overconfidence, personal pride, and lack of patience. On December 16, Tecumseh received the bad news of Tippecanoe while retrieving his sister Tecumapese, who had run away from her war-hero Shawnee husband to join a white man at New Madrid. He had just found Tecumapese that night in the arms of a Frenchman. At midnight, according to Allan W. Eckert, he said to his men, "We will go in the morning back to Apple River, where we will leave Tecumapese. Then we will return to Tippecanoe and see what can be done to salvage our union, and what will be done to Tenskwatawa."[22] It was minutes later that the earth buckled beneath them, and Tecumseh, his sister, and men found themselves in the epicenter of one of the greatest earthquakes of all time.

As the shell of Turtle Island cracked open, Tecumseh's family-run Ohio Valley Alliance that had survived fifty years against impossible odds was split, and the Algonquin Confederacy, which had withstood seven thousand years of invasion and disaster, was finally broken. Within two more years, Tecumseh, now a president without a country, was dead, betrayed by his brother and many of his former allies. Judging from the records and firsthand accounts, Tecumseh—who had used his will to live to crush many who wished for him and his people to die—grew to wish that same death for himself. He told his men that he would die this day in battle and that many of them would die as well, and encouraged them to go home to their families. Many did leave, yet many others stayed at his side. He then walked, unadorned but for a simple buckskin outfit, into the furious Battle of the Thames against impossible odds, and was soon dead. Sixteen different accounts of his death exist, most of them less than convincing.

Recently Munsee elder Floyd Case took me to the Tecumseh memorial on Ontario Provincial Highway 2 overlooking the Thames River battlefield where Tecumseh was slain in 1813. There, standing in the snow, looking out at the now-famous field of battle, we discussed Tecumseh's death. It was there that he told me about a letter that was found among his grandfather's papers after his death, written hurriedly with a dark pencil on a legal pad, perhaps in his last days. It was an account of how Tecumseh had been buried, as he had learned it from eyewitnesses as a young man. Grandfather John Case was a long-time chief of the Munsee and a schoolteacher who could speak fluently in English, Iroquois, Anishinabi, and Lenape tongues. He was a highly respected man known for his integrity and credibility. The story he left for posterity should be taken very seriously.

It appears that once again it fell upon the shoulders of the Munsee Nation to be the guardians of that which is sacred to the Native American. For the letter reveals that it was the Munsee who witnessed the burial, and knew its secret which they now keep, and it was two Shawnee cousins of Tecumseh who carried him to the grave and buried him, both of whom then remained to live with the Moraviantown Munsees for the rest of their lives, keeping the secret among their closest friends and relatives. The ground where Tecumseh fell and was buried is only a few miles from that Munsee reserve, which still stands today. In the previously unpublished letter, created in 1924, John Case wrote:

Moraviantown was completely evacuated. Old men, women, and children were removed to Wau-lah-ha-mu-kong, or Danda's near Hamilton [Ontario]. A messenger was sent to the Munsees of the Thames, calling for aid to resist the invaders or "Long Knives." Chief Dolson [the Munsee Chief from Munsey Town where John Case lived] immediately collected a war party.

The Indian line held out for twenty or twenty-five minutes. Colonel Johnston made this claim very prominent in his electoral campaign for Congress some time later. I have not the space here to mention the arguments of the various claimants. Suffice it to say Colonel Johnston's claim was the most likely according to Drake's findings.

The letter states that a Potowatomi chief had been mistaken for Tecumseh and was killed, abuse heaped on his dead body in the field of battle, his apparel stolen from him, but that Tecumseh was carried while still alive to a rather unusual grave. John Case writes:

The whereabouts of the grave was [sic] known only to those who visited the grave. Great care was taken in that the ground was not disturbed or anything left there to indicate the location of the grave. Tecumseh was said to have been mortally wounded in the early part of the battle, but did not die until he had been carried some distance in the rear. A burial place was found for his body farther in the woods. A large tree had fallen, carrying the top of a smaller tree with it to the ground, consequently bending and uprooting this second tree so a large cave was formed under the trunk of the smaller tree. This cave was hurriedly prepared for the burial. Here then was the dead chief's grave. The entanglements of this tree were cut loose from the larger tree thus allowing it to spring back to its original position. All protruding roots of the tree were carefully removed, thus sealing for all time to the knowledge of man the whereabouts of this grave. Those two men, Timoo and Pah-Pah-Coosh, were said to have assisted in this burial. Tecumseh wanted to leave his bones here, meaning that he wanted to rest here in peace. Who then would be so indiscreet as to remove them, if such has been done? This was the idea of the secrecy of the grave so that no intruders would ever trespass there. The fears of his nearest friends were born out by what happened in respect to the supposed body of Tecumseh on the battlefield.

He was placed here in full dress with all his equipment at his side save his sword. Previous to the battle, in conversation with his friends, he expressed the thought that he would not survive this action. He warned them not to be dismayed but to continue the struggle until victory was won. This accounts for the stubborn resistance of the Indian line in the face of such terrible odds, even after our Chief fell.

There is a map of the battlefield and where the woods are located in Dark Rain Thom's book *The Shawnee: Kohkumthena's Children*. However, no information about the exact location of Tecumseh's grave has ever been published, nor is it known to any but a select few. It is said that a flood occurred at the site a few years after the battle, further obscuring the location. The location of the burial of Tecumseh's troubled brother Tunskwatawa, however, has been found, but it is a grave without honor. The body was dumped in a hole in a ravine bisecting Ruby Avenue in the block west of 38th Street in Kansas City, Kansas.[23]

The fall of Tecumseh marked the fall of the Eastern Algonquin civilization as a political power in the world. For four miraculous decades, this remarkable leader had been able to help prevent that downfall though constantly surrounded and outnumbered. Now he was dead and buried in a place known only to the Munsee and those they wished to tell, mainly Tecumseh's next of kin.

Once again, the Delaware were scattered to the four winds. Many small bands of Munsees had been wandering in the wilderness look-ing for a home before 1813, but after the Battle of the Thames was lost, each family had to struggle on its own as best it could. Many would foresake their Lenape identity and the honor and responsibility of that heritage, and claim various exotic European lines of descent, depending on their skin color. Some claimed Italian ancestory, some Turkish, some Spanish. For years, they had held together against all odds, an organized nation on the move, marching from the sea, heading somewhere to the west, ever in search of a land to call their own. Now they entered an era of diaspora, and though they were scattered like seeds, those anonymous seeds were to fall on fertile soil in all fifty states, and all over Canada. The Munsee, who had established New York City and gave rise to the Delaware Nation, were about to help build the very nation that had defeated them: the United States of America.

EPILOGUE

How the Munsee were defeated or made to disappear is a story with two sides to be told. Their history was suppressed, their language driven out of them, their New York settlements, in the words of New York State Historian James D. Folts, "cartographically submerged."[1] In spite of, and partially because of, their precarious situation, the decendants of the Munsee were to make a number of startling contributions to the history of the United States, which historians are only now beginning to piece together. I call them "true founders of America," although space does not permit more than an encapsulated summary of their heroism.

TRUE FOUNDERS OF AMERICA

On their way west, the Lenape who founded New York City also founded (with help from a variety of Algonquin relatives) New Paltz, Kingston, Binghamton, Suffern, Hillburn, Elmira, and Corning, New York; Wilkes-Barre, Shamokin (Sunbury), Harrisburg, Sharon, Pittsburgh, Kittanning, and Punxsutawney, Pennsylvania; Cashoctin, Chillicothe (first capital of Ohio), Delaware, Gnadenhutten, Upper Sandusky, Mansfield, Dayton, and, to some extent, Youngstown, Ohio. They settled Muncie, Indiana, and Muncie, Ontario, as well, to name only a few. Typically the Munsee were pushed into the wilderness or into areas adjacent to existing reservations. There they created entire towns of log cabins, often with stone chimneys and other niceties, and then found their towns destroyed by arson or war, forcing them to move west to the next town, and ultimately to Canada. It is from the ashes of these towns that many American cities rose.

The Munsee and other Delaware also played an important role in the early story of Asbury Park, New Jersey; Buffalo, New York; Cleveland, Columbus (which the Lenape knew as Sekunk), Toledo (which the Lenape called Fallen Timbers), Ohio; Fort Wayne, Indiana (which the Lenape knew as Kekionga[2]); Leavenworth, Topeka, and Lawrence, Kansas; Kansas City, Missouri; Dallas, Texas; and Texarkana, Arkansas. They even lent one of their words to name the state of Wyoming.

They Founded Ohio

In 1764, the Delaware, along with their cousins the Shawnee, signed the Treaty of Pittsburgh. In it, the Delaware promised to remain neutral in the war between the French and British. The British colonists promised the Ohio River would be a permanent western boundary of white settlement, in accordance with King George's proclamation; west of that boundary would be virtually a country all their own. The Delaware began to settle Ohio in great numbers, leaving most eastern lands remaining to the Americans. The Great Council of the Delaware was moved to Ohio during that time. Full of hope for the future, the Delaware and Shawnee built many Indian towns throughout Ohio. Most, if not all, of those towns are now significant Ohio cities today.

They Saved Texas

The Delaware, descendants of the original founders of New York City, befriended Stephen F. Austin, the future founder of the state of Texas, as a child and taught him Native ways that later saved his life. Later the Delaware helped him to manage conflict with the Comanche, making possible the establishment of Texas.[3]

Texas is not alone in its debt to its Delaware founders. Eleven of our twenty-five Indian state-names refer to the Algonquin people of which the Lenape are considered "grandfathers."[4] This is only a small indication of the importance of the Algonquin in founding those states. In fact, the Lenape played an important role in the history of at least half the states in the United States.[5]

THE ORIGINAL LONE RANGERS

According to *The Story of the Texas Rangers: A Century of Frontier Defense* by Walter Prescott Webb, the Delaware and Shawnee were the first people to be hired and placed on the payroll of the newly formed Texas Rangers, to be scouts, and to accompany white "irregular militia" on horseback to guard the northern frontier from Comanche raiders.

Black Beaver, Suk-tum-mah-kway, is an example of those Delaware frontiersmen whose ancestors once lived around Manhattan. Fluent in English, French, and eight separate Native American languages, he was considered perhaps the best scout and interpreter in North America. He had been the most celebrated and skilled scout before the Civil War. He was born in Belleville, Illinois, in 1806. From 1824 onward, his name appears frequently in historical records. In 1834, he served as a guide and interpreter for General Henry Leavenworth and interpreter for Colonel Richard Dodge's councils with the Comanche, Kiowa, and Wichita Indians on the Upper Red River. He was an employee for the American Fur Company in the 1830s and 1840s. He "visited nearly every point of interest within the limits of our unsettled territory."[6]

When the Rocky Mountains fur trade declined in the 1840s, Black Beaver turned to guiding wagon trains westward. He also guided the expeditions of the naturalist painter John J. Audubon. During the Mexican-American War at San Antonio, he raised a company of Delaware and Shawnee Indians, called Beaver's Spy Company—Indian-Texas Mounted Volunteers. As captain of the unit, he served under General William S. Harney during the fighting. After the war, he continued to serve the United States Army under contract as a scout. In the mid-1860s, Randolph Marcy, a Union general in the Civil

War, dubbed Black Beaver "the great Delaware," and kept the public abreast of his exploits.

According to Marcy's journals, the old Indian was "a meager-looking man of middle size, and his long black hair framed in a face that was clever, but which bore a melancholy expression of sickness and sorrow...." Marcy commented that Black Beaver had seen the Pacific Ocean seven times, and served the Americans in three wars. He described Black Beaver as a "cosmopolite," a modest, "resolute, determined, and fearless warrior," and as a "competent" guide.[7] He helped found the Texas Rangers as a scout—his exploits becoming part of the mythical "Tonto" character's life story as well—and then joined the Union Army as a scout and brought the North the first victories and captives of the Civil War. These exploits are detailed in Dr. Laurence M. Hauptman's *Between Two Fires*.

GOOD SCOUTS

Much of the lore and tradition of the Boy Scouts was adapted from the Delaware, or Lenni Lenape, who were known for their sense of duty and honor, and whose prowess as wilderness scouts was unmatched anywhere. Captain Ben Simon was a Delaware scout who helped bring the Mormons to Salt Lake City when they were being persecuted by the government. Simon was a much-loved captain in the Union Army who was referred to in Indian petitions after 1864 as "chief." He had been a Rocky Mountain trapper for years, and had a long track record as guide and scout. He had been employed by the great Brigham Young and his politically beleaguered Mormon community while working in the Great Basin. Such an assignment would have been no Sunday picnic; the Mormons were frequently under semimilitary attack until their settlement in Salt Lake City.[8] Ben Simon was impressed with the charismatic Brigham Young and became one of the early members of the church, playing a role in white religious history as well as the Native American.

"Although a significant portion of the Delaware fought against the Americans during the French and Indian War, Pontiac's Rebellion, the American Revolution, and the War of 1812, an equal if not greater number joined the Americans as allies."[9] They served as scouts for Roger's Rangers in the French and Indian War; received commendations from George Washington for their heroism during the American Revolution;[10] signed the first Indian treaty of alliance with the fledgling United States in 1778; joined the United States Army fighting Florida's Indians in the Second Seminole War in the 1830s; and aided the Americans in the Mexican War. In most cases, they were promised land if victorious, helped win the war, and were left homeless and with empty pockets afterward. Ironically the only leader to make good on such a promise was America's enemy, King George III. He gave the Munsees land in Canada as many of them helped in the war effort, but then placed them on Chippewa land, which was later sold out from under them in 1820. The wampum treaty belt commemorating the promise now stands on display at New York City's Museum of American History, on land which the Munsees once possessed but lost.

Fall Leaf, Panipakuxwe, or "He Who Walks When Leaves Fall," (1807–80) was a great Delaware scout and captain in the Union Army who became known as "Falleaf." He was second only to Black Beaver in fame and respect among the Delaware people. He was a scout for John C. Fremont, who explored and surveyed much of the great Southwest.

ONLY A CRUST OF BREAD

In spite of the extensive Native American settlements in Ohio and many postwar treaties, Americans continued to pour into the Ohio Valley. After the disastrous Battle of Fallen Timbers in western Ohio, the Delaware were forced to leave the area. By 1801, the main body of the Delaware were living along the White River between Muncie and Indianapolis, Indiana.[11] Again the Munsee were never granted land of their own, only land belonging to other nations. After their own

Delaware brothers were persuaded to sell off the Munsee portion of their land in Indiana in 1849, the once-proud spokespersons for Algonquin liberty and justice were reduced to desperate poverty and starvation as never before.

In return for all their loyalty, the Munsee were treated severely. In 1849, a group of Munsee in Indiana wrote a letter to President Zachary Taylor, begging for "a crust of bread," as they put it. The complete contents of this letter are included in Appendix III, but here is an excerpt:

> Your Excellency will please permit us to remind you of our ancient Covenant of Friendship which was established at East Town, Pennsylvania and which was to be good forever to remain as long as the Sun would be seen and as long as Rivers run and Trees grow. The Commissioner's name was Capt. Bullen, who acted on the part of the government of the United States, in making the said important Covenant of Peace. He told our people to commit it to memory in their feeble way of entering into record, such important national matters.
>
> Thus a Wampum Record was made out directly to that effect, which now still remains in our hands to this present day. He also did let our people have the Flag of the United States which likewise remains in our possession to this present time. The said Commissioner told our forefathers never to lose this Record of Peace and relationship, but to keep it safe always for our remembrance, because he further states that at some future period of time, the Munsee Nation might somehow unfortunately become overshadowed with a cloud of trouble, then in such a perilous time, if they should be able to show this Record of Peace and Friendship, their Great Father would certainly at such a time, release and Comfort his Munsee Children. The said Commissioner further stated that at some future time, if even a Small Munsee boy would only be able to show this Covenant of Friendship to our Great Father, and if only partly convince him of the reality of our Covenant, even to such a young lad, favor should

be granted. He further told our people that if even our Great Father hereafter, would have but a small piece of bread, he would divide a part of it to his Munsee Children. Our said Wampum is divided into thirteen parts, which signifies Friendship strongly, established by the authorized Commission of thirteen Governors of the thirteen original states.

THEY HELPED PRESERVE THE UNION

In spite of the conflicts over land issues with the United States, the Delaware were largely pro-Union at the outbreak of the Civil War, and contributed greatly to the war effort in the west, serving mainly as scouts and home guards. Black Beaver, Captain Fall Leaf, Ben Simon, and Jim Ned are the best known heroes of this era.

In 1860, Suk-tum-mah-kway, or Black Beaver, part of whose history we've already heard, was the most famous Delaware Indian in North America. He continued as peacemaker among the Natives on behalf of the United States until the Civil War broke out in 1861. Suddenly the Unionists in Indian Territory were worried about Confederate invasions from secessionist Arkansas and Texas. Soon William W. Averell's Texas Mounted Rifles were marching north toward the Wichita Agency undetected, preparing to ambush the forces of Colonel William H. Emory. The aging Black Beaver was about to enjoy the greatest success of his long military history. Black Beaver scouted the advancing column, informed Emory, and gave him the information needed in order to capture the enemy's advance guard. In fact, they became the first prisoners captured during the Civil War on either side. Black Beaver then guided Emory, his troops, and their prisoners through five hundred miles of inhospitable country without the loss of a single man, horse, or wagon.

Unfortunately for Black Beaver, his success was a little too well noticed. The Confederate Army retaliated by seizing his cattle, horses, and crops, destroyed his ranch at the Wichita Agency, and placed a bounty on his head, which remained throughout the war,

prohibiting him from returning home. The estimated $5,000 in dam-
ages were never compensated, though Black Beaver continued to
press for help until his death in 1880.[12]

When the Civil War came, the Delaware could have sat it out
with impunity. Surprisingly, out of 201 eligible Delaware males in
1862, 170 volunteered for service with the Union Army. Apparently
"to a small, weak, and often removed Indian nation, the strategy of
currying favor with 'the Great Father' in Washington was the only
survival option open to them."[13] Prominent Delaware were given
commissions and authorized to raise their own companies of volunteers. In 1862, Indian Agent Fielding Johnson claimed that the high
rate of enlistment among the Delaware was a direct result of "a patri-
otism unequaled in the history of the country."[14]

Though most of the Delaware heroes in the Union Army assisted
their rise to position by converting to Christianity, Falleaf clung to
the traditions of the Big House ceremonies in the face of much prej-
udice and scorn from the white military hierarchy. In 1861, he raised
a company of fifty-four Delaware for the Union Army and guided
them from Sedalia, Missouri, to Springfield without being spotted by
Confederates. He raised eighty-six Delawares to serve under him as
Company D of the Second Kansas Indian Home Guard. In 1862, they
served in the first Union attempt to capture the Indian Territory.

They Invented Groundhog Day

According to one of the original Creation stories of the Delaware, the
Lenni Lenape began life as animals down inside Mother Earth and
emerged ages later to hunt and live as men. Thus it was that Oijik
(Wejak) or Wojak came to be recognized as the "grandfather" of the
Lenape. The Lenape word *wojak* is where "woodchuck" comes from.
The woodchuck is also known as a groundhog. In Lenape stories, the
groundhog is a very smart, clever animal and knows whether it's
going to be a long winter or not.

The Lenape watch certain animals for signs to predict the weather. If the groundhog comes out in February and sees that the sky is still blue—in other words, the sun is so bright he can't look at it, but he can see his shadow—that means it is still winter, and it will not change for a long time. It is always cloudy in the spring, and it rains a lot. In the dead of winter, the sky is usually blue and clear. If the groundhog comes out and sees no shadow, that means the clouds have already started to roll in, and that's a sign that spring is on its way. February 2, or Groundhog Day, is the exact middle of the winter season, right between winter solstice and the spring equinox, and it is the coldest time of the year. After that, the light begins to return, and it gets gradually warmer.

Punxsutawney, Pennsylvania, a town about fifty miles northeast of Pittsburgh on Pennsylvania State Route 119, used to be a "border" or no-man's-land between Indian nations. Around 1723, however, displaced Delaware settled the area in large numbers. The big migration west followed between about 1740 and 1760. According to Lenape legend, it was during this time that an Indian sorcerer first appeared in various forms and attacked travelers from the East. He was hunted and killed in combat by a young chief, somewhere near Stump Creek. The sorceror was not afraid of anything. They tried to burn the sorcerer's body to destroy the "evil medicine" he carried. But miraculously, he turned into a swarm of searing sand flies, or *ponksad*, which plagued the whole area and the Indians, especially. Sand flies still plague the area today. From then on the Lenape called this place Ponksaduteney, which means the "town of the sand flies." The name is a warning to travelers. Today it is spelled Punxsutawney and once a year, all the major television networks bring their cameras there to spot Punxsutawney Phil, the groundhog.

The Munsee Today

There are currently three distinct Munsee settlements in North

America, where people solely identified as Munsee can still be found living together: the Moraviantown band of Munsee near Thamesville, Ontario; the Munsee Delaware Nation of Munsey, Ontario (also known as "Munsee Town") and; the Stockbridge Munsee of Stockbridge, Wisconsin. A number of Munsee also live on the Six Nations Reserve on Grand River in Ontario. However it is only at Moraviantown, Ontario, that the language is still spoken. It is a miracle of human endurance that these people were able to survive the ordeal and find each other on the other side of the mountains and lakes. Many of the Munsee of the core Pennsylvania group never made it in one piece to a permanent home. They lost their cultural identity and either intermarried with the Shawnee and Miami, became Delaware, or entered fully into the white world. The ones who retained their Munsee language and identity had to go into hiding for generations, endure starvation and hardship, rebuild their burned villages over and over again, fight in many wars, perform favors that were never returned, and ultimately flee to Canada.

The journey that led the first Munsee into Canada started in 1784. According to Chief Mark Peters of the Munsee Delaware Nation, "It is likely that around that time the Munsee who had come by way of Niagara began to fear for their independence and pushed on to the Thames to create their own villages. They may have been joined by a group of Munsee, Delaware, Nanticoke, and Conoy (Piscataway) who had settled with the western Indian nations before that."[15] Other Munsee arrived there from the Miami River, the Sandusky in northern Ohio, Cattaraugus in western New York, the Susquehanna Valley in Pennsylvania, and the Minisink area near the Delaware River tri-state region.

"The first survey of the Thames was ordered in 1790, to be carried out by the Munsee-speaking Patrick McNiff. His starting point was to be the Delaware village. This village was also called 'the Delaware Castle' by Lieutenant-Governor Simcoe when he passed through Munsee in 1793. He offered the Munsee a fourteen-hundred-acre tract on the south bank of the Thames, and bought the land in his own name. He was then sent to Santo Domingo in 1796, and the title was never transferred."[16] This ambiguity led to disputes in 1820 between the Chippewa and Munsee. The Chippewa were moved to part of the new land, but the Munsee were not mentioned in the papers. In 1829, there were 160 Munsee living on that small tract of land, all of whom could trace their ancestory back to the Minisink, from Port Jervis southward along the Delaware. Others may have come to Canada in the aftermath of the Gnandenhutten massacre of March 8, 1782, in which ninety mission or "praying" Delaware were killed inside the church of the Moravian mission.

Although the Munsee were among the largest holders of what is now New York land at contact, and among the most generous and helpful, the colony of New York never granted or acquired for them a single reservation all their own during its entire history. Instead New York drove them completely out of the state by every means possible. In fact no Munsee group has ever been granted federal recognition inside the United States except where they were mixed with other Native people.

It is important to remember that Native Americans were not allowed to marry whites until the 1960s and were not allowed to own land until 1924, and only then if they were U.S. citizens. The original Native New Yorkers were therefore placed between a rock and a hard place. Without a reservation of their own, they could either go to the shared reserves as they were told, or blend in with other indigenous nations as individuals, thereby losing their cultural identity, language, and history. Or they could pretend to be white, falsify their records, and marry into white families. Or they could starve to death, which many likely did.

Even in Canada, the process of adoption and abandonment served to demoralize the Munsee. The Chippewa of the Thames who adopted the Munsee in the late 1700s were influenced to sell off that part of their land on May 9, 1820, leaving the Munsee homeless once again. Many years earlier, the Moravians of Ohio and Pennsylvania were allowed to create a missionary settlement in Ontario, where Munsees who had converted to Christianity and foresworn their Indian ways could exist and speak their language. On the other side of the border, the United States seemed bent on erasing all memory of the Munsee language. The attempt was successful. At this writing, south of the Canadian border there is an almost complete vacuum of understanding concerning the nature of the Munsee language and its relationship to Unami or Delaware in general. This language, which may have had fifty- to sixty-thousand speakers at one time, now has only six. Once in possession of one of the largest and most beautiful territories of any unified Native peoples on the east coast, the Munsee now have a few square miles of land spread across three reserves in Ontario, and one in Wisconsin.

The true story of their seven-thousand-year occupation of what is now New York State is no longer remembered, but as long as the language remains there is hope of reconstructing some of that history.

RETURN OF THE NATIVES

Today the number of Native Americans living within the five boroughs is larger than in 1500 C.E., and growing.[17] In the 2000 census, the total Native American population of New York City was 41,289, with an additional 17,711 in the immediate vicinity. The statewide figures were nearly double that of the five boroughs: 82,461. The census tallied 10,752 Native Americans in Manhattan alone in that year.

The Lenape belief in our roles as Land Keepers for the sacred, living Mother Earth still finds expression through the many environmental and civic activities of the various Algonquin nations around New York: most notably the Ramapough, Poospatuck, Montauk, Matinecock, and Shinnecock. However, to hear the words and teachings of the most ancient traditions of the Land Keepers, we must now turn to the distant cousins of the Lenape, the Mayan peoples or the Hopi, both of which are still very close to the ancient ways. Mercedes Barrios Longfellow, a spokesperson for the Maya who now lives in the United States, gave a moving and eloquent talk in Maniwaki, Quebec, Canada, on the role of the Mayan Land Keepers. For me, hearing her words was like being in the presence of one of New York's Land Keepers from a thousand years ago. It confirmed everything I'd been able to glean about the nature of these Lenape sages over several years of receiving visions, gathering fragments, and talking to Native people. I feel that Mercedes's words speak for the benevolent spirit watchers of the people of New York to whom this book is dedicated, and its message is the message of this book.

> We are the Land Keepers, but we cannot do it alone. We need help from everyone. We are all responsible to keep the Mother healthy. The trees are Grandmothers and Grandfathers whose spirits live in each of those trees. We can draw much wisdom and knowledge from them, which they willingly share, once we stop seeing them as inanimate objects. When we cut them down, we are killing the spirit of each Grandmother and Grandfather, which is the spirit of the Creator, and which is our own spirit as well. If we keep doing what we are doing, there won't be those spirits here any longer. Our strength will leave us and we will all die. Those spirits cannot speak out loud; we must listen, say our prayers. Praying does not mean just sitting still and chanting, it can mean being very kind to each other, or serving all life here on earth. Keep the trees where they are, be aware of how you use the products of the trees. Be kind to the earth, and you will begin to be the defenders of the earth with all of us—you can be helpers and watchers of the earth.

Mercedes Barrios Longfellow
Maniwaki, Quebec Canada
August 5, 2001

Postscript

While the focus of this book is on the past, it's impossible to ignore the fact that part of New York City's skyline "disappeared" while this book was being prepared for publication. The World Trade Center stood twenty blocks north of the site of one of New York's first Dutch buildings—a trading post—which in turn reflected the trading patterns of the Lenape at what was then the foot of Manhattan.

Native Americans have never left New York. In fact, the attack on the twin towers was witnessed from the fiftieth floor of a nearby construction site by some of the same Mohawk ironworkers who had proudly taken part in the construction of the World Trade Center years earlier.

The city I was writing about in the Spring of 2001 was a brusque, self-assured city on a tight schedule of its own. Today, in the wake of the awful events of September 11, 2001, it is a city in a healing crisis, both physically and emotionally. To those who live in or love New York City and feel wounded or fearful because of what has happened, I can only say; take heart: The Lenape Land Keepers are close by. I was awakened around 9:00 A.M. that morning by a vision of a Lenape Land Keeper who exclaimed to me in Munsee, *"Ne Mat Townee!"* which could be translated as "Oh my God!" (or "I swear!"). I felt especially guided that day, as I know many did, and I continue to feel their guidance, as well as that of other native ancestors. I have since received messages that others in New York saw the Land Keepers helping in the healing process.

New York and its tenacious people will survive, now more than ever, guided by Divine Spirit, the Great Mystery, as they rebuild their city. Mayor Rudy Giuliani said it best: "New York was here yesterday, it is still here today, and it will be here tomorrow and forever!"

I hope that this book may in some way help readers embrace that same conviction.

Evan Pritchard
October 2001

MUNSEE VOCABULARY

Beulah Timothy is eighty-five years old. She spoke only Munsee before the age of seven when she went to a boarding school. There were no other Munsee-speaking children at the school, but she would speak Munsee with her family during the summer. Today she is one of six fluent speakers of the Munsee language in the world. All of the fluent speakers today live at Moraviantown, Ontario. This word list was recorded in her home on March 16, 2001.

Here is a brief guide to pronunciation of the letters in Standard Phonetic Algonquin, which is designed for standard English typography and English sound recognition. The syllables in bold type are stressed. Please note that *x* is pronounced like the *ch* in the Scottish *loch* or the German *buch*.

A like the a in bat
B like the b in boy
Bp hard b or soft p
C not used in Standard Phonetic Algonquin
Ch like tch in watch
D like the d in dog
Dt hard d, soft t
E like the e in best
Ee like the ee in heel
F (rare in Munsee) like fox
G like the g in go
Gk hard g or soft k
(g) at the end of a word, like the g in Cavanaugh
H like the h in house, except when following a vowel, when it is a silent
    aspiration on the previous vowel

I like the i in kit

J like the j in jack, often spelled dj for clarity

K like the k in kit

Gk soft k like the k in

L like the l in lion

(L) like the soft French L in meilleur

M like the m in man

N like the n in nut

(n) nasal n like the French n in *monsieur,* or non, or manger

O like the o in so

Oo like the oo in cool

Oh like the o in sow

P like p in Paul

Bp soft p like the b in bullet

Q a popping sound in the back of the throat, like Iraq

Q(w) popping sound in the back of the throat but with lips pursed as if to
    whistle

R does not exist in Munsee

S like the s in saw

T like the t in toy

Dt soft like the t in water

U schwa sound, like the u in but

V does not exist in Munsee

W is like the wo in two

(w) is an aspiration of air with lips pursed as if to whistle, after a hard con-
    sonant. The lips are pursed before the consonant is sounded.

X is like the ch in the German *buch*

Y is like the y in why

Z is like the z in zoo

' often used, as in ak'n, to show the lack of a schwa, or where a consonant is
    replaced by a glottal stop. For example, in Cockney, button becomes
    bu'on. This happens often in modern Algonquin, however the Munsee
    do not do this often.

ANIMALS

animal	**wess**
bear	**maxk**-(w)
big tail	**kwal**
butterfly	ka-**ka**-pish
cat	**pou(g)**-sheesh
crow	**a**-haas
dog	**mwa**-ka-nayo
duck	(w)-**shee**-weao
ducks	**sheek-weao**
fish	na-**maes**
more than one fish	na-**maes-suck**
fox	**kwal-wess**
frog	sh'**kwal**
geese	**shee**-weh-wuk
flying	**peh**-mee-lax-**teet**
I saw the geese flying	**neo**-wa-wuk **shee**-weh-wuk **peh**-mee-lax-**teet**
little people	**womp**-tcha-ka-**nee**-sha
lizard	**twe'**q
mourning dove	**moo**-hwee-lehsh
mosquito	**skee**-maeo
owl	**ko**-kos
robin	**tsheesh**-ko-kosh
snake	**axk**-kok
little snake	**axk**-ko-kish
squirrel	sak-quil-**lin**-djay-o
swan	**wap**-so-**weao**
tail (animal or bird)	esh-**ko(n)**-mai
turkey	pu-**leao**
turtle	t'**kxwaqx**

BODY

blood	**mux**
my ear	**nee**-to-wak
your ear	**kee**-to-wak

one ear	**neks**-kee-to-wak
your ears	**kee**-to-wak-al
my eyes	**nis**-keen-shkwal
your eyes	**kes**-keen-shkwal
his eyes	**ma**-ka-wis-keen-shkwal
heart	(w)-**teh**
my mouth	g'**don**
your mouth	g'**do(n)g**
my nose	nee-**kee**-wun
your nose	kee-**kee**-wun
his nose	wee-**kee**-wun
my teeth	nee-**beet**-l
your teeth	**gee**-**beet**-l
their teeth	**wee**-**beet**-l

COLORS

blue	**oh**-lin-kaeoh
gray or brown	**wee**-pung-gwaeo
green	usk-kusk-**kwaeoh**
orange	o-linj-**ap**-mo-**qut**
	(the color of an orange. The p is hard)
red	**mox**-kaeoh
white	**wap**-paeoh
yellow	**wee**-sa-**waeoh**

FOOD

corn	**hwask**-kweem
tea	tee

FRIENDS AND FAMILY

angry	men-**no(n)k**-suk
I am angry	na-**men**-no(n)k-see
He is angry	**mun**-no(n)k-sil
big	a-**kxun**-dja
The food is delicious	**ween-gun**
The food is good	**nee-tchyen-ween-gun**

The food is bad	moo-**ween**-gun-**nul**
going around	**wee**-woo-**nee**-a-xun
good feeling	woo-**lay-len**-dum
Have a good day	**xan**-eel-**wel**-ee-**geesh**-kway
hello	there's no word for hello in Munsee
He is a boy	**neh**-ka **ska**-han-zo
He is a man	**neh**-ka **len**-no
He is looking away	lax-**heen**-gwa-**x(l)een**
He is looking	pat-**teen**-gwa-**x(l)een**
towards you	(the l is rolled slightly)
He jumped up	**tis**-bax-tche
I jumped up	**tis**-bax-tcha-**kee**
I sit down	**lump**-ta-peh
I am digging	no-**ual**-he
I am digging in the earth	no-**ual**-he-a-**kee**-te-la
I am sleeping	**ga**-ka-wo(n)-**kwee**
I'm washing my hand	**gu-see-len**-jeh
I'm washing my clothes	**gu**-shee-ux-**tee**-keh
I forget	no-**wun**-see
I saw	**neo**-wa-**wuk**
I saw something	**peh**-mee-la-**teet**
It is dead	me-**neek-leh**-o
I'm glad to see you	**kwee(n)**-ga-**nay**-oh-weh
I love you	**k'tah**-wah-**lelx**
Love me	**k'tah**-wah-**lee**
man	**len**-no
men	**len**-nu-ak
one day	**Gu**-tak-a-**maeo**
round	**p'tuk**-kwaeo
See you again	la-**pitch**-ka-**nae**-o-wul
See you all again	la-**pitch**-ka-**nae**-o-wul-**lung**-wa
She is a girl	ox-**quae**-sis
sorrow	ne-**mut**-te-**len**-dum
Thank you	**en**-na-**shee**
woman	**ox**-quae-oh

HOUSE

boards	**p'see**-ka-**kway**-o-way
chair	**ap-pong**
door	**t'ka**-hu(n)
fence going around	**mel**-laq-wee-**woo**-nee-**a**-xun
firewood	**xhoss**-ul
house	**wee**-kwam
table	e-**hen**-da-**q'ong**
window	**ay**-heh-shan-**day**-kin
wood	**xhoss**

NATURE

bow (hunting bow)	**wheep**
clouds	**a**-kum-**maxk**(w)
cold	**dap**-tchee
cold day	taq-o-maeo
cold night	deet-**bpeh**-q't
forest	**ko**-pee
grass	nee-**xashq**(**w**)
ground	**ha**-kee
leaf	wu-**nee**-po
leaves	wu-**nee**-p'**kwak**
moonlight	**wax-aeo**
mud	a-**sees**-q'wol
it is muddy	a-**sees**-q'wo-**ul**
rain	**sok**-laan
river	**see**-poh
snow	**koh**-wun
snowing, it is	**wee**-nay-oh
snowing, it has stopped	**ek**-wal-**wee**-maeo
solid face mask (tree spirit)	may-**sing**-gwaeoh
stream	**shee**-po-shish
sun	**gkeesh**-oq(w)
sunlight	woo-**lahn**-daeo
trees	**meet**-qwuk
water	**bpee**

the water is dirty	**neesk**-peh-q'ot-**bpee**
water, edge of	**tshy**-ta
windy	**sha**-k'n

NUMBERS

one	goh-**tah**
two	neesh-**shaw**
three	**n'xah (or n'xo(n))**
four	**naeo**-wa
five	**noa**-lin
six	gut-**tash**
seven	nee**sh-ash**
eight	na-**xash**
nine	**noa**-lee
ten	**weem**-but
one hundred	goh-tah ho-ka

SPIRITUAL

book	pom-**beel**
burning	lo-taeoh
circle, ring	**tay**-tee-owq(w)
Creator	Mun-**ih**-toh (Men-i-to is the Devil)
He is dancing	**gkunt**-ta-kaeo
I am dancing	**gkunt**-ta-ka
elder	**keek**-ess
fire	**tun**-daeoh (like a torch)
in	**ox**-teo
fire in my heart	**tin**-deao(n) (w)**tea**-xun-da-**ox**-teo
from	**woounj**
from my heart	**woounj** (w)**tea**-hu(n)g
I give	k'meel-**lelx**
good	no-la-**lee**-huk
That's good	oo-**let**
grandfather	ma-**xo**-mis
my grandfather	**nu**-ma-**xo**-mis
your grandfather	**ka**-ma-**xo**-mis

his grandfather	**ma**-xom-**tsal**
medicine	**tcha**-piq
I'm sorry	**jee**-wel-**len**-dum
Indian Medicine	Le-**na**-pay **wap**-see-q'n
new	**whuss**-ka
old	xo-**wee**-ae-oh
story	**ex**-la-**tcheen**-wing
strong (someone, animal)	**mask**-ka-neh-**so**
strong (rope or object)	**mask**-ka-**nae**-oh
weak due to sickness	**bees**-a-la-ma-**less**-n
strong, not	**ma**-mask-ka-**nae**-oh
thoughts	a-**lee**-ta-**haeo**
thinking big thoughts	a-**kxun**-dja **lee**-te-**haeo**
tobacco	**k'shah'**-taeo
wisdom, somebody with	xspo-**waeo**

TRAVEL

boat	na-**muk**-q'ol
I'm going	**dax**
journey (I'm going a long way)	**wha**-la-**dax**
little boat	na-**muk**-q'ol-ish
long way	**wha**-lax
path	**aan**-esh
road	**aan**-nai
running	gush-**shee**-la

TWELVE LEVELS OF ALGONQUIN HISTORY IN NEW YORK STATE

Phase (Arch.)	Year	Description	Remanent Language
I. The Dawn of Time	19000 B.C.E.	Unknown People	proto-Micmac
II. The Clovis Era	14000 B.C.E..	Spear Point People	proto-Naskapi
III. Early Great Lake	6000 B.C.E..	Bison People	Cheyenne/Arapaho
IV. Oka	5000 B.C.E..	Fire People	Okanogan/proto-Mohican
IVb. Alumette	4000 B.C.E..	Old Copper Culture	Cree/Algonquin
V. Ojibway	3000 B.C.E..	The Scroll Drawers	Ojibway/Potowatomi/Ottawa
VI. Orient Point	1000 B.C.E..	People of the Sun	Corchaug/Mohican
VIb. Red Bank	1000 B.C.E..	Red Ochre People	Micmac II
VIc. Sebonac	700 B.C.E..	People of Ground Nuts	Shinnecock
VII. Fox Creek	100 B.C.E..	River People	Mississippian
VIII. Owasco	900 C.E.	Pottery People	Mohawk/Munsee
IX. Minisink	1000 C.E.	The Grandfathers	Munsee
X. Bowman's Brook	1100 C.E.	The Real People	Unami/Unalatchtigo/ Micmac III
XI. Clason Point	1300 C.E.	East Bank People	Renneiu (Wappinger, Canarsie, Quinnipiac, Siwanoy, etc.)
XII. Colonial Era	1600 C.E.	People of the Delaware	Delaware

EXPLANATION OF THE TWELVE LEVELS CHART

This chart represents a reconstruction of the core Algonquin language of New York City as it passed through various stages of development. The first four phases mentioned were not necessarily spoken in New York City, but represent source languages from which those forms of speech derived. There may have been a tongue spoken millennia ago in New York which has no modern remnant.

In evolution theory, species, languages, tools, and ideas generally begin in a more cumbersome but profound form. These earlier forms have fewer parts but are complex to use, requiring considerable skill. As the idea or language is passed on, new parts are added, new letters, etcetera, while at the same time it becomes more streamlined and easier to use. Such is the case with languages. Using this principle as a guide, I have been able to reconstruct the development of the Lenape language from early times, using existing remnant tongues in northern and western Canada as approximations of the older forms.

There are three major types of Algonquin languages in the region, the N language, the L language, and the R. The N or Mohican type is associated with those developed before 1000 B.C.E., the L type after 1000 C.E. and the R type after 1300 C.E.

Here are fifty-two sample Algonquin languages and the category to which they belong:

1043 B.C.E.	1000 C.E.	1300 C.E.
N dialects (Ancient, Pre-L)	L dialects (Mississippi)	R dialects (East Bank)
Cheyenne	Munsee	Wappingers
Blackfoot	Unami	Quinnipiac/Quiripi
Ojibway	Micmac (modern)	Canarsie
Mohican	Abenaki	Matinecock
Potowatomi	Nipmuck	Siwanoy
Wampanoag	Nanticoke	Rockaway
Massachusetts	Powhatan	(All Matouac)
Narragansett/Niantic	Hatteras	Merrick
Algonquin	Passamaquoddy	Unquachaug (Y)
Ottawa	Penobscot	Nissequogue
Naskapi	Maliseet	Patchogue
Montagnais	Pennacook	Massapequa

1043 B.C.E.	1000 C.E.	1300 C.E.
Quabaug	Shawnee	Secatogue
Pequot/Montauk (Y)	Miami	
Arapaho	Illinois (R)	
Cree		
Menominee		
Sac/Fox/Kickapoo		
Corchaug		

MOHICAN: ONE OF THE MOST ANCIENT LANGUAGES

Proto-Mohican covered a wide area and is the substratum of the Lenape-type southern language, and probably the northerly L languages as well. In its original form, it was not much like Lenape today, but probably more like Ojibway, Massachusetts, Niantic, Wampanoag, and Quabaug, which are N languages like Mohican. I also believe that Corchaug is related to an older form of Mohican. It means "Ancient Ones," so I'm told. Western Abenaki is part Mohican, but with lots of L's. Shinnecock was probably a unique variation on Corchaug "Mohican."

Munsee, Unami, Piscataway, Powhatan, and Hatteras possess a linear aspect of their diffusion from north to south. But there is much more to the picture. Powhatan has a lot of words in common with the Pequot, who speak a Mohican-related tongue. Pennacook and Nipmuck are both L dialects like Munsee, although Pennacook is basically the same as Abenaki. Micmac is an L language, but very different from most other Algonquin tongues. It stands to reason that the words that northern and southern tongues have in common would be the old N words, since both groups can pronounce them.

Wappingers, Quiripi, Matouac, Canarsie, Rockaway, and Matinecock are all R dialects, the latest form of Algonquin developed during what I call the Golden Age of Algonquin Culture, between 1300 and 1500 C.E. There is a preponderance of anecdotal evidence to make the assumption that Wappingers was halfway between Mohican and Quiripi, and closely related to the Mohican by blood. Other R speakers also claim a historical link to the Mohican as well. However, the R words would have been adapted from the Munsee or Mississippian type, and not from Mohican words. The Y dialect groups all claim Mohican heritage as well. Again there are times when we have to make a distinction between language and culture.

THE VERRAZZANO DIARY LETTER TO FRANCIS I OF FRANCE

According to *Verrazano, Explorer of the Atlantic Coast* by Ronald Symes, Verrazzano's diary was found in a private Roman library in 1900 by a prominent Italian scholar, Alessandro Bacchiani. Written in Italian, it was one of several copies that Verrazzano had sent to friends in Florence during his lifetime. One copy was translated into French and presented to the king of France. New maps of the Americas were drawn and given to the king as well, and later to King Henry VIII.

The ship was named *The Dauphine* after Dauphin Charles Orland (1492–95) born in the year of Columbus's first landing in the New World. Son and first child of King Charles VIII and Anne of Bretagne, Dauphin Charles Orland disappeared at three. This Francis I, to whom Verrazzano writes, is the king who brought the Renaissance to France. He married Claude de France, the daughter of Louis XII in 1514, and was coronated the year after. She was of the family of the lost "dauphin."

The letter to Francis I in the Morgan Library in New York City was probably copied by the navigator's brother Gerolamo. The original is also housed at the Morgan Library as part of the Cellere Codex. It is twenty-four pages long, written on twelve pieces of 11 ⅜" x 8 ½" paper, and highly legible, but in old Italian. I have removed the last paragraphs as they didn't pertain to the Lenape or their close cousins.

Giovanni da Verrazzano's Report to Francis I, July 8, 1524

[From a translation by E. H. Hall, 1910. The only remaining sixteenth-century copy in Italian longhand is held by the Morgan Library, New York.]

To King Francis I of France:
The History of the Dauphine and Its Voyage

After the tempest suffered in the northern parts, Most Serene King, I have not written to tell Your Majesty that which was experienced by the four ships which thou hadst sent by the Ocean to explore new lands, as I thought you had already been informed of everything—how we were compelled by the impetuous force of the winds to return to Brittany with only the distressed Normanda and Dauphine; where having made repairs, Your Majesty will have learned the voyage we made with them, armed for war, along the coasts of Spain; later, the new disposition with the Dauphine alone to continue the first navigation; having returned from which, I will tell Your Majesty what we have found.

From the deserted rock near to the Island of Madeira of the lost Serene King of Portugal (commencing 1524) with the said Dauphine, on the XVII of the month of January past, with fifty men, furnished with victuals, arms and other instruments of war and naval munitions for eight months, we departed, sailing westward by an east-south-east wind blowing with sweet and gentle lenity. In XXV days we sailed eight hundred leagues. The XXIIII day of February (perhaps 16 hours) we suffered a tempest as severe as ever a man who has navigated suffered. From which, with the divine aid and the goodness of the ship, adapted by its glorious name and fortunate destiny to support the violent waves of the sea, we were delivered. We pursued our navigation continuously toward the west, holding somewhat to the north. In XXV more days we sailed more than 400 leagues where there appeared to us a new land never before seen by anyone, ancient or modern.

Land Sited: 34 Degrees Latitude: At first it appeared rather low: having approached to within a quarter of a league, we perceived it, by the great fires built on the shore of the sea, to be inhabited. We saw that it ran toward the south; following it, to find some port where we could anchor with the ship and investigate its nature, in the space of fifty leagues we did not find a port or any place where it was possible to stay with the ship. And having seen that it tended continually to the south, in order not to meet with the Spaniards, we decided to turn about to coast it toward the north, where we found the same place. We anchored by the coast, sending the small boat to land. We had seen many people who came to the shore of the sea and seeing us approach fled, sometimes halting, turning back, looking with great admiration. Reassuring them by various signs, some of them approached, showing great delight at seeing us, marveling at our clothes, figures and whiteness, making to us various signs where we could land more conveniently with the small boat, offering us of their foods.

We were on land, and that which we were able to learn of their life and customs I will tell Your Majesty briefly:

They go nude of everything except that at the private parts they wear some skins of little animals like martens, a girdle of fine grass woven with various tails of other animals which hang around the body as far as the knees: the rest nude; the head likewise. Some wear certain garlands of feathers of birds. They are of dark color not much unlike the Ethiopians, and hair black and thick, and not very long, which they tie together back on the head in the shape of a little tail. As for the symmetry of the men, they are well proportioned, of medium stature, and rather exceed us. In the breast they are broad, their arms well built, the legs and other parts of the body well put together. There is nothing else, except that they tend to be rather broad in the face; but not all, for we saw many with angular faces. The eyes black and large, the glance intent and quick. They are not very strong, but they have a sharp cunning and are agile and swift running. From what we were able to learn by experience, they resemble in the last two respects the Orientals, and mostly those of the farthest Sinarian [Chinese] regions. We were not able to learn with particularity of the life and customs of these people because of the shortness of the stay we made on land, on account there being few people and the ship anchored in the high sea.

We found on the shore, not far from these, other people whose lives we think are similar. I will tell Your Majesty about it, describing at present the site and nature of said land. The maritime shore is all covered with fine sand XV feet high, extending in the form of little hills about fifty paces wide. After going ahead, some rivers and arms of the sea were found which enter through some mouths, coursing the shore on both sides as it follows its winding. Near by appears the spacious land, so high that it exceeds the sandy shore, with many beautiful fields and plains, full of the largest forests, some thin and some dense, clothed with as many colors of trees, with as much beauty and delectable appearance as it would be possible to express. And do not believe, Your Majesty, that these are like the Hyrcanian Forest or the wild solitudes of Scythia and northern countries, full of rugged trees, but adorned and clothed with palms, laurels, cypresses, and other varieties of trees unknown in our Europe; (we baptized this land "Forest of Laurels" and a little farther down on account of the beautiful cedars it was given the name "Field of Cedars.") which, for a long distance, exhale the sweetest odors; (we smelled the odor a hundred leagues, and farther when they burned the cedars and the winds blew from the land) the property of which we were not able to learn, for the cause above narrated, not that it was difficult for us to travel through the forests, because their density is not so great but that they are entirely penetrable. We think that partaking of the Orient on account of the surroundings, they are not without some medical property or aromatic liquor. And other riches: gold, to which land of such a color has every tendency. It is abundant of many animals, stags, deer, hare; likewise of lakes and pools of living water, with various numbers of birds, adapted and convenient for every delectable pleasure of the hunt.

This land stands in 34 degrees (like Carthage and Damascus). The air salubrious, pure and moderate of heat and cold: in those regions gentle winds blow and those which prevail most continuously are west-north-west and west in summer time, at the beginning of which we were; (in those regions) the sky clear and serene with infrequent rains, and if sometimes with the south winds the air gathers in clouds or darkness, in an instant, not lasting, it is dispelled, again becoming pure and clear; the sea tranquil and not boisterous, the waves of which are placid. And although the shore always tends to lowness, and is barren of ports, it is not therefore troublesome for sailors, being entirely clean and without any rocks; deep, so that within four or five paces from land are found, exclusive of flood or ebb, XX feet of water, increasing in a uniform proportion to the deep of the sea; with such good holding-ground that any ship whatsoever afflicted by the tempest can never perish in those parts unless it breaks its rope. And this we have proved by experience; because many times in the beginning of March when the force of the wind usually prevails in all countries, being anchored in the high sea oppressed by storms, we found the anchor broken before it dragged on the bottom or made any movement.

We left this place continually, skirting the coast, which we found turned to the east. Seeing everywhere great fires on account of the multitude of the inhabitants, anchoring there off the shore because it did not contain any port, on account of the need of water we sent the little boat to land with XXV men. Because of the very large waves which the sea cast up on the shore on account of the strand being open, it was not possible without danger of losing the boat for any one to land. We saw many people on shore making various signs of friendship, motioning us ashore; among whom I saw a magnificent deed, as Your Majesty will hear.

Sending ashore by swimming one of our young sailors carrying to them some trinkets, such as little bells, mirrors, and other favors and being approached within four fathoms of them, throwing the goods to them and wishing to turn back he was so tossed by the waves that almost half dead he was carried to the edge of the shore. Which having been seen, the people of the land ran immediately to him; taking him by the head, legs and arms, they carried him some distance away. Where, the youth, seeing himself carried in such a way, stricken with terror, uttered very loud cries, which they did similarly in their language, showing him that he should not fear. After that, having placed him on the ground in the sun at the foot of a little hill, they performed great acts of admiration, regarding the whiteness of his flesh, examining him from head to foot. Taking off his shirt and hose, leaving him nude, they made a very large fire near him, placing him near the heat. Which having been seen, the sailors who had remained in the small boat, full of fear, as is their custom in every new case, thought that they wanted to roast him for food. His strength recovered, having remained with them awhile, he showed by signs that he desired to return to the ship; who, with the greatest kindness, holding him always close with various embraces, accompanied him as far as the sea, and in order to assure him more, extending themselves on a high hill, stood to watch him until he was in the boat. Which young man learned of this people that they are thus: of dark color like the others, the flesh more lustrous, of medium stature, the face more clear-cut, much more delicate of body and other members, of much less strength and even of intelligence. He saw nothing else.

We called it Annunciata from the day of arrival, where was found an isthmus a mile in width and about 200 long, in which, from the ship, was seen the oriental sea between the west [before had been written "the east"] and north. Which is the one, without doubt, which goes about the extremity of India, China and Cathay. We navigated along the said isthmus with the continual hope of finding some strait [after this word was written "to the end of," but was cancelled] or true promontory at which the land would end toward the north in order to be able to penetrate to those blassed shores of Cathay. To which isthmus was given by the discoverer (the name Isthmus) Verazanio: as all the land found was named Francesca for our Francis.

Having departed thence, following always the shore which turns somewhat toward the north, we came in the space of fifty leagues to another land which appeared much more beautiful and full of the largest forests. Anchoring at which, XX men going about two leagues inland, we found the people through fear had fled to the woods. Seeking everywhere, we met with a very old woman and a damsel of from XVIII to XX years, who through fear had hidden themselves in the grass. The old one had two little girls whom she carried on the shoulders, and back on the neck a boy, all of eight years of age. The young woman had as many of the same but all girls. Having approached toward them, they began to cry out (and) the old woman to make signs to us that the men had fled to the woods. We gave them to eat of our viands, which she accepted with great gusto; the young woman refused everything and with anger threw it to the ground. We took the boy from the old woman to carry to France, and wishing to take the young woman, who was of much beauty and of tall stature, it was not however possible, on account of the very great cries which she uttered, for us to conduct her to the sea. And having to pass through several woods, being far from the ship, we decided to release her carrying only the boy.

These we found whiter colored than those of previous ones, dressed in certain grasses which hang from the branches of trees, which they weave with various ends of wild hemp. The head bare in the same form as the others. Their food in general is of pulse with which they abound, differing in color and size from ours, of excellent and delectable flavor; also from hunting, fishes and birds, which they take with bows and with snares. They make (the bows) of tough wood, the arrow of reeds, placing at the extremities bones of fishes and of other animals. The beasts in this part are much wilder than in our Europe because they are continually molested by the hunters. We saw many of their boats constructed from a single tree twenty feet long, four feet wide, which are not fabricated with stones, iron or other kind of metals, because in all this land, in the space of two hundred leagues which we traveled, only one stone of any species was seen by us. They aid themselves with the fourth element, burning such part of the wood as suffices for the hollow of the barge, also of the stern and prow, so that, navigating, it is possible to plough the waves of the sea.

The land in situation, goodness and beauty, is like the other; the forests open: full of various kinds of trees, but not of such fragrance, on account of being more north and cold. We saw in that (land) many vines of natural growth which, rising, entwine themselves around the trees, as they are accustomed in Sialpine Gaul; which, if they had the perfect system of culture by the agriculturists, without doubt would produce excellent wines, because (of) finding many times the dry fruit of those (vines) sweet and agreeable, not different from ours. They are held in esteem by them, because where ever they (the vines) grow, they lift up the surrounding bushes in order that the fruit may be able to mature. We found wild roses, violets and lilies, and many sorts of herbs, and fragrant flowers different from ours. We did not learn about their habitations on account of their being within, inland. We think, on account of many signs we saw, they are composed of wood and grass, believing also from various conjectures and signs, that many of them, sleeping on the ground, have nothing for cover except the sky. We did not learn else of them. We think all the others of the land passed live in the same manner.

Having remained in this place three days, anchored off the coast, we decided on account of the scarcity of ports to depart, always skirting the shore which we baptized Arcadia on account of the beauty of the trees, toward the north and east, navigating by daylight and casting anchor at night. We followed a coast very green with forests but without ports, and with some charming promontories and small rivers. We baptized the coast "di Lorenna" on account of the Cardinal; the first promontory "Lanzone," the second "Bonivetto," the largest river "Vandoma'" and a small mountain which stands by the sea "San Polo" on account of the Count."

Land of Angouleme, Bay of Santa Margarita. In Arcadia we found a man who came to the shore to see what people we were: who stood hesitating and ready for flight. Watching us, he did not permit himself to be approached. He was handsome, nude, with hair fastened back in a knot, of olive color. We were about XX [in number] ashore and coaxing him he approached to within about two fathoms, showing a burning stick as if to offer us fire. And we made fire with powder and flint-and-steel and he trembled all over with terror and we fired a shot. He stopped as if astonished and prayed, worshipping like a monk, lifting his finger toward the sky, and pointing to the ship and the sea he appeared to bless us.

Note: Some scholars believe Vandoma was Verrazzano's name for what later became known as the Delaware River. It could be safely speculated then that the Lenape might have ended up as Vandoma Indians had history twisted another way. This is not far-fetched, in that the area known as L'Acadie in Nova Scotia was named Arcadia by Verrazzano and the Indians from that place later came to be called "Cajuns" (short for Arcadians).

The following section was translated by Susan Tarrow and published in the 1970 Morgan Library edition of Lawrence Wroth's *The Voyages of Giovanni da Verrazzano 1524–1528.* Her translation is modern and easy to understand.

After a hundred leagues, we found a very agreeable place between two small but prominent hills; between them a very wide river, deep at its mouth, flowed out into the sea; and with the help of the tide, which rises eight feet, any laden ship could have passed from the sea into the river estuary. Since we were anchored off the coast and well sheltered, we did not want to run any risks without knowing anything about the river mouth. So we took the small boat up this river to land which we found densely populated. The people were almost the same as the others, dressed in birds' feathers of various colors, and they came toward us joyfully, uttering loud cries of wonderment and showing us the safest place to beach the boat. We went up this river for about half a league, where we saw that it formed a beautiful lake, about three leagues in circumference. About xxx (30) of their small boats ran to and fro across the lake with innumerable people aboard who were crossing from one side to the other to see us. Suddenly, as often happens in sailing, a violent unfavorable wind blew in from the sea, and we were forced to return to the ship, leaving the land with much regret on account of its favorable conditions and beauty; we think it was not without some properties of value, since all the hills showed signs of minerals.

We weighed anchor and sailed eastward since the land veered in that direction, and we covered LXXX (80) leagues, always keeping in sight of land. We discovered a triangular shaped island ten leagues from the mainland similar in size to the island of Rhodes; it was full of hills covered in trees, and highly populated to judge by the fires we saw burning continually along the shore. We baptized it in the name of your illustrious mother, but did not anchor there because the weather was unfavorable. We reached another land XV (15) leagues from the island where we found an excellent harbor before entering it, we saw about XX (20) boats full of people who came around the ship uttering various cries of wonderment. They did not come nearer than fifty paces, but stopped to look at the structure of our ship, our persons, our clothes; then all together they raised a loud cry which meant that they were joyful. We reassured them somewhat by imitating their gestures, and they came near enough for us to throw them a few little bells and mirrors and many trinkets, which they took and looked at, laughing and then they confidently came on board ship. Among them were two kings, who were as beautiful of stature and build as I can possibly describe. The first was about XXXX (40) years old, the other a young man of XXIIII, (23) and they were dressed thus; the older man had on his naked body a stag skin skillfully worked like damask with various embroideries; the head was bare, the hair tied back with various bands, and around the neck hung a wide chain decorated with many different-colored stones. The young man was dressed in almost the same way. These people are the most beautiful and have the most civil customs that we have found on this voyage. They are taller than we are; they are a bronze color, some tending more towards whiteness, others to a tawny color; the face is clear-cut, the hair is long and black, and they take great pains to decorate it; the eyes are black and alert, and their manner is sweet and gentle, very like the manner of the ancients.

The things we gave them that they prized the most were little bells, blue crystals and other trinkets to put in the ear or around the neck. They did not appreciate cloth of silk and gold, nor even of any other kind, nor did they care to have them; the same was true for metals like steel and iron, for many times when we showed them some of our arms, they did not admire them, nor ask for them, but merely examined the workmanship. They did the same with mirrors; they would look at them quickly and then refuse them, laughing. They are very generous and give away all they have.

We made great friends with them, and one day before we entered the harbor with the ship, when we were lying at anchor one league out to sea because of unfavorable weather, they came out to the ship with a great number of their boats; they had painted and decorated their faces with various colors, showing us that it was a sign of happiness. They brought us some of their food and showed us by signs where we should anchor in the port for the ship's safety, and then accompanied us all the way until we dropped anchor.

We stayed there for XV (15) days, taking advantage of the place to refresh ourselves.

Every day the people came to see us at the ship, bringing their women, of whom they are very careful; because, entering the ship themselves, remaining a long time, they made their women stay in the barges, and however many entreaties we made them, offering to give them various things, it was not possible that they would allow them to enter the ship. And one of the two Kings coming many times with the Queen and many attendants through her desire to see us, at first always stopped on a land distant from us two hundred paces, sending a boat to inform us of their coming, saying they wished to come to see the ship; doing this for a kind of safety. And when they had the response from us, they came quickly, and having stood awhile to look, hearing the noisy clamor of the sailor crowd, sent the Queen with her damsels in a very light barge to stay on a little island distant from us a quarter of a league; himself remaining a very long time, discoursing by signs and gestures of various fanciful ideas, examining all the equipments of the ship, asking especially their purpose, imitating our manners, tasting our foods, then parted from us benignantly. And one time, our people remaining two or three days on a little island near the ship for various necessities as is the custom of sailors, he came with seven or eight of his attendants. watching our operations, asking many times if we wished to remain there for a long time, offering us his every help. Then, shooting with the bow, running, he performed with his attendants various games to give us pleasure.

Many times we were from five to six leagues inland which we found as pleasing as it can be to narrate, adapted to every kind of cultivation grain, wine, oil. Because in that place the fields are from XXV to XXX leagues wide, open and devoid of every impediment of trees, of such fertility that any seed in them would produce the best crops. Entering them into the woods, all of which are penetrable by any numerous army in any way whatsoever, and whose trees, oaks, cypresses, and others, are unknown in our Europe. We found Lucullian apples, [cherries, which Verrazzano had not seen before] plums and filberts, and many kinds of fruits different from ours. Animals there are in very great number, stags, deer, lynx, and other species which, in the way of others, they capture with snares and bows which are their principal arms. The arrows of whom are worked with great beauty, placing at the end, instead of iron, emery, jasper, hard marble, and other sharp stones, by which they served themselves instead of iron in cutting trees, making their barges from a single trunk of a tree, hollowed with wonderful skill, in which from fourteen to XV men will go comfortable; the short oar, broad at the end, working it solely with the strength of the arms at sea without any peril with as much speed as pleases them.

Going further, we saw their habitations, circular in form, of XIIII to XV paces, compass, made from semi-circles of wood (i.e., arched saplings, bent in the form of an arbor) separated one from the other, without system of architecture, covered with mats of straw ingeniously worked, which protect them from rain and wind. There is no doubt that if they had the perfection of the arts we have, they would build magnificent edifices, for all the maritime coast is full of blue rocks, crystals and alabaster; and for such cause is full of ports and shelters for ships. They change said houses from one place to another according to the opulence of the site and the season in which they live. Carrying away only the mats, immediately they have other habitations made. There live in each a father and family to a very large number, so that in some we saw XXV and XXX souls. Their food is like the others: of pulse (which they produce with more system of culture than the others, observing the full moon, the rising of the Pleiades, and many customs derived from the ancients) also of the chase and fish. They live a long time and rarely incur illness; if they are oppressed with wounds, without crying they cure themselves by themselves with fire, their end being of old age. We judge they are very compassionate and charitable toward their relatives, making them great lamentations in their adversities, in their grief calling to mind all their good fortunes. The relatives, one with another, at the end of their life use the Sicilian lamentation, mingled with singing lasting a long time. This is as much as we were able to learn about them.

Munsee Letter to President Zachary Taylor, March 29, 1849

The text of this previously unpublished document filed in the National Archives on behalf of the Office of Indian Affairs should convey to the reader the feeling of shock the White River Munsee felt upon becoming suddenly homeless again. The letter to President Zachary Taylor that follows contains not only some fascinating highlights of the Munsee's contributions to North American history, but also the horror of the situation they were placed in. It is as if the Munsee Nation were begging for mercy or for their very lives, and had reached the end of their rope, after two hundred and some odd years of relentless persecution. I have transcribed it from the longhand manuscript, so I apologize for any misinterpretations of letters that might be found. Most of the original letter is legible.

To his Excellency, Zachary Taylor,
President of the United States of America

Father:

The undersigned memorialists are members of the Munsee Tribe of Indians, now presently residing in the Delaware Country, Indiana Territory, who now humbly beg leave to inform your Excellency in regard to the welfare of their Nation. We would in the first place inform you how that many years ago, our people were scattered throughout many parts of the United States, but in the course of time our places of residence have become quite altered.

Part of our people here, many years ago, resided in the northern part of the state of Ohio, and now presently residing with the Delawares in their country. We would here make the preliminary remark in regard to our inconvenience by living with the said Delawares. In the first place we do not feel welcome to the enjoyment of the privileges of their country, and we would likewise observe that our Munsee tribe are naturally an enterprising and industrious people, but now living as they do with a different tribe of Indians they do not feel themselves at liberty to practice and exercise their industry, though they have made great improvements already on the said Delaware lands.

The said Delawares have sold their part of their country where we reside to the Wyandots, and in this sale of their lands to the said Tribe, there has not been the least kind of calculation made, by which our people might be paid for the valuation of the improvements that they have made on the said Delaware lands. Our people have built good comfortable houses and all the improvements are generally valuable and they have also built a good and commodious House of worship, and where they attend at every Lord's day to the preaching of the good words of eternal life by their kind Missionary. We would further observe that whereas a part of our Nation have for many years past received the gospel that they have likewise enjoyed the good effects of it, and by it many of us have been enabled to see the advantages of civilization. We would further state that whereas we have been told that there will be no remuneration allowed to our people for their dwelling houses and fields, that this is a great discouragement to our people for making further improvements on the Delaware lands, because it is nothing else but wasting our strength and industry, and also throwing away labor for nothing.

Your Excellency will please permit us to remind you of our ancient Covenant of Friendship which was established at East Town, Pennsylvania and which was to be good forever to remain as long as the Sun would be seen and as long as Rivers run and Trees grow. The Commissioner's name was Capt. Bullen, who acted on the part of the government of the United States, in making the said important Covenant of Peace. He told our people to commit it to memory in their feeble way of entering into record, such important national matters.

Thus a Wampum Record was made out directly to that effect, which now still remains in our hands to this present day. He also did let our people have the Flag of the United States which likewise remains in our possession to this present time. The said Commissioner told our forefathers never to lose this Record of Peace and relationship, but to keep it safe always for our remembrance, because he further states that at some future period of time, the Munsee Nation might somehow unfortunately become overshadowed with a cloud of trouble, then in such a perilous time, if they should be able to show this Record of Peace and Friendship, their Great Father would certainly at such a time, release and Comfort his Munsee Children. The said Commissioner further stated that at some future time, if even a Small Munsee boy would only be able to show this Covenant of Friendship to our Great Father, and if only partly convince him of the reality of our Covenant, even to such a young lad, favor should be granted. He further told our people that if even our Great Father hereafter, would have but a small piece of bread, he would divide a part of it to his Munsee Children. Our said Wampum is divided into thirteen parts, which signifies Friendship strongly, established by the authorized Commission of thirteen Governors of the thirteen original states.

Father, your Excellency will please to permit us to state further in regard to other particulars concerning our Nation. Previous to your arrival into our vast Continent, our Ancient Prophets and wise men had a Vision and Revelation in regard to your coming, though they did not understand fully the meaning of it, whether it was to be the almighty himself or our fellow men, this was a matter of deep consideration for a while with our forefathers until you did arrive. Our ancient wise men without any delay made a Song concerning their expectation of your coming. Likewise a Drum was made for the purpose, out of the shell of a Sea Turtle. The drumming and their singing of the song were connected together and were performed jointly together, and also dancing, which was performed with great solemnity in honor of your coming. This foreknowledge of our forefathers of your coming was one year previous to your arrival; our forefathers collected together frequently and performed these celebrations until you did arrive, and when the vessel came at last in open sight to the eyes of our forefathers at the shore, the appearance of the vessel at sea was truly a great mystery to our forefathers, and immediately many wise men and counselors of high respectability among our ancient forefathers were called and collected together by the rumors and influential men of our

Nation in order to ascertain what that mysterious sight could be, which was making progress toward the shore by the distant appearance of the sails of the vessel our forefathers first concluded that it was some great water fowl, and as the vessel came nearer to fair open view, they concluded that it must be their God, coming to bring them some new kind of game, and when the vessel reached the shore, they saw the Captain of the Ship, and then concluded that he must be the almighty himself, and as he had blue eyes, this was another great wonder, and by it they further concluded that he must certainly be the Great God. Our forefathers highly respected the arrival of their Great Father, and did instantly spread white Beaver skins from the shore where the vessel landed to a certain tent where the wise men and counselors were assembled together; for the Captain to walk on. The kind disposition of the Captain induced him to tell our forefathers that he was not the almighty, but that he was their brother, that in ancient times he was with his brethren, and by the various changes that frequently occur in this life, he had some how got separated from his brethren, but he expressed great joy, that he had now arrived and found his brethren again, and hoped that he would never be again separated from his brethren. He further told our forefathers that he had merely come in search of his red brethren and seeing that he had discovered his brethren he would then return to his people, and inform them how that he had discovered their brethren on the great Continent and which would cause great joy throughout the nations who were situated beyond the Deep Waters. He gave our forefathers many presents such as hoes and axes and tin buckets and the next year he came again in company with a large number of his people in order to come and reside among their red brethren, at which time they saw our forefathers wearing hoes and axes and covers to the tin buckets about their necks. He then showed our forefathers the design of the hoes and axes. Handles were put into them, and large trees were cut down before them, which created a general time of laughing, to think how greatly they had been mistaken in regard to the design of the presents that had been given to them.

Father we do further beg leave to state, that when you first arrived onto our vast American continent, you was destitute of land, but your Munsee children were always liberal towards you in granting you their lands according to your necessity. You first requested your Munsee children to grant you as much land what a Bullock Skin would cover, and which was cut into small cords, which was laid in the form of a circle on the land which you desired to have, and we your Munsee children directly complied to your request for

said land. Furthermore, your Excellency will please permit us to state further
that at another time afterwards, you did that is figuratively speaking, your
Nation applied to our Munsee Tribe again for more land, which was our
Father then promised, that we should grant him as much land as a middling
sized lad could travel around a tract of land in one day's journey, and again
your Munsee children did likewise grant this earnest request for more land.
And now, Father, you have got all our land, and we at this time are very poor,
have no land at all, not so much as to set one foot on, and you have plenty
of land lying waste, and we think it would be better for us to have some of
it than to have it lying useless as it presently does, and by our persevering
industry, we think we may get our living on it.

We would further state in relation to our destitute (state) that the present amount of annuity allowed to us is nothing as it were in proportion to
the annuities allowed to other tribes, because some of them now yearly
receive form thirty to seventy and one hundred dollars a head, while we the
poor Munsees receive something like one dollar a piece, which is almost a
trifle, and likewise these tribes never had no more land than us.

Further, your Excellency will please permit us to speak plainly to you
of our needy circumstances and as you have always told us, not to be back-
ward in telling you of our desires, as you had no distinction toward your
red children, and that you had feelings of compassion for them. Just as
much as you did for your own children of your flesh and blood, and we
have always rejoiced to see the kind feelings of the Government towards us,
therefore, we would also refer your kind attention to the latter part of our
ancient Covenant of Friendship, where you told us that hereafter if you
only had a small piece of bread, that you would divide a part of it to your
poor Munsee children, therefore we would humbly request you, under your
kind feelings for us, in order to better our condition that you will please to
grant us wagons and working cattle, chains [?] narrow and broad axes,
ploughs and harrows, saw mill and grist mill, likewise crosscut saws, grind
stones, [?] to [?] shingles with, and likewise black smithing. Likewise that
our rising young may be educated by the kindness of the Government of
the United States.

Again, your Excellency will please permit us to speak in regard to the
Delawares having sold us out to the Wyandots, that the said Wyandots will
want all the land that they have bought of the Delawares. Thus you see that
we are entirely destitute of home. And on account of our living with the
said Delawares in their Country, not having no right to form regulations

for the good of our Nation, we would observe that it is a disadvantage to us in living in the Delaware lands, and because many of our rights are kept down. The total number of our Munsee tribe including all that are settled in various places is probably about eleven hundred.

And again we would further humbly beg leave to remark in connection to what has already been said in regard to the Munsee Tribe being liberal toward their Great Father, when he first came to them on this our vast continent, and made applications to our forefathers for a sufficient quantity of land for his subsistence, that his earnest request was freely granted by our forefathers. And we would further say that we do rejoice with exceeding great joy to think that our forefathers were able to show kind favor to our Great Father on his arrival to this Continent, and not only this but we likewise rejoice that our Great and kind Creator has so highly favored him in prosperity, since he has come to this Continent and has rendered him to become a great Nation.

And now our Great Father, your Excellency will please permit us to say further in regard to this important subject, that we observe that your stature as it were [figuratively speaking] almost reaches the heavens, and your arms extending from the rising of the sun and to the going down of the same, and we are sensible that it is the Almighty who is now building you up, on the foundation where our forefathers once stood. Our forefathers first had this greatness granted to them by the good will of the Almighty, but he is now granting it to you. And now in all your splendor and greatness, we do entreat you most tenderly as our father that you will never forget your poor red children.

We the Munsees, were the first tribe that you came to on this continent, and we were the first ones that listened to your wants for land, and we were the first Indian nation that received you, our forefathers were then living on Manhattan Island where the City of New York now stands.

Therefore, Father, be not indifferent or unmindful to the humble entreaty of your poor Munsee children; and now Father we do further humbly entreat you to provide a way to collect and gather your scattered Munsee children that is we sincerely request your kind feelings towards us, to grant us land of a sufficient size where the whole of our Munsee Tribe can be collected together. And if we are collected together as a tribe, it will turn out as we hope, for our best good. We do therefore further entreat you as our Father that your Excellency will please to permit us to explore the vacant land in the Indiana Territory and that you will please to send us the permission through the hands of our Agent of the Fort Leavenworth Agency. And we would here further entreat your Excellency that you will be so kind as to lay the foundation for the lasting residence of your Munsee children. We would likewise humbly entreat your kindness that if you grant us home that you will be so good as to remove us there and to allow us one year's provisions.

We would further beg leave to inform your Excellency that a few years ago, we sent one of our influential men to the seat of Government, for the purpose of laying before the United States the object of high importance, which we had in view for many years past, which was concerning the said Treaty, which the said Government made with our Munsee tribe in connection with some other tribes of Indians, when our people together with the other tribes did sell the large territory of land about one hundred and twenty miles square, which was situated and inlaid on the north part of the state of Ohio, commonly called lower Sandusky; and our people never have received nothing at all yet, from the avails of said treaty, which was made on the fourth of July, 1805. Our Delagate was told, by the government that he had come unexpected, that nothing could be done for our people then at that time, under the said Treaty, because Government was unprepared to act on it then, and that our people were required to send again to the said Government in two years' time, and by all means the next time they send, to notify the Government that such a one was coming again for that purpose, and Government agreed by their kind Officers, likewise to hear the expenses of such Delegates going on this important purpose. Now we inform you that we want to send again next winter, and that Government would be so kind as to befriend us some how in order to enable our Delegates to go to the Seat of Government.

We would further state to your Excellency that our Tribe did actually own the said immense territory of land the Shawanese and Senecas had but a small right to it, because they were few in number, and they were living with the Wyandots; as to the Chippeways, Ottawas, and Potawatomies, they were nothing but hunters on the said territory, the Delawares had no right at all, no more than this, our Munsee Tribe under the kind respect they had for the Delawares, who were agreeable to the ancient customs of our forefathers, politically related to us in our distress, for this reason they inserted the Delawares into the said Treaty. It will soon be forty four years since the said Treaty was made, and up to the present time our Munsee Tribe have never yet received the least benefit from the avails of said Treaty. We think that we are entitled to all the back annuities, and likewise we would recant, disannul, revoke and exclude the Delawares entirely out of the said Treaty, because they never owned or ever were in possession of the said territory of land. And furthermore we would inform your Excellency that our Munsee tribe was the legal and rightful owners of the said vast territory of land, and they were the only ones that ever held possession of the said country of land, and likewise the only owners of it. Therefore we think that it would be just and right for us, from henceforth forever to receive annually the one thousand dollars stipulated in the said Treaty.

Our people have really been patient for nearly half a century, while the other tribes have probably been drawing annuities from the said Treaty, who had but a small right to it. There were thirty-two families of our Munsee tribe then actually residing on the said Territory of land, and their population was two hundred at the time the said Treaty was made; and vast improvements were made by our people on the said Territory of land, amounting to one thousand acres without the least shadow of doubt. Some of our people are yet living among us , who were born and raised in the said Territory of land, and did reside there until it was sold to the Government of the United States.

We would likewise further state in regard to the other tribes who were included in the stipulations of said Treaty that they really are better off in circumstances than what we are at this present time, and they can do better without the benefit of said Treaty than what we can.

We would further inform you of the names of our Chiefs who signed the said Treaty. The name of the first was Pucconsittona, and the other was Pamehlot. The first was the head Chief of the Nation who died on the place before our people moved from there. The other was our War Chief. We do further remark that we shall ever consider ourselves to be under the peaceable and quiet protection of the United States.

We would further inform your Excellency that our Munsee Tribe did also own land in Genesee County in the State of New York, which was a place of residence of one Long Arm, an ancient Chief of our Munsee Tribe, who resided near Rochester some time before the revolutionary war. Our Munsee tribe have never yet received benefit from the avails of said Country of land.; We would therefore inquire in regard to that land, and in what position it lies in the eyes of the Government; because it is altogether likely that the Unites States must have had some kind of Jurisdiction over that part of the state of new York at the time our said Chief Long Arm resided there on the land. We do further humbly pray that your Excellency will be so kind as to take particular notice of our important inquiries and that you will please to send us answers to our inquiries as soon as convenience will become favorable. By this complying to our humble Memorial, you much oblige your unworthy Memorialists and Munsee Children. There are seven important inquiries in our Memorial, the first inquiry is in regard to the implements of husbandry, the second in regard to one year's provision, the third in regard to our being removed by the kindness of Government. The fourth in regard to permission from Government for exploring vacant land in the Indiana Territory. The fifth in regard to the said mentioned Treaty, the sixth in regard to the land in Genessee [sic] County in the State of New York. The seventh in regard to our kind Father granting us land. May your Excellency please to send us answer to our Memorial, to the hands of our Agent as soon as practicable. And we your unworthy Memorialists as in duty bound will ever pray. In testimony of the same we have hereunto set our hands this 29th day of March, 1849.

Done at the Munsee Settlement, Indiana Territory

This was written by John W. Newsom [?] a Mohekunuk or Stockbridge Indian who was educated at [?] and who writes these words at the request of his Munsee friends.

Gideon Williams John Quadrobe John Killsnake Joseph Francis John Wrightman S. Williams John Henry John Brown Easgr. Nicodemus Leonard Snake Daniel Anderson Thomas Hill Yaptaw Hill John Thomas John Lewis John Daniel John Wilson Doctor Block John Young

[A copy of this document was provided to me by the Munsee of the Thames River band of Delawares, who received it from Siegrun Kaiser of Germany. The document is originally from the Office of Indian Affairs. At least four of the people who signed the letter ended up having to leave the United States, settling with the Thames River band of Munsee in Ontario.]

The Nimham Lineage

The Nimhams, a long line of sachems of the Wappinger people (although the term "Wappinger" didn't come into use until the mid–eighteenth century) are among the most legendary of all Native New Yorkers. I am indebted to historian J. Michael Smith for his explanation of the Nimham sachem lineage, often mentioned by historians, but a puzzle to almost everyone. Some of Smith's research on the Nimham family has been published in *Hudson Valley Regional Review*.

THE NIMHAM SACHEMS WERE:

Nimham I of Long Island, Sachem approximately from 1667 to 1703.

Nimhammau, originally of New Jersey, Sachem approximately from 1677 to 1744. Probably the son of Nimham I, he began negotiating land in Dutchess County in 1721. By 1744 he was called King Nimham. He died in 1750, then known as Old Nimham, as he was in his late nineties.

Nimham II was probably Old Nimham's eldest son, One Shake. He became sachem around 1745 and served in that capacity until 1762.

Daniel Nimham was probably the eldest son of "Nimham II" (or "One Shake"). He was Sachem from 1762 until his death in 1778. He had followed in his grandfather's footsteps, trying to challenge land fraud in association with treaties in the South Ward area of Dutchess County. He went to New York City to argue his claims, but was unsuccessful. He led the Wappingers to Stockbridge, Massachusetts, to live with their old allies the Mohican around 1757 and was granted land in the township in 1762. He served under George Washington in the Revolutionary War, and is said to have been killed in a surprise engagement with the Queen's Rangers and British cavalry, along with his son Abraham Nimham, Captain of the Stockbridge Indian Company.

Aaron Nimham was probably the second eldest son of Nimham II, and brother of Daniel. He became sachem in 1778, and led the Wappingers people to a new settlement called New Stockbridge (in Oneida territory near Rome, New York). He was still active in 1794.

Hendrick Nimham was probably the son of Aaron Nimham. According to Sheila Powless, a Mohican historian at the Stockbridge Munsee Reservation in Bowler, Wisconsin, Hendrick Nimham was sachem after Aaron. She suspects he died in 1825, which was the year most of the New Stockbridge Mohicans (and Wappingers) moved to Wisconsin. From that point on, the name Nimham seems to have become an Oneida family name through intermarriage.

TIME LINE OF
LENAPE HISTORY

This material has been collected from many sources, notably Herbert C. Kraft's *The Lenape: Archaeology, History, and Ethnography* for precontact entries. However, some are my own estimations based on probability; these are marked "probable" or noted with an asterisk. I use modern place-names for toponymic clarity, but I have placed them in brackets out of respect for the fact that they are anachronistic and culturally biased. These brackets replace the words "what is now called," and are not used for words familiar to Native people of the time. Archaeologic terms have not been bracketed. I use B.C.E. (before common era) and C.E. (common era) out of respect for Lenape and Mohican individuals today who may not find the term B.C. relevant to their history.

PRECONTACT PERIOD
Lithic Period: 50,000-11,000 B.C.E.)

50,000–11,000 B.C.E.	[Bering Strait] open
50,000–25,000 B.C.E.	Pre-Projectile; no spears or bow-and-arrow weapons used.
18,000 B.C.E.	Land exposed near [Labrador] due to drop in sea level.
15,000 to 13,000 B.C.E.	Meadowcroft Rock Shelter (south of [Pittsburgh]) and [Cactus Hill, Virginia] inhabited.

Clovis Culture Period (Lithic-Algonquin): 15,000–8,000 B.C.E.

Clovis develops in [New Mexico]. As Wisconsin Glacier recedes, these hunters follow it to the northeast, possibly through the Ohio Valley into the [Great Lakes,] and possibly to [New York City] area about 10,000 B.C.E. (Clovis remains were found in [Intervale, New Hampshire,] dated at between 10,000 and 7000 B.C.E. Some say the Micmacs were able to settle [Nova Scotia] by 10,000 B.C.E., while others say that the Clovis didn't appear even in [New Mexico] until 9,200 B.C.E. However Clovis people inhabited [Cactus Hill,Virginia] about 8925 B.C.E.

11,000 B.C.E.	Possible human habitation of [Santa Rosa] island off the coast of [California.] Average temperature was 18° colder than today.
10,500 B.C.E.	[Dutchess Quarry Cave] site in [Monroe, NY] radiocarbon dated to 10,580 B.C.E. (only true rock shelter in region, found by archaeologists in unspoiled condition). [Monte Verdi, Chile] inhabited.
10,000 B.C.E.	[New York City's] first settlers arrive. [New York] first used as hunting ground for big game. A site in [Peru] is inhabited and another one in the [Amazon].
9000 B.C.E.	Evidence of mastodon hunting in [Hyde Park, New York]. Eight mastodons have been found off the coast of [New Jersey], dating 7860–10,730 B.C.E., and over 300 Clovis points suitable for hunting mastodons have been found in [New Jersey] alone. Debert Site in [Nova Scotia,] dated to 8600 B.C.E. (Proto-Algonquin).
8000 B.C.E.	Clovis people may have reached [Labrador]. From here, several waves of Proto-Algonquin culture expanded and spread across the continent in the following millennia. First occupation of the Shawnee-Minisink site (near Dreamer's Rock, [Pennsylvania]) carbon-dated 8590–8750 B.C.E. Possible continuous occupation (Kraft) by ancestors of the Munsee. Fishbones found dating back to ancient times. Vail site in [Maine] dated to 9120 B.C.E. Warming trend in [New York City] area; big-game hunters leave.

Archaic Period: 8000–1000 B.C.E.
(some define as 7000 to 1000 B.C.E.)

Defined by hunting and gathering as opposed to cultivating plants. Dog is only domesticated animal. People seasonally nomadic. Geographic cultural areas include Great Lake Archaic, Maritime Archaic, and Eastern Woodland Archaic.

Early Archaic: 8000–6000 B.C.E.

8000–7000 B.C.E.	Folsom Culture develops in Southwest. Probable* spread of Proto-Algonquin culture in first wave from [Labrador] to Oka, near [Montreal]. Micmac culture today probably retains remnants of this. People collect clams, make seaworthy dugouts, catch swordfish.
7500–4500 B.C.E.	Plano Culture develops in Midwest. Trade goods reach Proto-Algonquin in the East. Stone tools found from this period at [Flint Mine Hill] near Coxsackie, [NY] probably continuous use for flint mining.
7000 B.C.E.	First occupation of Plenge site near [Washington, NJ,] rock shelter at [Inwood and Port Mobil] site on [Staten Island.] Corn (maize), beans, and squash—the "three sisters"—first developed in Central America, reach [NJ/NY] area about 1000 C.E.
6980–6210 B.C.E.	Hunters using "Hardaway-Dalton" points and "bifurcated" points arrive in [New Jersey] and on [Staten Island] from the more populous southeast region; also called Piedmont culture.

Middle Archaic: 6000–4000 B.C.E.

Due to low sea levels, [New Jersey] is wider extending roughly 25 to 50 miles into what is now the [Atlantic Ocean]. [New York] extends 15 to 30 miles past [Long Island].

Major sites along [Delaware River] (north to south) include Rockelein, Faucett, Miller Field, Shawnee-Minisink, Harry's Farm, and Byram. Near [Philadelphia] is Koens-Crispin and Savich Farm sites.

6000 B.C.E.	Uninterrupted occupation of some areas with open rock shelter sites in the [Hudson] Valley.
5000 B.C.E.	Flora and fauna of region appears much as it does today. Natives begin to use readily available sedimentary rock to make tools, using the new pecking-and-grinding method. Axes appear. Proto-Mohican group probably headed west. Proto-Algonquin head south along Hudson Valley, settle near Dreamer's Rock, [Delaware Water Gap area]; continuous occupation developing into Munsee culture.
4500 B.C.E.	New people, small game trappers, enter [New York City] region.
4280 B.C.E.	Second wave of Proto-Algonquin spread to [Alumette Island] in Ottawa River—first permanent settlement of the Algonquin, early ancestors of the Lenape and Mohican.

Late Archaic: 4000–2000 B.C.E.

Mortar and pestle become popular food processors. Grinding stones also popular. Ulu or slate knife is introduced. Atlatls, counterbalanced with a "bannerstone" or "atlatl weight" were the first known machines that greatly accelerated the velocity of the spear, become more popular. Bolas, three grooved round stones attached together by yardlong tethers, are adopted from the Piedmont people as hunting devices. Large weirs used for fishing as well as nets with sinker-weights. People live near water.

4000–1500 B.C.E.	Old Copper Culture [Lake Superior].
4000 B.C.E.	First great river culture in North America develops at [Alumette Island], at same time as Harrappian, Chinese, and earliest Mesopotamian river cultures elsewhere. Copper mined from the south shore of [Lake Superior] and [Isle Royal, Michigan] begins to appear. Alumette Island people control trade with the east and possess large amounts of copper goods. (Gaffield) Much of this reaches the eastern Algonquin. They also handle fur and corn as trade goods. [Alumette and Oka Islands] overpopulate,

proto-Mohican and Lenape head south to [Manhattan] along Mohican Trail and west to [British Columbia].

3000 B.C.E. Oldest burials in [Hudson Valley] yet discovered.

2300–1900 B.C.E. 52 cremation burials at Savich Farm site, [Marlton, NJ]. (Not typical Lenape, probably "Piedmont" people.) Tribes have more defined home areas, but trade more widely.

Terminal Archaic: 2000–1000 B.C.E.

Next wave of Algonquin, from [Alumette and Oka], probably arrive in [NY, NJ] Broadspears appear from Piedmont people to the south. "Susquehanna River culture." Bolas and net sinkers less used. Soapstone from [Maryland] popular.

Woodland Culture: 1,500 B.C.E.–1,534 C.E.

1500 B.C.–400 B.C.E. **Early Woodland Period.** First use of bow and arrow, according to some.

1500 B.C.E. Domesticated dog throughout Algonquin regions. Red Bank Mound burials; "red ochre burials" with bodies interred, sprinkled with red ochre, and presented with mortuary gifts possibly by this time in [New Brunswick, Canada].

1000 B.C.E. Algonquin intermarry with NW coast people, create Salishan, Kwakiutl cultures. Culture spreads wherever large inlets (rivers that flow both ways) and fjords exist, as far south as [Navarro River] in [California]. More Algonquin come down from the north, interact and intermarry with local relations in [NY], form distinct tribal groups. Territories more defined. "Orient Point, or Long Island Phase" dominant from Potomac River to [New England]—small tribes and close-knit family units typical of Lenape. Fish is cured. Some trade with sophisticated Adena culture to the west.

1000 B.C.E.–500 C.E. Ceramic period introduced by Orient People. Pots made from marine clay along coast, with flat bottoms (to imitate soapstone bowls, according to Kraft). Snowshoes developed, stone from [Labrador] and copper from [Great Lakes] traded across Algonquin world, now extended to [British Columbia.] Introduction of fishhook. Sites include (Delaware River) Rockelein, Minisink, Faucett, Rosenkrans, Miller Field, Pahaquarry, Harry's Farm Abbot's Farm [Newark], Salisbury, Goose Island, Raccoon Point [Lower Delaware River.] Indian Head, Riggins, St. Jones River. Also Orient Point, [Long Island], Bowman's Brook, Tottenville, (Staten Island).

1200 to 300 B.C.E.

Meadowood Phase. People from NW and central [New York State] travel to [Delaware, Walkill, and Hudson Valleys] by boat. According to Kraft, they introduced a tubular clay tobacco pipe to the Lenape, tobacco from South America, which gives birth to the great Lenape horticulture tradition; slate pendants, and birdlike atlatl stones, which may have transferred ritual "flying"magic to the spear. They introduce triangular pottery, left large caches of unfinished spearpoints or "blanks" buried near the riverbanks, used red ochre burials with mortuary gifts like the people of [New Brunswick, Canada], but cremated the body.

800–300 B.C.E.

Adena-Middlesex Phase. Adena refers to the great mound-building culture of Ohio, but Middlesex indicates the less sophisticated versions of Adena culture attempted in the Mid-Atlantic region. Their burials and camps have been found on the [Jersey] shore, (including a mound) and from [Delaware] and [Maryland] up to New Brunswick, Can. Burial mound at [Trenton.] Extensive use of copper.

400 B.C.E.–1000 C.E.

Middle Woodland Period. Fox Creek Phase. Formation of Algonquin confederacies; creation of the different tribes as we know them. Many different types of arrowheads developed. Introduction of red sandstone "platform" pipes (similar to Plains pipe). Highly elaborate,
flamboyant pottery similar to Hopewell pots created at Abbot's Farm site near [Trenton, NJ].

150 B.C.E.–1 C.E.	Wave of people speaking Algonquin migrate from eastern [Great Lakes] in all directions. These are the Anishinabi people. Arapaho leave Minnesota (?). Cree eventually reach Rockies. Micmac, Innu reach Maritimes. Maliseet, Passamaquoddy split off later. Ojibway in east.
300–850 C.E.	Triangular Jack's Reef points used. Widespread use of bow and arrow begins. Population increases as food more plentiful. Estimated diffusion of Lenape-type languages. (E. Pritchard).
500 C.E.	Possible arrivals from [British Columbia] arrive in Ohio.
800 C.E.	Oldest flex burials yet discovered in [Hudson] Valley.
900 C.E.	Iroquois/Owasco enter Susquehanna Valley from [Pittsburgh] area, take over area. "Old Mohican" cultures scatter eastward, become part of Abenaki, Penobscot, Massachusett, Narragansett, Nipmuk, Wampano or Quiripi, Pequot, Weckweesgeek cultures.
1100 C.E.	Hatteras Algonquin of coastal North Carolina split off from Powhatan, intrude into Catawba/Cherokee/Tuscarora region.
1000–1524 C.E.	**Late Woodland Period**. Beginning of the "golden age" of Mohican/Lenape culture, which lasts for several hundred years, reaching its peak at about 1524. Early contact. Development of Lenape farming practices, which they eventually mastered. Farming drastically changes their way of life, but increases the population.
1100 C.E.	Illinois split off from Ohio group, head west. Unami split off from Munsee, head southeast. Nanticoke and Piscataway speakers split off from Unami, go to [Maryland]. Powhatan split off from Nanticoke, intrude into Tidewater [VA] area.
1200 C.E.	Oldest pet burials yet found in [Hudson] Valley. Warlike Oak Hill and Chance cultures from [Ontario (Huron?)] spread to eastern NY.

CONTACT PERIOD

996   Norse land in [Nova Scotia, Labrador.]

1010   Norse spend three winters under Thorfinn Karlsefni. According to Barry Fell and others, they build stone towers as far south as [Rhode Island.]

1000–1350   Pahaquarry phase of Munsee pottery, collarless but with cord impressions. Shawnee move into [Cumberland Gap] region of east Tennessee, conflicting/blending with Cherokee.

1300   Possible date when the prophets of the seven fires began to appear to the Algonquin people of the Northeast, urging them to move westward "to the land where food grows on the water" to avoid destruction from invaders from the east. Creation of Ottawa, Algonquin, Ojibway, Potowatomi, Menominee as separate nations. The Lenape are not generally part of this movement, but gradually become aware of it.

1300s   [Oak Island] settlement of Europeans of Knights Templar in [Nova Scotia.] They train Micmacs in Masonry skills and Masonic lore.

1350–1650   Minisink Phase of Munsee pottery, incised with square collar.

1492   Columbus "sailed the ocean blue." Observes tobacco ceremony in the [Caribbean.]

1493   Horses and other livestock introduced at Hispaniola. Columbus' second voyage.

1497   John Cabot explores Canada, meets Micmac who speak European languages, but no contact with Lenape.

1500   Gaspar Corte Real of Portugal explores coast, discovers [Hudson] River, calls it Deer River.

1500   Peak of Mississippian culture. Lenape benefit from Mississippian knowledge, probably borrow longhouse construction from them. Probable migration of some Shawnee from Ohio.

1501   Corte Real's second voyage. He is lost at sea. Portuguese fishing boats off coast.

1502   Montezuma II ruler of Aztecs. Columbus's fourth voyage.

1504   French fishing boats off coast of [North America.] Contact with Algonquin. Term "America," after Amerigo Vespucci, coined by German mapmaker.

1513   Ponce de Leon claims [Florida] for Spain.

1513   Balboa discovers [Pacific] for Europeans.

1517   Cordoba discovers Yucatan, battles the Maya.

1521   Ponce de Leon fatally wounded in "Florida."

1524	Giovanni da Verrazzano explores [North America] from the [Carolinas] to [Nova Scotia] under a French flag. Sails into [New York Harbor] trades with Lenape, writes a diary account of his meetings, almost discovers [Hudson River]. Diary published in France, Italy. This marks the high point and downfall of the Lenape culture, as European-carried disease begins to destroy their society.
1526	Verrazzano killed by Natives in the West Indies.
1534	Jacques Cartier lands on Gaspé Peninsula, claims land for France.
1535	Jacques Cartier winters at Quebec area and sees Hochelega, a Huron town near [Montreal].
1536	Jacques Cartier's second voyage.
1537	Pope Paul III tries to outlaw Indian slavery to no avail.
1539	De Soto begins exploration of New World.
1540	Basque whalers visit the coast of [Labrador] until 1610.
1541	Third voyage of Cartier. Founded [Quebec] city, conquered native town of Saguenay.
1546	Mayan revolt crushed by Spanish army.
1570	First European mention of Iroquois Confederacy, latest possible date of its creation, founded at Onondaga Lake, near [Rochester]. Some Native elders estimate its creation as early as 900 B.C.E.
1576	Martin Frobisher sails to the Arctic, to [Baffin Bay].
1579	Cortés captures Tenochtitlan [Mexico City].
1581	Demand for beaver hats in Paris increases greatly.
1584	Walter Raleigh sends expedition to [Virginia].
1586	Potato introduced to Europe from [New World]. English colonists rescued at [Roanoke Island.]
1587	Virginia Dare born at [Roanoke], first English child born in the [New World].
1588	Thomas Harriot, member of [Roanoke Colony], describes Native culture in his journal.
1590	Croatan Lost Colony, southern relatives of Lenape.
1598	Dutch make first visit to [Hudson River] area.
1603	Samuel de Champlain's first voyage.
1603	[American Indians] paddle a canoe on England's River Thames near London.
1605	Port Royal set up by Sieur de Monts in [Nova Scotia.]
1607	First permanent English colony at [Jamestown].
1608	Champlain establishes permanent French colony at Quebec. Captain John Smith writes first American book published in London.

1609	Iroquois repelled at Quebec by combined forces, but this pushes the Iroquois to the south and into the Mohican territory, greatly affecting their fate, and ultimately, that of the Lenape.
1609	Henry Hudson explores [Chesapeake Bay], [Delaware Bay], and [Hudson River] to [Albany.] John Smith decrees that colonists must grow corn (maize).
1610	Captain Samuel Argall names Delaware Bay after Lord De La Warr III, first governor of the English colony at Jamestown. The river that feeds into it is then named Delaware. Soon all the people along its 300-mile-length are called Delawares. Two hundred and ten colonists in North America. Santa Fe established. Jamestown famine; some whites join Algonquin, become Melungeon people.
1613	Dutch establish trading post on south tip of Manhattan. Pocahontas converts to Protestantism.
1616	Smallpox kills 90 percent of Natives in [New England].
1617	Criminals sent from England to Virginia settlement as punishment.
1620	Pilgrims chartered by Virginia Company of London to settle in [Virginia], but after three month voyage land at Pawtuxet, which they name [Plymouth Rock].
1621	Treaty with Massasoit, kept for twenty years.
1623	Only 200–300 Lenape left on Manhattan, by some accounts.
1624	Dutch settle [New Amsterdam] on Canarsie land called Kapsee. Verhulst becomes first governor. [Fort Orange] created on Mohican land called Schodack [Albany, NY]. Drinking first becomes a problem among Lenape. Virginia made a royal colony
1625	Lenape hunted all available furs on Manhattan Island. By some accounts, Verhulst is fired, replaced by Peter Minuit. Minuit becomes director-general in May of this year.
1626	Peter Minuit reputedly buys Manhattan for $24 of beads (60 guilders). No deed ever produced.
1627	Mohican Wars, fought over fur trade with the Lenape.
1628	Mohican Wars over; the Mohawk win, demand tribute.
1628	Puritans settle at Salem, led by John Endicott, who rules with an iron hand.
1636	Van Twiller becomes director-general, begins buying land from Lenape.
1637	[New Sweden] established on 60 miles of [Delaware River] shore, among friendly Lenape.
1638	Van Twiller fired, Kieft becomes director-general of [New Amsterdam]. Long war between Mohawk and Mohican ends. Kieft demands protection money from Lenape.

1639	First colonial printing press in Massachusetts Bay Colony. A Lenape chief takes a single piece of tin from the Dutch fort at Swanendael and is murdered, setting the stage for Kieft's War.
1640	Kieft's War in [New York] begins, rages on and off (till 1649, according to some sources).
1643	Kieft initiates numerous major massacres all over Manhattan and surrounding area. Anne Hutchinson and many other settlers in the [New York City] area are killed by Lenape as retribution.
1645	August 30, 1645, Kieft makes treaty with Lenape. Susanna Hutchinson apparently released. War drags on.
1647	Peter Stuyvesant arrives with high expectations, finds "New Amsterdam" in ruins. He rules with an iron hand until 1664, when he is defeated by the English.
1649	Kieft's War concluded with treaty.
1654	Dutch capture [New Sweden] from the Swedes.
1663	Some Esopus driven from the [Kingston] area and move in with the Minisink.
1664	English capture New Amsterdam, rename it New York. Names of many towns and rivers changed.
1668	Old Conference House built on the south shore of [Staten Island] at ancient village and burial site.
1672	[Old Boston Post Road] created out of Lenape trails.
1674	Some Shawnee move to Savannah River area.
1675	European glass beads spread among Lenape, gradually replacing quillwork. Secretary of Indian Affairs and Board of Commissioners established at [Albany, NY].
1675–76	King Philip's War in New England. Metacom (King Philip) killed.
1676	Bacon's Rebellion leads to defeat of both the Susquehannocks, enemies of the Lenape, and Virginia Tidewater tribes, allies of the Lenape, in Virginia Colony.
1680	Esopus Chief Ankerop leaves [Rosendale], dies about 1700.
1682	William Penn's First Treaty creates friendly relations with Lenape. Unami begin to move west.
1683	Tamanend signs land treaty with William Penn.
1686	The Charter of the English Governor Dongan declares New York "an anciente citie."
1689–97	King William's War, first between England, France, and Indians, begins a period of 75 years of such conflicts called the French and Indian Wars.

1690	First group of Munsee to go west, settle with the Ottawa, join the French Alliance.
1693	Governor Ben Fletcher of New York offers bounty on scalps of "dead Indians." Frederick Philipse builds an inn at the corner of the two post roads, Albany and Boston.
1699	Kuckeno (Montauk), who assisted John Eliot in translating the Christian Bible into Algonquin, dies.
1700	Susquehannock people leave the Susquehanna valley and move north to join other Iroquois. Teedyuskung is born. Marameg people of Anishinabi disappear.
1702–13	Queen Anne's War, also between England, France, and Natives.
1709–1742	Lenape move from Delaware River Valley and settle in Susquehanna River Valley with the blessing of the Iroquois. Two major settlements, Shamokin (founding the city of [Sunbury]) and Wyoming (founding the city of [Wilkes-Barre]). Smaller third settlement to south (in wilderness), Paxtang, grows over thirty years into large town, becomes [Harrisburg, PA]. Last Lenape group leaves Susquehanna Valley in 1768.
1710	A Mohican chief, Aroniateka (or "Hendrick") along with three Mohawk, is received in Queen Anne's court as "The Four Kings" of the New World.
1714	Fort Stanwix Treaty— Shawnee lose [Cumberland Gap] territory, migrate in all directions.
1718	The Delaware cede land in several treaties with Pennsylvania.
1720	War with Iroquois. Pontiac born in [Ohio].
1724	Iroquois force some Delaware to cross Alleghenies to Kittanning.
1732	Lenape cede more land to Pennsylvania colony.
1737	The Infamous "Walking Purchase" by Penn's sons.
1742	Last Delaware River Lenape group leave Lehigh and Delaware area (Easton, PA) and head for Susquehanna Valley at the request of Governor George Thomas.
1744	Treaty of Lancaster; all Unami along the lower Delaware are to "leave the waters of their river and move to Shamokin (where Sassoonan lived) or Wyoming.
1744–48	King George's War, between English, French, and Natives.
1747	Lenape Chief Sassoonan dies in Shamokin, [PA].
1751	Unami, Munsee settle in [East Ohio]. Ben Franklin cites Iroquois League as a model for his Albany Plan of Union. Lenape influences are also obvious.
1754–63	French and Indian War involves colonies. Many Lenape move west

beyond Alleghenies, some settle Kittanning. Less than a thousand stay in New Jersey.

1756   William Johnson appointed superintendent of Indian affairs. Persuades Iroquois to ally with England. Governor Robert Morris declares war on Delaware April 14. On September 8, John Armstrong burns down village at Kittanning. Delaware move to Shanango near [Sharon, PA].

1758   Treaty of Easton; Delaware disperse to Ontario, Wisconsin, and Kansas, with much hardship.

1758   English Colonel Forbes attacks French fort of Duquesne. French retreat, burn their own fort, can no longer protect Lenape. Lenape must make peace treaty with the English. Forbes begins work on Fort Pitt. Pittsburgh expands.

1760   First white settlers move into Minisink, NY, after untold centuries of Munsee control.

1763   Chief Teedyuskung burned to death in fire, probably arson. France loses Seven Years' War at Treaty of Paris, loses Louisiana to Spain and New France to England. King George III declares in proclamation that no Indians be displaced without crown consent, attempts to keep settlers east of the Continental Divide, and establish protected Indian country to the west.

1763–64   Pontiac's Rebellion against the British in the Great Lakes, inspired by the Delaware prophet, Neolin. Pontiac takes nine out of eleven British forts in the Great Lakes region easily.

1764   Ojibway lose western Niagara region by treaty.

1768   Lenape give up control of Susquehanna Valley.

1769   Founding of Dartmouth College in New Hampshire, encouraging Indian enrollment. Pontiac assassinated in Illinois.

1775   Continental Congress formulates Indian policy. Treaty of Pittsburgh; Delaware promise to remain neutral, Americans promise Ohio River as permanent western boundary of white settlement.

1776   Missionary David Zeisberger creates his famous Delaware spelling book. U.S. Declares independence from Britain.

1778   Treaty between U.S. and Delaware Indians, led by Chief White Eyes, the first U.S. and Indian treaty, offering the Delawares possible statehood. White Eyes is assassinated while serving with the patriots. Delaware discouraged that U.S. takes no action to prevent settlers from taking land west of the Ohio. Joseph Brant and British attack settlers in western New York.

1779   Generals Sullivan and Clinton, and Colonel Broadhead lay waste to most Indian towns in New York State, and break the power of the Iroquois League, in retaliation for Brant's move. This is considered George Washington's greatest offense against Natives; however it is not clear how many were killed.

1780   Ribbonwork style of dress becomes popular in Great Lakes region, spreads south and becomes popular with Lenape and other Natives.

1782   Massacre of pacifist Christian Lenape "praying Indians" at Gnadenhutten, Ohio.

1782–86   Some Lenape live in Clinton River area (with Chippewa, near Chippewa River south of Akron, Ohio), some move to Pilgerroh near Pittsburgh, then to Pettquotting, then in 1791, they move to Canada.

1783   Continental Congress issues proclamation warning against squatting on Indian lands. British defeated. Munsee try to return to Ohio, but are not welcome, and settle in Ontario at the suggestion of Chief Joseph Brant, Mohawk leader. Most settle on a six-mile-deep tract along the length of the Grand River. Other Munsee join the Cayuga on the Thames River in Ontario (Six Nations).

1784   Ojibway lose southern Ontario by treaty, piece by piece. First white settlement in Ohio: Marietta.

POST-REVOLUTIONARY PERIOD

1789   New U.S. Constitution goes into effect, George Washington elected,inaugerated in Manhattan. He lives at #1 Cherry Street, named after Munsee cherry orchard. Congress establishes a Dept. of War and grants Secretary of War authority over Indian affairs. Only government can negotiate with Indian tribes and foreign powers. Some Delaware move to Cape Girardeau, in south Missouri, at Spanish invitation.

1790   Algonquin cede Detroit area on Canadian side.

1791   St. Clair defeated with help from Buckongahela and 400 Delaware warriors.

1794   Battle of Fallen Timbers, ending Little Turtle's War 1790-94. Lenape sign treaty of Fallen Timbers. Lenape raids on Pennsylvania, Virginia, cease.

1795   Treaty of Greenville signed August 3, with 381 Delaware present; it acknowledges that the Delaware and their allies were "owners of most of present Ohio, Indiana, and Illinois." So many settlers move in illegally that Delaware join Piankashaw (Miami) at White River, Indiana, establish town of Muncie, Indiana.

1798	A few Delaware move back to Tuscarawas River area.
1799	Handsome Lake of the Seneca forms Longhouse Religion, not dissimilar to Big House ceremony practice of Lenape.
1800–21	First Delaware arrive in Wisconsin. Shawnee removed from northern Kentucky.
1801–02	With 63 Lenape left at Brotherton Reservation, they sell the land and join the Mohicans at New Stockbridge near Oneida Lake, NY May 10, 1802.
1807–15	Delaware from Missouri move to Texarkana area and stay until 1854.
1808	John Jacob Astor forms American Fur Company and trades with Natives extensively.
1809	Treaty of Fort Wayne. Future President Harrison obtains 2.5 million acres of Ohio and Indiana territory from Natives. Lenape still owed 1.2 million dollars for Western Ohio. Cherokee and Shawnee are owed a similar amount.
1811	Tecumseh's brother Tenskwatawa is defeated at Tippecanoe by Harrison. New Madrid earthquake follows shortly thereafter.
1812	Second war between British and U.S.
1813	Tecumseh, brigadier general for British, is killed in battle with Harrison. The eastern Algonquin resistance, led in part by Lenape chiefs, is broken. Future president Jackson defeats Creeks. Council fire at Brownstown, MI taken into hiding.
1818	Treaty of St. Mary, Ohio, August 3; Delaware, Munsee, plus remnant Mohican and Nanticoke forced to give U.S. occupancy rights to Indiana. Moved to southern Missouri on Mississippi River within three years.
1819	Great Kickapoo Resistance in Illinois to 1824.
1821	Thirteen hundred and forty-six Delaware of White River, Muncie, Indiana move across Mississippi to Cape Girardeau southern Missouri. Then move to the James Fork of the White River, southwestern Missouri. In 1830 they are moved again to a location near Leavenworth, Kansas.
1822	Forty Brotherton Delawares leave New Stockbridge and move to Green Bay, in Michigan territory, where they purchase land from Menominee. BIA (Bureau of Indian Affairs) is created, federally recognized in 1832.
1829	Indian Removal Act Treaty of 1829.
1830	Last Esopus Indian dies on Rondout Creek. Indiana Delaware moved from Missouri to Leavenworth, Kansas, where they stay until

	1868, becoming accomplished buffalo hunters and horsemen, skirmishing with Osage and Pawnee.
1831–39	Jackson removes Cherokee and "The Five Civilized Tribes" to Oklahoma. The Cherokee later "adopt" Absentee Delaware.
1831	Main body of Delaware moved to a new reservation on the north bank of the Kansas River, joined by some Delaware from Ohio (between Kansas City and Topeka).
1832	Brotherton group at Green Bay go bankrupt, so remaining monies are granted from New Jersey to help them. Final severance of ties between the Lenape and New Jersey.
1832	Black Hawk War in Illinois and Wisconsin.
1835	Main Delaware group joined by those removed to Missouri in 1789.
1837	Some Munsee move from Moraviantown and Muncey Town in Ontario to Kansas.
1854	Manypenny Treaty moves Texarkana Delaware on Red River to location near Dallas. More land ceded 1860, 1864. Stay till 1875.
1859	Government moves Delaware from Texas to Washita River area near Anadarko, OK.
1861	Anadarko Delaware forced to flee during Civil War. Return in 1874.
1865	U.S. gives Protestants contract to create Indian schools.
1866	July 4th, Delaware sign treaty to move to Oklahoma.
1867	Delaware sell land in Kansas, buy rights as members of Cherokee in Oklahoma. By this time there are only about 3,000 Delaware members. Each adult gets 160 acres at $1 per acre. 985 Delaware buy land along the Little Verdigris (or Caney) River in Washington County, northeast Oklahoma.
1868	14th Ammendment denies Indians the right to vote. Delaware of Leavenworth, Kansas, move to Dewey, Oklahoma, where they still reside.
1871	Congress passes law prohibiting treaties with Indians. General Sheridan issues orders forbidding western Indians (which now include some Lenape) to leave their reservations without permission. White hunters begin wholesale killing of buffalo.
1874	Four hundred and seventy-one of original 1491 return to Anadarko, now possessed by their old enemies, the Caddo. They are now called the Absentee Delaware, or Western Oklahoma Delaware.
1875	Delaware settled in Dallas are moved to Anadarko, Oklahoma, where they continue to live with Cherokee to this day.
1877	Nez Perce flee to Canada under Chief Joseph.

1879	Carlisle Indian School opens its doors in Pennsylvania.
1885	Last great herd of buffalo slaughtered.
1887	Jim Thorpe born in a log cabin in Prague, Oklahoma, near the town of Shawnee.
1890–1910	Lowest point of Indian population in North American history. According to some estimations, the reduction is forty to one, based on a 10 million population for 1500.
1907	Oklahoma Territory, including its Indian territories, becomes a state. Citizens try to have Indian lands placed on the open market and subjected to taxation.
1912	Jim Thorpe, a graduate of the Carlisle School near old Paxtang Delaware Village, participates in the Olympic games at Stockholm, Sweden, winning gold medals in the pentathalon and decathalon.
1913–19	Jim Thorpe plays four complete seasons with the New York Giants baseball team, while also playing with the New York Giants football team.
1917	Jim Thorpe's Giants play in World Series, but Thorpe has to play football that week. He takes the field for only one game.
1924	Big House ceremony discontinued.
1945	Big House ceremony revived temporarily in spring.
1951	Canadian Indian Act grants Munsee and other Indians the right to vote and makes them subject to the same laws as other Canadians. American Indian Movement founded in Minneapolis. Delaware treaty claims reach U.S. Supreme Court.
	The Nanticoke, close cousins of the Unami, entered New Jersey around the time of the Civil War, mostly into Salem and Cumberland counties to do sharecropping. Although their language is lost, they incorporate on August 7 as the Nanticoke-Lenni-Lenape Indians of New Jersey, and continue to have powwows in the area.
1980	On October 16, the New Jersey legislature recognizes the Powhatan-Renape Nation, who claim that their ancestors had come into the area after 1642.
1992	Columbus Day: "500th Anniversary Friendship Circle" at Otisville, NY. Many chiefs and elders speak, including Chief Redbone Van Dunk of the Ramapough Nation, who are kin to the Lenape.
1999	September 17, Munsee Chief Mark Peters gives talk at the Open Center in New York City. First oration in Manhattan by its indigenous leader in 250 years.

NOTES

INTRODUCTION

1. Sora, Steven. *The Lost Treasure of the Knights Templar: Solving the Oak Island Mystery.* (Rochester, VT: Inner Traditions International, Ltd.) As Sora writes, it is generally thought that a number of European fishing vessels explored the Atlantic coast without reporting or drafting maps, as they were not funded or equipped to do so.

2. Letter from Giovanni da Verrazzano to King Frances I, July 8, 1524. This letter is in the general collection of the Morgan Library in New York City. English translation by Susan Tarrow from Lawrence Wroth's *The Voyages of Giovanni da Verrazzano 1524–1528,* (New Haven, CT: Morgan Library/Yale University Press, 1970), p. 19.

3. Edwin G. Burrows and Mike Wallace, *Gotham: A History of New York City to 1898* (London, England: Oxford University Press, 1999), p. 6.

4. This information came from my conversations in July of 2000 with William Commanda, Algonquin Wisdom Keeper and Holder of the Seven Fires Wampum Belt, as well as from a display, *Beads, Bones, and Ancient Stones* (1999–2000) at the Abbey Museum in Bar Harbor, Maine. The exhibit included a skull from a Pilot whale, a small whale hunted between 3,000 and 500 years ago in what is now Maine. William Commanda explained that many whales were too big to be hauled in by canoe, but that the "bottlehead" whale, only seven to ten feet long, was an ideal catch for canoe-going Algonquin whalers. According to Raymundo Wesley Rodriquez, a Native marine biologist, the modern name of the bottlehead whale is "Baird's Beaked Whale," a cross between a beluga and a porpoise. It has pegged teeth, a bottlenose, and a bubble head, and is not aggressive. It was hunted nearly to extinction by white whalers in the 1800s. (Per telephone conversation, October 2001.)

5. Richard Adams, *Legends of the Lenape—Legends of the Delaware Indians and Picture Writing,* (Washington, DC, 1905, reprinted Syracuse: Syracuse University Press, 1997. Edited with an introduction by Deborah Nichols with translations by Nora Thompson Dean and Lucy Parks Blalock, comments and transcriptions by James Rementer). See also Alanson Skinner, *Indians of Manhattan Island and Vicinity* (1913; reprint, Port Washington, NY: Ira J. Friedman, 1968).

6. Reginald Pelham Bolton's maps from *Indian Trails in the Great Metropolis*, map viii. Item 1. (New York: Heye Museum Indian Notes and Monographs.) Available at the Heye Museum Research Room. Smithsonian, National Museum of the American Indian (NMAI), New York, NY. Also Arthur C. Parker, *Archaeological History of New York* (Albany, NY: State Museum Bulletin, nos. 237-238, September, October, 1920, bound book), p. 627 and plate 192.

7. This information came from displays at the Mashantucket Pequot Museum and Research Center, Pequot War Gallery permanent exhibit and film, "The Witness," in the same gallery, Mashantucket, CT.

8. Dean Snow, *The Archaeology of New England* (New York: Academic Press, 1980).

9. Burrows and Wallace, *Gotham*, p. 5.

10. For examples, see the books of Laurence Hauptman, Ray Fadden, and Paul Wallace in bibliography listings.

11. To their credit, the Peabody is repatriating all or most of these skeletons under the guidelines of the Native American Grave and Pottery Repatriation Act (NAGPRA) and the enlightened leadership of Dr. Dean Snow and others.

12. The term *Lenape* has been translated in many different ways, but no one, to my knowledge, has suggested the obvious: *len*, "human," plus *nape*, "that water there"—in other words, "We are the people of that water there."

13. Anthropologists often use the spelling "Mahican" to refer to this group, but the legal incorporated name of this group in the United States is Mohican. Therefore, I will use this spelling except when quoting other texts.

14. James D. Folts, "Westward Migration of the Munsee Indians in the Eighteenth Century" (lecture given at the Mohican Conference, Albany, NY, March 10, 2001).

15. There is an entire genre of stories among the Munsee on the theme of starvation. One story tells of two men gambling over whose horse would be eaten, and then which of the men would eat the other man. John Bierhorst, in his *Mythology of the Lenape: Guide and Texts* (Tucson, AZ: Arizona University Press, 1995), mentions four such stories of famine. There are many more in John Bierhorst, *The White Deer and Other Stories Told by the Lenape* (New York: William Morrow and Co., 1995).

16. Gregg Cantrell, *Stephen F. Austin: Empresario of Texas* (New Haven, CT: Yale University Press, 1999).

17. In order of significance: (my analysis) New York, New Jersey, Pennsylvania, Connecticut, Maryland, Delaware, Ohio, Indiana, Illinois, Michigan, Wisconsin, Texas, Kansas, Oklahoma, Massachusetts, Wyoming, Kentucky, Arkansas, Missouri, West Virginia, Idaho, California, Colorado, Vermont, Utah, and possibly Nebraska, a total of twenty-six states. In 1977 there were 119 enrolled Delaware living in Washington State, 13 in Virginia, 25 in Nevada, 32 in Louisiana, and less in the remaining twenty-two states.

18. Walter Prescott Webb, *The Texas Rangers: A Century of Frontier Defense* (Austin, TX: University of Texas Press, 1965), pp. 21, 30. Originally published under the title, *The Story of The Texas Rangers: A Century of Frontier Defense;* (New York: Grosset and Dunlap, 1957).

19. Burton J. Hendrick, *Statesmen for a Lost Cause; Jefferson Davis and His Cabinet* (Boston: Little, Brown, and Co., 1939).

Chapter 1: The Naming of Things

1. Nora Thompson Dean. Her definition of the word Lenape appears in many texts. My primary reference for this usage, including "men and women," comes from Herbert. C. Kraft, ed., *The Lenape Indian: A Symposium* (South Orange, NJ: Archaeological Research Center/Seton Hall University, 1984, Publication no. 7) where he quotes Dean on pages 1, 63.

2. Charles A. Weslager, *The Delaware Indians: A History* (New Brunswick, NJ: Rutgers University Press, 1972), p. 234. See also *King of the Delawares: Teedyuscung, 1700-1763,* by Anthony F. C. Wallace (Philadelphia: University of Pennsylvania Press, 1949).

3. *Webster's New World Dictionary,* 2nd College Ed. (New York: Simon & Schuster, 1982) s.v. "title."

4. I will be using what I call Standard Phonetic Algonquin spelling throughout the text (except where the word has become part of the geographic or conversational lexicon). This spelling is explained in Appendix I, Munsee Vocabulary. Hyphenation is used where it will assist the reader in breaking up syllables and letter groups correctly.

5. According to Joseph Campbell in *The Masks of God: Creative Mythology* (New York: Viking Penguin, 1968), the wound is always in the thigh. For example, Tristan, Odysseus, and Wotan were all wounded in the thigh; pp. 123–128 go into remarkable detail.

6. According to *Webster's New World Dictionary*, the Walloons were a Protestant Celtic people from Belgium and parts of France. They spoke a Romany dialect of French. They were not ethnically "Dutch" at all.

7. According to *Webster's New World Dictionary*, the word *Walloon* comes from the Old High German *Wahl*, or Walah, per Mirriam-Webster's 10th Ed., "foreigner."

8. The term used by the people of Japan is Nippon. *Japan* is not a Japanese word but a Mongol one.

9. Given the soft *k* in Lenape, which sounds like a *g*, and the soft *r* in the old Hudson Valley accent of Dutchess County (now only found in the northern half of the county), Wapp-ing-ers isn't so far off. Unfortunately most people in the town of Wappingers Falls pronounce it "Wapp-in-jer Fawlz," and then spell it with an apostrophe *s* ('s), which they fail to pronounce. The apostrophe is incorrect. The solution is to pronounce it "Wappinge(r)s Falls—with a silent *r* and a hard *g*.

10. Chief Mark Peters, "A History of the Munsee Delaware," 2000, p. 16. This booklet will soon be available to researchers at the Munsee Delaware Nation Office in Muncey, Ontario, Canada.

11. Iatwenta was Onondaga by birth but was adopted into the Mohawk Nation, as was the Peacemaker.

12. The old maps say Sansquehanna or Sasquesahanoug, "the people of the place where water crosses the plain." This information is from John Ogilby's self-published "America," published in London in 1671.

13. Conversation with Dr. Dorothy Miller, a Cherokee, Friday, April 13, 2001.

14. This information was gathered from the State of Wyoming Web site http://www.state.wy.us, and email correspondence on January 16, 2001, with K. Murphy, librarian at Wyoming State Library, quoting from Wyoming History Blue Books (Cheyenne, Wyoming, Wyoming State Archives, Dept. of State Parks and Cultural Resources, Barrett Bldg.), pp. 1163-1170.

15. Delaware was named after an English baron, Wyoming is one of the few states the Lenape never lived in, and Indiana derives its name from the mistaken idea that the Lenape were people of India.

16. *Min* is berry. *Etche* is sandy, related to *Rechkawik*, "sandy place" in Renneiu dialects, which became Rockaway. In Unami the same word is *Letchewik*. *Rechewanis* is another word for the Manhattan tribe.

17. *Massa-pe-qua* means "big-water-shallow" in the Renneiu language. The *at* or *ut* syllable means "at" as in English. The suffix *anoag* means "the people." Therefore it is clear that "people at the shallow water" is accurate.

Chapter 2: How Green Was Manhattan

1. From a permanent display outside, near the Bowling Green park at the Smithsonian, National Museum of the Native American, Heye Foundation, New York, NY.

2. According to Carla Messinger, the director of the Museum of Indian Culture in Allentown, Pennsylvania, the people of the Delaware Confederacy—the Munsee, Unami, and Unalatchtigo—lived in harmony with nature along the Delaware and Hudson Rivers. They were hunters and gatherers, and then for one thousand years before European settlers arrived, they farmed the regions east of the Appalachians in what is now New Jersey, Pennsylvania, parts of New York, and Delaware. The sparks from their council fires lit the fires of the Mohican, Piscataway, Nanticoke, and Powhatan nations as well. All of them are children of "the grandfather" Lenape. According to most Lenape I've asked, this term "grandfather" means that they were peacemakers, the wise ones, and not that they had the oldest origins. Some, however, such as Darryl Stonefish and Ojibway teacher Eddie Benton-Banaise, hold that it does mean the oldest.

3. Edwin G. Burrows and Mike Wallace, *Gotham: A History of New York City to 1898* (London: Oxford University Press, 1999), p. 3.

4. *Webster's New World Dictionary,* 2nd ed., s.v. "blunderbuss."

5. Burrows and Wallace, *Gotham,* pp. 3–4.

6. Floyd M. Shumway, *Seaport City: New York in 1775* (New York: South Street Seaport Museum, 1975), p. 11.

7. Ric Burns and James Sanders, eds., *New York, an Illustrated History* (New York: Random House, 1999), p. 9, quoting Johannes de Laet, a company official of the Dutch East India Company, from his report to Amsterdam, circa 1626.

8. Burns and Sanders, *New York, An Illustrated History,* p. 14.

9. Burrows and Wallace, *Gotham,* p. 4.

10. The New York Aquarium in Brooklyn, New York, has at various times been home for gigantic lobsters, turtles, and other marine life indigenous to the area. Their staff marine biologists stated that the reports of the six-foot-long lobsters were most likely accurate. They housed a lobster until recently that was four feet six inches long and almost one hundred years old.

11. Gladys Tantaquidgeon, *Folk Medicine of the Delaware and Related Algonquin Indians* (Harrisburg, PA: Pennsylvania Historical and Museum Commission, 1972). The whippoorwill was an important part of Delaware folklore. It was said that when the whippoorwill sings in the evening, it is time for children to go to bed, (p. 89) and that the first cry of the whippoorwill in spring marks the time to plant corn (p. 101).

12. Mike Bastine, Algonquin elder, from conversation at Maniwaki, Quebec, Canada, August 1, 1999.

13. Burrows and Wallace, *Gotham,* p. 4.

14. Letter from Giovanni da Verrazzano to King Francis I, dated July 8, 1524. This letter is in the general collection at the Morgan Library, New York, New York.

15. From the writings by Judith Aldofer Abbott, a Lenape woman of the Esopus River valley, read from untitled ms. at Alf Evers's home on May 8, 2001.

16. *They Lied to You in School* (documentary film). Ray Fadden, writer and narrator, produced by Nathan Konig (Woodstock, NY: White Buffalo Productions, 1999).

17. *Owasco* is an archaeological term linked to both the early Minisink culture of the Munsee, and the Mohawk. Little is known of their origins, and nothing of their language. The notes in the transcript of Edward V. Curtin's lecture at the Mohican Seminar at New York State Archives in Albany, March of 2000, discussed this problem (p. 12, note 2 of transcript, "The Ancient Mohicans in Time, Space and Prehistory"). Curtin is an archaeological consultant in Saratoga Springs, NY.

18. European population figures are based on B. Leonard W. Cowie, *Seventeenth Century Europe* (New York: Ungar, 1964).

19. Dr. Laurence Hauptman, "The Lenape of the Hudson Valley," lecture, Marist College, Goletti Theater, December 1999.

20. In an e-mail to me on June 5, 2001, Dr. Snow indicated the number 5,300 for the Mohican, however this seems to be a post-decimation number.

21. Shumway, *Seaport City*, p. 17.

22. Ibid., p. 20, caption.

23. Ibid., p. 21. It was in fact called "Breedewegh."

24. Elizabeth Chilton, (slide presentation given at Mohican Seminar 2001, State Archives, Albany, NY, March 10, 2001.)

Chapter 3: A Paradise for the Living

1.John Heckewelder, *An Account of the History, Manners, and Customs of the Indian Nations,* (Philadelphia: 1819; new and revised, 1881). Weslager quotes from this work in *The Delaware Indians: A History* (New Brunswick, NJ: Rutgers University Press, 1972) and Kraft provides a similar quote from Heckewelder's *Account,* p. 154–157 on pp. 128–9 of his book, *The Lenape: Archaeology, History, and Ethnography* (Newark, NJ: New Jersey Historical Society, 1986. Collections of the New Jersey Historical Society, Volume 21).

2. Kraft, *The Lenape,* p. 227, quoting William Penn's letter to the Committee of the Free Society of Traders, 1683, from Albert Cook Meyers, ed., *William Penn's Own Account of the Lenni Lenape or Delaware Indians* (Somerset, NJ: Middle Atlantic Press, 1970), p 233.

3. Weslager, *The Delaware Indians,* p. 158.

4. Robert S. Grumet, *The Lenapes* (Indians of North America Series, Frank W. Porter, ed., New York: Chelsea House Publishers, 1989), p. 13, quoting a Dutch observer in 1655.

5. Weslager, *The Delaware Indians,* p. 166.

6. Ibid., p. 166.

7. Alanson Skinner, *Indians of Manhattan Island and Vicinity* (Port Washington, NY: I. J. Friedman, 1961).

8. Description recorded by The Netherlands Office, as quoted in Alanson Skinner, *The Indians of Greater New York,* American Museum of Natural History (Cedar Rapids, IA: Torch Press, 1915, reprinted 1925).

9. Alanson Skinner, *Indians of Greater New York.*

10. Alanson Skinner, *Indians of Manhattan Island and Vicinity.*

11. James Folts, *The Westward Migration of the Munsee Indians in the Eighteenth Century* (Albany, NY: New York State Archives, lecture, March 10, 2001), pp. 16–17.

12. This information is from a telephone conversation with John Bierhorst in August 2001 on the geography of story.

13. All four of these tales are referred to in John Bierhorst, *Mythology of the Lenape: Guide and Texts,* (Tucson, AZ: Arizona University Press, 1995), pp. 28–29.

14. These stories are from the Pequot Village diorama, a permanent exhibit at the Mashantucket Pequot Museum and Research Center at Mashantucket, CT.

15. Dr. Larsen offered no translation of "Sushumna." It refers to one of the seven solar rays in Sankrit. Also, more relevant to the story, it is the name of the spinal nerve that connects the heart and the crown of the head in kundalini yoga. This would identify the Empire State Building as the backbone of New York City. See Stephen Larsen, *The Mythic Imagination* (New York: Bantam, 1990), p. 132.

16. Larsen, *Mythic Imagination,* p. 208

17. Larsen has observed over the years that clients with even one-sixteenth of "native blood" tend to have distinctly different experiences than most others. He feels that bit of ancestry "draws shamanic experiences" to them. On several occasions, after noting a particular dream configuration he's come to know, he's asked clients with no visible ethnicity, "Do you have any Native American ancestry?" The answer has always been yes. He wonders if that blood or DNA leaves some inner doorway open to the shamanic in a unique way. See Larsen, *Mythic Imagination.* My observation is that it is a two-way street: at least some of those persons' ancestors are Native American, and the belief system of those ancestors compels them to reach out and help those in their lineage.

18. Stephen and Robin Larsen, in *The Fashioning of Angels: Partnership as Spiritual Practice* (West Chester, PA: Chrysalis Books, Swedenborg Foundation Publishers), pp. 90–91, describes at length how a Lenape spirit guide helped a young woman through a nervous breakdown. He also described to me in a conversation in August of 2001 an incident where a group of Aboriginal Australian dancers performing in the Shawangunks region were visited by a Lenape "bloke," in spirit form, who was seen by all the dancers and who entered into the choreography with them.

Chapter 4: A Walk around Old Manhattan

1. Sheridan Square was named after General Philip Henry Sheridan (1831–88), celebrated for killing Native Americans in the frontier Indian wars.

2. The rest of Manhattan is excluded. That front gate, with its cold black ironwork, is, as you might imagine, square.

3. Information from "The Deal of the Millennium," a display in 2000 at the New-York Historical Society, New York, NY.

4. This Lenape expression, "share the pot," is still used today.

5. This story shows up from time to time, but it is not considered any less questionable than the $24 deal.

6. There are at least two types of wildcats in the lower New York region, the bobcat, related to the lynx, and the cougar. There was also a red wolf that was indigenous to the area, which is now extinct.

7. Reginald Pelham Bolton's map viii, item 113, from *Indian Trails in the Great Metropolis* (maps on file at the Heye Museum Research Room) shows the spelling as Paggank, whereas in *New York City in Indian Possession* by the same author, the name of the island is Paggunk. Reginald Pelham Bolton, *Indian Trails in the Great Metropolis* (New York: New-York Historical

Society); *New York City in Indian Possession* (1920, Indian Notes and Monographs, Vol. 2 no. 7; reprinted, New York: Museum of the American Indian / Heye Foundation, 1975).

8. Howard B. Furer, editor and compiler, *New York: A Chronological and Documentary History, 1524–1970* (Dobbs Ferry, NY: Oceana Publications, 1974).

9. Sanna Feirstein, *Naming New York: Manhattan Places and How They Got Their Names* (New York: New York University Press, 2001), p. 29.

10. From information displays at the site of Fraunce's Tavern, Pearl and Broad Streets, New York, NY, 2001.

11. Feirstein, *Naming New York*, p. 25.

12. The shade was provided by a now-legendary buttonwood tree, which Lenape traders had apparently gathered under for years. Many Wall Street firms proudly trace their origins back to the Dutchmen who continued to exchange stock under its branches after the Lenape left.

13. Based on the standard design of an Algonquin village, the site chosen by Washington for the presidential mansion may well have been not only the former site of a Kapsee chief's house, but the site of a council fire and a council elm as well. (See Introduction, note 6.)

14. Cornel Adam Lengyel, *Presidents of the United States*, (New York: Bantam/Golden Books, 1964), etching p.13. Compare with inside front cover photograph of White House.

15. Herbert C. Kraft, *The Lenape: Archaeology, History, and Ethnography,* also David de Vries, *New Netherlands Journal* (New-York Historical Society Collections, 1857-58), series 2, p. 89.

16. The early Dutch settlers understood *Werpoes* to mean "by the thicket." However, in the Renneiu language, *wer* generally means "good, beautiful and *po* refers to a "field" or "plain." Iron Thunderhorse, *A Complete Language Guide and Primer to the Wampano/ Quinnipiac R Dialect of Southwestern New England* (Milltown, IN: Algonquin Confederacy of the Quinnipiac Tribal Council/Algonquin Confederacies' Language Institute ACQTC/ACLI, 2000), pp. 34, 76.

17. Floyd M. Shumway notes the evolution from Alehouse to State House in his book, *Seaport City: New York in 1775* (New York: South Street Seaport Museum, 1975), p. 17.

18. Feirstein, *Naming New York*, p. 35.

19. Bolton's maps from *Indian Trails in the Great Metropolis* show this as Sapohannikan territory and Nora Thompson Dean, a Unami Delaware speaker, recognizes the place-names associated with the Sapohannikan as Unami; in Herbert C. and John T. Kraft's *The Indians of Lenapehoking* (South Orange, NJ: Seton Hall University Museum, 1985), inside back cover.

20. The use of this name Lapinikan is noted by *Benton's New York*. Lapinikan is very close to *Lapexican,* the word for "plough" in David Zeisberger's *Essay of a Delaware-Indian and English Spelling Book* (Philadelphia: Henry Miller, 1776; reprint, Ohio Historical Society, 1991).

21. Feirstein, *Naming New York*, p. 84

22. Ibid. Minetta Street and Lane follow the Dutch spelling, which means "little one." The name of Manetta in Munsee may derive from Mun-ih-toh, or Spirit. It is some kind of spirit, though not a good one.

23. It is commonly believed that there was tobacco on the back of the dollar bill at one time.

24. See Alanson "Buck" Skinner, *Indians of Greater New York* (Cedar Rapids, IA: Torch Press, 1915, reprinted New York: Museum of Natural History, 1925), for Nanabush and Manetta. In his version of the story, Nanabush creates a turtle that kills the great snake, Manetta (Lenape); Eddie Benton-Banaise, *The Mishomis Book: The Voice of the Ojibway* (Hayward, WI: Indian

Country Communications, 1988) (Ojibway); Evan T. Pritchard, *No Word for Time* (San Francisco: Council Oak Books, 1997, reprinted, 2001), p. 191 (Micmac); Joseph Bruchac, *Gluskabe and the Four Wishes* (New York: Cobblehill Books, 1988); *Gluskabe Stories* (Cambridge, MA: Yellow Moon, 1990); and *The Wind Eagle and Other Abenaki Stories,* (Greenfield Center, NY: Good Mind Records, Greenfield Press, CD and book, 2001) (Abenaki); Stephen Larsen, *The Mythic Imagination,* (New York: Bantam, 1990), p. 207 (Innu/Naskapi).

25. This firsthand account provided in March 1999 conversation with former Village tenement dweller Janet Jappen, who lived near Minetta Lane in 1969.

26. Archaeological evidence is not available, so I have used logic to determine the location of the gathering spot. The Sapohannikan Trail was an important one; it was used to haul water to what is now Fourteenth Street. The watering place where two villages interacted would have been a significant gathering spot. In Burns and Sanders, *New York, an Illustrated History* (p. 9), we find the statement, "To facilitate fur trading with [the Lenape], the Dutch colonists soon widened an ancient hunting trail that ran north from the fort, calling it Heere Straat and later Breede Wegh. It would become Broadway."

27. The Shepmoes were a group of Canarsie people; the name we know them by is a late feature, probably from the name of a Dutch farmer. Their original name has been lost.

28. Feirstein, *Naming New York,* p. 90.

29. A woman named Sevestet opened The Village Tannery in 1974 and her shop is still going strong in 2002. She is the last leatherworker in Manhattan still working from scratch. She cuts all the leather herself from whole tanned sides (made from half of the animal); however, no brain tanning is allowed in New York City; her tanning is done in Gloversville, Orange County, New York.

30. The debate as to whether the Manhattan people were really Munsee speakers or not is unresolved. It is recognized that they were people of Munsee origin, and they probably adopted the Renneiu language at a late date.

31. The American Indian Community House includes an art gallery with new exhibits by Native artists each month, a modest book and magazine selection, plus a number of offices that provide a variety of community services for Native Americans. The organization publishes the *AICH Newsletter.*

32. According to archaeological maps created around 1911 for *Indian Trails in the Great Metropolis* by R. P. Bolton (map viii, item 99) there was what might be considered a prehistoric traffic island at this spot, possibly created to make space for a large tree, such as a council elm, or for other aesthetic reasons.

33. In 1858 Lincoln had engaged in eight debates over slavery with Stephen A. Douglas. These brought him some national recognition, but he had won only one election in his entire career other than for state assembly. The Cooper Union Address made him an overnight sensation.

34. President Buchanan, refusing to take sides, was waffling on the issue of slavery and the Constitution.

35. An anonymous eyewitness, whose words are recorded in "The Speeches of Abraham Lincoln" (available at Lincoln Online http://showcase.netins.net/web/creative/lincoln/speeches/cooper.htm, said, "His face lighted up as with an inward fire, the whole man was transfigured. . . .[F]orgetting myself, I was on my feet like the rest, yelling like a wild Indian, cheering this wonderful man."

36. Mount Sinai's doctors are pioneers in utilizing the "Bedscape" concept of simulating a natural environment for the quicker healing of the patient. This is similar to the healing lodge concept of the Algonquin, which used real landscapes.

37. The high, tawny cliffs that grace the New Jersey shores of the Hudson River on its western bank, down to Fort Lee, New Jersey, are called "The Palisades."

38. Near this site today is the Dykman Farm Historic Site, open to visitors.

Chapter 5: Exploring the Ancient City

1. This translation comes from Reginald Pelham Bolton, in reference to a shell midden at the Cold Spring rock shelter. Some translate Shorakapkok as "a cover," from a Mohican word.

2. Sanna Feirstein, *Naming New York: Manhattan Places and How They Got Their Names* (New York: New York University Press, 2001), p. 178. Bolton, Feirstein, and others spell Rechgawawanc with a *c*, but I use a *k* to make it consistent with other spellings in this book. In *New York City in Indian Possession* (p. 11), Bolton implies that Harlem was a central location of the Rechgawawanc, and that this group constituted the real "Manhattan" Indians. The spelling varies from one location to another according to dialect. B. A. Botkin tells several interesting tales about how Spuyten Duyvil got its colorful name in *New York City Folklore* (New York: Random House, 1956), p. 20-22. The most likely explanation given is that before it was widened into a canal, the waves rushing into the Muscoota River from the Hudson River crashed against the downstream current, creating an occasional spout of water.

3. Robert Steven Grumet, *Place Names of New York City* (New York: Museum of the City of New York, produced by Center for Cultural Resources, 1981).

4. Ibid.

5. This is a Unami translation based on David Zeisberger, *Essay of a Delaware-Indian and English Spelling Book* (Philadelphia: Henry Miller, 1776. Reprint, Ohio Historical Society, 1991), pp. 9, 24.

6. Ibid. *Mosch* means "clear"; *moschachgayoo* means "it is ground that is clear of trees" (p. 48) plus *loosasoo,* "it is burnt," (p. 20).

7. Ibid. *Auchsu* means "in the wild" (p. 15) and *wiki* is translated as "home" or "where you live." (p. 12).

8. The Cock's Tavern was apparently a nickname, according to *Old Homesteads and Historic Buildings, Genealogy and Family Lore,* by Daughters of the American Revolution, NY, Manhattan Chapter, (Parsons, KS: The Commercial Publishers Co., 1930). The reference to James Fenimore Cooper was without other explanation. The site is at 230th and Broadway.

9. This information comes from Bolton's maps for *Indian Trails in the Great Metropolis,* available at the Smithsonian/National Museum of the American Indian, Heye Foundation Research room, and from Grumet's *Place Names of New York City.*

10. Grumet, *Place Names of New York City.*

11. Ibid. I interpolated "open" to make the meaning clearer.

12. Reconstructing precontact history through linguistic and archaeological models, it seems evident that the Lenape of 1300 C.E. had contact with ocean-going traders and whalers from the south. The warm trade winds, which form a great clockwise circle in the north Atlantic, take vessels from balmy locations like Trinidad and Puerto Rico and carry them northward along the coast, making contact with land at Cape Hatteras, North Carolina; Montauk Point on Long

Island; and Peggy's Cove in Nova Scotia. It is the southernmost two of these points where we find the introduction of the letter *r* into the Algonquin languages.

This letter "r" seems to have originated in the sacred Nahautl language of the Inca of Peru. *Interami* is an ancient Incan term for the ceremony of the sun, while Rumenyawi is the name of a great leader among the Incan-related peoples of Ecuador. As Thor Heyerdahl proved in *Kon Tiki,* the Peruvians have had the means for long-distance ocean travel for some thousands of years. In 1995, traces of coca and nicotine, both products of Peru, were found in Egyptian mummies thousands of years old.

By tracing the letter *r,* we can see that at some point—some would say after the destruction of the city of Tiuhtihuanaco, which fell into Lake Titicaca when an underground fissure split, opening up a large aquifer—thousands fled northward, sailed down the Oronoco River, and found themselves in Trinidad, which still possesses remnants of a high culture from seven thousand years ago. From there, the *r* spread through the islands, particularly the Island of Mona off the coast of present-day Puerto Rico. A branch of Cherokee oral tradition, another *r* bearing culture, holds that the Island of Mona was once the home of the Cherokee ancestors.

Once these highly advanced travelers found the trade winds, it is reasonable to assume they headed northward to see what they could find. Variations on what I call the Renneiu language, all with the *r* letter and all with anomalous words not typical of Algonquin, appear in these coastal trading areas. Clason Point is one of those areas, as are Manhattan and the five boroughs.

What is interesting about Clason Point is that it was there that a new type of projectile and material culture, now bearing the name "Clason Point," was first identified. A projectile, forming a one-inch triangle of stone that was attached to the end of an arrow shaft, was carbon-dated to around 1300 C.E. (After contact, these same people made triangular points out of copper.) The one-inch triangle was a very important shape in Taino "Cemi" (spiritual) ritual at that time, and often was used—as a hooking device, as part of a strap, or at the end of a launcher, and in the design of the atlatl, a spear-throwing device. [A "hand-held forked throwing cradle;" Norman Bohan, Edith Smith, contributors to Town of Esopus Bicentennial Committee's *The Town of Esopus Story: 3000 B.C. – 1978 A.D.* (Esopus, New York: Hillcrest Press, 1979) p. 19.] The design evokes the shape of a volcanic mountain, which in turn represents the journey of life. The foot of the mountain—the edge of the arrowhead—represents the first stage in life where we crawl very low to the ground. The peak of the triangle represents the top of the mountain, the age where we stand up tall and straight and accomplish great things. The opposite edge represents the end of the journey where we stoop more and more, and slow down until we find ourselves one with the earth. (This interpretation of the triangle's significance in Taino culture is by Roberto Borrero, Taino leader and director of Native Programming at the American Museum of Natural History, New York, NY.)

What is so startling is the almost exact coincidence between the geographical region encompassed by Clason Point culture archaeologically and that of the Renneiu language at time of contact. According to Algonquin/Taino Raymundo Wesley Rodriguez, there was a Taino chief named Keibiaga who left the village later to be called Arecibo (which still exists in Puerto Rico) around the year 1300 C.E., bringing with him many men. He headed north on the trade winds, never to return. If there is truth to this story, which Rodriguez claims is part of ancient oral tradition, it would seem that the Taino were the ones who settled in and around Manhattan, bringing new elements of culture to the Algonquin.

Unfortunately the languages of both the Taino and the Renneiu speakers were quickly scattered at the time of contact and are only now in the process of being resurrected. The number of possible cognates between the two are many, but I have yet to find any identical matches that can be verified at this time.

13. Grumet, *Place Names of New York City.*

14. The widespread form of contact-period Algonquin speech which I refer to as Renneiu, "they are the people," has long been referred to by one of its main languages, the Quiripi, of southwest Connecticut, a term which Iron Thunderhorse defines as "in the main river." He defines *sewan* as "clam and oyster shells" and *siwanoy* as "wampum-makers," on p. 87 of *A Complete Language Guide and Primer to the Wampano/Quinnipiac R Dialect of Southwestern New England* (Milltown, IN: Algonquin Confederacy of the Quinnipiac Tribal Council/Algonquin Confederacies' Language Institute ACQTC/ACLI, 2000).

15. According to Raymond Ballinger, author and descendant of the Ballingers who first settled New Jersey, such stones were used as boundary markers by the Lenape, often depicting foxes, wolves, turtles, raccoons, and snakes with considerable skill. The Unami ("Turtle Clan") presence receded after 1300 C.E.

16. Bolton avoids translating the term Canarsie in his book *New York City in Indian Possession,* whereas Iron Thunderhorse, in *A Complete Language Guide and Primer to the Wampano/Quinnipiac R Dialect,* translates it as "in the main river."

17. Reginald Pelham Bolton, *New York City in Indian Possession* (1920; reprint, New York: Museum of the American Indian/Heye Foundation, 1975), p. 89. The gorget is now at the Smithsonian National Museum of the American Indian, Heye Foundation, New York, NY.

18. Alanson Skinner, *Indians of Greater New York* (Cedar Rapis, IA: Torch Press, 1915, reprinted New York: Museum of Natural History, 1925).

19. Bolton, *New York City in Indian Possession,* map insert at back cover, also map for *Indian Trails of the Great Metropolis* (New York: New-York Historical Society).

20. Arthur G. Adams, *The Hudson through the Years* (Westwood, NJ: Lind Publications, 1983), p. 1.

21. It was the second "First Dutch Reformed Church." The first was at New Amsterdam.

22. To get an idea of how crowded Brooklyn is now, consider its population. At 2,266,300, it is larger than the thirty-fourth most populous state, Utah, at 2,071,500. Utah's population is spread out over 82,168 square miles, whereas Brooklyn is a tilted eight-mile by eight-mile square, approximately sixty-four square miles. Chicago's population is now larger—at 2,746,200—but at one time Brooklyn claimed the title of America's largest city. *Rand McNally Road Atlas 2000* (Skokie, IL: Rand McNally, 2000).

23. "Massebackhun," according to Grumet. See Grumet, *Place Names of New York City.*

24. Ibid.

25. Ibid.

26. Many links between an original Native term and the Dutch-derived name Coney Island have been proposed: Maxono Island, in reference to a Canarsie Bear Clan (or Band) is suggested by B. A. Botkin's *New York City Folklore.* (New York: Random House, 1956), p. 28, which describes how the Dutch sold the area now known as Gravesend to Lady Moody, who was worried about this "Bear Band" (Konoh) of Canarsie Indians roaming wild: "They told her, 'We call it Konijn Hok, the Rabbit's hutch, or breeding place,'....punning on the fact that genuine rabbits—or coneys—shared the beach with the Indians." This is an example of what I call "double Dutch." Coneh-ho Island, from a Mezzo-American/Aztec word for "rabbit." (The Spanish word for rabbit is "conejo" (pronounced cone-**nay**-ho).

27. Grumet, *Place Names of New York City.*

28. Ibid., although I have often heard "broken-up ground," a variation on Mannahatting.

29. It is generally supposed that *Yau-may-ko,* "Place of the Beaver," (Bolton spells it *yemacah* on p. 47 of *New York City in Indian Possession*), became Jamaica because of confusion with the Dutch use of the letter "j" for the "y" sound. However, given the preponderance of Caribbean sounds in the dialects of Queens, it may have been named after the Islands of Jamaica in Hispaniola, either by Native American slaves who returned to their homeland after serving in the islands, or by Taino and Carib explorers who headed north on the trade winds long before Christopher Columbus. The Taino territory Jumacao is as likely a link as Jamaica itself.

30. Information on the Astoria area trails is taken mostly from Bolton's maps for *Indian Trails in the Great Metropolis,* although others have been consulted.

31. Grumet, *Place Names of New York City;* also *Jackson Heights: From Ice Age to Space Age: A History for Children* (Queens, NY: Jackson Heights Beautification Group, 1999). Maspeth's water was presumably "bad" because it was salty, like the East River, at least halfway inland.

32. There were thirty Lenape families living at Flushing in 1650. Bolton, *New York City in Indian Possession,* p. 54; also *Jackson Heights: From Ice Age to Space Age: A History for Children.*

33. *Jackson Heights.*

34. My translation is based on several words in Zeisberger's Unami text. *Metch* is "great" and *kenta* is from *kentacoy,* or "ceremonial gathering," and *woom* is from "woo-lay" or beautiful.

35. This translation is by Bolton. See *New York City in Indian Possession,* p. 50. He calls it *Shawcopshee.*

36. Alanson Skinner, notes from excavation and photographs. From the Lenape Indians display of 2000, at the Staten Island Institute of the Arts, Wall Street, St. George, Staten Island, New York.

37. This information is from Bolton's maps and others. See *New York City in Indian Possession,* map insert.

Chapter 6: Verrazzano and His Legacy

1. In a lecture at Marist College in December 2000, "Lenape of the Hudson Valley," Dr. Laurence Hauptman stated that there were fourteen epidemics between 1640 and 1680 alone. Herbert C. Kraft writes that the lethal pathogens—against which the Indians had no resistance—introduced by *The Dauphine* and subsequent sailing ships to this "utopia" included smallpox, measles, bubonic plague, cholera, typhus, pleurisy, scarlet fever, diphtheria, mumps, whooping cough, cold, venereal diseases (syphilis, gonorrhea, and chancroid), pneumonia, and some unusual influenza and respiratory diseases. See Kraft, quoting Henry Dobyns, *Their Numbers Become Thinned* (Knoxville, TN: University of Tennessee Press, 1983) and Russell Thornton, *American Indian Holocaust and Survival: A Population History Since 1492* (Norman, OK: University of Oklahoma Press, 1987) and Kraft, *The Dutch, the Indians, and the Quest for Copper: Pahaquarry and the Old Mine Road* (South Orange, NJ: Seton Hall University Museum, 1996), pp. 2, 4.

2. Stephen R. Bown, *All Is Not Gold That Gliseneth, Frobisher's Fool's Errand to the Arctic* (Eugene, OR: Mercator's World, 1999) www.mercatormag.com/301_glitter.html.

3. Steven Sora, in his book, *The Lost Treasure of the Knights Templar: Solving the Oak Island Mystery* (Rochester, VT: Inner Traditions, 1999), p. 48, states that Orkney Island fishermen reached the Maritimes of Eastern Canada in 1371, and that Basque whalers had been exploring the north Atlantic coast since 1450.

4. In my book *No Word for Time* (San Francisco: Council Oak Books, 1997, reprinted, 2001), I mention that the Noose are now called the Coharie. The Coharie were finally recognized for the first time by the state of North Carolina in 1971, and they now have four communities.

5. Also called the Pintouac, the Pomeetuoc people helped the Jamestown Colony survive, then later, during a famine, were able to bring selected individuals into the mountains to the west, where they became Malungeons, a mixed-blood group that still survive to this day. The story of the Malungeons is being researched by Raymond Ballinger for a proposed book on his family history, titled *Earth Bound.*

6. The description and spelling San Polo is from Ronald Symes, *Verrazano, Explorer of the Atlantic Coast,* illustrated by William Stobbs (New York: Morrow, 1973).

7. In 2001, a new minor league baseball stadium was built at the approximate spot, between St. George and Tompkinsville.

8. Adapted from Sora, *Lost Treasure,* p. 194. Arcadia was a "Garden of Eden" with an underground stream, once extolled in a poem by Jacopo Sannazaro. This legend was also celebrated by Renaissance scholar and king, Rene d'Anjou.

9. Samuel Elliot Morison, *Lost Treasure,* p. 62-3

10. Sora, p. 20.

11. Ibid., pp. 18, 106.

12. Bonacorso Rucellai's struggle in protecting the interests of Jews is recounted in Sora, p. 200.

13. Conversation with Jack Dempsey, July 2001. He is a professor at Wheaton College and editor of the book, *Good News from New England, and other writings of the killings at Weymouth Colony* (Scituate, MA: Digital Scanning, Inc., 2001) based in part on the writings of Edward Winslow, one of the first white settlers of Cape Cod.

14. Sora (quoting Bacon), *Lost Treasure,* p. 201.

15. Steven Sora, however, obviously believes the secret island is Oak Island, Nova Scotia, which is really secret—millions of dollars have been spent trying to find its secret buried treasure, to no avail.

16. Jeff Schechter, a spokesperson for the American Jewish Communities Organization of New York, per e-mail, June 2001.

17. Cornel Lengyel, *Presidents of the United States* (New York: Bantam/Golden Books, 1964), p. 14.

18. Ric Burns and James Sanders, eds., *New York, An Illustrated History* (New York: Knopf, 1999), p. 15. Under sanction from bigotry, the Jewish people of the city developed the New York banking system, contributed to the New York literary scene, created the famed Diamond District north of Grand Central Station, and helped develop the fur market and the fashion district. Their talents contribute to every university and college in the five boroughs. They gave us the Gershwin brothers and cast members and crew to most Broadway plays and musicals now running. Jewish people were the principal creators of the medium of television, an industry that presents New York City as a truly international city, multicultural in every way.

19. Kraft, *The Dutch, the Indians, and the Quest for Copper,* p. 21. Also, from telephone and e-mail communications with Cherokee traditionalist Charlene Kelly, 2001.

20. Lengyel, *Presidents of the United States,* p. 14.

Chapter 7: We Belong to the Earth

1. Herbert C. Kraft, *The Dutch, the Indians, and the Quest for Copper: Pahaquarry and the Old Mine Road* (South Orange, NJ: Seton Hall University Museum, 1996).

2. According to Heckewelder's *History, Manners, and Customs,* quoted on p. 197 of Herbert C. Kraft's book *The Lenape: Archaeology, History, and Ethnography* (Newark, NJ: New Jersey Historical Society, 1986, Collections of the New Jersey Historical Society, Volume 21), Henry Hudson visited the Hudson River in 1609 and then again in 1610. However, *New York: An Illustrated History,* Burns and Sanders, eds., (p. 6) states unequivocally, "Hudson himself [leaving in 1609] would never again see the great bay or the majestic waterway that would bear his name." It seems that someone came from Europe to sail the river in 1610, but it wasn't Hudson, and the Lenape could not tell the difference. According to *History of the State of New York,* (vol. 1, Alexander Flick, ed., New York: Columbia University Press, 1933), p. 165, "Immediately after Hudson's return, Isaac Le Maire sent out a vessel named the *Little Fox* to follow the explorer's track, but there is no record of her having reached the American coast."

3. Lee Francis, *Native Time: A Historical Time Line of Native America* (New York: St. Martin's/Griffin, 1996), p. 33.

4. Charles A. Weslager, *The Delaware Indian Westward Migration* (Wallingford, PA: Middle Atlantic Press, 1978), pp. 105-6.

5. Many people, including Mormons, Native American Christians, and those of other faiths, believe that Christ walked across North America two thousand years ago to teach the citizens of Turtle Island. How were they to know if this visitation was of a similar nature, or a threat?

6. Allan W. Eckert, *A Sorrow in Our Heart: The Life of Tecumseh* (New York: Bantam Books, 1992), amplified note 50, p. 824.

7. Gladys Tantaquidgeon, *Folk Medicine of the Delaware and Related Algonquin Indians* (Harrisburg, PA: Pennsylvania Historical and Museum Commission, 1972) pp. 85-87, 100-01.

8. Kraft, *The Lenape,* p. 180.

9. Albert Cook Myers, ed., *William Penn's Own Account of the Lenni Lenape or Delaware Indians* (Somerset, NJ: Middle Atlantic Press, 1970), p. 49.

10. Herbert C. Kraft, ed., *The Lenape Indian: A Symposium* (South Orange, NJ: Archaeological Research Center / Seton Hall University, 1984. Publication no. 7), Nora Thompson Dean's lecture, p. 45. Also, Frank G. Speck, with Jesse Moses Jr. and Joshua Montour, *The Celestial Bear Comes Down to Earth, The Bear Sacrifice Ceremony of the Munsee-Mahican in Canada as Related by Nekatcit.* Reading [Pennsylvania] Public Museum and Art Gallery, Scientific Publications number 7, 1945, p. 9.

11. From displays at the Mashantucket Pequot Museum and Research Center, Pequot War Gallery permanent exhibit, and movie *The Witness* in the same gallery, Mashantucket, CT.

12. From displays at the Mashantucket Pequot Museum and Research Center, Pequot War Gallery permanent exhibit, Mashantucket, CT. Also, see p. 147, Weslager, *The Delaware Indians: A History.*

13. The Pequot War display at the Mashantucket Pequot Museum and Paul Wallace *The White Roots of Peace: The Iroquois Book of Life,* (Santa Fe, NM: Clear Light Publishers, 1994) p. 82. Frank G. Speck recorded the Native American axiom, "Wampum is our heart."

14. Wallace, *The White Roots of Peace,* p. 82.

15. Isaack de Rasieres, 1628, from Pequot Museum. The Pequot War display at the Mashantucket Pequot Museum and Research Center, Mashantucket, CT.

16. Mashantucket Pequot Museum, Pequot Village display.

17. Mashantucket Pequot Museum.

18. Edmund B. O'Callaghan, ed., *Documents Related to the Colonial History of the State of New York: Albany, 1853–1857*, p. 14:470. This multi-volume set is in the New York State Archives in Albany, New York. Quoted in Mashantucket Pequot Museum permanent display, The Pequot War.

19. The Pequot War display at the Mashantucket Pequot Museum.

20. Verhulst was the first politician in New Amsterdam after Cornelius May, who was more of a ship captain.

21. There's an old joke about the selling of Manhattan, told to me by Jim Davis of the Munsee Davises, whose family has survived over four hundred years of wars, plagues, treaties, real estate developers, and even the flooding of their land by New York City's reservoir. The Davises are still a strong presence in the Esopus Valley. Needless to say, there is some tinge of bitterness to the humor:

  Old sly Peter Minuit comes to this beautiful island with tall trees, green grass, and fresh water flowing in the streams. Blue sky overhead, hills and rocks in the distance, and the sound of birds in the air—you can imagine how much like paradise it is. He arranges a meeting with the local subchief of the people and offers him a real estate contract to sell for $24 cold hard cash. Surrounded by his assistants, the Indian chief agrees. Minuit says, "Don't read the fine print. It's just a rental agreement." The chief says, "Sure, buddy. We know about your European agreements. I'll sign." He hands the paper back to Minuit, who grabs it greedily. The chief then turns to his assistants and yells in a loud voice, "OK! STRIKE THE SET!" The men pull down the blue-sky scrim, roll up the Astroturf, turn off the prerecorded bird-call tape, and roll away the papier-mâché rocks and boulders. Peter finds himself surrounded by miles of flat concrete, not a sign of life. "Thanks for the wampum!" the chief says as he leaves.

22. According to Ric Burns and James Sanders, eds., *New York: An Illustrated History* (New York: Knopf, 1999) p. 9. The $24 was recently calculated, adjusted for inflation, to equal $669.42 in 1999 U.S. funds.

23. *Rome and the Vatican,* Casa Editrice Lozzi, Roma, Italy, (circa 1982, nd), p. 36.

Chapter 8: The Two-Colored Snake

1. A schoolteacher of the colony also made money on the side by running a bleachery, or laundry service, at the site of the small creek where the Dutch "maidens" or *Mädchen* generally did their laundry. Today, Maiden Lane now stands at that spot. There is every reason to think that, in earlier times, the Canarsie "maidens" of lower Manhattan did their washing there as well.

2. E. M. Ruttenber, *Indian Tribes of Hudson's River to 1700, vol. 1* (Saugerties, NY: Hope Farm Press and Book Shop, 1992), p. 1:113. I have researched this passage, but have not been able to determine its original source. A researcher at the State Archives suggested Ruttenber may have had exclusive access to a letter or piece of correspondence from the time period.

3. Ibid., p. 1:113

4. This nickname, "Willem the Testy," was reported by Washington Irving in 1809 in his *Knickerbocker Tales.*

5. Ruttenber, p. 1:119.

6. This is from the Munsee as noted in Frank G. Speck, *The Celestial Bear Comes Down to Earth:The Bear Sacrifice Ceremony of the Munsee-Mahican in Canada as Related by Nekatcit.* Reading [Pennsylvania] Public Museum and Art Gallery, Scientific Publications number 7, 1945, p. 28.

7. His expedition of 130 men swept through the section of Connecticut Mayanes had come from, but did not find any Lenape. The expedition then continued north to Pound Ridge.

8. Three hundred eventually died at Wounded Knee, many from wounds that were not treated. Most of the victims were of the Minneconjou Nation. Read Dee Brown, *Bury My Heart at Wounded Knee* (New York: Simon & Schuster, 1970), p. 416.

9. Burns and James Sanders, *New York.*

10. Ibid.

11. Ibid.

12. The Dutch had taken over Swanendael in New Jersey by force ten years earlier, driving out the Swedes.

13. Henry H. Kessler and Eugene Rachlis, *Peter Stuyvesant and His New York* (New York: Random House, 1959) and Burns and James Sanders, *New York.*

14. B. A. Botkin, *New York City Folklore* (New York: Random House, 1956), pp. 27-28. See also Kessler and Rachlis, *Peter Stuyvesant.*

15. In another version, both men are holding spears in their right hands, and the Dutchman has crossed straps over his vest, indicating a military inclination.

Chapter 9: The World of the Lenape

1. One documentary film I saw many years ago at the museum at the Oneida reserve at Salamanca, I believe, showed an Iroquois woman making a complete ash basket in minutes.

2. Alanson Skinner, *Indians of Greater New York and Vicinity,* (Cedar Rapids, IA: Torch Press, 1915; reprint, New York: American Museum of Natural History).

3. Munsee Chief Mark Peters explained this to me in September of 1999 while viewing the new Munsee longhouse at Mohawk State Reserve in New Paltz, NY, a rather accurate reconstruction.

4 Herbert C. Kraft, *The Lenape: Archaeology, History, and Ethnography* (Newark, NJ: New Jersey Historical Society, 1986). Similar description in Skinner, *Indians of Greater New York.*

5. This is according to Captain John Smith of Virginia, in his notes.

6. Skinner, *Indians of Greater New York.*

7. Ibid.

8. The Minisink Indians lived where Pennsylvania, New Jersey, and New York now meet, an area then called Minisink.

9. William Ritchie shows this in his archaeological studies. See *Archaeology of New York State* (Garden City, NY: Natural History Press, 1969; reprinted, Fleischmanns, NY: Purple Mountain Press, 1994).

10. Edward V. Curtin, "Ancient Mohicans in Time, Space, and Prehistory." Paper presented at the Mohican Conference, New York State Archives, Albany, New York, March 2000, pp. 5-9.

11. Alanson Skinner cites the Labadist ministers, Jasper Dankers and Peter Sluyter, *Journal of a Voyage to New York, 1679-1680* (Ann Arbor, MI: University Microfilms, reprint, 1966) who went to "Najack" (Nyack, now Fort Hamilton) in 1676 and met a bean pounder, a woman of better than eighty years, and were impressed with her excellent health and muscular strength. She thought nothing of it. See Skinner, *Indians of Greater New York.*

12. "Believe It Or Not's" talented Mr. Ripley, who lived on an island near New York City, made this statement in his newspaper series, "Ripley's Believe it or Not," which reran the item for years.

13. Susun Weed, *The Menopause Years, The Wise Woman's Way: Alternative Approaches for Women, 30-90* (Woodstock, NY: Ash Tree Publications, 1992).

14. Trudy Lamb Richmond, "Sweat Lodge," a display at the Mashantucket Pequot Museum, Pequot Village.

15. Nicolaes van Wassenaer, a journalist and physician who visited the New Netherlands colony, quoted in *Documentary History of New York* III: 28, quoted in E. M. Ruttenber, *Indians of Hudson's River*, vol. 1 (Saugerties, NY: Hope Farm Press, 1992), p. 1: 27.

16. Ibid, p. 1:21.

17. In 1902, Wickham Cuffee found the Shinnecock still maintaining this practice. Caitlin, the artist, found the same practice maintained by the Sac and the Fox, relatives of the Lenape, out west. Most who have tried it say it is slow and painful. The Lenape were therefore somewhat interested in scissors and shavers when they arrived. Skinner, *Indians of Greater New York.*

18. The Lenape shown were residents of Manhattan in 1654. This drawing is now at the Smithsonian/National Museum of the American Indian, Heye Foundation in lower Manhattan. A similar drawing, if not identical, by Peter Lindestrom first published in *Geographia Americae,* (1653) appears on p. 15 of Kraft, ed., *The Lenape Indian.*

19. This information came from David Pietersen de Vries' *Voyages from Holland to America,* 1655, quoted in Skinner, *Indians of Greater New York.*

20. During the Civil War, individuals searching for sources of saltpeter found a turkey feather coat buried in a cave in Kentucky.

21. Skinner, *Indians of Greater New York.*

22. Paul Bailey in his book *The Thirteen Tribes of Long Island* (Syosset, NY: Friends for Long Island's Heritage, 1959) p. 9, attributes this description to the mate on Henry Hudson's *Half Moon* (1609), from his journal.

23. Based on comments by Wickham Cuffee, written in 1902, quoted in Bailey, *The Thirteen Tribes of Long Island,* p. 9, and Skinner, *Indians of Greater New York.*

24. Quillworking workshop 1989 with Gaylen Drapeau, Yankton Sioux, now of Pipestone, Minnesota, Rhinebeck, New York.

25. Eddie Benton-Banaise, from conversation, Sarnia, Ontario, Canada, February 1999.

26. The Menominee, Sac, Fox, and Micmac women were still occasionally seen wearing such hats in 1915. Skinner, *Indians of Greater New York.*

27. Ruttenber, *Indian Tribes of Hudson's River,* p. 1:22. Ruttenber implies the Lenape women

had the same high regard for pearls as the Dutch women did, but the tale of Pearl Street and Algonquin lore in general suggests a less materialistic slant.

28. Charles Wolley (Bailey spells it Wooley), a priest of the Church of England, spent the years 1678 and 1679 on Long Island. He wrote the following account: "Most of them are between five and six feet high, straight bodied and strongly composed." Bailey, *The Thirteen Tribes of Long Island*, p. 9.

29. Ruttenber, *Indian Tribes of Hudson's River*, p. 1:22, quoting Van der Donck (source or document not specified, but presumably his *Description of the New Netherlands, 1655*), "Here and there they lay upon their faces black spots of paint."

30. Skinner, *Indians of Greater New York*.

31. Mashantucket Pequot Museum, Pequot Village permanent exhibit.

32. I received the acorn recipe from herbalist Janet Jappen, May 2001, and from Phoebe Legere, Wampanoag musico-historian, also May 2001.

33. Ruttenber, *Indians of Hudson's River*, p. 1:24.

34. Conversation with Burton Ward, Eel Ground Micmac Reserve, October 2000. Mr. Ward is a tour guide at the Metipenagiak Heritage Center in Red Bank, New Brunswick.

35. Skinner, *Indians of Manhattan Island and Vicinity*.

36. Robert S. Grumet, *The Lenapes*, Indians of North America Series, Frank W. Porter, ed., (New York, NY: Chelsea House Publishers, 1989), p. 13.

37. Trudy Lamb Richmond, "Hubbub" display at the Mashantucket Pequot Museum, Pequot Village.

38. One can easily see the "three cherries" of the gambling hall one-armed bandits evolving out of this game. Also, the New York expression "hubbub" may have come from this (as in "making such a hubbub"). The word may also have Celtic parallels, but there is every reason to believe it is of Algonquin origin.

39. Skinner, *Indians of Greater New York*.

Chapter 10: Sweet and Full of Meaning

1. According to the 1996 *Guinness Book of Records* (New York: Facts on File, 1996), the most difficult major language in the world today is Ojibway. One could say that Lenape is like Ojibway, but with more letters and more pieces of other Algonquin languages thrown in.

2. Robert S. Grumet, *The Lenapes*, Indians of North America Series, ed., Frank W. Porter (New York: Chelsea House Publishers, 1989), p. 25.

3. The origins of American Sign Language (ASL) are considered to be about 40 percent Native American Sign Language and 60 percent French Sign Language (FSL). Much of early ASL was developed on Martha's Vineyard, Massachusetts, home of the Wampanoag Confederacy of Algonquin Indians, but its roots are otherwise difficult to trace—little is known about the individuals who preserved this great tradition.

4. Taught to me by Talking Leaves, Fire Keeper for the Ramapough Mountain Indians and the foremost storyteller of that nation. He began to show me basic hand signing at his home off reservation in Florida, New York, on May 22, 2001.

5. Ibid.

6. Judith Aldofer Abbott in reference to use of "youse"; Abbott quoting (conversation with) Nora Thompson Dean in reference to "you-all"; and Abbott quoting O'Meara in reference to *kee* and *keeloowa*. John O'Meara, *Delaware-English, English-Delaware Dictionary* (Toronto: University of Toronto Press, 1996). My experience, and those of others I have asked, confirm this.

7. Some other expressions we use have translations in Munsee, but it is not clear if they are used as slang or not: "Low down" is *"Aah-kink."* "I bet" is *"Aax-koo-kus."* "Small town" is *"Chung-oo-te-nesh."* "I guess so" is *"Sha-kee-et."* "He is crabby or irritable" is *"Me-tche-ent."* (From Beulah Timothy, March 16, 2001, Moraviantown Reserve, Ontario, Canada.)

8. David Zeisberger, *Essay of a Delaware-Indian and English Spelling Book,* (Philadelphia: Henry Miller, 1776; reprint, Ohio Historical Society, 1991).

9. The area includes Fifth Avenue, Park Avenue, York Avenue, East Side Drive, and FDR Drive from Fifty-ninth up to Ninety-sixth—that "golden rectangle" of real estate. *Rechgawonk* in Munsee really means "sandy place," but it is a remarkable coincidence nonetheless.

10. It is "warm day" but with the *r* turned to an *l* (as the Lenape had no *r*), plus "it is" at the end. Zeisberger, *An Essay.*

11. The Munsee now say "O" as in the word "tone" instead of *ay-yoo*. (Ives Goddard, "Nasalization of PA (Proto-Algonquin) in Eastern Algonquin." *International Journal of American Linguistics,* part 1, vol. 37, #3 (July 1971): pp. 139–151.

12. John Bierhorst, ed., *The White Deer and Other Stories Told by the Lenape* (New York: William Morrow and Co., 1995), p. 11.

13. There are versions of this story all over North America. This is my own adaptation of the Lenape version.

14. Of course these numbers of years are merely symbolic, representing the average. Some race through the wheel to get to the end, only to find it is an infinite circle and there is nowhere to go. Likewise some go slow, fearful of reaching the end, only to find there is nothing to fear and that nothing ends.

15. This is the translated Australian Aborigine term, but the word in Algonquin is very old and may have been lost. The Algonquin term basically translates as "walkabout."

16. I tried an exercise with my Native American history class, offering them a chance to write a poem or letter in Lenape, with English translations, based on a word list. The results were very good, except that one or two were frustrated with the lack of the word *the*. They search for it on the list and couldn't find it, so they wrote in the missing word in English. It opened my eyes to the importance of *the*. It changes everything.

Chapter 11: Native New Yorkers East of the Hudson River

1. Route 23A would have been a mountain hiking trail, not for the weak-hearted. There were no villages along this route—at least there is not archaeological or written historical record of one.

2. Dr. Leonard Eisenberg, former director of SUNY New Paltz Department of Archaeology, writes in *The History of Ulster County,* that "the first [Algonquin] settlers chose places with a superb view."

3. The Hudson River begins at Lake Tear of the Clouds on Mt. Marcy, in Essex County, approximately 1,000 feet from the peak. See Hudson River Sloop Clearwater's website, www.clearwater.org.

4. *Rand McNally Road Atlas 2000* (Skokie, IL: Rand McNally, 2000), pp. 70-71.

5. I noted this information from a conversation circa 1994, with the Reverend James Davis, an indigenous Munsee person, and resident of the Catskills, at the Wittenberg Center for Alternative Resources, Bearsville, New York.

6. This comes from *nape,* as in Lenape. *Ape* means "people" and *kamak* means "field." E. M. Ruttenber in *Footprints of the Red Man: Indian Geographical Names of New York* (New York: New York State Historical Society, 1906) notes that *nape* could mean "that water there," as explained in the introduction to this book. "That water" would have to refer to the Bronx River at the edge of Yonkers.

7. *Westchester Heritage Map* 1778–80. Indian Occupation-Colonial and Revolutionary Names, Structures, and Events. Map made by Robert Erskine, 1778-1780. (Reprint, Westchester, NY: Westchester County Historical Society, Stephen A. Estrin, Inc., 1978).

8. Ruttenber, in *Footprints of the Red Man,* says the *wan* ending (of Kitchewan) is a part of speech, but I believe it is a Munsee pronunciation of *run,* a run of water, as it usually shows up in place-names where there is a run. The *k* ending in Kitchewank, which means "this place," is sometimes added and sometimes not. It is a variant on the old Algonquin *q* ending, with a click in the back of the throat. Croton Point has been the site of human occupation for about nine thousand years. Shell middens appear to be that ancient. Other ancient shell deposits indicating early human occupation can be found at Rocky Point in Saugerties, Shagabok in Hyde Park, Barren Island, and other places along the Hudson. Herbert Kraft mentions the downstream middens in *The Lenape: Archaeology, History, and Ethnography* (Newark, NJ: New Jersey Historical Society, 1986), Collections of the New Jersey Historical Society, vol. 21, p. 78.

9. *Westchester Heritage Map.*

10. Ibid.

11. Ibid.

12. Reginald Pelham Bolton, maps for *Indian Trails in the Great Metropolis* (New York: New-York Historical Society, Smithsonian Institute, National Museum of the American Indian, Heye Foundation; research room).

13. *Westchester Heritage Map.*

14. B. G. Trigger, ed., in *Northeast,* vol. 15, W. C. Sturtevant, general ed., *Handbook of North American Indians* (Washington, DC: Smithsonian Institution, 1978). Map from Bert Salwen, *Indians of Southern New England and Long Island: Early Period.*

15. Many historians classify these people as Munsee, including the esteemed Ives Goddard. However, their Quiripi-type language, which I call "Renneiu," and their Clason Point culture are so different from Munsee that the term confuses more than it enlightens. I refer to them as Munsee 2.0, a radically different type of Lenape but still anchored in Munsee beliefs and traditions. In fact in Salwen's map (see above) the Wappingers language is referred to as "r 2."

16. The following, except for translations and unless otherwise specified, is from my original analysis of the information on the *Westchester Heritage Map.*

17. James Hammond Trumbull, *Indian Names and Places In and On the Borders of Connecticut* (1881; reprint, Derby, CT: Archon Books, 1974), p. 85-86.

18. Patricia Edwards Clyne, *Hudson Valley Tales and Trails* (Woodstock, NY: Overlook Press, 1990), page 33. According to Iron Thunderhorse, *chappa* does mean "separate place" in the R dialect; *A Complete Language Guide and Primer to the Wampano/Quinnipiac R Dialect of Southwestern New England, Milltown, Indiana* (Algonquin Confederacy of the Quinnipiac Tribal Council/Algonquin Confederacies' Language Institute ACQTC/ACLI, 2000), p. 76.

19. The Roaton were Wappingers, as were the Tankitekes, both between Wilton and Fairfield, Connecticut.

20. J. Michael Smith, "The Highland King Nimhammaw and the Native Indian Proprietors of Land in Dutchess County, NY: 1712–1765," presented as a lecture in March 2000 at the annual Mohican seminar at the State Archives at Albany, New York, and later converted into an article of the same title for *The Hudson Valley Regional Review, A Journal of Regional Studies,* vol. 17, #2 (Sept. 2000), pp. 69-108.

21. The Quinnipiac translation of *wech-qussuk-auk* is from Iron Thunderhorse, *A Complete Language Guide,* p. 83.

22. Conflict with the Dutch however, was the telling blow. In 1626, a Weckweesgeek warrior was murdered in a robbery attempt by some of Minuit's men. His nephew avenged his death many years later (upon an innocent Dutchman, Claes Smit), and it triggered a campaign against the Weckweesgeek, in 1640. E. M. Ruttenber, *Indian Tribes of Hudson's River,* vol. 1, p. 1:101-102.

23. Clyne, *Hudson Valley Tales,* p. 30. If Mamaroneck means "stripes on his arms" then Clyne is almost certainly correct about it being a sachem's name.

24. Ibid., p. 30.

25. This is based on John O'Meara, *Delaware-English, English-Delaware Dictionary* (Toronto: University of Toronto Press, 1996), s.v.—under the term shippa. Smith, "Highland King," p. 5, indicates that the term "a long stretch" was commonly used in land deeds, and was used for such a shoreline in what is now Poughkeepsie, New York.

26. Bolton, maps for *Indian Trails.* Definition as "Place of Stringing [beads]" can be found in Clyne, *Hudson Valley Tales,* p. 28.

27. To learn how these rock overhangs were transformed into comfortable living quarters, I recommend visiting the rock shelter at Boudoin Park on Sheafe Road near the Hudson River in Wappingers, New York. With reeds and mats on a sturdy framework of saplings, a rock shelter can approach the longhouse in comfort and convenience, as the Boudoin reconstruction demonstrates.

28. Papequanaehen was an Esopus chief from what is now Kingston, and from this general time period. A connection between the village Pequenahunc and the sachem Papequaneahen is likely.

29. The Bear Rock petroglyph at Ward Pound Ridge, a full profile of a bear which mimics the shape of the rock itself, was thoroughly investigated, and found to be authentic Lenape handiwork. The soil underneath and around it was excavated by Nicholas Shoumatoff and others, revealing a deboutage (stone chips) pit , a charcoal pit, and other signs of Lenape encampment. A piece of sharpened quartz, which was determined to be the same one used to create the peck-and-groove petroglyph on the rock surface, was found in one of the pits. See Nicholas A. Shoumatoff's article, "The Bear Rock Petroglyph Site," *The Bulletin, New York State Archaeological Association,* no. 55 (July, 1972): pp. 1-5.

30. Clyne's *Hudson Valley Tales,* p. 28, is the source for the translation of Tuckahoe as "jack-in-the-pulpit." Joanne Menchini, an Ojibway woman living in Tuckahoe, is the source of the literal translation of "a root that is good to eat" and the information concerning its preparation. The translation of jack-in-the-pulpit as "Indian turnip" and *sigabun* is from Evan Pritchard, *Aunt Helen's Little Herb Book* (Woodstock, NY: Resonance Communications, 1994).

31. This information is from the Putnam County Historical Society website: http://hvol.com/putnamhistorian/

32. *Maaxk(oo)-pak-mpeesos* would mean "bear-flats lake" in Munsee. See O'Meara *Delaware-English, English-Delaware Dictionary*, s.v. bear, flat, and lake.

33. Many roads in wealthy Putnam County are still narrow dirt roads, which discourages development, and many real estate deals are still carried out on a cash basis or high down payment, which keeps prices down. Therefore this twelve-mile-wide strip of land between Connecticut and the Hudson is still rather pristine, with Cold Spring as the only town over 2,000 in population.

34. E. M. Ruttenber, *Indian Tribes of Hudson's River to 1700, vol. 1.* (Saugerties, NY: Hope Farm Press and Book Shop, 1992), p. 93, and John Ogilby, *America* (London: 1671, published by the author. Available in the Gilder-Lehrman collection housed at the Morgan Library).

35. Arthur C. Parker, ed., *Archeological History of New York* in Albany, NY *State Museum Bulletin*, nos. 237-238 (September, October, 1920): p. 547. A map published in the 1666 book *America* approximates the Waoranecs in northern Putnam County as well. Ogilby, *America*.

36. Clyne, *Hudson Valley Tales*, p. 30.

37. Ibid., p. 30. J. Michael Smith, "Highland King," confirms this, referring to mid-1700s litigation against the heirs of the Rombout, Beekman, and Philipse Patents.

38. Parker, *Archaeological History of New York*, p. 548, item 24.

39. Ibid., p. 547, item 2.

40. Local historians have always held that *Poughkeepsie* means "sheltered spring" in Wappingers, and identify the spring at Spratt Park as the one being referred to. In *Our Historic Hudson* (Roosevelt, NY: James B. Adler, 1968), p. 15, John S. Dyson states that the place-name Poughkeepsie derives from the Mohawk word *A-po-keep-sing,* or "safe harbor." The *ing* ending, however, is unique to the Algonquin. Nonetheless, it is remarkable that a city of 27,600 has been able to keep such a difficult Algonquin word in circulation so long.

41. J. Michael Smith, "Highland King," pp. 7–8.

42. Ibid., p. 9.

43. Parker, *Archaeological History of New York*, p. 547, item 4.

44. Shirley W. Dunn, *The Mohicans and Their Land: 1609–1730* (Fleischmanns, NY: Purple Mountain Press, 1994), p. 52.

45. Sepasco, or Sepascot, means "little river," and refers to a Lenape group that lived along the Landman's Kill River, just to the south of today's route 308, whose looping side roads are remnants of the Sepasco Trail. Most of these roads now have Dutch street names, are still intact, and preserve the flavor of the old trail. Sepasco Lake, further up 308, was not connected to the "little river" but the Sepasco Indians lived there until 1867, when the last Sepasco died in his hut near Welch's cave on the east side of Sepasco Lake. See Nancy V. Kelly, *A Brief History of Rhinebeck* (Rhinebeck, NY: The Wise Family Trust, 2001), p. 4.

46. J. Michael Smith, "Highland King," p. 13.

47. Parker, *Archaeological History of New York*, p. 547, item 1. The location of this ruin is unclear. Indian Lake is on the Connecticut border. Pine Plains, which is on the Shekomeko Creek, is further west.

Chapter 12: The Head of the Wolf

1. There is no *r* in Munsee, so upon checking *A Complete Language Guide and Primer to the Wampano/Quinnipiac R Dialect of Southwestern New England* by Iron Thunderhorse, (Milltown, IN: Algonquin Confederacy of the Quinnipiac Tribal Council/Algonquin Confederacies' Language Institute ACQTC/ACLI, 2000) under place-names, I found the prefix *warra*, which is the equivalent of the Munsee *woo-lay*, i.e., "good, peaceful, beautiful." *Neck* means "those" or "they" at least in Munsee, according to O'Meara. See John O'Meara, *Delaware-English, English-Delaware Dictionary* (Toronto: University of Toronto Press, 1996), s.v. neck. Iron Thunderhorse interprets it as a corruption of *ent*, or "camp," in Quinnipiac, translating waoraneck as "peaceful camp."

2. The name Warranawongkong comes from *warra* meaning "good and peaceful" in the Renneiu dialect, plus *wongkong*, "place near a mountain," in Munsee. (See O'Meara, *Delaware-English, English-Delaware Dictionary*, s.v. *wongkong*. E. M. Ruttenber says the place-name means "a hollow or concave site." (See Ruttenber, *Footprints of the Red Man* (New York: New-York Historical Society, 1906), p. 93) Iron Thunderhorse translates the place-name as "people of the good bay or cove." See Thunderhorse, *Complete Language Guide and Primer*, p. 88.

3. Eisenberg in *The History of Ulster County, with the Emphasis on the Last One Hundred Years, 1883-1983*; compiled by the historians of Ulster County for the Tercentenary (Kingston, NY: Ulster County Historians, 1983-4).

4. *Danskammer* is Dutch for "dance chamber." Henry Hudson observed the ritual there and nicknamed it "The Devil's Dance Chamber." According to Bellows, the proper spelling is Duyvil's Dans-Kamer.

5. There were ten years of unrest after the conclusion of Kieft's War in 1645. In 1655, a Munsee woman was shot by Hedrick Van Dyck at New Amsterdam for picking a peach from an orchard that had been sold to the Dutch. Her family chose the path of "blood redemption," a form of capitol punishment, to avenge the death, and conscribed a war party of Wappingers to help them find Van Dyck. The murderer was not to be found, and a war broke out while Peter Stuyvesant and his troops were away, one that was to rekindle itself again and again, right up to the Second Esopus War. SeeE. M. Ruttenber, *Indian Tribes of Hudson's River to 1700, vol. 1* (Saugerties, NY: Hope Farm Press and Book Shop, 1992), p. 1:121.

6. Ibid., p. 151.

7. Charles Skinner, *Myths and Legends of Our Own Land* (Philadelphia: J. B. Lippincott, 1896), pp. 31-33.

8. Kit Davits, or "Davis," came over on a boat that followed the *Mayflower*. He first settled in Plymouth, Massachusetts, per Stone Ridge, New York resident and historian, Darryl Britten. The "Great Plot" of land is mentioned on p. 146 of Ruttenber, *Indian Tribes of Hudson's River*, stating that the new village of Dutch was built on the northeast portion of "The Great Plot," and a village and fort at the Ronduit, at Ponckhokie, which still bears that name. The new village at the Great Plot was soon torched by the Lenape.

9. The source of this information is Carla Messinger, a Unami elder and historian, in the 1999 brochure for the Museum of Indian Culture, Allentown, PA. The three symbols are depicted on sassafras leaves in the Wanaque, because the sassafras plant saved them from extinction due to smallpox, according to Native historian Charlene Kelly, in a conversation in July 2000, and also Herbert C. Kraft, *The Dutch, the Indians, and the Quest for Copper: Pahaquarry and the Old Mine Road* (South Orange, NJ: Seton Hall University Museum, 1996), p. 30.

Tuxedo, or *p'tuxseepu*, is translated as "crooked water" by J. H. Salomon in *Indians of the Lower Hudson Region: The Munsee*, p. 85, but the local white "settlers" of today still preserve the oral tradition of "round-footed ones." *P'tuxito* means "they are the round-footed ones, the Munsee!" (The *ayoo* ending meaning "they are" was replaced by the sound *oh* later in Munsee, according to Ives Goddard.) See Julian Harris Salomon, *Indians of the Lower Hudson Region: The Munsee* (Suffern, NY: Rockland County Historical Society, 1982), and Ives Goddard, "Nasalization in PA (Proto-Algonquin) in Eastern Algonquin, *International Journal of American Linguistics*, pt. 1, vol. 37, #3 (July 1971): pp. 139-151.

10. Mamakating is difficult to translate. In Quiripi/Renneiu, *mamau-qu-tuck* means "where they gather at the tree (or river)," according to Iron Thunderhorse's *A Complete Language Guide*," s.v. "mamakating," p. 89. This is similar to *mayomeek* "gatherings," *ut*-"at," *ing* "place" in old Algonquin, but *memakochcus-ing* is "place of the red-headed woodpecker" in Unami per David Zeisberger in *Essay of a Delaware-Indian and English Spelling Book* (Philadelphia: Henry Miller, 1776; reprint, Ohio Historical Society, 1991), p. 47. I, however, believe local lore supports "gatherings at the river."

11. According to conversations with the Hudson Valley's foremost historian, Alf Evers, author of *Woodstock, History of an American Town* (Woodstock, NY: Overlook Press, 1987) and other books, the area surrounding Middletown and Goshen was known for enduring endless streams of squatters and freeloaders until 1760, when Robert Livingston bought the land and drove them off. Needless to say, the white squatters didn't keep records. Therefore we can say very little about how the land was used by the Lenape and how it transited into the hands of the interlopers

12. *Wi(n)eg-te-ko(n)k*: good fire place. (My use of (n) indicates a nasal *n* and nasal preceeding vowel.) The non-initial *t* was often soft, like a *d* so, combined with the nasal n, the word would sound like wegdkok, or woodcock. Woodcock is an English mnemonic for Wegdkok.

13. A drawing of the Maringoman "castle" appears on p. 1:94 of Ruttenber's *Indian Tribes of Hudson's River, vol. 1*. According to several telephone conversations throughout 2001 with Raymundo Wesley Rodriguez and Paula Broset, who researched the history of Blooming Grove, there is a deed between the English and the Ramapough, dated August 10, 1700, which unfortunately clarifies little. Of the two sachems who signed it, Maringoman is spelled several different ways, and Nanawaron is referred to as both "she" and "he" throughout the text of the deed. Although its credibility is questionable, it seems to be one of our few links to the Native people of the area. Maringoman may have been a racial epithet or perhaps even a mispronunciation of nearby Murderer's Creek in Dutch. Rodriguez suggests that the name Nanawaron means "rock that stands proudly on a cliff" in the Nahautl (Taino) language, however it could also mean "good grandmother leader" in pidgin Renneiu.

14. Skinner, *Myths and Legends*, pp. 40-41.

15. A historic marker on Route 209 reads: "Route taken by NY, NJ militia in pursuit of Col. Brant for raid on Minisink (Port Jervis) July 21, 1779."

16. In 1641 in the *Journal of New Netherlands*, it was recorded that "[i]n the interior are pretty high mountains exhibiting generally strong indications of minerals." On August 31, 1645, a Dutch official wrote that "[t]he West India Company is determined to investigate . . . having received from savages some specimens of minerals, which we think valuable, and being informed by the savages that the mountains from which they had brought the specimens is [sic] inland near the Raretang [sic], we have considered it best, most advantageous and profitable for the West India Company to use all diligence to discover the said mine and when found and it is valuable, it is resolved to take possession thereof for the said Hon'ble Company

and build a fort there." Fourteen years later, on April 25, 1659, the director in Holland wrote to Peter Stuyvesant, "We have lately been shown a small piece of mineral which is said to have come from New Netherlands and which we found to be good and pure copper...." C. G. Hine, *The Old Mine Road* (New Brunswick, NJ: Rutgers University Press, 1909, reprinted 1963), pp. 2–3.

17. Albany records of April 25, 1659, briefly mention a copper mine at Minisink. Given this lack of enthusiasm—fourteen years to come up with a single piece of copper—it is unlikely that there is anything to the legend. One mine is on the Delaware River, where one of the Shawangunk Mountains nearly approaches the lower part of Pahaquarry Flat, now in New Jersey. The other is at the north foot of the same mountain, near the halfway point between the Delaware and Esopus Rivers. Copper, lead, and even silver may have been mined there at one time, but they are of poor quality and even today it is economically unfeasible to mine them. Kraft, *The Dutch, the Indians.*

18. The Reverend James Davis, a Munsee of the Shawangunks, passes on this oral history along with the observation that the people Verrazzano and the Dutch met were wearing "an awful lot of copper" at the time of contact. (Based on 1994 conversations at the Wittenberg Center for Alternative Resources.)

19. Marc B. Fried, *Tales from the Shawangunk Mountains: A Naturalist's Musings, a Bush Whacker's Guide* (Glens Falls, NY: Adirondack Mountain Club, 1981).

20. C. G. Hine, *The Old Mine Road* (New Brunswick, NJ: Rutgers University Press, 1909, reprinted 1963), p. 88.

21. Kraft, *The Dutch, the Indians,* p. 127.

22. Ibid., pp. 75-78.

23. The Dutch women learned many herbal medical cures from the Esopus women, and this was passed down. Local Stone Ridge resident Don Traver, whose family has some Native ancestry, told me his mother accidentally cut two of her uncle's fingers off when she was a child. Her "Dutch" grandmother said, "Go out and get the fingers and we'll set them in blood!" She used Indian herbs such as boneset to mend the bones, and the fingers were repaired. Don Traver related this story in a conversation with author at the Stone Ridge Library, at the site of the old Minisink Trail, route 209, Stone Ridge, New York, June 2001.

24. Although the history books tell us there were munitions in the fort, other history books tell us the Lenape had no guns. Either they had captured guns and ammunition during some previous skirmish, or they were holding the munitions as some kind of bargaining chip. This is a matter for further research.

25. Marc B. Fried, *The Early History of Kingston and Ulster County* (Marbletown, Kingston, NY: Ulster County Historical Society, 1975), pp. 87-91.

26. Ibid., pp. 92-93.

27. *Wiltmeet* is Dutch for "gathering-place of savages."

28. Ruttenber, *Indian Tribes of Hudson's River,* vol. 1, p. 1:95.

29. Charles A. Weslager, *The Delaware Indian Westward Migration* (Wallingford, PA: Middle Atlantic Press, 1978), pp. 89, 165.

30. Thunderhorse, *Complete Language Guide,* p. 89.

31. Ruttenber, *Indian Tribes of Hudson's River, vol. 1,* p. 1:95. See also Parker, *Archaeological History of New York,* p. 569.

32. Shirley W. Dunn, *The Mohicans and Their Land: 1609–1730*. (Fleishmanns, NY: Purple Mountain Press, 1994), p. 54.

33. This is based on comparisons with O'Meara, s.v., *neepaahum- moon*, also Zeisberger, *nee-pa-hum*.

34. Hine, *Old Mine Road*.

35. See Zeisberger, *Essay of a Delaware-Indian and English Spelling Book*. Zeisberger translates *win-ayoo* as "it is snowing" (p. 32), plus *sook* for "fall" (as in rainfall, waterfall, etc.). *Sok* means "to pour" (p. 56, see also p.78). The story is from Skinner, *Myths and Legends*.

Chapter 13: A Walk Down the Minisink Trail

1. Marc B. Fried, *The Early History of Kingston and Ulster County* (Marbletown, Kingston, NY: Ulster County Historical Society, 1975), p. 45, explains that *wilt* refers to "wild or savage, or Indian," and defines *wyck* broadly as "a quarter, ward, parish or district, or a retreat or refuge."

2. E. M. Ruttenber, *Indian Tribes of Hudson's River to 1700, vol. 1* (Saugerties, NY: Hope Farm Press and Book Shop, 1992), p. 150.

3. George Van Sickle, respected local historian, passed this valuable piece of information on to me in conversation, while exploring the cornfields at Wyltmeet, now near Tongore Road in Marbletown, June 2001.

4. Fried, *Early History of Kingston and Ulster County*, footnote p. 34.

5. This is information from the Punxsutawney, Pennsylvania, website: http://users.penn.com/~mweimer/history.html, and from Groundhog Day website, http://www.groundhog.org/history/tradition.shtml. *Ponckees* are usually biting sand flies, not mosquitos. Hocking means "country" or "territory," i.e., land. Alf Evers, author of *Woodstock: History of an American Town*, and other books, agrees and in conversation in his home near Woodstock, June 2001, related that they are still known by the name *Ponckees* in the Adirondacks. He comments, "The black flies come first, followed by the *ponckees*, or little sand flies."

6. Alf Evers, conversation with author, June 2001. He showed me a photograph of "Chief Ponckhokie" from a clipping of *The Kingston Freeman*. I did not note the date of publication, but the likeness to an "Indian Chief" was unmistakable.

7. This is based on Fried, *The Early History of Kingston and Ulster County*, p. 51. He suggests it may have been part of a trail connecting to the Ponckhockie Path.

8. Alf Evers, at his home, June 2001. Conversation with author.

9. Ibid. Fried employs the spelling *Atharhacton* in *The Early History of Kingston*, p. 10, and appendix 3, p. 179. *Atkarkarton* is the spelling used by Ruttenber, *Indian Tribes of Hudson's River, vol. 1*, p. 1:125.

10. One spot along the road is called Spook Hollow, because during Dutch colonial times, a horse was "spooked" there. Apparently it saw something in the bottom of the gully near the Elmendorf mansion and was unable to pass the spot. Hurley has always been known for its witches, ghosts, and supernatural beings, many of them Indian. From C. G. Hine, *The Old Mine Road* (New Brunswick, NJ: Rutgers University Press, 1909; reprinted 1963), pp. 36, 145.

11. *Squaw* does indeed indicate female, and the term *sunk* seems to mean "high up," in Lenape. *Sunksquaw* is the term used for female sachem by author John A. Strong in *The Montaukett Indians of Eastern Long Island* (Syracuse, NY: Syracuse University Press, 2001), p. 8, quoting Burt Salwen, "Indians of Southern New England and Long Island." In *Handbook of the North*

American Indians, vol. 15, *The Northeast,* ed. Bruce Trigger (Washington, DC: Smithsonian Institution Press, 1978), pp. 164-170. Author Robert Grumet (see bibliography) reportedly also interprets its meaning as "top, or high-ranking woman."

12. Town of Esopus Bicentennial Committee, *The Town of Esopus Story: 3000 B.C. – 1978 A.D.* (Esopus, NY: Hillcrest Press, 1979), pp. 199-201.

13. Hine, *The Old Mine Road,* p. 57.

14. Trowbridge ms. in Heckewelder, *History* p. 474, quoted in John Bierhorst, *Mythology of the Lenape: Guide and Texts* (Tucson, AZ: Arizona University Press, 1995), p.32.

15. From conversations with Stephen J. Augustine, Hereditary Micmac Chief, in February of 1990. Augustine is now director of Native American research at the Museum of Civilization, in Hull, Quebec, Canada.

16. Bierhorst, *Mythology of the Lenape,* p. 32. "Captain Pipe" is the translation of his name *Hopocan,* but he was also known as "seeker of light."

17. David Zeisberger, *Essay of a Delaware-Indian and English Spelling Book* (Philadelphia: Henry Miller, 1776; reprint, Ohio Historical Society, 1991), p. 55, v.s. *shawaneu;* p. 5 v.s. *aan.* The interpretation of *gunk* as "near or on the side of a mountain," was confirmed in a conversation with Alf Evers in June of 2001, at his home. Many Lenape mountain names have *konk, gunk,* or similar endings.

18. Historical marker on Route 209.

19. Ruttenber for "rock," Hine for "tree." See Ruttenber, *Indians of Hudson's River, vol. 1,* and Hine, *Old Mine Road,* p. 59.

20. There is an impressive bust of an Indian at the famed Mohonk Mountain House, New Paltz, New York, a distinguished inn, meeting place, and home to conferences on Native American issues at the beginning of the twentieth century. Research, however, has shown that the man depicted, although a hero of sorts who was known for his impeccable honesty, is an Ojibway from the Great Lakes and does not represent local history.

21. Hine, *Old Mine Road,* p. 72.

22. Per conversation with Carolee Schneeman, historic home owner, Springtown, New York, June 2001.

23. Per historian Darryl Britten of Marbletown, New York, in conversation at his historic home, June 2001.

24. This fanciful version comes from Arnold Bellows, *The Legend of Utsayantha and Other Folk Tales of the Catskills* (Margaretville, NY: Catskill Mountain News, 1945).

25. Conversation with Darryl Britten at his historic home in Marbletown, New York, June 2001.

26. John Bierhorst, telephone conversation with author, May 2001

27. *Ashokan,* Unami for a rapids, waterfall, strong current. *Acho* as a prefix is a unique sound in Unami Delaware which always carries the meaning "it is strong, hard, or difficult"; the *o* means "it is," therefore "it is strong." Zeisberger, *Essay of a Delaware-Indian and English Spelling Book,* pp. 14, 38, 63. The *kan* ending, if accurate, means "a state of being," i.e. "-ness" in Proto-Algonquin (strongness or strength).This would be a likely personal name for a chief, and lends at least a shred of credibility to the folktale. However it also sounds like *kong,* "near or on a mountain," or *hong,* "a waterfall." Therefore, it could refer to a strong mountainside "rapids," difficult to travel by canoe. Winchell's Falls was such a "strong rapids" and would have earned the

name "Ashokan." Ironically, according to Richard Frisbee, publisher/editor of E. M. Ruttenber's books and a Hudson Valley historian, that falls is now far beneath the surface of the Ashokan Reservoir which bears its name. Further proof of the "rapids" hypothesis lies in the fact that nearby Shandanken was thought to mean "strong rapids," even though it clearly does not.

28. John Bierhorst, telephone conversation with author, May 2001.

29. Zeisberger, *Essay of a Delaware-Indian and English Spelling Book*, p. 6. *Schind* is translated as "spruce," or in some dialects "hemlock." *Akee* is "land."

30. According to author Charles Skinner, *Myth and Legends of Our Own Land* (Philadelphia: J. B. Lippincott, 1896), Chief Shandanken's wigwam was located at the site of the famed Catskill Mountain House.

31. Arnold Bellows, *The Legend of Utsayantha* and other folk tales of the Catskills, illustrated by Lamont A. Warner (Margaretville, NY: Catskill Mountain News, 1945), p. 30.

32. Hine, *Old Mine Road*, p. 107.

33. Fried, *The Early History of Kingston and Ulster County*, p. 78, mentions that the town was named after a stream named Kerhonkson Kill, earlier spelled Kahakasnik (misspelling of Kahaksink, "Place of the Wild Geese").

34. Joseph Montour, a direct descendant of Ulster County's Esopus Munsee, explained the origin of the Maysingway mask in Frank G. Speck's *The Celestial Bear Comes Down to Earth*: *The Bear Sacrifice Ceremony of the Munsee-Mahican in Canada as Related by Nekatcit*; (Reading, PA: Public Museum and Art Gallery, Scientific Publications number 7, 1945), cited in Bierhorst, p. 49.

35. Marc B. Fried, in *Tales from the Shawangunks*, writes that "when viewed from the northwest, the profile is unmistakable." He speculates it is a giant portrait of Preuwamackan, the oldest and greatest of the Esopus sachems, or perhaps Seuwackenamo the Peacemaker. See Fried, *Tales from the Shawangunk Mountains* (Glens Falls, NY: Adirondack Mountain Club, 1981).

36. Like the Lenape, the Bacchants incorporated dancing and singing into their worship. Using alcohol in conjunction with ceremony, however, has always been taboo for the Lenape and all Algonquin people.

37. Fried, *Early History*, p. 77.

38. Ruttenber, *Indian Tribes of Hudson's River*, p. 138.

39. Hine, *Old Mine Road*, p. 69, quotes E. M. Ruttenber's *Footprints of the Red Man: Indian Geographical Names of New York*. (New York: New York State Historical Society, 1906) stating that Wawarsing means "at a place where the stream bends." The word for blackbird in Lenape is *Teokali*.

40. Hine, *Old Mine Road*, p. 82–83.

41. "Rondout Valley in the Old French War" published in *Olde Ulster*, April 1907, vol. 3 no. 4, by the editor, Benjamin Myer Brink (Kingston, NY: R.W. Anderson and Sons), pp. 104-113. (Facsimile provided by Wendy Harris, Cragsmoor Archaeological Consultants, Cragsmoor, New York, June 2001.)

42. Kay Olan, Mohawk instructor at Kanatsiohareke, Fonda, New York. Story told to author in April 2001, at New Paltz, NY.

43. "Rondout Valley in the Old French War," pp. 103–113.

44. Wilhelm Benignus, *Shawangunk Mountain Stories* (1916), quoted in Fried, *Tales from the Shawangunk Mountains.*

45. Fried, *Tales from the Shawangunk Mountains.*

46. Sam Gonsalus changed the spelling of his family name—from Gonsalez, which his grandfather had used, to Gonsalus. His father, Manuel II, used both spellings interchangeably. This information according to documents read in telephone conversations with Wendy Harris of Cragsmoor Archaeological Consultants, June 2001.

47. Fried, *Tales from the Shawangunk Mountains,* p. 89. Thanks to Wendy Harris of Cragsmoor Archaeological Consultants for further details, told at the edge of the cliff itself, looking down upon the pinetops below. Hine wrote that some believed the first white settler was a Spaniard, claiming at least to be Protestant (possibly a refuged Morano or Spanish Jew) named Don Manuel Gonsal[ez], who came to Kingston before 1689, and settled at a place called Rochester, although the dates seem a bit late. Don Manuel then built a log house in Mamakating Valley after 1728, though again the exact date is uncertain. Sam, living in the middle 1700s, would have been one of his grandsons. See Hine, *Old Mine Road,* pp. 9, 15, 105.

48. Wendy Harris provided the information as to the whereabouts of Sam's father, and Hine writes on pp. 104-105 of *Old Mine Road* that old Manuel Gonsalus's blue flagstone tombstone still stands "behind a barn," inscribed with the words, "Manuel Gonsalus is Gestorven De 18 April Anno 1758"; (Manuel Gonsalus was buried here on April 18, 1758). That barn gave way to the airport. Hine's grave is that of Sam's father, whose surname changed spelling intermittently between Gonsalez and Gonsalus. Sam kept the spelling Gonsalus.

49. *Aiap-ayoo* means "it is a buck," and *osxum-mo-wall* is "horns" in Munsee. See O'Meara's *Delaware-English, English-Delaware Dictionary,* s.v. aiapayoo, osxummowall.

50. Wendy Harris, conversation of June 2001 at Sam's Point.

51. Hine, *Old Mine Road,* pp. 126–129, recounts the story of Brant's attack on homes along the Old Minisink Trail. Wendy Harris states that Levi Pawling wrote a surveillance report to Governor George Clinton in 1778 describing plans for Joseph Brant (and at least twenty other Indians) to be joined by Sam Gunsales [*sic*] in a raid on the village of Rochester. This document is found at the New York State Archives at Albany, in *The Public Papers of George Clinton, First Governor of New York, #1578,* (Albany, NY: James P. Lyons, State Printer, 1900).

52. Based on Hine, *Old Mine Road,* p. 101.

53. The church grounds were established in 1737, and the first church and cemetery were established in 1743. The church was already forty-two years old when Joseph burned it down on July 20, 1779—ironically just ten years before the Delaware Valley finally became safe for occupation by Christians. It was rebuilt at that time, and stood until the early twentieth century. Today its large "pumpkin field" cemetery is an attraction for tourists and history buffs.

Chapter 14: Native New Yorkers of Stony County

1. This information is from the Rockland County Historical Society website, www.rootsweb.com/~nyrockla/

2. No translation is given in the historical records for the meaning of Tappan. The Tepanecs, however, were a warlike tribe who conquered Tezcuco in what is now Mexico and created a great city-state. The *ec* ending is found in many tribal names throughout the Hudson Valley. Some interpret this to mean "camp" (in Waoraneck); it is at the very least a locative, or place-name ending such as "berg" in German, "ville" in English, the *ik* ending in Mohican

place-names, such as Hoosic, and the *ing* ending in Lenape, as in Sintsing. Therefore it seems possible that this is another Lenape word of Central American origin.

3. Julian Harris Salomon, *Indians of the Lower Hudson Region: The Munsee* (Suffern, NY: Rockland County Historical Society, 1982), p. 31. On p. 15, Salomon states emphatically that the Tappan, Haverstraw and all related tribes down to the Raritan were Munsee-speaking and Munsee-related peoples. He also notes that the Munsee were often distinguished from other Delaware, (p. 14). Although Skinner, Bolton, and others entertained conflicting theories in 1900, there is no reason to doubt Salomon's statements today

4. Salomon, *Indians of the Lower Hudson Region*, p. 71.

5. Salomon, *Indians of the Lower Hudson Region*, p. 52.

6. E. M. Ruttenber, *Indian Tribes of Hudson's to 1700, vol. 1*(Saugerties, NY: Hope Farm Press and Book Shop, 1992), n. 2, p. 1:92, quoting O'Callaghan's *New Netherlands, V II*, p. 509.

7. Ibid., p. 55.

8. Springtown, New York resident Carolee Schneemann was told this story during her childhood by elderly men and women born before 1880. They specified a certain cliff just west of Springtown Road as one of the signal fire cliffs. (From conversation near the rock itself, May 30, 2001.) Signal Rock in Gallatin, New York, Columbia County, was another such Algonquin signal-fire hill, per Patricia Edwards Clyne's *Hudson Valley Tales and Trails* (Woodstock, NY: Overlook Press, 1990), p. 34.

9. Salomon, *Indians of the Lower Hudson Region*, page 84.

10. The territory of Hillburn, New York, crosses the pass to the northwest, and Suffern, New York, crosses it to the southeast.

11. Talking Leaves, Fire Keeper of the Ramapough Nation, conversation with author, at his home in Florida, New York, May 2001.

12. The only other railroads along the lower New York border are at Nanuet to the east and at Port Jervis near the Delaware to the west. This central alley was and still is of strategic importance to transportation of goods and persons in and out of New York.

13. Talking Leaves, Fire Keeper of the Ramapough Nation, conversation with author, at his home in Florida, New York, May 2001.

14. Ibid.

15. Ibid. Also, Chief Walter Van Dunk and Talking Leaves, conversation with author, May 22, 2001, Ramapough Mountain Band Office, Mahwah, NJ.

16. Ibid. Talking Leaves via telephone, June 2001.

17. In conversation with Chief Walter Van Dunk at Ramapough Mountain Indians Band Office, Mahwah, NJ, May 22, 2001.

18 .The Paramus Trail follows Paramus Road (near the crossing to Manhattan) to East Saddle River Road to West Saddle River Road and then to Cherry Lane Road in New York, which becomes Spook Rock Road.

19. Salomon, *Indians of the Lower Hudson Region*, pp. 10-11.

20. Ibid.

21. There is a bronze tablet that says, simply, "To insure the preservation of Spook Rock as a public monument, the plot of ground has been donated to the Rockland County Historical Society by David Carlough, July 23rd, 1931." See Salomon, *Indians of the Lower Hudson Region,* p. 10.

22. Salomon, *Indians of the Lower Hudson Region.*

23. Ibid., p. 10 Salomon states, in reference to the bronze plaque, "Few stop to read it and fewer still know that this ledge and stone heap are the remains of a rare and authentic Indian landmark, perhaps the most important one remaining in the entire New York metropolitan area."

24. Talking Leaves, Fire Keeper of the Ramapough Nation, conversation with author, while exploring Spook Rock, May 22, 2001.

25. Salomon, *Indians of the Lower Hudson Region,* p. 11.

26. Ibid., with clarification by Talking Leaves, Fire Keeper of the Ramapough Nation, conversation with author at Spook Rock, May 22, 2001.

27. Ibid., p. 66.

28. Some Ramapough are clearly of Munsee stock. Shortly after returning from a trip to the Munsee reservation at Moraviantown, Ontario, I saw Ramapough Indian Talking Leaves standing on the streets of Manhattan. Although I had never met him before, I walked up to him and asked if he was Munsee. His face, which to me was unmistakably Munsee, suddenly brightened with surprise and he answered, "Yes! I am!" I responded, "What are you doing here in Manhattan?"—knowing full well about the five hundred years of persecution and removal. He answered quite correctly, "This is the land of my people! We have always been here. We have never left!"

29. Chief Walter Van Dunk, conversation with author, May 22, 2001, Mahwah, NJ.

30. Salomon, *Indians of the Lower Hudson Region,* p. 67, quoting Frank G. Speck's article in *The Southern Workman.*

31. Ibid., p. 70. Salomon indicates that Johnsontown, like other Ramapough settlements in the 1950s, was nothing more organized than log cabins scattered through the wilderness.

32. Ibid., pp. 70–71.

Chapter 15: Native New Yorkers of the North—the Mohican

1. The Siwanoy are closely linked to the Munsee, but their language is unknown. It is undoubtedly a Renneiu dialect, probably of the Connecticut type.

2. Lion Miles, author of a new Mohican dictionary to be published in 2002; telephone conversation with author, June 21, 2001.

3. An Orient Point "fishtail" projectile was recently found at Sam's Point, near Ellenville, New York, according to Wendy Harris; conversation with author at base of Sam's Point.

4. Orient Point culture was present in Manhattan by 1000 B.C.E. and coincides in many ways with the development of Mohican culture. The Mohican language is of an ancient northern Algonquin variety and would have been a foundation for the later Lenape vocabulary.

5. Shirley W. Dunn, *The Mohicans and Their Land: 1609–1730* (Fleischmanns, NY: Purple Mountain Press, 1994), p. 52. Dunn states that the various Mohican villages of this northeast corner of Dutchess County were closely associated with the Mohican of Weatogue (now Salisbury, CT). Arthur C. Parker, ed., *Archaeological History of New York,* (Albany, NY State Museum Bulletin,* nos. 237-238, September, October, 1920), p. 547, item 1, mentions "an

Notes 463

Indian mission house at the north end of Indian Lake." (The remains were still visible on Douglas Clark's farm in 1920. This source notes the approximate date 1740 for the Pine Plains mission.)

6. Wabanaki is the name for the Confederation of Algonquin people from Maine and the Maritimes, plus parts of New Hampshire and Vermont. See Pritchard, *No Word for Time.*

7. Louisa A. Dyer, *The House of Peace* (New York: Longmans, Greene, 1956), pp. 4-5.

8. Ibid., p. 13.

9. Ibid., p. 14.

10. Ibid., pp. 14-15.

11. *Shaman* is a word for "mystical healer" in the Altaic language of Siberia, and has since spread throughout much of the world, particularly in Turkey, northern India, and Tibet. I use "Shamanic" here in the adverbial sense, i.e., "done in a similar way to..."

12. Dyer, *House of Peace,* p. 46.

13. Pritchard, *No Word for Time,* pp. 52-53, revised edition. *Eenoodahain* is the Micmac word for the sacred dance.

14. James Hammond Trumbull, *Indian Names and Places In and On the Borders of Connecticut* (1881, reprinted Derby, CT: Archon Books, 1974), via Mohican scholar and author, Lion Miles.

15. Lee Miller, *From the Heart: Voices of the American Indian* (New York: Knopf, 1995), p. 63, quoting George H. Loskiel, *History of the Mission among the United Brethren Among Indians in North America,* vol. 2 (London: Brethren's Society for the Gospel, 1794), p. 14.

16. Lion Miles, per telephone conversation with author, June 21, 2001.

17. A similar address is made to the bear throughout northern Asia and in the entire circumpolar region of the north. In each case, the bear is killed either with a bow and arrow or an ax. Most of the N dialect Algonquin are of the bear-cult type, whereas most of the L and R type are not. The Munsee are not, except those intermarried with the Mohican.

18. Speck notes that this behavior is otherwise unnatural to bears and constitutes a "miracle," an article of faith for the Mohican and Wabanaki. See Frank G. Speck and Jesse Moses, Jr., *The Celestial Bear Comes Down to Earth: The Bear Sacrifice Ceremony of the Munsee-Mahican in Canada as Related by Nekatcit,* Reading, PA Public Museum and Art Gallery, Scientific Publications number 7, 1945, p. 64.

19. The painted turtle is called *tkway* in Algonquin. The Munsee called the painted turtle rattle *kuxwunee-kan,* a "shaken instrument." Speck, *The Celestial Bear Comes Down to Earth,* p. 4.

20. Dyer, *House of Peace,* p. 47.

21. Ibid., pp. 48-49. Dyer writes that the Mohican form of government provided for "their protection and common interests but left them free from too much interference in their daily lives."

22. The first fire was created when lightning struck an old dead tree. The ancient Micmac story of the ancestor Gluscap and the original fire was first published in *Introductory Guide to Micmac Words and Phrases,* compiled by Evan Pritchard with annotations by Stephen Augustine, observations by Albert Ward (Woodstock, NY: Resonance Communications, 1991, revised, 1998), p. 67 of revised ed., based on Stephen Augustine's recounting of the story.

23. Dyer, *House of Peace*, p. 6.

24. Lion Miles, telephone conversation with author, June 21, 2001.

25. Aepjin was a sachem. It is a Dutch epithet (or mnemonic) meaning "little ape," yet another "double Dutch" term. The prevailing notion is that he was called Aptun, which means "he speaks," by his fellow Mohican. The great Wilhelm Apamut, perhaps the foremost of all the Mohican, who lived in the 1800s and who preserved much of what is known about his Native language, may have been named after Aptun/Aepjin, or descended from him. Apamut means "speaker."

26. E. M. Ruttenber, *Indian Tribes of Hudson's River, vol. 1* (Saugerties, NY: Hope Farm Press and Book Shop, 1992), p. 1: 88.

27. The Wappingers dialect, like other Renneiu dialects, is one-third Mohican and one-third Delaware, with the *l* replacing the *l* in the Delaware words, and *r* replacing *n* in the Mohican. The final one-third or less comes from various southern influences.

28. J. Michael Smith, "The Highland King Nimhammaw and the Native Indian Proprietors of Land in Dutchess County, NY: 1712–1765" (New York State Archives, Albany, NY). Article based on lecture given at Mohican Seminar, March 2000, later published with same title, in *The Hudson Valley Regional Review, A Journal of Regional Studies*, vol. 17, #2 (Sept. 2000): pp. 69–108.

29.The common translation of Sepascot is from *seepus-coq*, or "small river place" in reference to the Landman's Kill, a small river which ran beside the old trail, now Route 308. Nancy V. Kelly, *A Brief History of Rhinebeck* (Rhinebeck, NY: The Wise Family Trust, 2001). *Sebun-us-koq* (*sebun* short for *segabun*, or ground nut) means "a specific place on the land of the ground nuts."

30. Lion Miles, telephone conversation with author, June 21, 2001.

31. Parker, *Archaeological History of New York*, p. 544, item 1. Taghkanik was renamed Tom's Mountain (or Tom's Hill) after a Mohican named Tom who lived there well into white occupation, at least according to local lore. See Patricia Edwards Clyne, *Hudson Valley Tales and Trails* (Woodstock, NY: Overlook Press, 1990), p. 34.

32. Parker, *Archaeological History of New York*, p. 673, describes these visitations to the tree "as late as the year 1850, and always accompanied by a very old squaw." The identification of the individual described in *Archaeological History* was made by Dr. Lucianne Lavin, Schaghticoke Historian, Director, American Cultural Specialists, LLC, Seymoore, CT, via telephone conversation, August, 2001.

33. See Newton Reed, *Early History of Amenia: Martyrs of the Oblong and Little Nine Partners* (New York: De Lacey and Wiley, 1875, 1948).

34. Parker, *Archeological History of New York*, p. 673, item 17.

35. Via telephone conversation June 21, 2001, with Lion Miles. *Sodus* is derived from *assoro-dus*, "silvery waters."

36. Clyne's *Hudson Valley Tales and Trails*, chapter 12, "Climbing the Indian Ladder Trail," describes the Helderberg Mountains of John Boyd Thacher State Park, which features the "upper and lower" bear paths, and the site of the famed Indian Ladder. The terrain she so vividly describes overlooks the city of Albany, New York.

37. Arthur G. Adams, *The Hudson Through the Years* (Westwood, NJ: Lind Publications, 1983).

38. Dunn, *Mohicans and Their Land*, p. 249.

39. A more likely translation of Coxsackie, is Kaak-hakie, "land of the goose," which is what E. M. Ruttenber says. See Ruttenber, *Footprints of the Red Man: Indian Geographical Names of New York* (New York: New York State Historical Society, 1906). "Hooting Owl" is from Parker, *Archaeological History of New York*. Owl in Unami is *gok-hoos*.

40. Although most of the burials of the "high" Orient Point culture were removed to the eastern point of Long Island in their day, there is reason to think this may be a link between them and the Alumette culture of the earlier phase. Mortuary gifts such as "killed pots" and wampum necklaces, were a distinctive feature of the Long Island burials.

41. The story was published in Charles Skinner's *Myth and Legends of Our Own Land* (Philadelphia: J. B. Lippincott, 1896), pp. 26-29. This is my own interpretation.

42. Clyne, *Hudson Valley Tales and Trails*, p. 34, reveals that Hop-O-Nose, a rocky promontory at the mouth the Catskill Creek, was named after a Mohican resident named Hopp, who was possessed with an impressively large nose.

43. Ruttenber, *Footprints of the Red Man.*

44. Arnold Bellows, *The Legend of Utsayantha and Other Folk Tales of the Catskills* (Margaretville, NY: Catskill Mountain News, 1945), note p. 22. Washington Irving also mentioned Garden Rock, a high precipice covered with flowering vines, as the abode of an old man Manitou, who would turn himself into wild game to fool hunters.

45. Iron Thunderhorse, *A Complete Language Guide and Primer to the Wampano/Quinnipiac R Dialect of Southwestern New England*, p. 88.

46. The source of this story is Bellows' fanciful book *The Legend of Utsayantha*, pp. 20-23. I have, however, told the story my own way here.

Chapter 16: The Mysteries of Long Island

1. Iron Thunderhorse, *A Complete Language Guide and Primer to the Wampano/ Quinnipiac R Dialect of Southwestern New England* (Milltown, IN: Algonquin Confederacy of the Quinnipiac Tribal Council/Algonquin. Confederacies' Language Institute ACQTC/ACLI, 2000), p. 90. *Paumanok* means the same thing as *Potomac* in the Powhatan language, "place where tribute is brought," as mentioned in Pritchard, *No Word for Time*, p. 270.

2. *Rand McNally Road Atlas 2000* (Skokie, IL: Rand McNally, 2000).

3. Because of these shifting boundaries, the use of the term "Long Island" today is completely ambiguous; sometimes it includes Queens and Brooklyn, sometimes it doesn't. Before 1900, it was all Long Island.

4. This information, and the station stops in the following chapter, are from the Long Island Rail Road website: http://www.mta.nyc.ny.us/lirr. Over four hundred of New York's localities (and twenty of its sixty counties) bear Indian names; this according to *History of the State of New York*, ed. Alexander C. Flick, p. 121, and nowhere is this tendency more visible than on Long Island.

5. Robert Redfeather Stevenson, tribal historian of the Montauk nation, on the other hand, believes that the famous story about Wyandanqx selling Gardiners Island to his friend Lion Gardiner for these simple items may be untrue. Apparently there is reason to believe that King George III gave the land to Gardiner over the head of Wyandanqx and without treaty. The United States took over Gardiners Island in 1790, and has since built military installations there and at Montauk. The Gardiner family still owns most of the island, and the heavy burden they pay in taxes has given rise to the inevitable discussion of development—condos, hotels, theme retirement villages, and the like. However, at this writing, much of that sacred

land "of many dead" is still in a pristine state under private ownership of the descendants of Lion Gardiner, the man who rescued Heather Flower from the Narragansett.

6. *King of the Montauks* was painted by E. L. Henry, and is in the possession of Bernard M. Feldman, Renaissance Galleries, Philadelphia. A reproduction can be seen on p. 18 of Paul Bailey's *The Thirteen Tribes* (Suffolk County, NY: 1959, reprinted by Friends for Long Island's Heritage, Suffolk County, NY, 1982).

7. Bailey, *The Thirteen Tribes of Long Island*, p. 24.

8. This is the wording handed down from "Bull" Smith descendant, Raymundo Wesley Rodriguez, conveyed in telephone conversation with the author, March 2001.

9. This information is from archaeological maps published in Arthur C. Parker, ed., *Archaeological History of New York* in Albany, NY *State Museum Bulletin*, nos. 237-238, (September, October, 1920): p. 624, plate 191.

10. Lee Miller, *From the Heart: Voices of the American Indian* (New York: Knopf, 1995), p. 60.

11. In one of the most intriguing pair of sentences yet written about the Lenape, E. M. Ruttenber wrote in 1872, that their "women were the most experienced star gazers, scarce one of whom could not name them all, give the time of their rising and setting, their position, etc., in language of their own....The firmament was to them an open book wherein they read the laws for their physical well-being, the dial plate by which they marked the years." E. M. Ruttenber, *Indian Tribes of Hudson's River to 1700, vol. 1* (Saugerties, NY: Hope Farm Press and Book Shop, 1992), p. 1:29.

Chapter 17: The Thirteen Tribes of Long Island

1. The definitions of the names of the thirteen tribes are in accordance with Paul Bailey, *The Thirteen Tribes of Long Island* (Suffolk County, NY, 1959, reprinted by Friends for Long Island's Heritage, Suffolk County, NY, 1982), p. 7.

2. The Iroquois, or Hodenosuannee, of New York State, perform their ceremonies circling counterclockwise. That is why the two civilizations and their ceremonies have never been successfully blended together. This matter of direction is too basic to be ignored or changed.

3. This is similar to Membertou, the eastern-most point of Micmac territory (in Onamagi, which splits into two "flukes" just as Long Island does), which was the traditional home of the Micmac grand chief. The Micmac of that region practiced similar burials at sunrise using red ochre, apparently before the Orient Point people did. The parallels between Long Island and the "island" of my Nova Scotia ancestors are numerous and fascinating to contemplate. In any case, the best-known of the Montauk grand chiefs was Wyandanqx, who "ruled" all of Long Island, except the Canarsies.

4. There is a burial place near the foot of Fort Hill, per Arthur C. Parker, ed., *Archaeological History of New York* in Albany, NY *State Museum Bulletin*, Nos. 237-238 (September, October, 1920): p. 699, item 47.

5. The Heather Flower saga was part of this war.

6. According to Native marine biologist Raymundo Wesley Rodriques, the name "right whale" derives from the fact that they were the "right whales" to hunt, as they were not very aggressive, and their compact twenty-foot frame was filled with whale oil.

7. This information is according to Bailey, *Thirteen Tribes of Long Island*, p.12.

8. Ibid.

9. In Cree lore, there are many similar stories about Weesuckerjack, the goose-man who helps the people. Sacajawea, the name of the woman who helped explorers Lewis and Clark, also means "goose."

10. George Dewan, "The Day the Montauk Indians Became Extinct," *New York Archives,* vol. 1, no. 1 (Summer 2001).

11. Mark R. Harrington, Director, American Museum of Natural History, quoted in William A. Ritchie, *Archaeology of New York State* (Garden City, NY: Natural History Press, 1969; reprinted, Fleischmanns, NY: Purple Mountain Press, 1994).

12. Parker, *Archeological History of New York,* p. 697.

13. Verne Dyson, *Anecdotes and Events in Long Island History* (Port Washington, NY: Friedman, 1969).

14. E. M. Ruttenber *Indian Tribes of Hudson's River to 1700, vol. 1* (Saugerties, NY: Hope Farm Press and Book Shop, 1992), p. 1:75.

15. Ibid., p. 1:73.

16. Parker, *Archaeological History of New York,* p.625 item 13.

17. According to historian Jacqueline Overton, Bailey, p. 70.

18. Ruttenber, *Indian Tribes of Hudson's River,* p. 1:73.

19. According to John H. Morice (his chapter on Long Island Indians cited in Bailey's *Thirteen Tribes of Long Island,* p. 6).

20. Ruttenber, *Indian Tribes of Hudson's River,* p. 1:73.

21. Ibid.

22. Ibid.

23. R. P. Bolton recognizes the Van Wyck Trail as the western border of the Matinecock territory; R. P. Bolton, *New York City in Indian Possession,* map insert, back cover. In addition Paul Bailey attributes to the Matinecocks all of Flushing Meadows and the area called Wandowenock ("they dig pits") extending the territory to the west end of Long Island. See Bailey, *Thirteen Tribes of Long Island,* p. 7.

24. Bernie Bookbinder, *Long Island, People and Places, Past and Present* (New York: Abrams Publishers, 1998).

25. Ibid.

26. Ruttenber, *Indian Tribes of Hudson's River,* p. 1:74.

27. Although it is tidal, the Nissequogue River seldom gets deeper than five feet.

28. The maiden name of Red Feather (Mary Francis Wheeler) was Funk-Evans; she was a descendant of Chief Mayanes. The surname "Maynes" on the Poospatuck rolls may be a variation on Mayanes.

29. Limonite is hydrated iron oxide, and was used as a pigment. It is known as "Indian Paint Pot" because it often erodes into a pot-like shape, which rainfall causes to fill with a reddish paint-like substance. See: http://mineral.galleries.com/minerals/oxides/limonite.htm

30. According to Dyson, *Anecdotes and Events in Long Island History.*

31. Based on my own archaeolinguistic reconstructions of Algonquin history, via the Center for Algonquin Culture, P.O. Box 1028, Woodstock, NY, 12498.

32. Ruttenber, *Indian Tribes of Hudson's River,* p. 1:75.

33. Parker, *Archaeological History of New York,* p. 699, states that this is "regarded as the spot where Poggatacut's head rested in 1651 when his body was sent down on the way to his grave. The hole was 1? feet deep and about the same width. It was regarded with reverence by the Indians in the locality who kept it clean up to the time of the American Civil War."

Chapter 18: Lenape Exodus

1. A source associated with New York's Department of Archaeology passed this story on to me in conversation, and it matches the oral history of the Munsee people of Canada.

2. There is no reason to believe the town is named after the descriptive Lenape word *Rockaway,* which means "sandy," as it is not very sandy there.

3. Wendy Harris lecture at Sam's Point, June 2001.

4. Herbert C. Kraft, *The Dutch, the Indians, and the Quest for Copper: Pahaquarry and the Old Mine Road* (South Orange, NJ: Seton Hall University Museum, 1996), p. 157.

5. Charlene Kelly, telephone conversation with author, April 2001.

6. Kraft describes the windings of this southward trail in his book *The Dutch, the Indians, and the Quest for Copper,* p. 148, although I first learned of it from a Native person, Charlene Kelly.

7. The *modern* town of Shamokin is a different village, which was built later.

8. Dick Shovel website; http://dickshovel.netgate.net/html

9. Charles A. Weslager refers to Sassoonan's "smokey cabin in Shamokin" but also describes him as "coming from Wyoming." See Weslager, *The Delaware Indian Westward Migration.* (Wallingford, PA: Middle Atlantic Press, 1978), p. 15.

10. Some translate Shingas as "swamp person," as it is ambiguous, but it carries a similar connotation. See: Weslager, *Delaware Indian Western Migration,* p. 17.

11. According to Weslager, "In October of 1753, twenty-one-year-old George Washington left Williamsburg, Virginia, with a message from Governor Robert Dinwiddie warning the commandant of French forces to leave the Ohio country, which the message said was the property of Virginia and the King of England. On this journey, Washington visited Shingas, whom he referred to as 'King of the Delawares,' at the chief's home about two miles below present Pittsburgh. . . . [H]e learned that the Indians were equally concerned about French intrusion in the Ohio Valley." Weslager, *The Delaware Indians: A History* (New Brunswick, NJ: Rutgers University Press), p. 212, also Weslager, *The Delaware Indian Westward Migration,* p. 47.

12. Weslager, *Delaware Indian Westward Migration,* p. 21.

13. Ibid.

14. There is some ambiguity as to the name of the treaty, but in the treaty of October 1764 between the Indians of Ohio and British Colonel Henry Bouquet, Bouquet demanded that all prisoners in the entire area be returned to Fort Pitt in twelve days. It is widely reported that most didn't want to go. At first, 110 returned, many reluctantly. In the end, Bouquet gathered up 310 white prisoners. See Allan W. Eckert, *Sorrow in Our Heart: The Life of Tecumseh* (New York: Bantam Books, 1992), p. 38.

15. Weslager, *Delaware Indians,* p. 233.

16. Ibid., p. 234.

17. E. M. Ruttenber, *Indian Tribes of Hudson's River 1700 to 1850, vol. 2* (Saugerties, NY: Hope Farm Press and Book Shop, 1992), p. 2:233.

18. Pontiac's Rebellion ended in 1764, due in part to the Treaty of Paris, which was signed on February 10. The treaty prevented the French from coming to Pontiac's aid against the British.

19. The French and Indians met the British troops only ten miles from the fort, killing 456 soldiers and mortally wounding General Edward Braddock. Four-hundred-twenty-one other British men were wounded in the defeat. On the French/Indian side, 3 officers were killed, 2 wounded, 27 soldiers and Indians killed, 27 wounded. Eckert, *A Sorrow in Our Heart,* p. 26.

20. The Delaware burned many houses west of the Susquehanna, specifically at Shippensburg and Carlisle, just west of Harrisburg, Pennsylvania. These had originally been Delaware campsites. The Shawnee under Tecumseh's father Chief Pucksinwah, however, were in favor of a peaceful settlement.

21. Weslager, *Delaware Indian Westward Migration,* p. 20, quotes the "disgraceful letter" from Lord General Jeffery Amherst to Colonel Henry Bouquet, as saying: "Could it not be contrived to send the small pox among the disaffected tribes of Indians? We must on this occasion use every stratagem in our power to reduce them." It would seem that Amherst was the first bio-terrorist.

22. Eckert, *A Sorrow in Our Heart,* p. 672.

23. The exact coordinates, according to Lee Sultzman, are NE 1/4 S30 T 11 S R 25 E, near White Feather Spring. See Dick Shovel website; http://dickshovel.netgate.net/html

Epilogue

1. James D. Folts, *The Westward Migration of the Munsee Indians in the Eighteenth Century* (Albany, NY: New York State Archives, lecture, March 10, 2001), p. 1.

2. Allan W. Eckert, *A Sorrow in Our Heart: The Life of Tecumseh* (New York: Bantam Books, 1992), pp. 267-269, with lavish descriptions of Kekionga on p. 274. Kekionga was formed in 1752 by the Miami. It was a major Native city called "the Glorious Gate" and was occupied by "a large number of Delawares" in 1780.

3. Gregg Cantrell, *Stephen F. Austin: Empresario of Texas* (New Haven, CT: Yale University Press, 1999); see also Walter Prescott Webb, *The Story of the Texas Rangers: A Century of Frontier Defense* (New York: Grosset and Dunlap, 1957), p. 132.

4. *Webster's New World Dictionary,* 2nd College Ed. (New York: Simon & Schuster, 1982) s.v. Ct., Del., Ill., Ind., Ma., Mi., Mn., Mo., Ms., Wi., Wyo., (Algonquin origins of state names) and ("Grandfathers") Richard C. Adams, *The Delaware Indians: A Brief History* (1906; reprinted Saugerties, NY: Hope Farms Press and Bookshop, 1995), p. 3; also Charles A. Weslager, *The Delaware Indian Westward Migration* (Wallingford, PA: Middle Atlantic Press, 1978), p. 125.

5. In order of significance: New York, New Jersey, Pennsylvania, Connecticut, Maryland, Delaware, Ohio, Indiana, Illinois, Michigan, Wisconsin, Texas, Kansas, Oklahoma, Massachusetts, Wyoming, Kentucky, Arkansas, Missouri, West Virginia, Idaho, California, Colorado, Vermont, Utah, and possibly Nebraska, a total of twenty-six. In 1977, there were 119 enrolled Delaware living in Washington State, thirteen in Virginia, twenty-five in Nevada, thirty-two in Louisiana, and less in the remaining twenty states, the historic impact of whose presence it is hard to determine.

6. Laurence M. Hauptman, *Between Two Fires* (New York: Simon & Schuster, 1996) p. 23. See also, Weslager, *The Delaware Indians,* p. 417. An excellent photograph taken of Black Beaver before 1869, one of the earliest photographs of a Delaware Indian, appears on p. 417.

7. Randolph Marcy, *Thirty Years of Army Life on the Border,* (New York: Harper & Bros., 1866), pp. 59-65. See also Marcy's *The Prairie Traveler* (New York: Harper & Bros., 1859), pp. 188-196. Quoted in Hauptman, *Between Two Fires,* p. 24.

8. *Legacy* (Salt Lake City, UT: The Church of Christ of Latter-Day Saints, circa 1990), a film. This film presents the Mormons' ordeal.

9. Richard White, *The Middle Ground: Indians, Empires, and Republic in the Great Lakes Region: 1650–1815* (New York: Cambridge University Press, 1991), pp. 277-295, quoted in Hauptman, *Between Two Fires,* p. 18.

10. John C. Fitzpatrick, ed., *The Writings of George Washington* (Washington, DC: U.S. Government Printing Office, 1937), pp. 44-45, quoted in Hauptman, *Between Two Fires,* p. 18.

11. Mark Peters, "A History of the Munsee Delaware" (Munsey, Ontario: Munsee Delaware Band Office, 2000), booklet, p. 18.

12. Grant Foreman, *Black Beaver* (Norman, OK: University of Oklahoma Press, 1933), pp. 279-280, quoted in Hauptman, *Between Two Fires,* p. 26.

13. Hauptman, *Between Two Fires,* pp. 23, 39.

14. ARCIA 1861/1862, p. 99, quoted in Hauptman, *Between Two Fires,* p. 23.

15. Peters, "History of the Munsee Delaware," p. 16.

16. Ibid., p. 16.

17. The 1990 census recorded 27,531 Native Americans in New York City. (American Indian Community House, New York City.)

BIBLIOGRAPHY

Adams, Arthur G. *The Hudson through the Years.* Westwood, NJ: Lind Publications, 1983.

Adams, Richard C. *The Delaware Indians, A Brief History.* 1906, reprinted Saugerties, NY: Hope Farms Press and Bookshop, 1995.

——. *Legends of the Delaware Indians and Picture Writing.* Washington, DC: 1905, reprinted Syracuse, NY: Syracuse University Press, 1997. Edited with an introduction by Deborah Nichols with translations by Nora Thompson Dean and Lucy Parks Blalock, comments and transcriptions by James Rementer.

Bailey, Paul. *The Thirteen Tribes of Long Island.* Suffolk County, NY: 1959, reprinted by Friends for Long Island's Heritage, Suffolk County, NY, 1982.

Ballantine, Ian and Betty, eds. *The Native Americans: An Illustrated History.* Atlanta, GA: Georgia Turner Publishing, Inc., 1993. With introduction by Alvin M. Josephy, Jr.

Bellows, Arnold. *The Legend of Utsayantha and Other Folk Tales of the Catskills.* Margaretville, NY: Catskill Mountain News, 1945. Illustrated by Lamont A. Warner.

Benignus, Wilhelm. *Shawangunk Mountain Stories.* Altoona, PA: Altoona Tribune Co., 1916.

Benton-Banaise, Eddie. *The Mishomis Book: The Voice of the Ojibway.* Hayward, WI: Indian Country Communications, 1988.

Bierhorst, John. *Mythology of the Lenape: Guide and Texts.* Tucson, AZ: Arizona University Press, 1995.

——, ed. *The White Deer and Other Stories Told by the Lenape.* New York: William Morrow and Co., 1995.

Bolton, Reginald Pelham. *Indian Trails in the Great Metropolis.* New York: New-York Historical Society.

——. *New York City in Indian Possession.* 1920, Indian Notes and Monographs, Vol. 2 no. 7; reprinted, New York: Museum of the American Indian / Heye Foundation, 1975.

Bookbinder, Bernie. *Long Island, People and Places, Past and Present.* New York: Abrams Publishers, 1998. Photographs by Harvey Weber.

Botkin, B. A. *New York City Folklore.* New York: Random House, 1956.

Bown, Stephen R. "All Is Not Gold That Glisteneth: Frobisher's Fool's Errand to the Arctic," (Eugene, OR: Mercator's World, 1999). www.mercatormag.com

Brink, Benjamin Myer, ed. "Rondout Valley in the Old French War" published in *Olde Ulster,* April 1907, vol. 3, no. 4, Kingston, NY. R.W. Anderson and Sons, Printers. (Facsimile provided by Wendy Harris, Cragsmoor Archaeological Consultants, Cragsmoor, NY.)

Brown, Dee *Bury My Heart at Wounded Knee.* New York: Simon & Schuster, 1970.

Bruchac, Joseph. *Gluskabe and the Four Wishes.* New York: *Cobblehill Books* (tape), 1988.

——. *Gluskabe Stories.* Cambridge, MA: Yellow Moon, (tape), 1990.

———. *The Wind Eagle and Other Abenaki Stories,* Greenfield Center, NY: Good Mind Records, Greenfield Press (CD and book), 2001.

Burrows, Edwin G., and Mike Wallace. *Gotham: A History of New York City to 1898.* London: Oxford University Press, 1999.

Burns, Ric, and James Sanders with Lisa Ades, ed. *New York: An Illustrated History.* New York: Knopf, 1999.

Campbell, Joseph. *The Masks of God: Creative Mythology.* New York: Viking Penguin, 1968.

Cantrell, Gregg. *Stephen F. Austin: Empresario of Texas.* New Haven, CT: Yale University Press, 1999.

Chilton, Elizabeth. Slide presentation given at New York State Archives, Albany, NY, March 10, 2001.

Clyne, Patricia Edwards. *Hudson Valley Tales and Trails.* Woodstock, NY: Overlook Press, 1990.

Cowie, Leonard W. *Seventeenth Century Europe.* New York: Ungar, 1964.

Curtin, Edward V. "Ancient Mohicans in Time, Space, and Prehistory." Paper presented at the Mohican Conference, New York State Archives, Albany, NY, March 2000.

Dempsey, Jack, ed. *Good News from New England, and Other Writings on the Killings at Weymouth Colony.* Scituate, MA: Digital Scanning, Inc., 2001.

Dewan, George. "The Day the Montauk Indians Became Extinct." *New York Archives,* vol. 1, no. 1 (Summer 2001).

Dunn, Shirley W. *The Mohicans and Their Land: 1609–1730.* Fleischmanns, NY: Purple Mountain Press, 1994.

Dutch Map, 1639. New York, New-York Historical Society.

Dyer, Louisa A. *The House of Peace.* New York: Longmans, Greene, 1956. Illustrated by Larry Toschik.

Dyson, John S. *Our Historic Hudson.* Roosevelt, NY: James B. Adler, 1968. Photos by A.E. Wooley, introduction by Stewart L. Udall.

Dyson, Verne. *Anecdotes and Events in Long Island History.* Port Washington, NY: Friedman, 1969.

Eckert, Allan W. *A Sorrow in Our Heart, The Life of Tecumseh.* New York: Bantam Books, 1992.

Fadden, John, writer, narrator. *They Lied to You in School.* Documentary film. Woodstock, NY: White Buffalo Productions, Nathan Konig, Producer.

Feirstein, Sanna. *Naming New York: Manhattan Places and How They Got Their Names.* New York: New York University Press, 2001.

Fitzpatrick, John C. *The Writings of George Washington.* Washington, DC: U.S. Government Printing Office, 1937.

Flick, Alexander C., ed. *History of the State of New York.* New York: Columbia University Press, 1933.

Folts, James D. "The Westward Migration of the Munsee Indians in the Eighteenth Century." Albany, NY: New York State Archives, lecture, March 10, 2001.

Foreman, Grant. *Advancing the Frontier, 1830-1860.* Norman, OK: University of Oklahoma Press, 1933.

Francis, Lee. *Native Time: A Historical Time Line of Native America.* New York: St. Martin's/Griffin, 1996.

Fried, Marc B.*The Early History of Kingston and Ulster County.* Marbletown, Kingston, NY: Ulster County Historical Society, 1975.

———. *Tales from the Shawangunk Mountains: A Naturalist's Musings, a Bush Whacker's Guide.* Glens Falls, NY: Adirondack Mountain Club, 1981.

Furer, Howard B., ed. *New York: A Chronological and Documentary History, 1524-1970.* Dobbs Ferry, NY: Oceana Publications, 1974.

Gaffield, Chad. *The History of the Outaouais.* Quebec: Institut Quebecois de recherché sur la culture, 1997.

Goddard, Ives. "Nasalization in PA (Proto-Algonquin) in Eastern Algonquin." *International Journal of American Linguistics,* part 1, vol. 37 #3 (July 1971): p. 139-151.

Grumet, Robert Steven. *Place Names of New York City.* New York: Museum of the City of New York. Produced by Center for Cultural Resources, 1981.

———.*The Lenapes.* Indians of North America Series, ed. Frank W. Porter. New York: Chelsea House Publishers, 1989.

Gugliotta, Guy. "Debate around the Old Campfire: Virginia Archaeological Find Challenges Theory of Migration." *Washington Post,* 5 April 2000, sec. A, p. 3.

Hauptman, Laurence M. *Between Two Fires.* New York: Simon & Schuster, 1996.

———.*Tribes and Tribulations: Misconceptions about American Indians and Their Histories.* Albuquerque, NM: University of New Mexico Press, 1995.

Heckewelder, John. *An Account of the History, Manners, and Customs of the Indian Nations,* new and revised. Philadelphia: 1881.

Hendrick, Burton J. *Statesmen of the Lost Cause: Jefferson Davis and His Cabinet.* Boston: Little, Brown, 1939.

Hine, C. G. *The Old Mine Road.* New Brunswick, NJ: Rutgers University Press, 1909. Reprinted 1963.

The History of Ulster County, with the emphasis on the last one hundred years, 1883-1983; Compiled by the historians of Ulster County for the Tercentenary. Kingston, NY: Ulster County Historians, 1984.

Hunter, Lois Marie. *The Shinnecock Indians.* Islip, NY: Buys Brothers, 1952.

Jackson Heights: From Ice Age to Space Age: A History for Children. Queens, NY: Jackson Heights Beautification Group, Publisher 1999.

Jones, Electa F. *Stockbridge Past and Present.* Springfield, MA: S. Bowles & Co., 1854.

Kelly, Nancy V. *A Brief History of Rhinebeck.* Rhinebeck, NY: The Wise Family Trust, 2001.

Kessler, Henry H. and Eugene Rachlis. *Peter Stuyvesant and His New York.* New York: Random House, 1959.

Kimetz, Vernon. *Timeline of Delaware Indian History.* Indian Historical Society.

Kirkpatrick, Katherine. *Trouble's Daughter: The Story of Susanna Hutchinson, Indian Captive.* New York: Delacorte Press, 1998.

Kraft, Herbert C. *The Dutch, the Indians, and the Quest for Copper: Pahaquarry and the Old Mine Road.* South Orange, NJ: Seton Hall University Museum, 1996.

———. *The Lenape: Archaeology, History, and Ethnography.* Newark, NJ: New Jersey Historical Society, 1986. Collections of the New Jersey Historical Society, vol. 21.

———, ed. *The Lenape Indian: A Symposium.* South Orange, NJ: Archaeological Research Center / Seton Hall University, 1984. Publication no. 7.

——, and John T. Kraft. *The Indians of Lenapehoking.* South Orange, NJ: Seton Hall University Museum, 1985.

Krech III, Shepard. *Ecological Indian: Myth and History.* New York: Norton, 1999.

Larsen, Stephen. *The Mythic Imagination.* New York, NY: Bantam, 1990.

——. *Shaman's Doorway, Opening Imagination to Power and Myth,* New York: Harper and Row, 1976.

——, and Robin Larsen. *The Fashioning of Angels: Partnership as Spiritual Practice.* West Chester, PA: Chrysalis Books, 2000.

Lengyel, Cornel. *Presidents of the United States.* New York: Bantam/Golden Books, 1964.

Lincoln, Abraham. "The Cooper Union Address." *The Collected Works of Abraham Lincoln.* Edited by Roy P. Basler. Lincoln Online: http://showcase.netins.net/web/creative/lincoln/speeches/cooper.htm

Long Island Railroad. Web site: http://www.mta.nyc.ny.us/lirr

Manhattan Yellow Pages Phone Directory, May 1999 to April 2000. New York: Bell Atlantic, 1999.

Marcy, Randolph. *The Prairie Traveler.* New York: Harper & Bros., 1859.

——.   *Thirty Years of Army Life on the Border.* New York: Harper & Bros., 1866.

Mavor, James W., and Byron E. Dix. *Manitou: The Sacred Landscape of New England's Native Civilization.* Rochester, VT: Inner Traditions International, 1989, 1992.

Miller, Lee. *From the Heart: Voices of the American Indian.* New York: Knopf, 1995.

Myers, Albert Cook, ed. *William Penn's Own Account of the Lenni Lenape or Delaware Indians.* Somerset, NJ: Middle Atlantic Press, 1970.

O'Callaghan, Edmund B., ed. *Documents Related to the Colonial History of the State of New York.* New York State Archives. Published in Albany, between 1853–1887, p. 14:470.

Ogilby, John. *America.* London: 1671. Published by the author. Available in the Gilder-Lehrman collection housed at the Morgan Library.

Old Homesteads and Historic Buildings, Genealogy and Family Lore. Daughters of the American Revolution, NY Manhattan Chapter. Parsons, KS: The Commercial Publishers, Co., 1930.

O'Meara, John. *Delaware-English, English-Delaware Dictionary.* Toronto: University of Toronto Press, 1996.

Parker, Arthur C., ed. *Archaeological History of New York,* Albany, NY *State Museum Bulletin,* nos. 237-238, September, October, 1920.

Peters, Chief Mark. "A History of the Munsee Delaware." Munsey, Ontario: Munsee Delaware Band Office, 2000.

Pritchard, Evan T. *Aunt Helen's Little Herb Book.* Woodstock, NY: Resonance Communications, 1994.

——. *Introductory Guide to Micmac Words and Phrases,* with annotations by Stephen Augustine and observations by Albert Ward. Woodstock, NY: Resonance Communications, 1991, revised, 1998.

——. *No Word for Time.* San Francisco: Council Oak Books, 1997, 2001.

Rand McNally Road Atlas 2000. Skokie, IL: Rand McNally, 2000.

Reed, Newton. *Early History of Amenia: Martyrs of the Oblong and Little Nine Partners.* New York: De Lacey and Wiley, 1875, 1948.

Ritchie, William A. *Archaeology of New York State.* Garden City, NY: Natural History Press, 1969; reprinted, Fleischmanns, NY: Purple Mountain Press, 1994.

Ruttenber, E. M. *Footprints of the Red Man: Indian Geographical Names of New York.* New York: New York State Historical Society, 1906.

——. *Indian Tribes of Hudson's River to 1700, vol. 1.* Saugerties, NY: Hope Farm Press and Book Shop, 1992.

——. *Indian Tribes of Hudson's River 1700 – 1850, vol. 2.* Saugerties, NY: Hope Farm Press and Book Shop 1992.

Salomon, Julian Harris. *Indians of the Lower Hudson Region: The Munsee.* Suffern, NY: Rockland County Historical Society, 1982.

Shoumatoff, Nicholas. "The Bear Rock Petroglyph Site." *The Bulletin, New York State Archaeological Association,* no. 55 (July, 1972): pp. 1-5.

Shumway, Floyd M. *Seaport City: New York in 1775.* New York: South Street Seaport Museum, 1975.

Skinner, Alanson "Buck." *Indians of Greater New York.* Cedar Rapids, IA: Torch Press, 1915, reprinted New York: American Museum of Natural History.

——. *Indians of Manhattan Island and Vicinity.* 1913, reprinted Port Washington, NY: Ira J. Friedman, 1961, 1968.

Skinner, Charles. *Myths and Legends of Our Own Land.* Philadelphia: J. B. Lippincott, 1896.

Smith, J. Michael. "The Highland King Nimhammaw and the Native Indian Proprietors of Land in Dutchess County, NY: 1712–1765." New York State Archives, Albany, NY. Article based on lecture given at Mohican Seminar, March 2000, later published with same title in *The Hudson Valley Regional Review, A Journal of Regional Studies,* vol. 17, #2 (Sept. 2000): pp. 69-108.

Snow, Dean. *The Archaeology of New England.* New York: Academic Press, 1980.

Sora, Steven. *The Lost Treasure of the Knights Templar: Solving the Oak Island Mystery.* Rochester, VT: Inner Traditions International, Ltd. 1999.

Speck, Frank G. *The Celestial Bear Comes Down to Earth: The Bear Sacrifice Ceremony of the Munsee-Mahican in Canada as Related by Nekatcit.* Reading, PA: Public Museum and Art Gallery, Scientific Publications number 7, 1945. With Jesse M. Moses, Jr. and Josiah Montour.

Strong, Duncan. *Indian Tribes of the Chicago Region.* Monograph of the Field Museum of Natural History. Chicago: Field Museum, 1938.

Strong, John A. *The Montaukett Indians of Eastern Long Island* (The Iroquois and Their Neighbors Series, Laurence M. Hauptman, series editor). Syracuse, NY: Syracuse University Press, 2001.

Symes, Ronald. *Verrazano, Explorer of the Atlantic Coast.* Illustrated by William Stobbs New York: Morrow, 1973.

Tantaquidgeon, Gladys. *Folk Medicine of the Delaware and Related Algonquin Indians.* Harrisburg, PA: Pennsylvania Historical and Museum Commission, 1972.

Thunderhorse, Iron. *A Complete Language Guide and Primer to the Wampano/Quinnipiac R Dialect of Southwestern New England.* Milltown, IA: Algonquin Confederacy of the Quinnipiac Tribal Council/Algonquin Confederacies' Language Institute ACQTC/ACLI, 2000.

Town of Esopus Bicentennial Committee, *Town of Esopus Story: 3000 B.C. – 1978 A.D.* Esopus, NY: Hillcrest Press, 1979.

Trigger, B. G., ed. *Northeast,* vol. 15. W.C. Sturtevant, general ed. *Handbook of North American Indians.* Washington, DC: Smithsonian Institution, 1978. Map from Bert Salwen, *Indians of Southern New England and Long Island: Early Period.*

Trumbull, James Hammond. *Indian Names and Places In and On the Borders of Connecticut.* 1881, reprinted, Derby, CT: Archon Books, 1974.

Voices of Indigenous Peoples: The Declaration of Indigenous People's Rights. Santa Fe, NM: Clear Light Publishers, 1994.

Waldman, Carl. *Atlas of the North American Indian.* Maps and illustrations by Molly Dean Braun. New York: Facts on File, 1985.

Wallace, Paul. *The White Roots of Peace: The Iroquois Book of Life.* Santa Fe, NM: Clear Light Publishers, 1994. Illustrated by John Kahionhes Fadden, Foreword by Chief Leon Shenandoah, Epilogue by John Mohawk.

Webb, Walter Prescott. *The Story of the Texas Rangers: A Century of Frontier Defense.* New York: Grosset and Dunlap, 1957.

Webster's New World Dictionary, 2nd college edition. New York: Simon & Schuster, 1982.

Weed, Susun. *The Menopause Years: The Wise Woman's Way.* Woodstock, NY: Ash Tree Publications, 1992 .

Weslager, Charles A. *The Delaware Indian Westward Migration.* Wallingford, PA: Middle Atlantic Press, 1978.

———. *The Delaware Indians: A History.* New Brunswick, NJ: Rutgers University Press, 1972.

Westchester Heritage Map. "1778–80. Indian Occupation-Colonial and Revolutionary Names, Structures, and Events." Map made by Robert Erskine, 1778-1780. Reprint, Westchester, NY: Westchester County Historical Society, Stephen A. Estrin, Inc., 1978.

White, E. B. *Here Is New York.* New York: Harpers, 1949.

Wilson, James. *The Earth Shall Weep: A History of Native America.* New York: Atlantic Monthly Press, 1998.

Wroth, Lawrence. *Voyages of Giovanni da Verrazzano, 1524-1528.* New Haven, CT: Morgan Library/Yale University Press, 1970.

Zeisberger, David. *Essay of a Delaware-Indian and English Spelling Book.* Philadelphia: Henry Miller, 1776, reprinted, Ohio Historical Society, 1991.

Other Sources

Abbott, Judy Aldofer. Musee Indian descendant, Ulster County, NY. Information from travel, New York State Historical Records, *Journal of New Netherlands,* as well as information on "the three sisters," corn, beans and squash.

Benton-Banaise, Eddie. Medicine Chief of Three Fires Midewiwin Society.

Case, Floyd. Munsee Indian eagle staff carrier.

Cheshire, Catherine. Director, Touch the Earth Foundation, aka Depsimana Hopi wisdom teacher.

Dean, Nora Thompson. Unami Delaware speaker, author, deceased; via tapes made by Nicholas Shoumatoff.

Evers, Alf. Woodstock, New York Historian of the Catskills.

Kelly, Charlene. traditional Cherokee, Information on northern NJ.

Lavin, Dr. Lucianne. Schaghticoke Historian and Director, American Cultural Specialists, LLC, Seymoore, CT.

Lonedog, Leota. New York City. American Indian Community House (AICH) census data.

Miskokomon, Roberta. Munsee Indian, a tribal historian.

Museum of Indian Culture, Allentown, PA, Carla Messinger, director.

Peters, Mark. Chief of Munsee-Delaware Nation, R.R. 1, Muncey, Ontario, Canada.

Richmond, Trudy Lamb. Program Manager of Education, Mashantucket Pequot Museum and Research Center, Mashantucket, CT.

Rodriguez, Raymundo Wesley. Nissequogue Indian and marine biologist.

Sagamore Hill National Historic Site, Oyster Bay, Long Island, NY. Amy Verone, office of the curator.

Schneemann, Carolee. Stone-home owner in Springtown, NY.

Snake, Dianne. Moraviantown Munsee Indian (fluent speaker of Munsee language) Moraviantown, Ontario, Canada.

Snake, Mike. Munsee-Delaware Nation, Muncey, Ontario, Canada. Delaware/Chippewa Indian.

Staten Island Institute of Arts and Sciences.

Timothy, Beulah. Moraviantown Munsee Indian (fluent speaker of Munsee).

Van Sickle, George. Local historian, Marbletown, NY.

Wells, Sunder. Corchaug Indian.

Wilkes, Brian. Flanders, NJ, Yona Gadoga Cherokee Deputy Chief, Eastern band Cherokee.

ACKNOWLEDGMENTS

I would like to express my gratitude to all the people and Land Keepers who have helped make this project a reality. There are so many who should be mentioned, I will pick out a few who acted above and beyond the call of duty.

To Mark Peters, Chief of the Munsee Delaware Nation of Munsey, Ontario, I send my thanks for sharing my vision, and for inspiring this project. Thanks to Pat Pritchard, my father, for his patience and support, to my mother Joanne for reminding me of the Algonquin spirit, to Talking Leaves for sharing the ways of Native New Yorkers with me, to James Babiarz for his help in historical research, Kevin Bentley for his editorial fortitude, Erika Sloan for enthusiasm for this project, Jennie Dunham for agenting this book, to Judith Aldofer Abbott for comparing notes with me, to Hugh Brodie for triggering the river of memories with his questions, to Shoshana Rothaizer for general research, and for bringing me back to the city of my youth, to Ian and Betty Ballantine for urging me to "make a difference," to Alf Evers for his stories of the Catskills, to Airy Dixon for being my prospector and finding nuggets of historic fact here and there, to Raymundo Rodriguez, culture-bearer of the Nissiquague, to Sunder Wells for opening my eyes to Long Island's ancient past, to Leota Lonedog, a woman of the Delaware, for strategic help, to Richard Frisbee of Hope Farms Bookstore, for letting me loiter on his premises (the best collection on New York anywhere), to Joanne Menchini for various leads and Anishinabic support, to Kay Olan for lending me half her library on the Lenape, to Fred and Maryanne Brusset for making me feel at home in Manhattan, to Chief Walter Van Dunk of the Ramapough for taking time, to Floyd Case for introducing me to the Munsee people of Ontario, to Chief Layton Hopkins for his hospitality, to Beulah Timothy for her patience in teaching me the Munsee language, and Dianne Snake as well, to David Pritchard, a typical Munsee, to Jack and Claire Patterson and all of their children, who knew all this long before I did, to Laurence M. Hauptman, for sharing his writings with me, to Steve Comer and Kate Hubbs for their scholarship and friendship, to Steve and Robin Larsen for their help as usual, to T.A.W. for configuring out my printer and letting me see the city through her eyes, to Jack Bierhorst for his generous sharing of knowledge, to Dr. Joseph Barber for "assisting the innate," to Louise and Valeria—the Staten Island sisters—for keeping me alive, to Oannes and Betty Pritzger for their devotion to our people, and to Gioia Timpanelli for her interest in learning the traditions of the people of "the Ancient Citie."

I would also like to thank the following individuals for their help and inspiration: Lynne Basik, Eddie Benton Banaise, Nancy Berne, Roberto Borrero, Joseph and Carol Bruchac, Grandfather *Ojigwano* William Commanda, Clare Danielson, Pat Darnley, Jim Davis, Martha Davis, Allan W. Eckert, Dina Fanai, Beth Herr, Iron Thunderhorse, Charlene Kelly, Phoebe Legere, Chris Lindner, Ken Little Hawk, Heather MacLain, Trudy Lamb Richmond, Roberta Miskokomon, Leo Nicholas, NJM Computers, Dr. Mar Peter-Roul, Michael Picucci, Shiela and Matt Powless, Lynn Pritchard, Nick Shoumatoff, Lori Siegel and all the fourth grade teachers who spoke up, Thyme Siegel, Michael Snake, Rose Snake, the Stone Ridge Library, Don Traver, Grandfather Turtle, Ron Welburne, Dr. Tom Wermuth, Tk'way White Eagle, Brian Wilkes, Henrietta Wise, and Joe Zeppetello.

INDEX